Marx and Nature

Marx and Nature

A Red and Green Perspective

Paul Burkett

Chicago, Illinois

© 2014 Paul Burkett

Haymarket Books
PO Box 180165
Chicago, IL 60618
773-583-7884
info@haymarketbooks.org
www.haymarketbooks.org

ISBN: 978-1-60846-369-5

Distributed to the trade in the US through Consortium Book Sales and
Distribution (www.cbsd.com) and internationally through Ingram Publisher
Services International (www.ingramcontent.com).

Special discounts are available for bulk purchases by organizations and
institutions. Please contact Haymarket Books for more information at
773-583-7884 or info@haymarketbooks.org.

This book was published with the generous support of Lannan Foundation
and the Wallace Action Fund.

Cover design by Josh On. Cover image from a painting by Shaun O'Dell,
Untitled, 2007, Ink & Gouache on paper, 29 3/4" x 22".

Library of Congress Cataloging-in-Publication Data is available.

Printed in the United States.

Entered into digital printing July 2019.

For my mother and father

Contents

JOHN BELLAMY FOSTER

Foreword

E very book more than a few years old needs to be seen within the historical context in which it was written—and works of social science most of all. Re-reading Paul Burkett's *Marx and Nature* today, nearly a decade and a half after its first publication, reminds me of how different in some respects the historical context was then, at the end of the twentieth century, from what we face today, in the second decade of the twenty-first century. Fifteen years ago the idea of a planetary ecological crisis still seemed fairly new and was being discussed by a relatively small number of environmentalists and scientists. Global warming was a world issue, but seldom hit the front page. Nowadays climate change is part of our everyday lives everywhere in the world—and history seems, if anything, to be accelerating in this respect. A decade and a half ago the contribution of Marx and Marxism to the understanding of ecology was seen in almost entirely negative terms, even by many self-styled ecosocialists. Today Marx's understanding of the ecological problem is being studied in universities worldwide and is inspiring ecological actions around the globe.

These changes are of course connected. As the environmental problems engendered by capitalist society have worsened, the necessary movements of ecological defense have radicalized and spread across the face of the planet. More comprehensive, dialectical explanations of the social destruction of the environment have thus been sought out, leading thinkers increasingly back to Marx. But today's widespread recognition of Marx's contribution to ecology can also be attributed to a considerable degree to Burkett's work and to that of a few other thinkers whom he influenced. In my own case the debt to Burkett is clear. As I wrote in the preface to my book *Marx's Ecology*, which appeared a year after *Marx and Nature*:

"Paul Burkett's magisterial work *Marx and Nature: A Red and Green Perspective* (1999) constitutes not only part of the background against which this work was written, but also an essential complement to the analysis provided here. If I have sometimes neglected to develop fully the political-economic aspects of Marx's ecology, it is because the existence of this work makes this unnecessary and redundant."[1]

Burkett provided for the first time a completely unified reading of Marx's value analysis that integrated its natural-material or use-value components within a general value-form theory, bringing the ecological aspects of Marx's political economy alive as never before.[2] The result was to sharpen the understanding of Marx's dialectic of natural-social metabolism, enhancing our knowledge not only of the ecological dimensions of Marx's critique but also of his political economy as a whole.[3]

Marx and Nature had both a negative and a positive character, and it was the negative aspect that stood out at first. Thus it was known at the outset more for its negative refutation of prevailing views than for its positive affirmation of Marx's ecological praxis. In the opening page of the book Burkett referred to three common criticisms of Marx's approach to nature that he proceeded to refute in his book: (1) the notion that Marx primarily advanced productivist or "Promethean" notions aimed at the conquest of nature; (2) the view that Marx's political economy, and especially the labor theory of value, downgraded nature's contribution to production; and (3) the idea that Marx's analysis of the contradictions and crises of capitalism had nothing to do directly with the natural conditions of production (vii).

In all of this Burkett was responding to what could be called first-stage ecosocialist analysis.[4] Although contributions to ecological thought within the Marxist tradition have existed since the beginning, going back to Marx himself, ecosocialism, as a distinct tradition of inquiry, arose primarily in the late 1980s and early '90s under the hegemony of green theory (and in the context of the crisis of Marxism following the downfall of Soviet-type societies). The general approach adopted was one of grafting Marxian conceptions onto already existing green theory—or, in some cases, grafting green theory onto Marxism. Thinkers such as André Gorz, Ted Benton, James O'Connor, Alain Lipietz, and Joel Kovel stood out in this respect for their important contributions to ecosocialist analysis.[5] Nevertheless, the problem with all such approaches from a socialist perspective was that they did not constitute genuine critiques (the passing through and transcendence) of prevailing environmental thought; nor did they systematically explore the radical roots of Marxian theory itself in order to build on its own materialist and naturalist foundations. Rather they commonly adopted various *ad hoc* means of bridging the gap between the red and the green (such as O'Connor's inspired introduction of the concepts of "conditions of production" and the "second contradiction of capitalism").

Eventually, such an artificially contrived, hybrid methodology, which hardly challenged more conventional green thought, led a number of first-stage ecosocialist thinkers to see Marxism as a mere hindrance to be discarded. Thus Gorz contended that Marx's approach to work, like Hegel's before him, was simply that of "the creative objectification of man's domination of nature." Not surprisingly, Gorz concluded: "As a system socialism is dead. As a movement and organized political force, it is on its last legs. . . . History and technical changes that are leading to the extinction, if not of the proletariat, then at least of the working class, have shown its philosophy of work and history to be misconceived." Likewise, in an article that appeared in O'Connor's journal *Capitalism, Nature, Socialism* only a year after the publication of Burkett's book, Lipietz claimed that Marx had fallen prey to "the Biblico-Cartesian ideology of the conquest of nature." Marx, Lipietz asserted, had underestimated the "the irreducible character of . . . external constraints (ecological constraints, to be exact)" to production and had thus failed to encompass the holism required by an ecological perspective. Hence, "the intellectual scaffolding of the Marxist paradigm, along with the key solutions it suggests, must be jettisoned."[6]

Burkett's *Marx and Nature* was written as a refutation of such first-stage ecosocialist views by means of a reconstruction and reaffirmation of Marx's own critical-ecological outlook. *Marx and Nature* thus represented the rise of a second stage of ecosocialist analysis which sought to go back to Marx and to uncover his *materialist conception of nature* as an essential counterpart to his materialist conception of history. The object was to transcend first-stage ecosocialism, as well as the limitations of existing green theory, with its overly spiritualistic, idealistic, and moralistic emphases, as a first step in the development of a more thoroughgoing ecological Marxism.

Behind the dispute between first-stage and second-stage ecosocialism was in fact a fundamental disagreement about the nature of socialism. First-stage ecosocialists argued that socialism was marred (some said irretrievably) in Marx's own work by his narrow productivism. A few went so far, as we have seen, to pronounce socialism dead. In this view ecosocialism was the heir apparent to socialism. In contrast, second-stage ecosocialists, beginning with Burkett, conceived ecosocialism not as a successor to Marxism but as a deeper form of ecological praxis arising out of the materialist foundations of classical Marxism. To the extent that the terms "ecological socialism" or "ecological Marxism" were used by second-stage ecosocialists, they did not refer to a break with Marxian theory and practice but represented a reinvigoration of its classical-materialist perspective. As Raymond Williams stated, the problem of our society is not that we are materialist, but that we are "not materialist enough"—in the use-value sense.[7]

Such differences in perspective naturally gave rise to considerable misunderstandings in the literature. For example, Kovel, who was to succeed O'Connor as editor-in chief of *Capitalism, Nature, Socialism,* observed in his book *The Enemy of Nature* (2002):

> An opposing point of view [to those who condemned Marx outright as antiecological], recently argued by Marxists such as John Bellamy Foster and Paul Burkett, energetically contests the indictment, and holds that Marx, far from being Promethean, was a main originator of the ecological world-view. Building their argument from Marx's materialist foundations, his scientific affinity with Darwin, and his conception of the 'metabolic rift' between humanity and nature, Foster and Burkett consider the original Marxian canon as the true and sufficient guide to save nature from capitalism. . . .
>
> A close reading will show Marx to be no Promethean. But he was no god of any kind, either. . . . Marxism today can have no greater goal than the criticism of Marx in the light of that history to which he had not been exposed, namely, of the ecological crisis.
>
> Here it needs to be observed that . . . there remains in his [Marx's] work a foreshortening of the intrinsic value of nature. Yes, humanity is part of nature for Marx. But it is the active part, the part that makes things happen, while nature becomes that which is acted upon. . . . In Marx, nature is, so to speak, subjected to labour from the start. This side of things may be inferred from his conception of labour, which involves an entirely *active* relationship to what has become a kind of natural substratum.[8]

For Kovel, "socialism, though ready to entertain that capital is nature's enemy, is less sure about being nature's friend." Such views led him to present ecosocialism as the historical answer to the serious defects of Marxism in this respect.[9]

Yet to contend that Burkett and I view "the original Marxian canon" as a "true and sufficient guide to saving nature from capitalism" is to attribute to us an absolute absurdity. No rational individual could believe that Marx's nineteenth-century analysis, notwithstanding all its brilliance, constitutes a "sufficient guide " to solving the global ecological crisis in an age of planetary climate change, ocean acidification, and fracking. Naturally, whatever methodological insights are to be derived from Marx's dialectic with respect to the ecological and social critique of capitalism—and as Lukács said, "orthodoxy [in Marxism] refers exclusively to *method*"—have to be synthesized with a vast body of historical and scientific knowledge that has arisen subsequently, and with the conditions of contemporary social praxis.[10]

But what about Kovel's criticisms of Marx himself in relation to ecology? Was Marx seriously ignorant with respect to ecological crisis? Was nature, in his analysis, properly conceived as a mere external object to be "subjected" by labor? Did he view nature as "passive" and inert, a mere "natural substratum"?

Recent scholarship, beginning with *Marx and Nature* itself, has demonstrated the error of contending that Marx was unaware of the major ecological crises in his time, or that he failed to learn from them—even if he could not possibly foresee the planetary ecological rift of today.[11] The idea that Marx saw nature as "passive" conflicts with his conception of nature as evolutionary and with the whole dialectical frame of his thought, which led him to point to what he called "the universal metabolism of nature."[12] Indeed, for Marx, the labor process, far from being viewed as a mere mechanistic force for the subjection of nature, was defined *in its essence* (as distinct from the alienated conditions of capitalist society) as "the universal condition for the metabolic interaction [*Stoffwechsel*] between man and nature, the everlasting nature-imposed condition of human existence."[13]

Reading *Marx and Nature*, one cannot fail to be impressed by the extent to which Marx's critique of political economy, as described by Burkett, incorporated the alienation of nature as an essential component of the critique of capital—so much so that this is embodied in the deep structure of Marx's value analysis. It was this that led Marx: (1) to point out that capitalism undermined "the original sources of all wealth—the soil and the worker"[14]; (2) to stress the contradiction between use value and exchange value; (3) to emphasize that human beings were themselves a part of nature; (4) to describe the labor and production process as part of the "universal metabolic process"[15]; and (5) to define socialism as the rational regulation by the associated producers of the metabolism between humanity and nature. According to Marx, no one, not all the people of the world put together, owned the earth; they held it only in usufruct as "good heads of the household" and were meant to pass it on in improved condition to future generations.[16]

Today it is possible to say that second-stage ecosocialism decisively won the great debate over the ecological significance of Marx and Engels's works. Nearly a decade and half after the first publication of Burkett's *Marx and Nature,* the abundant evidence of the deep and pervasive ecological critique embedded in Marx's work is now so well recognized that much of the debate in this respect is over. Ecological notions attributable to Marx, such as the metabolic rift and the natural-material basis of use value, have now entered into the basic conceptions of ecological movements themselves.[17]

Nevertheless, the fact that the basic analysis of *Marx and Nature* has now been widely affirmed by scholars does not make Burkett's work any less valuable to us today. Nor does it make it less important to continue to examine the works of Marx himself—or those of subsequent Marxists who can be said to have contributed to ecological thought. What it does suggest is that that the significance of Burkett's *Marx and Nature* today lies less in its *negative critique* of first-stage ecosocialism than its *positive contribution* to the urgent task of developing a socialist alternative to capitalism's destructive ecology. The focus has thus shifted to what can be considered a third stage of ecosocialism research (the logical outgrowth of the second) in which the goal is to employ the ecological foundations of classical Marxian thought to confront present-day capitalism and the planetary ecological crisis that it has engendered—together with the ruling forms of ideology that block the development of a genuine alternative.

Again Burkett led the way. Building on the foundational view established in *Marx and Nature,* he went on to develop a Marxian critique of existing ecological economics, with the goal of developing a distinctly Marxian ecological economics more equipped to address the environmental contradictions of our time. In 2006 he published his masterwork in this realm, *Marxism and Ecological Economics: Toward a Red and Green Political Economy.* This critique, aimed at neoclassical economics—together with those forms of environmental (or ecological) economics insufficiently opposed to the former—was developed with regard to four central issues: "(i) the relations between nature and *economic value*; (ii) the treatment of *nature as capital*; (iii) the significance of the *entropy law* for economic systems; (iv) the concept of *sustainable development*."[18] In all of this Burkett extended the deep understanding of classical Marxian insights already evident in *Marx and Nature* in order to critique and transform ecological economics in a more radical and uncompromising direction—in relation to both society and nature. His landmark article "Marx's Vision of Sustainable Human Development," in the October 2005 issue of *Monthly Review,* gave perhaps the most comprehensive view of Marx's larger ecological conception of socialism, conceived in terms of a world of substantive equality and ecological sustainability.[19]

It is a testimony to the power of Burkett's contribution that others are now attempting to follow in his footprints, extending Marx's socio-ecological dialectic and ecological-value analysis to the scrutiny of today's environmental problems.[20] We live in a time of great ecological peril, but we are also seeing a great flowering of socialist ecology and of more radical forms of environmental practice, particularly in the global South.[21] Burkett's work has made possible a kind of spiraling movement in which critics of the status quo are able to move back to Marx's radical materialist critique and then move forward again, newly inspired, to engage in revolutionary ecological and social praxis in the present. Mainstream environmentalism only describes the ecological crisis engendered by today's society; the point is to transcend it.

2013
Eugene, Oregon

Introduction
to the Haymarket Edition

A s John Bellamy Foster observes in his foreword to the current edition, *Marx and Nature* had both negative and positive goals. On the negative side, it aimed at refuting the main criticisms of Marx that had been posed by environmental thinkers. At the same time, this refutation positively affirmed Marx's method of incorporating nature into his analyses of economic history in general and of capitalism in particular. In effect, the goal was not only to clear away the main misconceptions regarding Marx and nature that had accumulated along with the rise of various strains of environmentalist thinking, but also to demonstrate what classical Marxism could "bring to the table" of contemporary environmental analysis.[1]

The Three Main Misconceptions

Responding to the charge that Marx embraced an ethic of productivist or "Promethean" domination of nature, I made three basic points in a defensive vein. First, for Marx, human wealth or use value was not reducible to labor; he always recognized nature as an inherent component of human wealth. Second, Marx was consistently aware that human production, under both capitalism and other systems, is constrained by natural, physical, biological, and even ecological laws. Even apart from human labor (itself a natural force), natural conditions actively shape the material-social forms of production and wealth under capitalism and all other modes of production. Third, Marx was highly cognizant of how the human development of productive forces, especially under capitalism, had wasted and destroyed natural wealth. Even more, he recognized that this resulted from a general break with the natural laws required for production to be ecologically sustainable, a break that reaches an extreme form under capitalist relations of production.

More affirmatively, I suggested that when Marx spoke of capitalism developing productive forces he took this largely as an empirical situation with which humanity and workers' movements have to grapple. This helps explain what appears as a paradox to some nondialectical environmental thinkers, namely that Marx emphasized the potential for human development created by capitalism's development of the productive forces while at the same time condemning *how* capitalism develops production—with respect not only to the exploitation of workers but also to the way capitalism treats nature. This point is of considerable contemporary relevance. If we are to do anything about environmental crises today, we can't treat capitalist development of the productive forces and its effects on nature as though it were a big mistake. Rather, we have to understand how it happens and look at the potential for a more sustainable system to grow out of this development of the productive forces. We need to look at how this development shapes things like class struggle and international conflict, instead of just condemning it on ethical grounds. We need to recognize, as did Marx, that humanity has a relatively autonomous relationship with nature compared to other species, due to the greater ability of human production to utilize and reshape the environment (and to damage it). Like Marx, we should not take this as something to be simply applauded *or* condemned; rather, we should treat it as an object of critical analysis and political struggle.[2]

Marx and Nature also employed defensive and affirmative postures in its response to the (then-) conventional wisdom that Marx's economic analysis of capitalism, especially his value theory, excluded or discounted nature's real contribution to production. On the defensive side, I argued that it is wrong to blame Marx for reducing value to abstract labor time; instead one should blame capitalism for this evidently antiecological form of wealth valuation. Marx's critics wrongly treat his value analysis as a normative assertion that, compared to nature, labor is a more primary or important element of production. But capitalism's reduction of the substance of value to abstract labor is not Marx's *a priori* preference; it is a result of his analysis of capitalist relations of production and exchange. In Marx's view, nature always contributes to wealth or use value, and labor is itself a metabolic relationship between people and nature. The tension between abstract labor as substance of value and the natural elements of wealth (including the wealth of human laboring capabilities) should be seen as a central part of the basic contradiction between use value and exchange value, as is emphasized by Marx.

Capitalist production relies on nature *and* human labor as material vehicles for the production of surplus value, yet in the aggregate it values commodities only according to the abstract labor they contain. This is a contradiction of capitalism, not a shortcoming of Marx's analysis. Once this is recognized, it becomes possible to interpret the value dimension of Marx's analysis not as an ecological embarrassment, but rather as a positive tool for analyzing the ecological contradictions of capitalism. *Marx and Nature* pursued this project by, first, unearthing from Marx's analysis several ecological tensions built into capitalist valuation of wealth by abstract labor as represented by money. To be specific, these forms of value are homogenous, divisible, mobile, reversible, and quantitatively unlimited. Contrast this with the qualitative variety (and ongoing variegation), indivisibility, locational specificity, irreversibility, and quantitative limits characterizing natural use values including ecological systems. The conclusion can only be that Marx's value analysis—which explicitly highlights these tensions in *Capital* and related works—demonstrates the *potential* for, the *possibility* of, environmental crisis under capitalism. I say "potential" and "possibility" because capitalism's concrete, historical interaction with its environment obviously cannot be read directly off the formal ecological contradictions of abstract labor, money, and monetary valuation. Analysis of actual environmental crises requires detailed study of the system's historical development as shaped by the system's specific pattern of technological change, as well as class and competitive struggles on both the national and global levels.

Marx and Nature provides important tools for such historical crisis analyses. It shows how the ecological tensions generated by capitalist valuation emerge again and again as Marx's analysis proceeds from the basic forms of commodity exchange, to the exchange of labor power for a wage, to the exploitation of labor power in production (creation of surplus value), to the use of machinery and management techniques to intensify this exploitation, to the complexities of the turnover and reproduction of the total social capital, and finally to phenomena involving commodity speculation, interest, and rents. At each step in his analysis, Marx is keenly aware that production remains a material process—that is, one reliant on *natural* wealth—even as it is converted into a vehicle for the accumulation of capital, of *abstract* wealth.[3] And he points out the various tensions, contradiction, conflicts and, yes, *crises* connected with this twofold character of capitalist production.

Marx observes, for example, that the very existence of wage labor presumes a forcible separation of workers from the natural conditions of production, starting with the land. That is, alienation from nature is a fundamental characteristic of capitalism. Marx goes on to characterize the essence of surplus value—the whole basis of capital accumulation—as the extraction of the vital force of workers and their families, i.e., explicitly as a material, biological, and energetic extraction process which, if prolonged or intensified beyond naturally determined limits, results in the vitiation, deformation, and even death of workers. Marx also emphasizes how capital accumulation relies on the free appropriation of any and all elements of natural and social wealth that can serve as material vehicles for the creation and realization of surplus value. Even when such productive wealth can be monopolized and yield a rent, it is still freely appropriated from the standpoint of capital as a social whole, since rents merely redistribute pre-existing values.

Marx's analyses of production time, the turnover of capital, and land rents emphasize how the forms of capital *in value terms* are actively shaped by natural conditions in industries where the labor process is interrupted by natural processes. The most notable instance is in agriculture, but Marx also considers productive activities that involve fermentation, dyeing, bleaching, and other chemical or biological stoppages in the direct processing of materials by labor and its tools.[4] He registers the tensions between these naturally given temporal-material requirements of production and the pressures of capital-as-value toward uninterrupted, flexible, and unlimited expansion. He emphasizes in particular the resulting tendencies toward depletion of soil fertility by capitalist agriculture and unsustainable harvesting of trees under capitalist forestry.[5]

One could go further with these kinds of examples. The point is that if we want to understand capitalism's specific forms of interaction with nature, we have to look at the complex dialectical interplay and interpenetration of the value and material dimensions of capital accumulation. It was on the basis of this materialist interpretation of Marx's value analysis that *Marx and Nature* responded to a third common criticism, namely, that Marx's diagnosis of the contradictions and crises of capitalism has nothing to do with the natural conditions of production. My response once again was partly defensive (see chapter 9 below). To begin with, I pointed out that since Marx had already integrated natural conditions into his materialist analysis of value and capital, these conditions were integral to *all* his discussions of accumulation crises. I then observed that Marx treated two kinds of specifically environmental crisis. In one type of crisis, capital accumulation is disrupted by shortages of raw materials—materials whose supplies are largely limited by natural conditions. Marx demonstrated how capitalism's development of mechanized industrial productive forces—the factory system—generated unprecedented advances in labor productivity that translated directly into historically huge increases in the throughput of matter and energy drawn from and emitted into the natural environment. He emphasized that this growing appetite for raw materials (including ancillary materials used as energy sources) inevitably results in shortages of these materials due to the dependence of materials production on natural conditions that cannot be reproduced by capitalist enterprise itself. The main example of such materials-supply problems Marx treated was the nineteenth-century cotton crises that afflicted England and other early industrializing countries. Marx's theoretical analysis of these crises was quite sophisticated, taking into account the interplay between value relations, technological and other physical production constraints, rents, and the role of the credit system and speculation in worsening materials shortages and price fluctuations. Moreover, it was in the context of such materials-supply disturbances that Marx made some of his strongest statements about the irrationality and unsustainability of capitalist agricultural practices. Accordingly, I concluded more affirmatively that Marx's treatment of environmental accumulation crises provides many useful hints for a materialist understanding of contemporary materials-supply disturbances, such as oil crises.

I then proceeded to a second type of environmental crisis Marx analyzed, involving damage inflicted by capital accumulation on the *natural conditions of human development*. Here, Marx showed that capitalism's spatial separation and industrial integration of manufacturing and agriculture resulted in a failure to recycle the nutrients extracted from the soil and the conversion of these nutrients into unhealthy pollutants, side by side with the vitiation of labor power by long and intensive worktimes and by enervating living conditions in both urban and rural areas. Marx saw this development as an unsustainable break in the circulation of matter and energy required for the reproduction of human-natural systems. This "metabolic rift" is of course an aspect of Marx's analysis about which we now know much more thanks to the monumental work of John Bellamy Foster.[6] As Foster showed, Marx clearly saw this rift as an outgrowth not just of agricultural practices, but of the whole pattern of "separation" or "antithesis" of town and country—the *combination* of industrialized agriculture with urbanized concentrations of manufacturing enterprise—generated by capital accumulation. Foster also documented how Marx's rift analysis was based on a very detailed study of the natural sciences of his time, especially the work of the great agricultural biochemist Justus von Liebig. In *Marx and Nature*, I was satisfied to merely establish that this rift analysis was not only consistent with, but an organic outgrowth of, Marx's materialist treatment of the basic forms of value under capitalism. In light of more recent work by Foster and others, it is now possible to affirm that Marx's metabolic rift approach—when properly reconstructed and updated to account for developments in technology, natural science, and the further globalization of capital accumulation—can help us understand the systemic roots of the contemporary problems of climate change, depletion and degradation of oceanic ecosystems by industrial fishing and aquaculture, and disruptions to the global nitrogen cycle brought on by overuse of inorganic fertilizers in industrial agriculture.[7] The rift approach has also been proven useful for demonstrating how *ecological imperialism* (the guano trade, sugar plantations, etc.) and resultant ecological crises have been central to the entire history of capitalist development and underdevelopment on a global scale.[8]

The distinction between profitability crises and crises in the natural conditions of human development has a resonance that goes far beyond any ecological defense of Marx's political economy. *Marx and Nature* demonstrated that the two types of crisis are based on the even more fundamental distinction made by Marx: that between the natural conditions that are required by capital accumulation and the conditions required for a sustainable, non-exploitative human development. As Foster and I have emphasized in subsequent work, this basic distinction is often missed by environmental thinkers. Many ecological economists and even some eco-Marxists tend to reduce the question of environmental crisis to one of capital accumulation crisis; that is, they treat environmental crises mainly in terms of their impact on capitalist profitability and sustainability of the profit-making system.[9] For Marx, however, capital accumulation can maintain itself through environmental crises. In fact, this is one thing that makes capitalism different from previous societies. It has the ability to continue with its competitive, profit-driven pattern of accumulation despite the damage this does to natural conditions, including, of course, the damage it constantly inflicts on the natural force of workers' labor power.[10] As I argued in *Marx and Nature*, this is in large part due to the minimal material conditions needed for capital accumulation (exploitable labor power and conditions enabling its exploitation) and to the way that capitalism treats workers and the natural conditions of production as separate inputs that can be mixed and matched spatially and technologically.

By contrast, previous societies (and workforces) were often tied more closely to particular ecosystems—regions of soil and water resources, for example—and if they overstretched these conditions, the entire system would be immediately thrown into a crisis. Capitalism has the ability, because of its global scope and more basically because of its treatment of labor power and its material conditions as separable inputs, to take a much more "slash and burn" attitude toward particular natural conditions, to continue accumulating on a global scale despite (and often because of) the damage it causes to nature.[11] When viewed in this way, the distinction between capital accumulation crises and the more general environmental crisis caused by capitalism is of the greatest importance for contemporary environmental politics. It is becoming more obvious in recent years that the natural conditions of human life (not to speak of other species of life) are increasingly threatened even as—indeed, precisely because—capital continues to accumulate. Although periodic environmental accumulation crises (due to materials-supply disturbances, for example) are no doubt on the horizon, it is both unjustifiably passive and ecologically suicidal for an environmental politics to place its hopes on a full systemic breakdown of capitalism—or, for that matter, on a "progressive" prevention of such a breakdown. The defense of and improvement in the quality of human life in all dimensions, environmental and otherwise, now requires a direct confrontation with capital accumulation (variously known as "progress," "competitiveness," and "economic growth") as the arbiter of natural and social conditions.

Thermodynamic Questions

At this point, I must pause for a moment to consider an additional criticism of Marx—one that grew in prominence after the publication of *Marx and Nature*. I am referring to the notion that Marx's political economy greatly downplays thermodynamic considerations in general, and has nothing to say about capitalism's reliance on massive increases of energy throughput in particular. The main source of this criticism has been the work of Joan Martinez-Alier, a Spanish environmental theorist. Martinez-Alier focused on two letters from Engels to Marx (at the very end of Marx's life) after Marx had sought Engels's opinion about the work of Sergei Podolinsky, a Ukrainian socialist working in France. In seeking to reconcile thermodynamics with Marx's analysis of surplus value, Podolinsky tried to quantify energetic inputs and outputs in agriculture. Podolinsky had sent Marx some of his work and asked Marx to comment. In replying to Marx, Engels criticized Podolinsky's attempt to reduce production to pure energy.

Strangely, Martinez-Alier, and many environmental theorists who were influenced by his argument, interpreted Engels's comments on Podolinsky as a point-blank rejection of the relevance of thermodynamic considerations in the analysis of (capitalist or noncapitalist) production, i.e., as a missed opportunity to bring thermodynamics into Marxist political economy. On this thin basis, Martinez-Alier and his followers promulgated the idea that Marx *and* Engels never took account of thermodynamics (including the first and second laws of thermodynamics) in their historical and political-economic writings. Martinez-Alier even claimed that Engels denied the truth of the second law of thermodynamics, the entropy law.[12] All of this was taken completely out of the context of Marx and Engels's writings, i.e., without engaging in any serious way with Marx's systematic development of production as a material-social process in *Capital* or with Marx and Engels's detailed studies of the natural sciences of their time, including those developments in physics and engineering that bore most directly on theoretical and practical thermodynamic issues. Yet by the early twenty-first century, the purported thermodynamic gaps and flaws of classical Marxism had become conventional wisdom among ecological economists and many other environmental theorists. In fact, given the demonstration of Marxism's ecological content in *Marx and Nature* and in John Bellamy Foster's book *Marx's Ecology*, Martinez-Alier's argument had become a kind of ultimate fallback position for those environmental theorists, including even some eco-socialists, who wished to distance themselves from classical Marxism.

Accordingly, in a series of coauthored articles beginning in 2004, John Bellamy Foster and I reconsidered Martinez-Alier's influential criticism in scholarly detail, in light of a fresh study of the relevant Marx-Engels correspondence, a detailed consideration of Podolinsky's work, and the actual treatment of thermodynamic questions by Marx and Engels as related to their studies of natural science.[13] With respect to the entropy law, Foster and I showed that what Engels was criticizing in an 1869 letter to Marx and in his *Dialectics of Nature* was not the law itself, but rather the hypothesis of the heat death of the universe, which is a quite distinct, though related, concept. Engels's criticisms of the heat-death hypothesis closely paralleled those voiced by several leading thermodynamic theorists of his time and anticipated later scientific criticisms of the hypothesis as well. Otherwise, that is, apart from the heat-death issue, Engels consistently adhered to and often directly endorsed the entropy law throughout his relevant writings, including the *Dialectics of Nature*—the main object of Martinez-Alier's critique.[14] Engels *did* criticize Podolinsky for reducing production to pure energy flows, but he also pointed out important thermodynamic phenomena that Podolinsky's energetic calculations had left out of account. Among these were the entropic dissipation of energy *within* the production process (and here Engels pointed out the need for constant awareness of the biochemical, not merely energetic, nature of human labor) as well as various forms of energy waste connected with the inefficient and unsustainable *extraction* of natural materials (including forests) under both capitalist and pre-capitalist production. In particular, Engels highlighted the "squandering [of] our reserves of energy," including "coal."[15]

There, is, moreover, a strong thermodynamic element in Marx's analysis of capitalism—even though *Capital* also repeatedly highlights those qualitative aspects of production that involve biological, chemical, and environmental systems that should not be reduced to purely quantitative energetic terms. For instance, Marx brings thermodynamics explicitly into his analysis of labor power (as shown by the very term *"labor power"*) and its exploitation by capital. Indeed, he shows very clearly how the extraction of surplus value is consistent with the conservation of energy; in other words, Marx had already answered the very question with which Podolinsky had begun his own energetic analysis of production![16]

Even more affirmatively, Marx provides important insights into what the prominent ecological economist Herman Daly has termed the "breaking of the solar budget constraint" through the utilization of fossil fuels, especially starting with the Industrial Revolution.[17] The causes of this development are highly relevant to any serious discussion of global climate change, not to speak of contemporary "oil shocks." Here, ecological economists basically take the discovery of fossil fuels as a given "original sin" and blame it—together with exogenous cultural factors such as the "ideology of growth"—for the system's shift onto an ecologically unsustainable path. Marx's analysis is quite different, and it goes far beyond the formal inclusion of fossil fuels under the category of *auxiliary materials*, as is noted in *Marx and Nature* (see chapter 9). In *Capital*'s chapter on "Machinery and Modern Industry," Marx shows that an essential precondition for greater use of fossil fuel-driven steam engines was the separation of workers from control over the tools used in production and the installation of these tools in machines, which could then be powered not just by human and other animate energy but by inanimate "motive forces." In other words, it was capitalism's specific production relations that both enabled and encouraged the break with the solar budget constraint. In this context, Marx draws on the research of natural scientists and industrial engineers (Ure and Babbage, for example) to treat capitalist factory production in explicitly thermodynamic terms as a system of energy transfer among machines, materials, and human labor power.[18] More recently, Andreas Malm has built on Marx's analysis, and his own brilliant synthesis of historical evidence, to show how capitalist relations of production and class struggle encouraged the transition from water power to coal-fired steam. Specifically, Malm establishes that coal-driven power, because it was more mobile and controllable than water power, provided a handy weapon to industrial capitalists seeking out supplies of exploitable labor power and/or ways of escaping more militant worker communities.[19]

Marx's metabolic rift analysis, too, is not only consistent with the first and second laws of thermodynamics, but also developed explicitly in energetic (as well as biochemical) terms. He argues, for example, that

> large landed property undermines labor-power in the final sphere to which its indigenous energy flees, and where it is stored up as a reserve fund for renewing the vital power of the nation, on the land itself. Large-scale industry and industrially pursued large-scale agriculture have the same effect. If they are originally distinguished by the fact that the former lays waste and ruins labour-power and thus the natural power of man, whereas the latter does the same to the natural power of the soil, they link up in the later course of development, since the industrial system applied to agriculture also enervates the workers there, while industry and trade for their part provide agriculture with the means of exhausting the soil.[20]

Space constraints prevent me from fully detailing our refutation of Martinez-Alier's thermodynamic claims against Marx and Engels.[21] Nonetheless, the inaccuracy of Martinez-Alier's interpretation and interpolation of the Podolinsky episode should be clear.[22] And with that, I hope we have cleared away the last remaining major polemical barrier to a broader recognition of the ecological resources of classical Marxism.

Ecology, Class Struggle, and Communism

Thus far this introduction has provided a summary and update of the first two parts, comprised of chapters 1 through 10, of *Marx and Nature*. It remains to deal with part III (chapters 11 through 14), with its somewhat more sweeping ecological interpretation of Marx's conception of class struggle and communism. The discussion in part III hinges not just on the prior response to Marx's environmentalist critics, but also on two major shifts in emphasis compared to the bulk of relevant literature.

The first major shift involved Marx's vision of class struggle. Here, the most common interpretation is that Marx held an essentially industrialist vision of class struggle. In this vision, capitalist industrialization would cause the proletariat employed in factories to become a more and more concentrated and conscious political force capable of leading a socialist revolution. This vision has, of course, been very influential in some twentieth-century socialist and social-democratic movements, especially in Western Europe. However, without denying that there is some evidence for this vision in Marx's writings, I argued that these writings also contain—and in fact more consistently champion—another, less narrowly industrialist vision of class struggle and revolutionary change. In this second vision, working-class struggles encompass all sorts of popular movements that (consciously or unconsciously) run counter to the economic, political, and cultural power of capital. I concluded that this broader vision is more consistent with ecological revolution as an integral part of the socialist revolution.

My argument was partly based on a rejection of simple "breakdown" interpretations, which would have Marx projecting socialist revolution as a direct outgrowth of a collapse of capital accumulation—a crisis to end all crises, so to speak. There is of course a long historical controversy in Marxism about breakdown theory which I did not wish to discuss in detail. In any case, I argued that rather than an automatic breakdown of capital accumulation, Marx foresaw a worsening contradiction between the conditions required by capital accumulation and the conditions required for a sustainable and healthy human development. For Marx, accordingly, the shift to a sustainable human development path required a revolutionary change in the relations of production, broadly conceived to include not just industrial production but rather the whole process of society's material reproduction—one that would place use value in command instead of capital's mindless competitive pursuit of exchange value.

My ecological interpretation of class struggle was also influenced by the important work of Michael Lebowitz, which emphasizes the structurally opposed positions of workers and capitalists vis-à-vis use value and exchange value. The capitalist's goal is to accumulate value in the form of money; use value is simply a means to that end. For workers, on the other hand, the goal is pursuit of use values, and the money wage is basically a means to the end of use value—of human needs and human development. Moreover, workers are constantly struggling to fulfill and develop their needs—to develop themselves as human beings—outside the realm of wage-labor itself, so this perspective fits in with the broader vision of class struggle mentioned above. In Marx's view, of course, nature and use value are inseparable. It becomes obvious that the working class—broadly defined to include non-waged workers in the household and cultural sectors—potentially has a more environmentally friendly position in the class struggle than capital does. Ecological struggles are part of the general struggle of working people and their communities for sustainable and fulfilling forms of human development.[23]

The second major shift in emphasis in part III of *Marx and Nature* was in chapter 14's discussion of Marx's vision of communism. Here, I tried to redirect the debate over Marx's vision from its prior focus on the allocative efficiency of planning versus the market and toward Marx's original emphasis on communism as a system of human development.[24] I showed that Marx did not see communism as simply a planned utilization of the productive techniques inherited from capitalism, but as a revolutionary transformation of production itself—an epochal, long-term process of qualitative changes in technology and socioeconomic relationships. For Marx, communism was about human development in a holistic, cultural, and ecological sense, not the piling up of more material goods for workers to consume. And Marx recognized the centrality of struggles against private ownership and exploitation of natural conditions ("the land") to this revolutionary process. This was the qualitative, human-developmental context in which Marx demonstrated the necessity not only of cooperative, democratic planning, but also of reductions in work time and development of more cultural-intellectual (and less ecologically damaging) forms of production, both of which would enhance society's planning capabilities.

Naturally Marx's vision is not a *blueprint* for a pro-ecological reengineering of production. Nor is it a certainty that a postcapitalist society of associated producers and communities will transform and undertake production in ecologically sustainable directions. A communist restructuring of the productive metabolism is a necessary but not sufficient condition of ecologically sustainable human development. It all depends on the explicit integration of ecological and other communal concerns into the anticapitalist revolutionary process itself. What I did argue in *Marx and Nature* is that, in order to be ecologically sustainable, an economy must: (1) acknowledge and internalize society's responsibility to manage its metabolism with nature sustainably, to protect the land as communal wealth for current and future generations; (2) diffuse scientific and technological knowledge among all producers and communities as required for this ecological responsibility to be fulfilled throughout the entire process of production and consumption; (3) recognize the uncertainty and incompleteness of our knowledge about ecological and biospheric systems and the corresponding need to follow the "precautionary principle" in all production decisions (taking no specific actions without a clear demonstration of the absence of significant ecological damages therefrom); and (4) respect the need for diversity in human economic relations, due to the variegation of natural conditions and the need for diverse paths of human fulfillment through productive and reproductive activities.

It was and is difficult for me to see how these four requirements can be fulfilled without a clear break from capitalism's monetary/profit calculus and anarchic competition, in favor of planning and cooperation in line with the imperatives of human development. The sustainable development of people as natural *and* social beings must be both means and end here. As Marx put it, "Freedom, in this sphere, can consist only in this, that socialized man, the associated producers, govern the human metabolism with nature in a rational way, bringing it under their collective control instead of being dominated by it as a blind power; accomplishing it with the least expenditure of energy and in conditions most worthy and appropriate for their human nature."[25]

Building on this ecological defense of Marx's vision of communism, I later argued more affirmatively that this vision "integrates three dimensions of sustainable development that have been more or less separately envisioned by ecological economists: (i) the 'common pool' character of natural resources; (ii) co-evolution of individual human beings, society, and nature; (iii) common property management of natural resources."[26] Marx clearly saw communism as a system of sustainable human development growing out of anticapitalist struggles. This is a real strength politically, given ongoing struggles by indigenous peoples around the world to resist transnational capital's "accumulation by dispossession" and to revivify their communal property systems and culturally embedded techniques for sustainable use of water, soil, plant varieties, and other common resources.[27] Industrial workers and communities can learn much from these largely rural movements as they themselves struggle to develop autonomous, self-sufficient, diversified, and cooperative democratic alternatives to capitalism's exploitative and ecologically disastrous production.[28]

New Acknowledgments

I am greatly indebted to John Bellamy Foster for honoring me with an insightful foreword. Thanks also to Sebastian Budgen, Anthony Arnove, and the Haymarket Books team for taking the time and effort needed to arrange for and bring out this paperback edition.

July 15, 2013
Terre Haute, Indiana

Preface and Acknowledgments

I n reconstructing Marx's approach to nature under capitalism and communism, this book responds to three common criticisms of Marx:

1. Marx fell prey to a "productivist" or "Promethean" vision under which (a) capitalist development of the productive forces allows human production to completely overcome natural constraints; (b) communism is projected as extending and rationalizing capitalism's drive toward complete human domination over nature; and (c) both capitalism and communism demonstrate an inevitable antagonism between humanity and nature.
2. Marx's analysis of capitalism excludes or downgrades the contribution of nature to production; this applies especially to Marx's labor theory of value.
3. Marx's critique of the contradictions of capitalism has nothing to do with nature or with the natural conditions of production.

The primary motivation of this book is to address these three claims and their most common corollaries in systematic, textually informed and politically useful fashion. I will argue that Marx's approach to nature possesses an inner logic, coherence, and analytical power that have not yet been recognized even by ecological Marxists.

Over the past several years, when asked about the subject of this work, my answer has normally been: "Green and Red." In a way, this response sums up my intellectual debts. I first became interested in environmental issues during my undergraduate days at Kalamazoo College, where in 1977 I wrote a senior thesis entitled "An Environmental Economist's Case for Organic Revolution." I want to thank Bob Brownlee and the late Louis Junker for their inspiration and encouragement at that time, which planted the seeds of the Green in the present work.

I began seriously studying Marxism while pursuing a graduate economics degree at Syracuse University. This interest was encouraged most of all by the late Jesse Burkhead, an outstanding teacher of the history of economic thought who was a beacon of intellectual openness to many Syracuse graduate students.

Given my earlier interests, it was inevitable that I would never see Marxism as an alternative to environmentalism but rather as a particular kind of environmentalism, one that considers people-nature relations from the standpoint of class relations and the requirements of human emancipation. For a number of reasons of a personal, political, and professional nature, however, only recently was I able to investigate this way of thinking in a scholarly fashion. My return to the Green by way of the Red has been greatly helped by John Bellamy Foster, who was kind enough to read and offer comments on the rough notes leading to this book. John has been a constant source of inspiration and encouragement in my work.

My gratitude is extended to my colleagues at Indiana State University for granting the leave time needed to finish this book. I also want to thank my immediate family members for putting up with me during the writing of it. Thank you, Suzanne, Shaun, Patrick, and Molly.

Although I owe much to the above-mentioned individuals, any errors or shortcomings in the book are my responsibility alone.

Portions of several chapters have previously appeared in scholarly journals. I thank their respective publishers for permission to reprint from *Science & Society,* Fall 1996 (Chapter 7); *Nature, Society, and Thought,* in press (Chapter 9); *Monthly Review,* in press (Chapter 12); *Capitalism, Nature, Socialism,* December 1995 (Chapter 13); and *Organization & Environment,* June 1997 (Chapter 13).

Finally, a stylistic note. Many of the passages quoted in this book contain emphasized words and phrases. To avoid cluttering up the presentation with an endless stream of qualifiers, it is simply indicated here that all emphases are in the original unless noted otherwise.

Terre Haute, Indiana
October, 1998

Introduction

This book reconstructs Marx's approach to nature, society, and environmental crisis. The focus on environmental issues needs little justification. There may still be disagreement about the threat to human survival posed by society's environmental impacts, but no one can doubt that individual ecosystems and the global biosphere are both increasingly shaped by human production and consumption (Vitousek, et al., 1997). Given the quantitatively limited character of natural conditions, it follows that the quality of human-social development will inevitably suffer if fundamentally new forms of social regulation are not applied to the human appropriation of natural wealth (Schnaiberg and Gould, 1994). In short, the environmental problem is not simply one of human survival versus human extinction (which is not to deny the latter possibility). It mainly involves alternative forms of co-evolution of society and nature, differing in terms of the human-developmental possibilities and restrictions they generate (Altvater, 1990, 26–8; Gowdy, 1994a and 1994b).

The reader may be bemused by the notion that Marx has something useful to say about environmental problems. The basic hypothesis informing this book, however, is that Marx's treatment of natural conditions possesses an inner logic, coherence, and analytical power that have not yet been recognized even in the ecological Marxist (or "eco-Marxist") literature. The power of Marx's approach stems, first, from its consistent treatment of human production in terms of the mutual constitution of its social form and its material content. While recognizing that production is structured by historically developed relations among producers and between producers and appropriators of the surplus product, Marx also insists that production as both a social and a material process is shaped and constrained by natural conditions, including, of course, the natural condition of human bodily existence. For example, Marx treats capitalist people-nature relations as necessary forms of the capital-labor relation *and vice versa;* the two are viewed as mutually constituted parts of a class-contradictory material and social whole.

The second key feature of Marx's approach to nature is his dialectical perspective on the historical necessity and limits of particular forms of human production. Hence, while indicating the new possibilities capitalism creates for human development, Marx also explains how capitalist relations prevent these possibilities from being realized. What makes this perspective dialectical is its recognition that capitalism's humanly restrictive properties are actually worsened insofar as production is developed under the sway of capitalist relations. Marx applies this method not just to the capital-labor relation and to competitive relations among capitalists but also to human relations with nature, insofar as these are shaped by and support capitalist exploitation and competition. In this way, Marx's approach leads to an historical analysis of capitalist environmental crisis.

The unutilized potential of Marx's approach for analysis of the historical co-evolution of society and nature is not widely recognized. As alluded to earlier, this is mainly due, I believe, to an inadequate grasp of the overarching logic of Marx's various statements dealing with natural conditions. At the risk of making claims only fully defended later, I will now establish in a preliminary way that many ecological commentators do indeed deny the methodological integrity of Marx's approach to nature.

Some Common (Partial) Interpretations of Marx's Approach

The notion that Marx never developed a coherent approach to nature has many guises. It appears most clearly in the treatment of Marx's statements on natural conditions as isolated observations inessential to his historical world-view or his analysis of capitalism. The renowned Marxist scholar Michael Löwy, for example, suggests that "in *Capital* one can find here and there references to the exhaustion of nature by capital" but that "Marx does not possess an integrated ecological perspective" (1997, 34). Similarly, Joel Kovel refers to "a number of strikingly prescient observations about the ecological relations of capital in Marx's writings" in apparent isolation from Marx's main analysis of value and capital accumulation (1997, 14). Left unanswered is the question as to why Marx would feel it necessary to make such observations (indicating their empirical relevance) yet not develop their importance in terms of the fundamental categories of capitalist production. Such a procedure seems completely foreign to anyone familiar with *Capital*'s systematic, logical development and empirical illustration of analytical categories (cf. Rosdolsky, 1977; Fine and Harris, 1979; Smith, 1990).

Instead of addressing this problem, or trying to reconstruct the role natural conditions actually play in Marx's critique of political economy, the ecological critics often engage in a kind of negative quotation-mongering in which Marx's ecological correctness is gauged by the volume of material in which he directly discusses various phenomena of contemporary ecological relevance (see, for example, O'Connor, 1994, 57–58). In this regard, Howard Parsons' *Marx and Engels on Ecology* (1977), a representative and indeed very useful compilation of some of Marx and Engels' most strikingly environmentalist passages, has unfortunately—and contrary to Parsons' original intent—served to reinforce the compartmentalization of these and other passages into the "isolated insights" category. Even many left ecological theorists find it sufficient to give a qualifying citation to Parsons (1977) before leaving Marx's works behind, otherwise untouched, or, worse yet, criticizing them without engaging them systematically.[1]

As a result, the interpretation of Marx's approach to nature as methodologically partial or one-sided is often more implicit among those voicing specific ecological criticisms of Marx. Consider James O'Connor's claim that "Marx tended to abstract his discussions of social labor . . . from both culture and nature" and that Marx's "conception of the productive forces also plays down or ignores the fact that these forces are natural as well as social in character" (1991b, 9). Apparently, "in his determination to show that material life is also social life, Marx tended to neglect the opposite and equally important fact that social life is also material life" (10). These assertions attribute to Marx a kind of non-dialectical dichotomization of material and social life. If, as Marx arguably suggests, social life and material life are mutually constituted aspects of a single class-contradictory whole, it makes no sense to pose their interaction in terms of a simple identity of opposites. For instance, if the material actually "is" the social and vice versa, as O'Connor seems to indicate, there would seem to be no possibility of systemic tension between the two. In this sense, the artificial dichotomization of the material and the social is the flip side of their non-dialectical commensuration. That this involves more than terminological hair-splitting is clear from O'Connor's argument that capitalism suffers from two separate fundamental contradictions, one stemming from capital's exploitation of labor, the other from capital's exploitation of natural and social conditions. Indeed, O'Connor suggests that capital's tendency toward intensified exploitation of labor and overproduction crises "has nothing to do with the conditions of production" (1991a, 107). (I return to this subject in Chapter 12.)

Marx's ecological critics also tend to downplay the role of historical specification in Marx's approach to human production. Enrique Leff, for example, suggests that "both conventional economics and historical materialism marginalize nature, hence when confronted with the environmental question, face theoretical problems" (1992, 109). The implicit presumption here is that conventional economics and Marx both treat "nature" and "the environmental question" as mere empirical givens definable without reference to historically specific production relations. Leff's interpretation also depicts nature as relevant only when "the environmental question" directly "confronts" Marxism. The nature of this confrontation and its apparent limitation to recent times is left unaddressed, as is the issue of precisely when and how historical materialism marginalized nature and whether this marginalization represented a logical development or a distortion of Marx's materialist and class-based approach.

Here again, these issues of historical specification involve more than methodological nitpicking. Their practical importance is clear from Ted Benton's influential argument that Marxism needs to be reconstructed to more effectively register "ultimate natural limits to population, or to human transformative powers vis-à-vis nature" (1989, 59). In Benton's account, Marx and Engels deliberately downgraded the importance of such limits for reasons of political convenience. As I discuss elsewhere, this interpretation never systematically addresses the class-relational specificity of the natural conditions and limits of production in Marx's view. As a result—and perhaps more than he intended—Benton's reconstruction presses Marxism into the mold of ahistorical Malthusian analysis and politics (Burkett, 1998a and 1998b).

The implicit downgrading of the historical specificity of Marx's analytical categories has had negative effects on the relations between socialism and environmentalism. For example, there is no doubt that a significant source of tension between Red and Green has been the notion that Marx's labor theory of value discounts nature's importance for human production and development (Leff, 1993, 46–48; Deléage, 1994, 48). In effect, Marx is deemed ecologically incorrect for establishing how *capitalism* represents wealth in the specific social form of abstract labor time. Marx is blamed for not doing the impossible: for not conducting a critical analysis of value that simultaneously, in the same breath, acts as a guide to a more ecologically sustainable and healthy co-evolution of society and nature than is achievable under capitalism (Skirbekk, 1994; Carpenter, 1997).[2] The ecological condemnations of Marx's value analysis often ignore or discount Marx's insistence on (1) the joint contributions of nature and labor to wealth production (with labor itself specified as a natural and social force), however much the value form of wealth disregards nature's contribution; and (2) the historical limits of value, rooted precisely in its inadequate representation of the contributions of nature and socialized labor to human production and development (see Chapters 7 and 12).

In short, it is not only Marx's insistence on historical specification that is often downgraded by the ecological critics of *Capital*'s value analysis; these critics also tend to downgrade Marx's historical-dialectical approach, under which the limitations of particular social forms of production emerge out of an analysis of their distinct features, compared to previous social forms and to projected future ones (see Ollman, 1993). Both forms of ahistoricism are implicit in what is undoubtedly the most influential ecological criticism of Marx, namely, his purported embrace of a "Promethean" industrialist outlook in which human progress corresponds to ever-greater human domination and control over nature. In this interpretation, Marx felt that human development must occur at nature's expense under both capitalism and communism (Benton, 1989, 76–77; McLaughlin, 1990, 95; Mingione, 1993, 86). Löwy, for example, suggests:

> There is a tendency in Marx (pronounced in the Marxism after Marx) to consider the development of the forces of production as the principal vector of progress, to adopt a fairly uncritical attitude toward industrial civilization, particularly its destructive relationship to nature. . . . His optimistic, "promethean" conception of the limitless development of the productive forces once the limits of capitalist relations of production are removed is today indefensible . . . above all from the standpoint of the threat to the ecological balance of the planet represented by the productivist logic of capital. (1997, 33–34)

The accuracy of Löwy's representative interpretation is addressed in later chapters. For my present purpose, its significance derives from its presumption that Marx treats capitalist and communist productive forces as qualitatively identical. This presumption downgrades the mutual constitution of productive forces (the material) and historically specific production relations (the social) that is arguably basic to Marx's approach (see Chapter 2). The downgrading of historical specification again goes hand in hand with the dichotomization of the material and the social; both are integral to the notion that Marx took a basically uncritical view of capitalism's material development of the combined productive powers of nature and human labor.

In sum, any evaluation of the various ecological criticisms of Marx must be based on a prior investigation of Marx's overall approach to human production and development from the standpoint of the role of natural conditions. Diverging from many of his critics, I argue that Marx did have a coherent method of dealing with natural conditions both transhistorically and under capitalism and, moreover, that this method definitely informs Marx's projections of communism. I also argue that Marx's approach provides original and useful insights into the sources of environmental crisis under capitalism, the relations between ecological struggles and class struggles, and the requirements of a healthy and sustainable co-evolution of humanity and nature.

Theme and Method

This book focuses on Marx's social-scientific approach to nature. That is, Marx deals with nature mainly as a condition of human-social production and development.[3] Marx sees the evolution of humanity as primarily shaped by the changing social forms of production, but he sees these social forms as being themselves reshaped by production as a material process dependent upon natural conditions.[4] Moreover, Marx treats social relations as material productive forces (see Chapter 2). Both the material content and the social forms of production therefore implicate specific social relations in Marx's view, and in this sense even the natural conditions of production are historically specific. Of course, some natural conditions (e.g., breathable air) are common to all human production, but even then one is talking about natural conditions of a series of specific social forms of production.[5]

Marx's approach automatically recognizes that all conceptions of "ecology" and "ecological crisis" are human-social constructs inevitably bearing the stamp of particular social forms of production (see Chapter 1). For Marx, the goal is not to evade this historical specificity in a misguided search for "value-free" conceptions of society and nature but rather to engage it consciously and critically in order to assist the transition to a nonexploitative society less restrictive of peoples' development as natural and social beings. Despite Marx's concern with historical specification, however, his approach never loses sight of the fact that human development occurs in and through nature, however much this development may be socially structured. In this sense, Marx's approach remains true to the "original meaning" of ecology, that is, "a study of the relations of living organisms, including human ones, with the external world" (Patel, 1997, 2388).

For example, Marx's emphasis on the role of specific social relations does not lead to a false social constructionism according to which human scientific and technological progress overrides the need for a balance with extra-human nature, thereby reducing the co-evolution of society and nature to a purely socially driven process. Instead, Marx's approach enables us to see how the social forms of production lend historical specificity to ecological processes, of which humanity is an increasingly determinant element. This is an important first step toward understanding the ability (or lack thereof) of particular production systems to ecologically sustain any given qualitative development of human life. Marx's perspective, although developed in more social-scientific terms, conforms to the spirit of Rachel Carson's response to those who would "dismiss the balance of nature as a state of affairs that prevailed in an earlier, simpler world":

> The balance of nature is not the same today as in Pleistocene times, but it is still there: a complex, precise, and highly integrated system of relationships between living things which cannot safely be ignored any more than the law of gravity can be defied with impunity by a man perched on the edge of a cliff. The balance of nature is not a *status quo;* it is fluid, ever shifting, in a constant state of adjustment. Man, too, is part of this balance. Sometimes the balance is in his favor; sometimes—and all too often through his own activities—it is shifted to his disadvantage. (Carson, 1962, 246; cf. Dasmann, 1968, 9–11)[6]

The following chapters repeatedly return to the theme of the unique synthesis of materialist and class-relational analysis in Marx's approach to nature. This synthesis provides a useful foundation for an eco-socialist perspective on contemporary capitalism and the political problems currently faced by environmentalists. Nonetheless, this book focuses on the reconstruction of Marx's approach rather than its application.

The present reconstruction is informed by a systematic and comprehensive investigation of the relevant texts. This investigation was systematic insofar as it was guided by the tentative hypothesis, based on a preliminary reading of the texts (especially *Capital*), that Marx's approach to human production combines materialist and social-relational elements in such fashion as to provide unique and politically informative ecological insights. An additional guiding force in my work was evaluation of the most common ecological criticisms of Marx in light of my textual investigation (see Burkett, 1996a and 1996b). The investigation was comprehensive in that it encompassed all significant passages in Marx and Engels' works and correspondence that deal with environmental issues from a materialist and social-scientific standpoint—at least insofar as these are available in English. Virtually all these passages appear in this book or in two recent companion papers (Burkett, 1998a and 1998b). Moreover, since Marx and Engels' environmental statements must be interpreted in terms of the system of historical-materialist categories in which they are inevitably enmeshed, much fresh study of the latter categories was required, leading to considerable auxiliary research into the primary texts. Within inevitable space constraints, this auxiliary work is also fully documented here; hence the following chapters contain much supportive material that, while not directly addressing ecological concerns, is nonetheless required to grasp Marx's approach to nature.[7]

Because my objective is to establish the coherence and usefulness of Marx's approach to nature, this book remains a work of interpretation and analysis, not simply of exposition. Although I do not want it to be known simply for its ample recording of Marx and Engels' statements about nature, my analysis can be classified as "Marxological" insofar as it is underpinned by a comprehensive and open presentation of what Marx and Engels really said about nature. In this sense, it is modeled after Hal Draper's (1977–90) monumental reconstruction of Marx and Engels' approach to revolutionary politics, even though I could never hope to replicate the sweep and power of Draper's work. The textual documentation will make this book useful even to those who don't agree with its interpretation of Marx's approach to nature. It was certainly written with the intent of giving readers sufficient information to make up their minds on the issues discussed, although this may also require engagement with the author's views. In short, although the book is more than a compilation, it may also serve as a kind of analytical reference work on Marx and nature. I hasten to add that readers less concerned with documentation can skip over the notes without losing the gist of the argument.

The "Marxological" character of the present work inevitably raises questions regarding the consistency of the primary texts. Here, the two most important issues involve possible differences between the "young" and "mature" Marx, and between Marx and Engels. Regarding the first issue, I agree with Paresh Chattopadhyay's comment that "the basic ideas on human liberation through the self-emancipation (self de-alienation) of the toiling people that Marx formulated in the forties he continued to hold till his last writings even though the way in which he expressed them and the corresponding vocabulary used were not always the same" (1992, 105).

Nonetheless, certain advances in Marx's thinking over the years did influence the methods of investigation and documentation I employed for this book. Most important, from 1845 onward, Marx appears to have utilized a more consistently historical and social-relational conception of human nature and human labor, as opposed to the somewhat abstract, generic concept of "species-being" exhibited in certain passages in the Paris Manuscripts of 1844. The crucial turning points in this connection seem to have been the *Theses on Feuerbach* and *The German Ideology* (Marx, 1976c; Marx and Engels, 1976; cf. Mandel, 1971). In addition, although the Paris Manuscripts contain many useful analyses of wage-labor and commodity exchange, there is no doubt that Marx's analysis of commodities and capital was only fully developed in the 1850s, especially in the *Grundrisse* (Marx, 1973).[8] Accordingly, this book only refers to those passages in Marx's (and Engels') earlier works that do not contradict Marx's mature conceptions of human nature and human labor, whereas all issues connected with value analysis are treated mainly with reference to Marx's mature critique of political economy as developed in the *Grundrisse* and thereafter.[9]

As for substantial differences between Marx and Engels, I believe that this problem has often been overestimated—at times gravely so.[10] Moreover, the potential difficulties in this connection are minimized insofar as my focus is on Marx's materialist and social-scientific approach to nature rather than questions of natural science as such, whereas it is Engels' investigations in the latter area that have provided the most grist for the mill of those who would substantially separate Marx and Engels.[11] In the course of my work, I was unable to find a single significant difference in Marx's and Engels' respective materialist and class-relational discussions of natural conditions, and here that is the crucial issue. Besides, as with Draper's reconstruction of Marx's revolutionary politics, Marx's approach to nature is one of those areas for which "it is impossible to give a thorough presentation of Marx's views without also including Engels' contributions" (Draper, 1977–90, I, 26).

An Overview

This book is divided into three parts: (I) Nature and Historical Materialism; (II) Nature and Capitalism; and (III) Nature and Communism. There is a twofold logic to this demarcation. The movement from historical materialism to Marx's analysis of capitalism reflects my belief that the latter is a consistent application of the former (especially insofar as Marx's study of capitalism shaped his approach to history in general). The movement from capitalism to communism parallels Marx's practice of projecting the general outlines of the future society out of the social contradictions and the possibilities for human emancipation that capitalism creates (Rosdolsky, 1977, Chapter 28; Ollman, 1993, 141–45). Overall, the book's sequence and content are shaped by the observation that Marx's overriding concern with human emancipation impels him to approach nature from the standpoint of materialist history, sociology, and critical political economy.[12]

Many ecological critics have condemned Marx's human-social perspective on nature as being overly "anthropocentric" and thereby anti-ecological (see, for example, Clark, 1989). In addition, espousal of a social and economic approach to nature does not in itself distinguish Marx from the many mainstream environmentalists (including Al Gore) who continuously harp on the need to alter production, consumption, and population dynamics to make our civilization more environmentally sustainable. Accordingly, this book explores the ecological connotations of Marx's human-developmental concerns, as well as the specific features distinguishing Marx's historical and class-based perspective from mainstream conceptions of society-nature relations. Chapter 1 begins this investigation by proposing four criteria for judging the adequacy of socio-ecological analysis: material and social specification, relational holism, qualitative and quantitative analysis, and pedagogical potential. The chapter then provides an overview of how Marx's approach to history, capitalism, and communism fulfills these criteria.

The remaining three chapters in Part I outline Marx's historical approach to nature and human development, focusing on those elements whose relevance is not limited to any one social system of production. Chapter 2 details Marx's conception of nature's contribution to the production of wealth or use value. This chapter also responds to the common view that Marx downgrades nature's importance for production by overestimating the autonomous powers of human labor. The next two chapters have more specific subject matter. After establishing Marx's general view of the natural basis of the surplus product under capitalism and all other modes of production, Chapter 3 responds to Benton's (1989) claim that *Capital*'s labor-process analysis downgrades the role of natural conditions, especially in eco-regulated forms of production. Chapter 4 then outlines Marx's conception of human labor and labor power as simultaneously natural and social forces. This conception is shown to have an in-built evolutionary and pro-ecological quality that is closely bound up with Marx's historical treatment of production as a combined material and social process.

Part II focuses on nature and capitalism, beginning with Chapter 5's outline of Marx's conception of capitalism as commodity production by wage labor employed in competing enterprises organized and operated to make a profit. In Marx's view, this system's class relations place their own stamp on people-nature relations, because the direct producers or laborers are socially separated from necessary natural conditions of production. Capitalist production entails a dual subsumption of labor and nature under capital, one that loosens the limitations previously placed on production by particular natural conditions, thereby extending the natural limits of production to the global level. Marx's perspective thus sheds light on capitalism's historically unprecedented tendencies toward biospheric crisis.

Chapters 6 through 8 investigate the ecological implications of Marx's value analysis. It is suggested that rather than reflecting anti-ecological biases, Marx's value analysis makes it possible to more clearly grasp the tensions between the true source of wealth (the combination of nature and social labor) and capitalism's monetary representation of wealth as abstract labor time. Within this general theme, Chapter 6 considers Marx's conception of natural conditions as "free gifts" to capital. *Capital's* references to the free appropriation of nature have been cited as proof that Marx discounts the opportunity costs of natural resources and ignores the natural limits to production (see, for example, Carpenter, 1997, 147). However, closer investigation reveals that for Marx, free appropriation merely refers to the fact that the production of many humanly useful natural and social conditions does not require any wage-labor time. The free appropriation category is Marx's way of recognizing that the contributions of society and nature to production are inadequately represented by value. This approach helps explain how capitalism attributes natural productive powers to capital itself. Indeed, Marx treats free appropriation as a crucial form of capitalism's alienation of natural and social conditions vis-à-vis the producers.

After showing the roots of the value-nature contradiction in capitalist production relations, Chapter 7 investigates the specific forms of this contradiction. Value and capital treat wealth as homogenous, divisible, and quantitatively limitless, thereby contradicting nature's qualitative variegation, ecological interconnection, and quantitative limits. My argument also suggests that the anti-ecological characteristics of value and capital cannot be remedied by market rents, whether these rents are generated privately or through government tax/subsidy schemes. Here, Marx's rent analysis is shown to possess a unique sensitivity to the importance, both materially and socially, of limited natural conditions of production. Chapter 8 shows that the most common ecological criticisms of Marx's value analysis fail to grasp Marx's basic demarcation of value, exchange value, and use value. Properly understood, Marx's analysis provides much keener insights into capitalism's environmental problems than do the essentially ahistorical approaches of those who would uncritically ascribe "value" to nature.

Overall, Marx's value analysis places him squarely in the camp of the growing number of ecological theorists questioning the ability of monetary and market-based calculations to adequately represent the natural conditions of human production and development.[13] That his analysis supports a replacement of market calculus with public deliberation and democratic negotiation of the uses of nature becomes clearer in Chapters 9 and 10, which reconstruct Marx's approach to capitalist environmental crises. Chapter 9 shows that Marx analyzes two distinct but interrelated types of environmental crisis under capitalism: (1) periodic crises in capitalist production and accumulation due to materials-supply disruptions; and (2) a secularly worsening crisis of the quality of human development, due to the unhealthy circulation of matter produced by the division of industrial cities and agricultural rural areas. Both forms of crisis implicate the anti-ecological characteristics of value and capital, as established in Chapters 6 and 7. Chapter 9 also considers the extent to which Marx's environmental crisis analysis can be comfortably extended to account for non-biodegradable synthetics as well as global issues, such as atmospheric warming from rising energy throughput. Marx's acute awareness of capitalism's tendency to overstretch its natural limits is further demonstrated in Chapter 10, in which *Capital*'s working-day analysis is interpreted as a model of environmental crisis. It is shown that Marx draws a parallel between capital's plundering of the respective natural forces residing in labor power and its natural conditions. For Marx, this dual plunder of (human and extra-human) nature verifies the class-exploitative character of capitalism's material and social relations, as well as the need for cooperative-democratic planning of society's labor and production.

In Marx's view, communism is the society that grows out of the collective appropriation and transformation, by workers and their communities, of the socialized conditions of production created under capitalism. This revolution is necessary because capitalism generates restrictions on human development that cannot be overcome without a replacement of wage-labor and competition with cooperative production-control by workers and communities. Part III investigates the place of environmental issues in Marx's vision of capitalism's historical necessity and limits, and in the projected communist transformation itself. Many critics have argued that it is precisely in treating capitalism's creation of necessary conditions for communism that Marx fell prey to a Promethean-industrialist viewpoint with distinctly anti-ecological implications. In response, Chapter 11 suggests that Marx in reality defines the progressivity of capitalist development in terms of the potential it creates for a *less restricted* development of people as natural and social beings. Far from being immanently anti-ecological, Marx's human-developmental vision is one of more universal and variegated people-nature relations. This vision cannot be reduced, as Marx's critics would have it, to orgies of mass consumption supported by a further development of anti-ecological production methods inherited from capitalism. In this connection, the ecological critics downplay the class-exploitative and alienated character of capitalist production and consumption along with Marx's corollary projection that the transition to communism involves a qualitative transformation of production and consumption, both materially and socially.

The next two chapters deal with two issues not directly theorized by Marx, namely, the role of natural conditions and environmental crises in capitalism's historical limits as a form of human production and in the class struggles shaping the development of communism out of capitalism. Although Marx and Engels did analyze capitalist environmental crises as well as the ongoing importance of natural conditions under communism, they did not systematically incorporate natural conditions into their discussions of the historical crisis of capitalism and accompanying struggles by workers and communities for a democratic socialization of production. This has led some critics to suggest that Marx's analyses of capitalist crisis and class struggle are barren of socio-ecological insight or even downright anti-ecological, insofar as they treat crises and struggles in economistic and industrialist fashion (Weisskopf, 1991; Mingione, 1993).

In response, Chapter 12 first argues that Marx does not reduce capitalism's historical limits to crises of accumulation. Instead, Marx sees capitalism's historical crisis as a more general culmination of the fundamental contradiction between production for profit and production for human needs. In brief, Marx argues that capital's development and socialization of production creates needs not satisfiable, human-developmental potentials not realizable, and social problems not resolvable within capitalist relations of private appropriation and competition. Capitalism's environmental crisis tendencies are then shown to be logically encompassed by Marx's historical-crisis approach. Moreover, unlike the "two contradictions" framework proposed by James O'Connor (1988, 1991a, 1998), Marx's approach does not draw any artificial dichotomies between capital's exploitation of labor and overproduction crises on the one hand, and crises of reproduction due to capital's despoliation of natural and social conditions on the other. Chapter 13 then considers the place of environmental crises and conflicts in Marx's vision of worker-community struggles for communal or associated production. While granting that certain passages in Marx and Engels' writings seem to espouse an industrialist vision of revolution with questionable ecological connotations, I suggest that Marx and Engels also developed a broader social vision of communist revolution more completely in tune with environmental themes. The relevance of this broader revolutionary vision for contemporary environmental struggles derives from its emphasis on the structurally opposed positions of labor and capital vis-à-vis use value and competition—an opposition arguably intensified by capital's exploitative socialization of production.

Chapter 14 reconsiders Marx's vision of communist society from an ecological standpoint. Marx projects communist production as being democratically planned by producers and communities no longer socially separated from necessary conditions of production including natural conditions. This new union of the producers with the conditions of production is to be socially validated by a new form (or forms) of communal property in these conditions. Marx's call for a system of directly associated social labor, unmediated by market relations, follows logically from the ecological shortcomings of the value form as outlined in Part II. Moreover, Marx and Engels' comments on communist production and planning often ascribe great importance to proper management of society's use of nature—especially the land—thereby undermining the Promethean-industrialist interpretations common among their ecological critics. Among the natural limits stressed by Marx are the limitations imposed by time itself. Marx places great emphasis on "economy of time" under communism—and not only in the sense of reduced work-time for its own sake or for greater enjoyment of consumption. Rather, Marx stresses the importance of increased free time for developing the producers' material and social capabilities, including their scientific mastery of production as a social process enmeshed with nature. This, along with his numerous calls for a more "rational" (read: ecologically sustainable) combination of industry and agriculture, suggests that Marx's vision of communism has more ecological potential than is commonly supposed.

PART I

Nature and Historical Materialism

CHAPTER 1

Requirements of a Social Ecology

By setting forth some basic analytical criteria, this chapter establishes the ecological usefulness of Marx's materialist approach to history, capitalism, and communism. The four requirements of a social ecology provide a structure from which some crucial elements of Marx's approach can be informally introduced as an overview for the subsequent chapters.[1] Chapters 2 through 4 then provide a more formal synopsis of the natural and social features of Marx's materialism that play key roles in his analysis of capitalism.

Material and Social Specification

The first requirement of socio-ecological analysis is that it be consistently social *and* materialist. On the one hand, it should treat people-nature relations as socially mediated in historically specific ways, thus avoiding crude materialist—whether technological determinist or naturist—conceptions of social reality as being naturally predetermined. On the other hand, it should not fall into a social-constructionist view one-sidedly emphasizing the role of social forms in shaping human history, to the neglect of the material content of these forms as constrained by the natural conditions of human production and evolution.[2]

A social ecology must recognize that "human consciousness and purpose," developed in and through society, "introduce a type of complexity . . . that is not found in the rest of nature" (Leacock, 1978, 66). In particular, it must recognize that all ecological values are human and social values, and avoid ascribing a quasi-human subjectivity or purposefulness to nature that it simply does not possess. Economic, cultural, and aesthetic valuations of nature must always be analyzed in connection with the specific social relations in and through which they are generated. At the same time, human valuations of nature are materially informed social constructions; they are inspired by a natural world whose objects, forces, and life forms are governed by objective, inalterable laws. Although ecological values are socially formed, it remains the case that "the natural world provides a rich, variegated, and permanent candidate for induction into the hall of universal and permanent values to inform human action and to give meaning to otherwise ephemeral and fragmented lives" (Harvey, 1993, 10).[3]

A combined social and material conception of people-nature relations is necessary to avoid the kind of technical and ethical dualism exhibited by mainstream environmentalism. In the mainstream view, "sustainable development" can be achieved through a combination of technical fixes ("green" tax and subsidy schemes, for example) and changes in individual values and behavior (promoting recycling along with consumption of more ecologically correct products), without changing the social relations connecting people with the conditions of their production. The assumption here is that ecological destruction is an inessential "external effect" of the dominant social relations of capitalism. By recognizing the mutual constitution of the social forms and material content of human-nature interaction, it becomes clear that technical and individual behavioral perspectives are not enough for society to become genuinely self-critical and self-transformative about its relations with nature. Rather, society must also become self-critical and self-transformative about its characteristic social relations.[4]

In focusing on the production and appropriation of society's surplus product, Marx's conception of history fulfills the first requirement of a social ecology. Surplus product denotes production in excess of that required to maintain the current level of production; this boils down to production above that needed to reproduce the human laborers and any produced means of production contributing to the current production. Marx analyzes the production and utilization of this surplus in terms of (1) the class relations between its producers and its appropriators; (2) the material and social conditions necessary for its production; and (3) the dynamic interactions between (1) and (2) as activated by and manifested in class struggles. This approach enables Marx to treat the development of society's productive capabilities and class relations in material *and* social terms, that is, as people-nature *and* people-people relations. Given that ecological crises involve excesses of human production and appropriation from nature relative to natural limits, and given the key role of the production and utilization of surplus in determining the changing level and forms of human production, the potential usefulness of Marx's materialist and class-analytic approach for social ecology is immediately evident. In sketching "the ecology of [pre-capitalist] tributary societies," for example, John Bellamy Foster is able to trace their "ecological collapse[s] . . . from the destruction of the soil" to "human interventions designed to extract a larger surplus product" (1994, 36–37; cf. Gowdy, 1995).

Marx's value-based analysis of capitalism abides by the first criteria of a social ecology by treating the forms of capitalist production (e.g., commodity, money, capital, wage labor) as historically specific, tension-filled unities of the material and the social. In Marx's conception, capitalism has a specific antagonism toward nature that is manifested in a particular kind of undervaluation of natural conditions, and this undervaluation is a basic form of the contradiction between use value and exchange value. Marx's perspective thus suggests that the struggle for a production system free of ecological crises must, in major part, be a struggle to overcome capitalist exploitation and the commodity form of the products of labor and nature.

Relational Holism

Social ecology should also utilize a holistic yet differentiated and relational approach to human production. Although holism is needed to conceptualize the natural conditions and limits of a total system of material production, differentiation is necessary to capture the dynamics (over space and time) of the interchange between society and nature. These dynamics are shaped by the evolving variegation of (human and extra-human) nature in conjunction with different groups' particular relations to natural conditions, based on their particular locations in a socially organized system of production. In short, differentiated people-nature relations—and any attendant conflicts among social groups—involve different *social and material positions* within the structure of human production and are not simply determined by the material variety of nature itself.

Recognition of internal differentiations and inequalities in human production is necessary to avoid overly sweeping ascriptions of environmental problems to all participants in an ecologically incorrect culture. In reality, the borders between society and nature, and the material content of social relations, look quite different depending on one's social position. One-sided ecological condemnations of entire civilizations run the danger of blaming the victim and thereby alienating potential forces in the struggle for a human production that does not rely on the intensive exploitation of human and extra-human nature. By downplaying the socially differentiated character of people-nature relations, overly totalistic approaches bypass the transformations in social relations required for an effective reintegration of human development and its natural conditions.[5]

Avoidance of an inadequately relational totalism need not and should not entail a complete rejection of holism as such. Ultimately, a holistic *and* relational approach is dictated by the human requirements of a viable and humanly progressive co-evolution of society and nature. Greater harmony between social and natural reproduction can only be achieved by people cooperatively appropriating, utilizing, and developing the social and material conditions of their production in line with certain agreed-upon ecological imperatives. People must grasp their production as a complex social and material totality. This individual and collective capability is not only a matter of fluency in the natural sciences (both theoretical and practical), though it certainly does involve this. It also involves people subjecting the development of the decision-making structure of human production to conscious cooperative-democratic control (Burkett, 1987). A holistic perspective, one that breaks down artificial barriers between natural and social sciences *and* between all science and the subaltern members of society, is absolutely essential for such development.

Marx abides by the criterion of relational holism by treating society and nature in terms of historically specific class-differentiated relations between people and necessary conditions of human production. Since relations between producers and appropriators of the surplus product are based on differential control over necessary conditions of *social* production, they are forms of human production as a class-divided whole. The same goes for all social forms of production connected with these fundamental class relations. The commodity, value, and capital, for example, become dominant forms of human production only with capitalism's extreme social separation of the direct human producers from necessary conditions of production—a separation placing its own stamp on the natural limits of production as a whole. At the same time, the natural *and* social variegation of the material world determines the differentiation of capitalism's socio-economic forms (e.g., the different forms of commodity use value, constant capital, and rent). Marx recognizes that these social forms are still forms of a material, hence natural, process of human production and need satisfaction. This recognition extends to Marx's vision of the new productive forces developed under communism (see Chapter 14).

Marx's relational holism is a key factor enabling him to treat the material and social features of human production as mutually constituted. The resultant dialectical conception of society-nature relations has been usefully summarized by Lucio Colletti:

> We can now understand how this *unity* of economics and sociology, of nature and history in Marx does *not* signify an identity between the terms. It involves neither a reduction of society to nature, nor of nature to society. . . . But we can also understand, conversely, how the avoidance of these two unilateral antitheses on Marx's part is due precisely to their organic composition, i.e., to their unification in a "whole." This whole is a totality, but a *determinate* totality; it is a synthesis of *distinct* elements, it is a unity, but a unity of *heterogeneous* parts. (Colletti, 1972, 13–14)

The conception of the totality of nature-society relations as a contradictory unity of material and social, objective and subjective, exploiting and exploited elements is what enables Marx to uncover the sources of tension and crisis in human production. It also enables Marx to establish how capital's development of labor and nature makes a transition to non-exploitative production relations more and more imperative both socially and ecologically.

Qualitative and Quantitative Analysis

Social ecology should give equal weight to qualitative and quantitative concerns. Nature's capacity to absorb or adjust to the human production process is itself largely determined by the combined qualities of the material objects, physical forces, and life forms constituting particular ecosystems and the terrestrial biosphere as a whole. The myriad forms, and the spatial and temporal unevenness, of human impacts on the biosphere can only be understood in terms of the qualitative variegation and differential resiliency of nature within and across ecosystems. Of course, uneven and differentiated human ecological impacts also implicate the specific features of human development, as compared to other species. The social division of labor, in particular, gives the level and qualitative differentiation of human production a peculiar momentum relative to extra-human nature.

Ecological crises are generated by the evolving pattern of spatial and temporal discords between the social differentiation and expansion of human production on the one hand, and the qualitative variegation, quantitative limits, and absorptive capacities present within nature on the other. Even at this general level, it is clear that the social relations of human production, through their shaping of the forms and levels of human appropriation from nature, are a prime determinant of the degree and pattern of human-ecological "mismatches."

The ecological influence of social production relations is clear from Gary Snyder's distinction between "ecosystem cultures" and "biosphere cultures" (Snyder, 1977, 20). The former cultures reproduce themselves within a particular ecosystem; that is, their appropriation from nature is limited to "a natural region, a watershed, a plant zone, a natural territory" which provides the "economic base of support . . . within which they have to make their whole living." A biosphere culture, by contrast, "spreads its economic support system out far enough that it can afford to wreck one ecosystem, and keep moving on" (21). Clearly, the two cultural types represent different forms of human production and ecological impacts, and different kinds of natural limits, that are explicable only with reference to specific social relations of production. Snyder himself suggests that human history can be conceived as a social evolution from ecosystem to biosphere cultures, with the latter based initially on slavery and the centralized state, and culminating in "imperialist civilization with capitalism and institutionalized economic growth" (21).

Marx's approach to human history helps account for the environmental disharmonies associated with human production. As long as the appropriation and allocation of society's surplus product is governed by antagonistic relations between the laboring and surplus-appropriating classes, and by competition among private-propertied interests, there is no reason to expect human production to resonate viably with the biosphere. According to Marx and Engels, a primary form of ecological disruption generated by class-formed human production is the separation of town and country. They argue that with capitalism's extreme social separation of the direct human producers from necessary conditions of production, the town/country separation is itself taken to an historical extreme. The vitiation of (human and extra-human) nature under this double separation and its correction under communism is a major concern of the founders of Marxism (see Chapters 9 and 14).

Marx's qualitative and quantitative analysis of capitalism's value form of wealth reveals that the commodity, money, and capital have peculiarly anti-ecological characteristics deriving from the separation of laborers from necessary conditions of production.[6] When combined with *Capital's* treatment of the separation of town and country, Marx's value analysis provides a framework for investigating the dual antagonism of capital accumulation toward nature and the needs of the human producers and their communities.

Pedagogical Potential

The development of society's self-critical and self-transformative capabilities, so important for the transition to a concordant co-evolution of society and nature, is determined largely in and through peoples' struggles for decent working and living conditions. This is where popular visions of the future are formed. Social capabilities, struggles, and visions are all essential, mutually constituted elements of an emancipatory ecological politics. From this perspective, the problem of social ecology becomes one of developing analytical tools that can be used not only by professional ecologists and social scientists but also by the popular sectors—students (undergraduates, high schoolers, and grade schoolers), labor and environmental activists, and general working-class readers. This requires straightforward conceptual frameworks that capture the system's development as observed from the angle of particular grassroots positions and struggles.

The pedagogical utility of Marx's approach derives from its holistic treatment of production relations as social relations and vice versa. For Marx, the way people relate to their material conditions is a fundamental aspect of the experience of class relations—relations that constitute the primary forms of human production as a whole. This perspective enables Marx to draw politically crucial connections between aspects of human production that are often treated in fragmented, partial fashion by mainstream social science (Ollman, 1993). Marx's treatment of commodity values and capital shows the necessary connections between the exploitation of wage-labor and the reduction of nature to a condition of capital accumulation, thereby revealing the fundamental kinship of working-class struggles and popular environmental struggles. Indeed, Marx's account of the capitalist extension of work time and of the struggle over the working day arguably represents a model of class-analytic social ecology of great political importance (see Chapter 10).

Although the remaining chapters represent an intervention into a theoretical debate rather than an attempt at popularization, they also clarify the political significance of Marx's approach to nature and human production.

CHAPTER 2

Nature, Labor, and Production

To understand how Marx incorporates natural conditions into his analysis of capitalism, it is necessary to first consider the place of nature in Marx's materialist conception of history. This chapter provides a broad outline of the natural and social elements in Marx's historical materialism, whereas Chapters 3 and 4 present in detail Marx's treatment of natural and human productive forces.

Nature and the Production of Wealth

Marx analyzes human history from the standpoint of the production of *wealth*, defined as *use values*, that is, anything that (directly in consumption or indirectly as means of production) satisfies human needs. As Marx indicates: "Use-values . . . constitute the substance of all wealth, whatever may be the social form of that wealth"; hence "an increase in the quantity of use-values is an increase of material wealth" (1967a, I, 36, 45). Wealth or use value encompasses not only basic requirements such as food, clothing, and shelter but also cultural and aesthetic needs. In short, "wealth consists . . . in the manifold variety of needs," and "use value[s] . . . can quite generally be characterised as the *means of life*" (Marx, 1973, 527; 1988, 40). Marx's materialism focuses first and foremost on the production of these means of life:

> The first premise of all human existence and, therefore, of all history [is] that men must be in a position to live in order to be able to "make history." But life involves before everything else eating and drinking, housing, clothing and various other things. The first historical act is thus the production of the means to satisfy these needs, the production of material life itself. And indeed this is an historical act, a fundamental condition of all history, which

today, as thousands of years ago, must daily and hourly be fulfilled merely in order to sustain human life. (Marx and Engels, 1976, 47)

Marx insists that both nature and labor contribute to the production of wealth or use values. The basic reasoning here is that "in so far as actual labour creates use values," it necessarily involves "appropriation of the natural world for human needs, whether these needs are needs of production or individual consumption" (Marx, 1988, 63). Labor can only produce wealth "by effecting exchange of matter between man and Nature"; it follows that "the worker can create nothing without nature, without the sensuous external world" (Marx, 1967a, I, 183–84; 1964, 109). The appropriate conclusion is clearly and firmly drawn by Marx: "We see, then, that labour is not the only source of material wealth, of use-values produced by labour. As William Petty puts it, labour is its father and the earth is its mother" (1967a, I, 43).[1]

It is true that in Marx's view, labor is a necessary condition of wealth production. According to some critics, this represents a downgrading of nature's use value. Carpenter (1997, 148), for example, argues that "Marx defined nature as possessing use-value only as its utility was realized through the transformative power of labor." Such criticisms neglect Marx's characterization of labor itself as "a process in which both man and nature participate" (1967a, I, 177). Specifically, the ecological critics tend to bypass five related features of Marx's human-natural conception of labor and wealth production.

First, the human capacity to work, or labor power, is itself "a natural object, a thing, although a living conscious thing"; hence labor is a process in which the worker "opposes himself to Nature *as one of her own forces*" and "appropriates *Nature's productions* in a form *adapted to* his own wants" (Marx, 1967a, I, 202, 177; emphases added). The second key feature, following directly from the first, is Marx's treatment of the primary appropriation of use values produced by nature as an inherent component of human labor. As Marx indicates: "All those things which labour merely separates from immediate connexion with their environment, are subjects of labour spontaneously provided by Nature" (178).[2] Through this recognition of primary appropriation as a necessary element of human labor, Marx's treatment of labor as "a necessary condition . . . for the existence of the human race" (42) becomes equivalent to the observation that in order to live, people must appropriate (and often work on) use values produced by nature without human assistance.

With the necessity of primary appropriation for human labor, a third feature of Marx's conception comes into view: the non-identity of labor and production. Marx emphasizes nature's distinct contribution to wealth by not subsuming production under labor; rather, he characterizes labor as "a natural *condition* of human existence, a *condition* of material interchange between man and nature, quite independent of the form of society" (Marx, 1970, 36; emphases added).[3] For Marx, the "labour-process . . . is human action *with a view to* the production of use-values," and this production requires an "appropriation of natural substances" not produced by labor (1967a, I, 183; emphasis added). Stated differently, Marx insists that the "universal metabolic process" of nature, with its production of myriad potential use values, "exists independently of labour" (1988, 63; 1973, 355).[4]

Fourth, in line with the non-identity of labor and production, Marx includes "among the instruments of labor" all conditions "necessary for carrying on the labour-process"—even those that "do not enter directly into the process . . . as conductors of activity" (Marx, 1967a, I, 180). He then specifies "the earth" as "a universal instrument of this sort" (180). In this way, Marx's conception of the labor process incorporates all those use values produced by nature without which "it is either impossible for [labor] to take place at all, or possible only to a partial extent" (180). In order to live and work, for example, people must breathe. "It is clear, however, that air which has been once breathed, can no longer serve for the same process until it has been purified in the great workshop of Nature" (482).

Fifth, it is simply not the case, *pace* Carpenter (1997, 148), for example, that Marx's insistence on labor as a condition of use-value production precludes a counting of currently unappropriated natural use values as part of wealth. Marx's conception of wealth incorporates not only natural conditions of labor not serving as direct instruments or subjects of labor (see last paragraph) but also all elements of "natural wealth" that, while potentially appropriable by labor, have not yet been appropriated (Marx, 1967a, I, 512–14).[5] All Marx suggests is that the significance of unappropriated natural wealth as potential use value hinges on its eventual combination with human labor, even if this is only the labor of primary appropriation.

In sum, nature's contribution to use value is not downgraded by Marx's recognition that "useful labour . . . is an eternal nature-imposed necessity, without which there can be no material interchanges between man and Nature" (Marx, 1967a, I, 42–43). Certainly, Marx's insistence on labor's necessity for wealth production does not prevent him from treating "the earth" as "the great workshop, the arsenal which furnishes both means and material of labour . . . the source of all production and of all being" (1973, 472, 106). At the same time, the significance of nature and labor as sources of wealth must be understood in terms of the social character of human labor.

Nature and the Social Character
of Human Production

To grasp human history, one must distinguish human production from the productive activities of other species. Marx does this by conceptualizing human labor and production as historically specific social processes. He suggests that "from the moment that men in any way work for one another, their labour assumes a social form," so that labor and production must be viewed as a "life-process of society . . . a social circulation of matter" (Marx, 1967a, I, 71, 80, 104).[6]

Marx draws attention to certain other characteristics of human labor that seem to qualify it as specifically human. For example, compared to other species, the human worker has an exceptional ability to preconceive the process and results of labor and, in doing so, to consciously "start, regulate, and control the material reactions between himself and nature" (177). Similarly, the conscious "use and fabrication of instruments of labour . . . is specifically characteristic of the human labour-process" (179). Nonetheless, it is only as descriptive shorthand that one may specify human labor in terms of the ability to mentally preconceptualize work, or to develop and utilize productive instruments.[7] For insofar as these capabilities have evolved to a greater extent for humans than for other species, this has occurred in and through a process of social evolution. As Engels indicates, the "new element" by which their "development has been strongly urged forward . . . and guided along more definite directions" was "the appearance of fully-fledged man, namely, *society*" (1964a, 177). The cumulative development of human production, "once humanity emerged from the mere animal condition," dictates a recognition that "human life has from the beginning rested . . . on *social production*" (Marx, 1994, 329).

Marx analyzes the social development of human labor and production in terms of the historically specific relations among the producers and between the producers and the appropriators of the surplus product. This conception is materialist insofar as the social form of production is itself affected by the development of society's productive forces conceived as a "process between man and Nature" (Marx, 1967a, III, 883). Marx's approach is neither crudely naturist nor technological determinist, however, since it sees the wealth-creating powers of labor and nature as being developed in and through specific relations of production themselves conceived as productive forces. As stated in *The German Ideology:* "A certain mode of production, or industrial stage, is always combined with a certain mode of co-operation, or social stage, and this mode of co-operation is itself a 'productive force'" (Marx and Engels, 1976, 49).[8] At the same time, the socio-historical conception of productive forces does not downgrade the natural, material content of production relations. Marx recognizes the mutual constitution of the social forms and the material content of human production, with the latter composed of human and extra-human natural forces. In short, he sees that "each stage" of human history "contains a material result, a sum of productive forces, a historically created relation to nature *and* of individuals to one another, which is handed down to each generation from its predecessor" (Marx and Engels, 1976, 62; emphasis added).[9]

Insofar as human production is shaped by its social forms in general and its class relations in particular, its evolution cannot be treated as a purely natural process. The production relation between people and nature must be treated as a socially mediated natural relationship:

> In the process of production, human beings work not only upon nature, but also upon one another. They produce only by working together in a specified manner and reciprocally exchanging their activities. In order to produce, they enter into definite connections and relations to one another, and only within these social connections and relations does their influence upon nature operate, i.e., does production take place. (Marx, 1933, 28)

Marx's conception suggests that the social form of production holds the key to the development of a specifically human production more and more distinguishable from the evolving natural world, which continues to provide its material substance and life forces. With each new "stage in the development of the productive forces of working subjects—to which correspond their specific relations amongst one another and towards nature," a certain "coherence arises in human history, a history of humanity takes shape which becomes all the more a history of humanity" not determined by nature (Marx, 1973, 495; Marx to Annenkov, December 28, 1846, in Marx and Engels [1975, 31]). This element of Marx's perspective is worth a detailed consideration.

Marx's Socio-Evolutionary Approach to Nature and Human Production

The divergence of human history from purely natural history in Marx's perspective can be restated as follows: the natural conditions required for human production have become increasingly distinct from those required for a reproduction and evolution of nature as unaffected by human intervention. Indeed, Marx indicates that there would be no need for a social scientific treatment of human production in the absence of this divergence: "It is not the unity of living and active humanity with the natural, inorganic conditions of their metabolic exchange with nature, and hence [with] their appropriation of nature, which requires explanation or is the result of a historic process, but rather the *separation* between these inorganic conditions of human existence and this active existence . . ." (Marx, 1973, 489).

This treatment of human production in terms of the historical divergence of its necessary conditions from nature as such has been a great source of discomfort for ecological thinkers. However, the separation of human existence from natural conditions that Marx refers to does not involve any material uncoupling of human production from nature. Rather, it signifies an *autonomization* of wealth production from nature in the sense that the combined roles of nature and labor in production—hence the natural requirements and limits of production—are not simply given from nature but are shaped by the social relations of production. Here, Marx emphasizes the historical separation of workers from control over necessary conditions of production, and the use of these conditions by surplus-appropriating classes as means of exploiting workers' labor, as the primary factor underpinning the development of the productive powers of labor and nature along a path not determined by nature as such (Marx, 1971, 422–23; 1973, 158–59; see Chapters 5 and 11 for further discussion).

The last point relates to another common criticism of Marx, namely, that by locating "the motive force of history" in the "dialectical tension between the productive forces and the relationships of production," he treats the "conditions of nature" as "a constant, static element in social development" (Skirbekk, 1994, 98). This critique confuses the social *divergence* of human production from nature's own reproduction with a static treatment of the latter. Marx does not suggest that nature is constant or static apart from human influences but rather that the social and class-exploitative character of human production has been the main force diverting human-material evolution from the (now largely counterfactual) evolution of extra-human nature.[10] It is difficult to see how Marx's view can be questioned, unless one wants to blame ecological crises on nature as such rather than on socially produced imbalances between human production and its natural conditions (more on this below). Besides, it is clear from *Capital's* various references to "subjects of labour spontaneously provided by Nature" and to "means of production, provided directly by Nature"—not to mention the definition of human labor as "a process in which both man and Nature participate"—that Marx recognizes nature's active role in human production (Marx, 1967a, I, 177–78, 182).[11]

Marx's perspective rests on the proposition that once one sees human production as social production, one can no longer speak simply of natural conditions and limits. Instead, the question as to which natural conditions count as use values, and which place limits on the production of wealth, must be answered with reference to the specific social relations structuring the productive nexus of labor and nature.[12] This approach does not discount the environmental impacts of production. Quite the contrary: only by recognizing how a particular social form of production uncouples its necessary conditions of production from the extra-human evolution of nature can one investigate the material sustainability of this form.

Consider the alternative assumption that nature can be identified with the natural conditions of a particular system of human production. Under this assumption, it becomes impossible to define environmental sustainability or environmental crises in terms other than those of the currently dominant relations of production. If one identifies nature with the natural conditions required by a particular system, then one cannot conceive of this system producing progressively worsening ecological crises precisely due to its treatment of (human and extra-human) nature merely as a condition of its own reproduction and growth. As is detailed in Part II, this example is not simply hypothetical, in Marx's view.

Ultimately, the social alienation of the human producers from the conditions of their production—and the attendant divergence of these conditions vis-à-vis nature—is not an anti-ecological aspect of Marx's materialist conception of history. We may *want* a harmonious co-evolution of society and nature, but it is misguided to blame Marx for recognizing and explaining why it has not historically taken place.[13] The movement toward a human production that does not exploit nature and labor demands a reconvergence of the conditions of human production with nature plus a pro-ecological redefinition of wealth, based on a social union of the human producers with their conditions of production. In this sense, the vision of a more concordant co-evolution of society and nature depends on the distinction between human production conditions, as formed by non-exploitative social relations, and nature as such (see Chapter 14).

CHAPTER 3

The Natural Basis
of Labor Productivity
and Surplus Labor

Despite the oft-made charge that he downgrades nature's contribution to production, Marx places great emphasis on the natural basis of labor productivity both transhistorically and under capitalism. Not only is labor power itself a natural force (see Chapter 4), but "material wealth, the world of use values, exclusively consists of natural materials modified by labor" (Marx, 1988, 40). "Different use-values contain very different proportions of labour and natural products, but use-value always contains a natural element" (1970, 36). It follows that the productivity of labor (the ability of human beings to produce use values in and through society) must be conceptualized in terms of definite natural conditions:

> Apart from the degree of development, greater or less, in the form of social production, the productiveness of labour is fettered by physical conditions. These are all referable to the constitution of man himself (race, &c.), and to surrounding Nature. The external physical conditions fall into two great economic classes, (1) Natural wealth in means of subsistence, i.e., a fruitful soil, waters teeming with fish, &c., and (2) natural wealth in the instruments of labour, such as waterfalls, navigable rivers, wood, metal, coal, &c. At the dawn of civilisation, it is the first class that turns the scale; at a higher stage of development, it is the second. (1967a, I, 512)

Similarly, in *Value, Price and Profit*, Marx includes "the *natural* conditions of labour, such as fertility of soil, mines, and so forth" as a principal factor determining "the productive powers of labour" (1976b, 34). The "progressive development of the *social powers of labour*" involves the "appliance of chemical and other natural agencies, . . . and every other contrivance by which science presses natural agencies into the service of labour." Natural conditions are thus integral to the process "by which the social or co-operative character of labour is developed" (34).

Of course, insofar as labor and production are developed socially, the productivity of labor cannot be treated as a purely natural phenomenon. "The productiveness of labour . . . is a gift, not of Nature, but of a history embracing thousands of centuries" (1967a, I, 512). This jointly social and natural conception of labor productivity is maintained in Marx's discussions of the natural basis of surplus labor.

The Natural Basis of Surplus Labor in General

Surplus labor means labor over and above that required to produce the current means of subsistence of the laboring class (including the labor needed to produce any requisite means of production). Such a surplus of labor and products is a prerequisite for the existence of exploiting classes, who live off the surplus produced by laboring classes:

> If the labourer wants all his time to produce the necessary means of subsistence for himself and his race, he has no time left in which to work gratis for others. Without a certain degree of productiveness in his labour, he has no such superfluous time at his disposal; without such superfluous time, no surplus-labour, and therefore no capitalists, no slave-owners, no feudal lords, in one word, no class of large proprietors. (Marx, 1967a, I, 511)

For surplus labor to exist, there must be "no natural obstacle absolutely preventing one man from disburdening himself of the labour requisite for his own existence, and burdening another with it" (511). Natural conditions must be such as to make possible the production of a surplus product—beginning with a surplus of means of subsistence:

> The natural basis of surplus-labour in general, that is, a natural prerequisite without which such labour cannot be performed, is that Nature must supply—in the form of animal or vegetable products of the land, in fisheries, etc.—the necessary means of subsistence under conditions of an expenditure of labour which does not consume the entire working-day. This natural productivity of agricultural labour (which includes here the labour of sim-

ple gathering, hunting, fishing and cattle-raising) is the basis of all surplus-labour, as all labour is primarily and initially directed toward the appropriation and production of food. (Animals also supply at the same time skins for warmth in colder climates; also cave-dwellings, etc.). . . . [In sum], since the production of means of subsistence is the very first condition of their existence and of all production in general, labour used in this production, that is, agricultural labour in the broadest economic sense, must be fruitful enough so as not to absorb the entire available labour-time in the production of means of subsistence for the direct producers, that is, agricultural surplus-labour and therefore agricultural surplus-product must be possible. (III, 632, 635)[1]

Here again, however, Marx hastens to interpret the natural basis of surplus labor in social and historical terms. Although natural conditions help account for the possibility of surplus labor, they are not sufficient to explain how this potential has been realized historically:

Favourable natural conditions alone, give us only the possibility, never the reality, of surplus-labour. . . . The result of difference in the natural conditions of labour is this, that the same quantity of labour satisfies, in different countries, a different mass of requirements. . . . These conditions affect surplus-labour only as *natural limits*, i.e., by fixing the points at which labour for others *can* begin. . . . The fewer the number of natural wants imperatively calling for satisfaction, and the greater the natural fertility of the soil and the favourableness of the climate, so much less is the labour-time necessary for the maintenance and reproduction of the producer. So much greater therefore can be the excess of his labour for others over his labour for himself. (1967a, I, 514–15, 512; emphases added)[2]

For Marx, the evolution of surplus labor is not a simple direct function of natural conditions; it is, rather, an outcome of the co-evolution of human needs and human laboring capacities in and through specific relations between the laboring and the exploiting classes under definite natural conditions:

At the dawn of civilisation the productiveness acquired by labour is small, but so too are the wants which develop with and by the means of satisfying them. Further, at that early period, the portion of society that lives on the labour of others is infinitely small compared with the mass of direct producers. Along with the progress in the productiveness of labour, that small portion of society increases both absolutely and relatively. (1967a, I, 512)

In short, Marx notes, "it is only after . . . labour has been to some extent socialised, that a state of things arises in which the surplus-labour of the one becomes a condition of existence for the other" (1967a, I, 512). Still, Marx stresses that "in no case would . . . surplus-product arise from some occult quality inherent in human labour" apart from its natural *and* social conditions (515).[3]

The Natural Basis of Surplus Value

For Marx, "the fact that the production of use-values, or goods, is carried on under the control of a capitalist and on his behalf, does not alter the general character of that production" as "a process in which both man and Nature participate" (Marx, 1967a, I, 177). It follows that "the bodies of commodities are combinations of two elements—matter and labour" and that "if we take away the useful labour expended upon them, a material substratum is always left, which is furnished by Nature without the help of man" (43). Given that surplus value, the capitalist form of surplus labor, must first of all be objectified in produced commodities, it is no great surprise to find Marx stressing the continuing natural basis of surplus labor (in the form of surplus value) under capitalism: "Thus we may say that surplus-value rests on a natural basis," namely, "on the naturally originating productivity of labour, which produces more than the absolutely necessary subsistence of the worker, a natural productivity which of course rests on qualities of its inorganic nature—qualities of the soil, etc." (1967a, I, 511; 1994, 155).

In Volume III of *Capital,* Marx specifies "the general conditions for the existence of surplus-value" as follows:

> These conditions are: the direct producers must work beyond the time necessary for reproducing their own labour-power, for their own reproduction. . . . This is the subjective condition. The objective condition is that they must be *able* to perform surplus-labour. The natural conditions must be such that a *part* of their available labour-time suffices for their reproduction and self-maintenance as producers, that the production of their necessary means of subsistence shall not consume their whole labour-power. The fertility of Nature establishes a limit here, a starting-point, a basis. (1967a, III, 634)[4]

Indeed, as part of his analysis of the origins of capitalist ground rent, Marx argues that this natural basis of surplus value represents the important kernel of truth in physiocratic doctrine:

The physiocrats, furthermore, are correct in stating that in fact all production of surplus-value, and thus all development of capital, has for its natural basis the productiveness of agricultural labour. If man were not capable of producing in one working-day more means of subsistence, which signifies in the strictest sense more agricultural products than every labourer needs, for his own reproduction, if the daily expenditure of his entire labour-power sufficed merely to produce the means of subsistence indispensable for his own individual requirements, then one could not speak at all either of surplus-product or surplus-value. An agricultural labour productivity exceeding the individual requirements of the labourer is the basis of all societies, and is above all the basis of capitalist production, which disengages a constantly increasing portion of society from the production of basic foodstuffs and transforms them into "free heads," as Steuart has it, making them available for exploitation in other spheres. (785–86)

The natural basis of surplus value is more than just an initial condition of capitalist production; it is an ongoing determinant of the *amount* of surplus value, hence of the rate of capital accumulation. As Marx indicates: "Capitalist production once assumed, then, all other circumstances remaining the same, and given the length of the working-day, the quantity of surplus-labour will vary with the physical conditions of labour, especially with the fertility of the soil" (1967a, I, 513). Surplus value must be objectified in commodity use values, which always have a natural basis and substance. Hence, it is only "by incorporating with itself the two primary creators of wealth, labour-power and the land" that "capital acquires a power of expansion" (604; see Chapters 5–6 for details).

However, the observation that "surplus-value rests on a natural basis" is valid "only in a very general sense," the reason being that "capital with its accompanying relations springs up from an *economic* soil that is the product of a long process of development" (1967a, I, 511–22; emphasis added). Production of surplus value is, like all forms of production, "a process between man and Nature"; but it is also a social process involving an historically specific "coercive relation" between capital and labor that "compels the working-class to do more work than the narrow round of its own life-wants prescribes" (508, 309):

Nature does not produce on the one side owners of money or commodities, and on the other men possessing nothing but their own labour-power. This relation has no natural basis, neither is its social basis one that is common to all historical periods. It is clearly the result of a past historical development, the product of many economic revolutions, of the extinction of a whole series of older forms of social production. (169)[5]

Despite the historically unique character of capitalist production, Marx always insists on its necessary material basis and substance in an interchange or metabolism between people and nature. Under capitalism, just as "on the first day of production, the original producer-formers, now turned into the creators of the material elements of capital—man and Nature—still work together" (1967a, I, 603). In showing how production is developed in and through capitalist social relations, Marx also establishes the historically specific character of capitalist people-nature relations (see Chapters 5–7).

Further Notes on Labor and Natural Conditions

Benton (1989) argues that Marx's labor-process analysis understates the dependence of human production on irreplaceable natural conditions. Benton's critique centers on "the 'labour process' as a transhistorical condition of human survival" (64), as demarcated in Chapter 7, Volume I, of *Capital*: "The elementary factors of the labour-process are 1, the personal activity of man, i.e., the work itself, 2, the subject of that work, and 3, its instruments" (Marx, 1967a, I, 178). Benton argues that this classification

> under-represents the significance of non-manipulable natural conditions of labour-processes and over-represents the role of human intentional transformative powers vis-à-vis nature. . . . Marx does, indeed, recognize such activities as felling timber, catching fish, extracting ore, and agriculture as labour-processes. . . . But in recognizing the necessity of [natural] conditions, Marx simultaneously fails to recognize their significance by including them *within* the category of "instruments of production." These conditions cannot plausibly be considered "conductors" of the activity of the labourer. (1989, 64, 66, 72)

In short, Benton's complaint is that

> the conceptual assimilation of contextual *conditions* of the labour-process to the category of "instruments of production" has the effect of occluding the essential dependence of all labour-processes upon at least some non-manipulable contextual conditions. . . . [T]he subjection to human *intentionality* which is implicit in the concept of an "instrument" is precisely what *cannot* be plausibly attributed to these contextual conditions of production. (72)

This critique is based on a partial dematerialization of Marx's labor-process conception. Specifically, it obscures Marx's internal differentiation of the "instruments" category to explicitly incorporate natural conditions that are *not* direct conductors of human labor:

> In a wider sense we may include among the instruments of labour, in addition to those things that are used for directly transferring labour to its subject, and which therefore, in one way or another, serve as conductors of activity, all such objects as are necessary for carrying on the labour-process. These do not enter directly into the process, but without them it is either impossible for it to take place at all, or possible only to a partial extent. Once more we find the earth to be a universal instrument of this sort, for it furnishes a locus standi to the labourer and a field of employment for his activity. (Marx, 1967a, I, 180)

Curiously, Benton *partially* quotes this passage—mentioning only that "Marx proposes to include . . . the earth itself (which 'furnishes a locus standi to the labourer and a field of employment for his activity') . . . among the instruments of labour ('in a wider sense')" (1989, 65–66). Benton thus conceals Marx's recognition of "all such objects as are necessary for carrying on the labour-process" as a distinct ("universal") category of productive instruments. This category includes not only "the earth" as "a locus standi and field of employment" but all natural conditions that, while not directly conducting human labor, are necessary for the labor process—as follows from Marx's terminology (not mentioned by Benton) in which the earth encompasses all forces and elements of nature.[6] The universal instruments category accords with *Capital's* earlier analysis of *commodity* use values, where Marx emphasizes that labor "is constantly helped by natural forces" (1967a, I, 43).

In short, far from *assimilating* natural conditions to a pre-determined productive instruments category, Marx *consciously variegates the instruments category* so as to distinguish those natural conditions that do not directly conduct human labor from those means of production that do serve as labor conductors. Similar problems emerge when Benton extends his rather liberal translation of Marx's Chapter 7 from the instruments to the subjects of labor:

> Marx concedes that some very elementary transactions with nature do not require artificial implements, and here human limbs themselves can be regarded as playing the part of "instruments of production." The "subject" of labour—the thing or material worked on—may be "spontaneously provided by nature," or, more commonly, it will have been "filtered through past

labour," in which case Marx speaks (somewhat misleadingly) of "raw material." (1989, 65)

Benton's description of produced instruments as "artificial" leaves the incorrect impression that for Marx, produced instruments have no natural basis or substance. Similarly, Benton sets up a false opposition between "spontaneously provided" and the ("more common") "filtered" subjects of labor—as if, for Marx, labor necessarily negates the natural characteristics of its nature-given subjects or reduces the importance of these characteristics for human production. Indeed, Benton's statement seems to suggest that Marx limited the importance of nature-provided means of production to those cases in which laborers use no instruments other than their own limbs! Here again, a far different picture emerges from Marx's text:

> The soil (and this, economically speaking, includes water) in the virgin state in which it supplies man with necessaries or the means of subsistence ready to hand, exists independently of him, and is the universal subject of human labour. All those things which labour merely separates from immediate connection with their environment, are subjects of labour spontaneously provided by nature. (Marx, 1967a, I, 178)

Notice that Marx in no way limits the role of "spontaneously provided subjects of labour" to "very elementary transactions with nature" in which labor uses no produced instruments, nor does Marx give any impression that the natural characteristics of these "universal subjects" become less important as a result of their being subjects of human labor.

Evidently, Marx needs to be reconstructed because, instead of using terms such as "non-manipulable contextual conditions" (Benton, 1989, 72), his terminology refers to natural conditions as universal "instruments and subject[s] of labour . . . means of production" (Marx, 1967a, I, 181). This despite the fact that Marx—far more intuitively than Benton—repeatedly insists on the irreplaceability of natural conditions by human labor:

> It appears paradoxical to assert, that uncaught fish, for instance, are a means of production in the fishing industry. But hitherto no one has discovered the art of catching fish in waters that contain none. (1967a, I, 181)
>
> In so far then, as its instruments and subjects are themselves products, labour consumes products in order to create products. . . . But, just as in the beginning, the only participators in the labour-process were man and the earth, which latter exists independently of man, so even now we still employ in the process many means of production, provided directly by Nature,

that do not represent any combination of natural substances with human labour. (1967a, I, 183)

In sum, Benton's critique seems to confuse terminological preference with conceptual assimilation. Certainly, Benton fails to demonstrate "defects in Marx's *concept* of the labour-process" from the standpoint of "non-manipulable contextual conditions" (1989, 72, 76, emphasis added; for further details, see Burkett, 1998b).

Marx on Eco-Regulated Labor and Production

Benton also suggests that "Marx's abstract concept of the labour process . . . assimilates all labour-processes to a 'productive' model" by not adequately encompassing "eco-regulatory" processes such as agriculture, in which

> human labour is not deployed to bring about an intended transformation in a raw material. It is, rather, primarily deployed to sustain or regulate the environmental conditions under which seed or stock animals grow and develop. There *is* a transformative moment in these labour processes, but the transformations are brought about by naturally given organic mechanisms, not by the application of human labour. (1989, 67)

Benton's point is that farming and other eco-regulatory labor processes have "an intentional structure which is quite different from . . . productive, transformative labour-processes" where the processing of the subjects of labor bears a more direct correspondence, both temporally and materially, with the direct operation of human labor on these subjects (1989, 67). Eco-regulatory labor "is primarily . . . a labour of sustaining, regulating and reproducing, rather than transforming"—a labor that "is applied primarily to optimizing the *conditions* for transformations, which are themselves organic processes, relatively impervious to intentional modification. The 'subject of labour' . . . is therefore *not* the raw material which will become the 'principal substance' of the 'product' but, rather, the conditions within which it grows and develops" (67–68).

An obvious feature of eco-regulatory processes is that the "spatial and temporal distributions of labouring activity are to a high degree shaped by the contextual conditions of the labour-process and by the rhythms of organic developmental processes." As discussed earlier, Benton argues that these conditions and processes are "not readily assimilable to Marx's tripartite classification (labour, instruments of labour, raw materials)" (1989, 68).

Responding to Benton's claim that *Capital* inadequately encompasses eco-regulatory processes, Grundmann (1991b, 108) suggests that "for Marx human interventions into . . . natural processes also count as transformative actions, since prepared ground is quite different from untouched nature." On one level, I agree with Grundmann on this point. For Marx, the utilization of natural conditions and processes for the production of use values must involve some contact of human labor with these conditions and processes at one moment or another—even in cases where such labor is limited to eco-regulation or, for that matter, primary appropriation (see Chapters 2 and 8). This necessary role of human labor in the production of use values explains why Marx is able to categorize the elements of the labor process in terms of their respective positions vis-à-vis the intended outcome(s) of this process.[7] That many conditions and processes of production are provided by nature does not change the fact that their appropriation and use is subject to human intentionality.

At the same time, I disagree with Grundmann's (1991b, 108) outright denial of any "significant difference between transformative and 'eco-regulatory' labour processes." The problem with this dismissal of Benton's argument is that it does not recognize how Marx formally analyzes the special role of natural conditions and processes in eco-regulatory production. In this connection, Grundmann fails to address one obvious question raised by Benton's critique. That is, if Marx's labor-process analysis inadequately encompasses eco-regulation, why was Marx able to use eco-regulated practices (agriculture, livestock raising, and the preparation of conditions for chemical and biological processes in industry) as *examples* of human labor in Chapter 7 of *Capital*, Volume I (1967a, I, pp.181–82)?

Part of the answer to this apparent puzzle is provided by the categorical distinctions Marx employs to differentiate eco-regulatory processes from other forms of production. Marx observes, for example, how "a particular product may be used in one and the same process, both as an instrument of labour and as raw material," as in the case of "the fattening of cattle, where the animal is the raw material, and at the same time an instrument for the production of manure" (182). Similarly, when referring to forestry and livestock production, Marx indicates that the "supply—a certain amount of standing timber or livestock—exists . . . simultaneously as instruments of labour and material of labour, in accordance with the natural conditions of its reproduction under proper management" (1967a, II, 244). Meanwhile, in order to distinguish the features of industrial eco-regulatory processes, Marx differentiates those "raw materials" forming "the principal substance of a product" from those which "enter into its formation only as an accessory":

An accessory may be consumed by the instruments of labour, as coal under a boiler, oil by a wheel, hay by draft-horses, or it may be mixed with the raw material in order to produce some modification thereof, as chlorine into unbleached linen, coal with iron, dye-stuff with wool, or again, it may help to carry on the work itself, as in the case of the materials used for heating and lighting workshops. The distinction between principle substance and accessory vanishes in the true chemical industries, because there none of the raw material re-appears, in its original composition, in the substance of the product. (1967a, I, 181)

Given Marx's categorization of the earth as the universal instrument and universal subject of labor, the above categorical distinctions can be applied to all natural conditions and processes "necessary for carrying on the labour-process" in eco-regulatory contexts (180).

Another distinction ignored by both Benton (1989) and Grundmann (1991b) is that between labor and production. Indeed, Benton's "eco-regulation" critique presumes that Marx identified the production process with the labor process. Actually, Marx specifies the "labour-process [as] human action *with a view to the production* of use values" and as a "*necessary condition*" for effecting exchange of matter between man and Nature"—a "*universal condition*" for the metabolic interaction between nature and man" (1967a, I, 183–84; 1988, 63, emphases added). That Marx does not reduce the production process to the labor process is clear from the examples of eco-regulatory production in Chapter 7 of *Capital,* Volume I, in which Marx speaks of the "gradual transformation [of] animals and plants . . . under man's superintendence," as well as the "modification" of (accessory and principal) raw materials by organic processes in industry (1967a, I, 181).

The labor/production distinction is clarified in Volume II of *Capital,* where Marx states that "the time of production naturally comprises the period of the labour-process, but is not comprised in it" (1967a, II, 121). Excesses of production time over labor time are not only due to "interruptions of the labour-process necessitated by natural limitations of the labour-power itself . . . by night for instance" (121, 238). Rather,

the process of production may itself be responsible for interruptions of the labour-process, and hence of the labour-time—intervals during which the subject of labour is exposed to the action of physical processes without the further intervention of human labour. The process of production, and thus the functioning of the means of production, continue in this case, although the labour-process, and thus the functioning of the means of production as instruments of labour, have been interrupted. This applies, for instance, to the grain, after it has been sown, the wine fermenting in the cellar, the labour-material of many factories, such as tanneries, where the material is exposed to the action of chemical processes. The time of production is here longer than the labour-time. (122)

Here Marx expressly states that during the excess of production time over labor time, means of production continue to function—that is, continue to produce use values—even though their functioning as instruments of labor has been interrupted.[8] In other words, Marx's analysis is quite capable of handling eco-regulatory processes based on his distinction between labor and production. Indeed, Marx often uses this distinction to emphasize the more naturally constrained role of human intentionality in eco-regulatory processes. For example:

The difference between production time and working time becomes especially apparent in agriculture. In our moderate climates the land bears grain once a year. Shortening or lengthening the period of production (for winter grain it averages nine months) itself depends on the alternation of good and bad seasons, and for this reason cannot be accurately determined and controlled beforehand as in industry proper. Only such by-products as milk, cheese, etc. can steadily be produced and sold in comparatively short periods. (1967a, II, 240)

In *Capital*, Marx only fully develops the above categorical distinctions applicable to eco-regulatory processes *after* Chapter 7, Section 1 of Volume I, that is, mainly in the context of analyses of specifically capitalist production. The reason is straightforward: the actual development of situations where means of production function as both instruments and raw material, of production processes involving different combinations of accessory and principal raw materials, and of the corresponding deviations between production time and labor time, can only be analyzed in relation to the specific social relations of production in and through which such developments occur.

Benton even forgets that Marx's labor-process classification in Chapter 7 of *Capital*, Volume I, could not incorporate eco-regulation as an intrinsic element for the simple reason that eco-regulatory labor is not a transhistorical element of human-social labor. If one follows Benton's suggestion and treats eco-regulation as transhistorical, one arbitrarily bypasses the possibility (and the historical fact) of human production on the basis of practices such as simple hunting and gathering—practices that do not require any "human labour . . . deployed to sustain or regulate the environmental conditions under which seed or stock animals grow and develop" (Benton, 1989, 67). Such primary-appropriative practices do, however—if socially organized—conform to Marx's conception of human labor, which is precisely why Marx includes them as examples of human labor in Chapter 7, Section 1 of *Capital,* Volume I (1967a, I, 178–83).

In short, since eco-regulation is not transhistorical in the sense demanded by Chapter 7, Volume I of *Capital,* it does not constitute a legitimate basis for a "critique and reconstruction" of Marx's transhistorical specification of human labor. As noted above, however, this does not mean that *Capital* contains no analyses of eco-regulatory processes. To see the logic of these analyses, one must remember the ordering of economic categories employed by Marx (Rosdolsky, 1977, 41–50; Burkett, 1991).

To begin with, insofar as capitalistic eco-regulation involves historically specific distinctions and relations between labor time and production time, it could only be formally treated in Volume II, where Marx analyzes the circulation and turnover of capital. The subject of Volume I is the basic class-exploitative nature of capitalist production; capitalism's reshaping of the material process of production is dealt with in this volume only insofar as is absolutely necessary to establish the historical specificity of capitalist exploitation and accumulation (see Marx, 1967a, I, 564–65, II, 23). However, that Volume I formally abstracts from divergences between production time and labor time does not mean this volume ignores eco-regulatory processes. Volume I's treatment of capitalism as a specific class form of production includes an analysis of capital's appropriation of natural conditions as a necessary condition of accumulation (see Chapters 5 and 6). In this context, Marx refers to "the purely mechanical working of the soil itself . . . on the amount of the product" as one of the "circumstances that . . . determine the amount of accumulation" (1967a, I, 599, 604).

In analyzing how, with industrial capital accumulation, "a radical change in the mode of production in one sphere of industry involves a similar change in other spheres" (Marx, 1967a, I, 383), Volume I of *Capital* deals with the capitalist division of labor between agriculture and industry. This includes the promotion of technological changes in agriculture by advances in eco-regulatory industrial methods and vice versa, and the attendant "separation between town and country" that, by "upsetting the naturally grown conditions for . . . the circulation of matter," winds up "sapping the original sources of all wealth—the soil and the labourer" (352, 505–7; see Chapter 9 for details).

In short, Volume I does treat eco-regulation insofar as is essential for establishing the "antagonistic character of capitalist production and accumulation" toward the producers and their natural environment (Marx, 1967a,

I, 673). Eco-regulatory processes are placed under a more powerful micro-scope in Volume II, where "excess[es] of the production time over the labour-time" arising from capital "functioning in the productive process without taking part in the labour-process" are a central concern in Marx's investigation of the circulation of capital (1967a, II, 122). Here Marx conducts detailed analyses of

> interruptions independent of the length of the labour-process, brought about by the very nature of the product and its fabrication, during which the subject of labour is for a longer or shorter time subjected to natural processes, must undergo physical, chemical and physiological changes, during which the labour-process is entirely or partially suspended. For instance grape after being pressed must ferment awhile and then rest for some time in order to reach a certain degree of perfection. In many branches of industry the product must pass through a drying process, for instance in pottery, or be exposed to certain conditions in order to change its chemical properties, as for instance in bleaching. Winter grain needs about nine months to mature. Between the time of sowing and harvesting the labour-process is almost entirely suspended. In timber-raising, after the sowing and the incidental preliminary work are completed, the seed requires about 100 years to be transformed into a finished product and during all that time it stands in comparatively very little need of the action of labour. . . . In all these cases therefore the production time of the advanced capital consists of two periods: one period during which the capital is engaged in the labour-process and a second period during which its form of existence—that of an unfinished product—is abandoned to the sway of natural processes. (238–39)

Chapter 13 of Volume II analyzes many cases where "differences between production time and working time" arise—a phenomenon that "admits of many variations" in terms of its effects on the circulation of capital materially and socially (1967a, II, 246). Numerous such analyses occur in other chapters of this volume, as when Marx discusses how "many raw materials, semi-finished goods, etc., require rather long periods of time for their production . . . especially . . . raw materials furnished by agriculture," or when Marx observes how in eco-regulatory spheres "varying amounts of capital [have] to be invested in different working periods, as for instance in agriculture" (143, 259). These analyses show great sensitivity to the special role of "contextual conditions" and "organic developmental processes" in eco-regulatory production (Benton, 1989, 68). The distinctive conditions of eco-regulated capital circulation are, in fact, central to Volume II's view that "the economic process of reproduction, whatever may be its specific social character, always becomes intertwined . . . with a natural process of reproduction" (Marx, 1967a, II, 359).

Even in Volume II, however, eco-regulation is treated in abstraction from the distinct roles of landed property, rents, and price fluctuations associated with market competition—all of which are only dealt with in Volume III. In the latter volume, Marx analyzes "the violent price fluctuations of one of the main elements in the process of reproduction . . . raw materials taken from organic nature . . . vegetable and animal substances whose growth and production are subject to certain organic laws and bound up with definite natural time periods" (1967a, III, 119–21). Marx roots both the origins and the materially disruptive effects of such price fluctuations in the contradiction between competitive capital accumulation and rational, sustainable agricultural practices. Volume III also extends Marx's analysis of the capitalist separation of town and country, paying close attention to the role of naturally variegated conditions in influencing the different forms of eco-regulatory production and corresponding rents (see Chapters 7 and 9).

When analyzing the productivity of agricultural investment, for example, Marx insists that "the peculiar nature of agriculture must be taken into account," since "it is not only a matter of the social, but also of the natural, productivity of labour which depends on the natural conditions of labour"; indeed, Marx emphasizes that "the increase in social productivity in agriculture" may "barely compensate, or not even compensate, for the decrease in natural power" (1967a, III, 766; cf. 691, 708–10, 733). Similarly, near the beginning of the section on differential rent, Marx emphasizes "climactic factors," differences in "the chemical composition of the top soil," and "location of the land" as factors—"quite independent of capital"—that influence "the unequal results of equal quantities of capital applied to different plots of land of equal size" (650–51). All of this is quite consistent with Marx's definition of a rent-yielding natural condition as a "monopolisable . . . condition for an increase in the productiveness of the invested capital that cannot be established by the production process of the capital itself" (645). Indeed, given that some of Marx's richest treatments of eco-regulation occur in his analysis of capitalist rents, Benton's failure to even mention Marx's rent theory is quite puzzling.

CHAPTER 4

Labor and Labor Power
as Natural and Social Forces

For Marx, labor is the creative, subjective factor in production conceived as a necessary part of the material metabolism between people and nature. Individual and collective human labors take place and evolve in and through definite social relations. Human production is thus constituted jointly by social production relations and the material characteristics of nature itself (see Chapter 2).

Marx often emphasizes the jointly material and social character of production by characterizing human labor and labor power as natural and social forces. Hence he describes labor power as a "natural force of human beings," or as a "living . . . social force," and human labor as "a social and natural force," or "human exertion as a specifically harnessed natural force" (1967a, III, 813, I, 239; 1977, 1056; 1973, 400, 612). While insisting that human laboring capacities are socially developed, organized, and utilized, Marx still emphasizes that "labour . . . is only the manifestation of a natural force, human labour power" (1966, 3).

Labor and Labor Power as Natural Forces

Human "labour-power or capacity for labor is to be understood [as] the aggregate of those mental and physical capabilities existing in a human being, which he exercises whenever he produces a use-value of any description" (Marx, 1967a, I, 167). This aggregate is a natural force insofar as it is subject to the physical and biological laws governing all of nature. Labor power "exists only as a capacity, or power of the living individual," as "a definite quantity of human muscle, nerve, brain &c.," and as such it is subject to "wear and tear and death" and must therefore "perpetuate [it-self] by procreation" (171–72). While "a certain mass of necessaries must be consumed by a man to grow up and maintain his life, . . . another amount" is required "to bring up a certain quota of children." In order "to maintain and reproduce itself, to perpetuate its physical existence, the working class must receive the necessaries absolutely indispensable for liv-ing and multiplying" (1976b, 39, 57). These "natural wants, such as food, clothing, fuel, and housing, vary according to . . . climactic and other phys-ical conditions" (1967a, I, 171).

Like all life forces, labor power represents "energy transferred . . . by means of nourishing matter," and this power "becomes a reality only by its exercise" (215, 171). Labor entails "expenditure of a certain amount of human muscles, nerves, brain, etc. [that] . . . exist in the [human] organ-ism . . . and these require to be restored" (1970, 31; 1967a, I, 44, 171). The worker's "means of subsistence must therefore be sufficient" not just for physical survival as such, but also "to maintain him in his normal state as a labouring individual . . . [since] he must again be able to repeat the same process in the same conditions as regards health and strength" (1967a, I, 171). Clearly, "free time to dispose of" is a natural means of subsistence of this sort, since a laborer "whose whole lifetime, apart from the mere phys-ical interruptions by sleep, meals, and so forth, is absorbed by his labour . . . is less than a beast of burden" (1976b, 54). It follows that for Marx, any reduction of workers' free time *or* material consumption "to the bare *physical minimum*"—any "diseased, compulsory, and painful . . . daily expenditure of labour-power" that "shorten[s] the extent of the labourer's life"—represents an unnatural "deterioration of [the laborer's] race" (1977, 1068; 1967a, I, 265; 1976b, 55). Such a "state of degradation" of people as natural beings takes place, for example, whenever insufficient free time "reduces the sound sleep needed for the restoration, reparation, refreshment of the bodily powers to just so many hours of torpor as the revival of an organism, absolutely exhausted, renders essential" (1976b, 54; 1967a, I, 265).

Labor and Labor Power as Social Forces

Labor and labor power are social forces insofar as (1) labor contributes to human-material reproduction in and through society; and (2) the repro-duction and evolution of labor power is itself a social process (Marx, 1978b). It is in terms of the first aspect that Marx refers to "the main force of production, the human being himself" (1973, 422). In their writings on the United States, for example, Marx and Engels emphasized the role of population as a socially harnessed natural productive force. They included the "energetic, active population" and the "personal energy of the individuals of various nations . . . transplanted to an already developed soil" as among the factors that "enabled the United States to exploit its tremendous industrial resources with an energy and on a scale that [would] shortly break the industrial monopoly of Western Europe" (Marx and Engels, 1979, 42–43, 256). This is in line with Marx's general inclusion of "the different natural energies and acquired working abilities of different peoples" as one of the forces on which "the productive powers of labour must principally depend" (1976b, 34). Given the requisite natural conditions, moreover, "the increase in population increases the productive power of labour, by making possible division of labour, cooperation, etc." (Marx, 1994, 17).

In *The Poverty of Philosophy*, Marx argues that the social productive force of human beings takes on a special form and significance in periods when "all the productive forces which could be engendered in the bosom of the old society" have been developed. During such intervals, "the productive powers already acquired and the existing social relations" tend to be "no longer . . . capable of existing side by side," so that the utilization and further development of these powers requires an "organization of revolutionary elements as a class" and "the creation of a new society." In this sense, "of all the instruments of production, the greatest productive power is the revolutionary class itself" (1978a, 169; cf. 1970, 21).

To fully understand Marx's conception of labor power as a social force, however, it is necessary to keep in mind Marx's historical approach to human production. Marx specifies and analyzes each form of production in terms of the specific social relations through which a "natural law" of human-material reproduction is fulfilled, namely, the necessity of a "distribution of social labour in definite proportions," enmeshed with natural conditions, so as to ensure a "volume of products corresponding to the different needs" (Marx to Kugelmann, July 11, 1868, in Marx and Engels [1975, 196]). Given this requirement, labor is a social productive force only insofar as it is "subordinate to" and forms part of "the *division of labour within society*" (Marx, 1976b, 30). The social character of human labor is shown by the fact that any particular labor (or any particular division of labor in a single workplace or industry) "is nothing without the other division of labour, and on its part is required to integrate them" (30–31). In sum, labor is a social force insofar as it contributes to the material reproduction of society by its participation in a social division of labor. This labor "must not only produce use-values, but use-values for others, social use-values" (1967a, I, 41). In this very specific sense, labor power is a central part of society's life forces.

It follows from this approach that "use-value itself . . . possesses an historically specific character" depending on "the form in which [the necessary] distribution of labour asserts itself," that is, on the specific social relations in and through which particular labors and products are integrated into the social division of labor (Marx, 1975, 199; Marx to Kugelmann, July 11, 1868, in Marx and Engels [1975, 196]). Under capitalism, the dominant form of use value is "the use-value of the commodity," the reason being that in this "social system . . . the interconnection of social labour manifests itself through the private exchange of individual products of labor" produced for a profit, so that the requirements of human need satisfaction are registered indirectly, "precisely [in] the exchange value of . . . products" (Marx, 1975, 199; Marx to Kugelmann, July 11, 1868, in Marx and Engels [1975, 196]). Use values that cannot be produced and sold at a profit—including many natural and social conditions required for or contributing to human production and development—tend to be undervalued or not valued at all, and this is an important source of ecological and social crises (see Chapters 6 and 7).[1]

Social production relations influence the development of human needs and laboring capacities in production. After all, in the process of production "not only do the objective conditions change . . . but the producers change, too, in that they bring out new qualities in themselves, . . . transform themselves, develop new powers and ideas, new modes of intercourse, new needs and new language," which "modify [their] functions and activities as the creators of material wealth" (Marx, 1973, 494; 1968, 288). Production "leads to new needs; and this creation of new needs is the first historical act" (Marx and Engels, 1976, 48).[2] The kinds of needs and capabilities generated in the production process will be conditioned jointly by the social relations among producers (both within and among individual workplaces) and the material characteristics of the production process. In this sense, too, labor and labor power are not only natural but also social forces.

Most directly, labor power is a socially constituted force insofar as the family within which labor power is reproduced is itself a fundamental social relation. Hence "the production of life," including "fresh life in procreation, now appears as a twofold relation: on the one hand as a natural, on the other as a social relation" (Marx and Engels, 1976, 48–49). The place of the family in conditioning the development of society's laboring class is apparent from Marx's analysis of the determination of the value of labor power under capitalism. In *Capital,* Marx suggests that "the number and extent of . . . so-called necessary wants, as also the modes of satisfying them, are themselves the product of historical development, and depend therefore to a great extent . . . on the conditions under which . . . the class of free labourers has been formed" (1967a, I, 171). Elsewhere, Marx reiterates that the "traditional standard of life" of the laborer involves "not mere physical life, but . . . certain wants springing from the social conditions in which people are placed and reared up" (1976b, 57). Clearly, family relations must be included as one of the basic "aspects of social activity" in and through which human laboring capacities have been developed, "and which still assert themselves today" (Marx and Engels, 1976, 48).[3]

The Natural and Social Force of Labor and Human Evolution

For Marx, human production is part of the material metabolism between people and nature—the part involving human labor operating in and through specific social relations and under definite natural conditions (see Chapters 2–3). Therefore, to say that labor and labor power are social and natural productive forces in no way implies the existence of two separate, autonomous realms or aspects of human production, one social and the other more natural or material. Labor can only operate as a social productive force—a force satisfying human needs developed in and through society— insofar as it is a natural force materially capable of appropriating, transforming, and ultimately conserving the actual and potential use values present in nature. As Marx says: "Use-values . . . are combinations of two elements— matter and labour," and labor "can only work as Nature does, that is by changing the form of matter" (1967a, I, 43). Human labor, "constantly helped by natural forces," only "changes the forms of the materials furnished by Nature, in such a way as to make them useful" (43, 71).

This leads to another sense in which labor and labor power are natural and social forces, namely, that the process by which society arose and evolved was itself a product of human labor developing out of the prehistoric animal-like unity of proto-humans with nature. As Engels puts it,

labour created man himself. . . . Hundreds of thousands of years—of no greater significance in the history of the earth than one second in the life of man—certainly elapsed before human society arose out of a troupe of tree-climbing monkeys. Yet it did finally appear. And what do we find as the characteristic difference between the troupe of monkeys and human society? *Labour.* (1964a, 172, 177)

It was indeed as a condition and result of "useful activity directed to the appropriation of natural factors in one form or another" that human society arose and developed—and with it the uniquely social and self-conscious character of human labor (Marx, 1970, 36; see Mandel, 1968, Chapter 1). In this sense, "all *natural forces of social labour* are themselves historical products" (Marx, 1973, 400). Marx's conception of labor and labor power as natural and social forces thus encapsulates the peculiarly historical character and potential of humanity as a natural yet self-positing and social species. This human-evolutionary angle is equally evident in Marx's vision of the "fully developed individual . . . to whom the different social functions he performs are but so many modes of giving free scope to his own natural and acquired powers"—a vision whose realization depends on "circumstances that allow all-round activity and thereby the full development of all our potentialities" (1967a, I, 488; Marx and Engels, 1976, 272). In Marx's projection, this "associated, social individual," for whom "the historic childhood of humanity, its most beautiful unfolding, as a stage never to return, exercise[s] an eternal charm," will have a much different, more healthy, and sustainable relationship with nature than is the case for individual workers (or capitalists) under capitalism, based on communism's democratic socialization of the conditions of production (1994, 109; 1973, 111). However, before considering this projection in detail (see Part III), it is necessary to establish the specific forms of alienation from nature that, in Marx's view, are characteristic of capitalism.

PART II

Nature and Capitalism

CHAPTER 5

Nature, Labor, and Capitalist Production

The common ground of Marx's materialism and Marx's analysis of capitalism is that all societies must allocate their labor among productive, that is, need-satisfying, activities entailing appropriation from nature. This allocation involves specific social relations in and through which each portion of society's total work-time is integrated into a division of labor enmeshed with natural conditions.[1]

Under capitalism, the division of labor takes the form of market (commodity and money) relations, based on the historically extreme social separation of the human producers from necessary conditions of production. Marx's analysis explains how this separation, by enabling labor and its natural and social conditions to be developed as conditions of competitive capital accumulation, leads to an historically unprecedented growth of their wealth-producing powers. At the same time, Marx emphasizes capital's tendency to plunder and vitiate its own human and natural conditions of existence. Chapters 6 and 7 establish capitalism's antagonism with nature from the standpoint of the value form of commodities, money, and capital. The present chapter focuses on the basic relations between workers' social separation from production conditions on the one hand, and the historical specificity of the natural conditions and limits of capitalist production on the other. Since these relations themselves implicate the conversion of use value into a condition and material vehicle of exchange value, we begin with a brief exposition of the necessary basis of generalized commodity production in the class relations of capitalism. This will also help set the stage for the value analysis.

Commodity Production and Capitalist Relations

In an economy in which social production occurs in private independent enterprises, the acceptance of any labor (including the labor of appropriating nature-provided means of production) as part of the reproductive division of social labor is only decided *ex post* by the exchange values that products command in the market. Exchange values validate particular labors as part of society's necessary labor time—"necessary," that is, to satisfy the needs that can be potentially satisfied with the total labor time at the disposal of society under given natural and social conditions.[2] This necessary labor time (as a whole or in particular portions) is what Marx calls abstract labor, and it constitutes the substance of value even though this substance is represented by money, the general equivalent form of value.[3] In short, when a commodity commands a money price, the particular concrete labor that went into its production is validated as socially necessary (abstract) labor "without regard to the mode of its expenditure" (Marx, 1967a, I, p.38).

The regulation of wealth production by exchange values presumes that individual members of society can obtain certain necessary use values only through the purchase of commodities with money obtained from commodity sales. A commodity economy thus precludes individuals (or households) from reproducing themselves independently of the market nexus.[4] This preclusion presupposes that both individually and collectively, the direct human producers lack access to some conditions required to produce necessary means of consumption outside the system of commodity production and exchange—that these necessary production conditions themselves take the form of commodities. This situation does not presuppose that *all* necessary use values and *all* conditions necessary for their production can only be obtained as purchased commodities but rather that a *significant portion* of them can only be so obtained. Indeed, the dependence of commodity production on conditions whose use values are not themselves validated by the market is a definite contradiction of such a system (see Chapters 6 through 8).[5]

Here, the key point about a social production process featuring commodified conditions of production is that it presupposes the social separation of the direct human producers from these conditions. It presumes, in other words, that the producers can only obtain necessary use values if they are united, as wage laborers, with the necessary production conditions after selling their labor power to the capitalists controlling these conditions (1967a, I, Chapters 26–33). In short, commodity production, with its regulation of the division of labor by monetary exchange values representing socially necessary labor time, can only be generalized and become the dominant form of production insofar as the dominant social relation of production is that between capital and "free" laborers:

> Free labourers, in the double sense that neither they themselves form part and parcel of the means of production, as in the case of slaves, bondsmen, &c., nor do the means of production belong to them, as in the case of peasant-proprietors; they are, therefore, free from, unencumbered by, any means of production of their own [sufficient for their own reproduction]. (1967a, I, 714)

"With this polarisation of the market for commodities," Marx adds, "the fundamental conditions of capitalist production are given" (714). Accordingly, Marx describes "the commodity-form of the product" as "the economic cell-form . . . in bourgeois society" (8). For Marx, it is only insofar as "production by means of wage-labour becomes universal, [that] commodity production is bound to be the general form of production" (1967a, II, 33). This is "because labour itself appears here as a commodity," so that "the money relation, the relation between the buyer and the seller, becomes a relation inherent in production" (116–17; cf. Marx, 1967a, I, 169, 587).

Some critics of Marx point to the possibility of production and exchange among self-employed business operators as proof that commodity production need not involve wage labor. Upon investigation, however, it becomes evident that *generalized* commodity production could not be underpinned by the reproduction of such petty bourgeois and/or peasant production. On the one hand, insofar as production by self-employed producers is oriented toward own use, with only the surpluses above necessary (production and consumption) needs being exchanged—and then mainly in order to obtain other use values rather than to accumulate money as an end in itself—it is inconsistent with a generalization of commodity relations to include a significant portion of the means of production. On the other hand, insofar as production becomes oriented toward monetary gain (and it must be remembered that this potential always exists even within a system of only partial production for monetary exchange), competition creates a powerful structural tendency toward its capitalization and wage-laborization. Of course, none of this precludes sizable incidences of petty bourgeois and/or peasant production within or on the margins of capitalist societies in which workers as a class have already been socially separated from necessary means of production.[6]

Labor, Nature, and Capital's Material Requirements

Having established the close affinity of generalized commodity production and capitalist relations in Marx's view, I will now consider the historically specific character of capitalism's natural conditions and limits. To begin with, among the production conditions from which laborers must be socially separated in order for capitalist production to commence, Marx assigns a prominent place to any natural conditions that might allow workers to reproduce themselves without becoming wage laborers. In *Capital*, Marx argues that "the expropriation of the agricultural producer, of the peasant, from the soil, is the basis of the whole process" by which "great masses of men are suddenly and forcibly torn from their means of subsistence, and hurled as free and 'unattached' proletarians on the labour-market" (1967a, I, 716). In this sense, "the expropriation of the mass of the people from the soil forms the basis of the capitalist mode of production" (768).[7]

Similarly, in an earlier consideration of "the historic preconditions for capital" in the *Grundrisse,* Marx suggests that "a presupposition of wage labour . . . is the separation of free labour from the objective conditions of its realization—from the means of labour and the material for labour. Thus, above all, release of the worker from the soil as his natural workshop" (1973, 471).

And further:

> The relation of labour to capital, or to the objective conditions of labour as capital, presupposes a process of history which dissolves the various forms in which the worker is a proprietor, or in which the proprietor works. Thus above all (1) *Dissolution* of the relation to the earth—land and soil—as natural condition of production—to which he relates as to his own inorganic being. (1973, 497)

Even in Engels' early *Outlines of a Critique of Political Economy,* the separation of the human producers from natural conditions of production is recognized as a fundamental basis of capitalism:

> To make the earth an object of huckstering—the earth which is our one and all, the first condition of our existence—was the last step toward making oneself an object of huckstering. . . . And the original appropriation—the monopolization of the earth by a few, the exclusion of the rest from that which is the condition of their life—yields nothing in immorality to the subsequent huckstering of the earth. (Engels, 1964b, 210)

With this social separation of wealth-creating labor from its natural conditions, "the objective moments . . . which labour needs at all for its realisation, appear as alienated from it, as standing on the side of capital, the means of subsistence no less than the means of labour" (Marx, 1988, 134–35). Means of subsistence "originally provided by nature free of charge" are now obtainable only by "earning" wages, i.e., through "the component of capital which buys labour capacity" (134). This is quite different from pre-capitalist societies, in which the individual worker relates "to the natural conditions of labour and of reproduction as belonging to him, as the objective, nature-given inorganic body of his subjectivity," even in those cases where this relation "appears mediated for him through a cession by the total unity . . . in the form of the despot, the father of the many communities—to the individual, through the mediation of the particular commune" (1973, 473). Under "slavery and serfdom," for example, the "separation" of workers from natural conditions of production "does not take place; rather one part of society is treated by the other as itself merely an inorganic and natural condition of its own reproduction . . . along with other natural beings, such as cattle, as an accessory of the earth"—so that the worker still "relates to a specific nature (say . . . earth, land, soil) as his own inorganic being" (489–90).

Capitalist production is therefore not constrained by the kinds of social ties between the laborers and natural conditions characterizing precapitalist societies. The material use-value requirements of capitalist production, in particular, are unencumbered by the producers' prior social ties to nature. The only *particular* use value *absolutely* required for capital accumulation is the use value of labor power, that is, the ability of human beings to expend surplus labor; without its appropriation of labor power's use value, there would be no source of profit for capital as a whole (1967a, I, Chapter 5).[8]

Of course, the existence of surplus labor, hence of surplus value, presumes that natural conditions are such that the entire work-time of the laborers producing means of subsistence is not absorbed in the production of *their own* means of subsistence (see Chapter 3). Exploitation of labor power's use value and its accumulation in the form of money also require that the labor expended by workers actually be useful labor, according to the judgement of the market. Capital thus requires not only exploitable labor power but also material conditions under which this labor power's use value can be objectified in *profitably vendible* use values. Nonetheless, these material conditions are only useful to capital insofar as they serve as vehicles for the exploitation and monetary realization of *labor power's* use value in the form of surplus value. As Marx indicates: "For money as capital, labour capacity is the *immediate use value* for which it has to exchange itself" (1987, 504; emphasis added).[9]

The tensions in the capital-nature relationship are already evident. On the one hand, capital requires living, physically functioning labor power and material conditions conducive to the embodiment of labor in need-satisfying products. Hence, like all forms of human wealth production, capitalist production is dependent on nature's contribution to use value (see Chapters 2 and 3). On the other hand, capital requires nature *only* in the form of "separate" material conditions for its appropriation of labor power's use value, not in the form of an organic social and material unity between the producers and their natural conditions of existence. This "separate" quality of natural conditions for capital corresponds to the social separation of the laborers from necessary conditions of their production, that is, to the fundamental class relation of capitalism. In short, capital's ranking of required use values, with exploitable labor power coming first, represents (1) a specifically capitalist abstraction from the necessary unity of human and extra-human nature; and (2) a social downgrading of nature *and* the human producers, of use value itself, to the status of mere conditions of money-making.

Capitalist Relations, Nature, and Human Needs

The conversion of natural conditions into a set of "separate" conditions for capital's exploitation of "free" labor power is, according to Marx, the flip side of the social separation of the human producers from necessary conditions of production. This specifically capitalist separation of labor and nature makes the material requirements of production much more autonomous from the extant evolution of extra-human nature than in pre-capitalist systems. In the latter, the social ties of the laborers to given natural conditions mean that the producers' (hence the system's) reproduction is more directly constrained by these conditions. This ecologically crucial difference between capitalist and pre-capitalist production can be approached from the standpoint of the needs of the human producers.

With production governed by capital's extraction of labor from free labor power and by the objectification of this labor in *vendible* use values, the subordination of use value (human need satisfaction) to exchange value is greatly enhanced.[10] True, commodity production and thus monetary exchange values can exist on the basis of non-capitalist production relations.[11] It is equally true that exchange value is always a social form of use value, which, given nature's necessary contribution to use value, means that exchange values always represent socially mediated people-nature relations.[12] But with capitalism, the laborers' access to necessary use values becomes dependent on the sale of their labor power to and its profitable exploitation by a capitalist controlling necessary production conditions. This relationship loosens the limitations formerly placed on exchange value by particular, given human needs more closely bound up with given natural conditions.

In a pre-capitalist economy, the scope for regulation of production by exchange values is limited by the social ties between the producers and the natural conditions of production—ties that tend to create a situation in which "production is *determined* by need" (Marx, 1967b, 277). Specifically, the pre-capitalist sphere of exchange value is limited by "the content outside the act of exchange . . . outside the specifically economic form" of exchange itself. This content "can only be: (1) The natural particularity of the commodity being exchanged; (2) The particular natural need of the exchangers, or, both together, the different use values of the commodities being exchanged" (1973, 242). Without capitalism's social separation of the laborers from necessary means of production, in other words,

> exchange-value does not acquire an independent form, but is still directly tied to use value. This is manifested in two ways. Use-value, not exchange-value, is the purpose of the whole system of production, and use-values accordingly cease to be use-values and become means of exchange, or commodities, only when a larger amount of them has been produced than is required for consumption. On the other hand, they become commodities only within the limits set by their immediate use-value. (1970, 50)

"It is," moreover, "clear that in any given economic formation of society, where not the exchange-value but the use-value of the product predominates, surplus-labour will be limited by a given set of wants which may be greater or less, and that here no boundless thirst for surplus-labour arises from the nature of production itself" (1967a, I, 235). In this sense, not only the material forms but also the general level of pre-capitalist production is limited by predetermined needs bound up with the laborers' social ties to natural conditions.[13] With capitalism's separation of labor power from necessary production conditions, by contrast, exchange value—specifically, the profitability of appropriating labor power's use value and objectifying it in salable use values—determines which (and whose) needs are satisfied. Exchange value and competitive monetary accumulation, not the given needs of the producers (or of anyone else), now regulate the growth and development of human production.[14] Under capitalism, the field of operation of exchange values is no longer limited to the "overplus of necessary use values . . . exchanged for what is superfluous as such" but may now penetrate the "bounds of immediate necessity" (Marx, 1987, 458). The *kinds* of use values produced, that is, the *kinds* of material and social needs to be satisfied, are no longer constrained by the laborers' former social ties to particular natural conditions. In this regard, too, capitalism is "a form of production not bound to a level of needs laid down in advance" by social bonds between the worker and natural conditions of production; hence the extant level and variety of needs "does not predetermine the course of production itself" (1977, 1037). Rather, if it is possible to profitably produce and sell a particular use value, then it will be produced in the absence of forcible social checks on such production. The social separation of the human producers from natural conditions and the attendant domination of exchange value over use value thus explain why, compared with previous forms of production, capitalism imposes "the compulsion to perform surplus-labour, labour beyond the immediate need . . . in a manner more favourable to production" (1963, 390). Below I consider this aspect of Marx's analysis from the standpoint of capital's development of the productive powers of labor and nature.

The Subsumption of Labor and Nature under Capital

Capitalism entails an initial separation or "freeing" of laborers from necessary conditions of production and their unification only in the production of commodities by the "freed" wage laborers whose labor power is purchased by the capitalists controlling the necessary conditions. In this process, surplus labor is extracted from workers and realized in the form of monetary surplus value if and when the commodities are profitably sold. Surplus value is the capitalist form of the surplus product—the social fund for investments in the growth and development of production. Marx shows how the accumulation of this fund and its allocation in line with monetary profitability not only reproduces the social separation of workers from necessary production conditions but also reproduces it on an ever-expanding scale.[15] Both the initial separation and its expanded reproduction in the process of capital accumulation enhance the commodification of wealth and the autonomy of production from the producers' predetermined needs associated with their erstwhile social ties to natural production conditions. The increasing domination of exchange value over use value thus progressively converts nature's contribution to wealth production into a new social form specific to capitalism—with natural conditions now appearing as "separate" conditions for the reproduction of "free" labor power and the objectification of its labor into vendible use values.

An economic system in which the laborers are socially separated from natural conditions of production can only accelerate the divergence of human production's evolutionary path from the (hypothetical) evolution of extra-human nature sans human intervention. The previous section considered this divergence in terms of the autonomy of the *social form* of capitalist (commodified) need satisfaction from predetermined needs more closely bound up with pre-capitalist producers' social ties to given natural conditions. However, it is just as important to investigate this divergence in terms of the connection between capitalist social relations and the *material content* of capitalist production. This connection is straightforward: based on its social separation of the human producers from necessary conditions of production including natural conditions, and its appropriation of the surplus product in the form of surplus value, capital is able to divide and rule over labor and nature because it determines the forms in which they are productively combined within and across individual production units according to the imperatives of exchange value and monetary profitability, not in line with any particular co-evolutionary path of human and extra-human nature.

Through its expansion of commodity production, capitalism develops specialization and division of labor among different production units to a historically unprecedented degree. This development, in which more and more necessary needs are satisfied (and can only be satisfied) through commodity exchange, presupposes the allocation of labor power and means of production according to relative monetary rates of return in different productive activities—unconstrained by any social ties between producers and the conditions of production.[16] Marx emphasizes this social basis of the capitalist division of labor in his analysis of the formation of a home market for industrial capital:

> Capital rapidly forms an internal market for itself by destroying all rural secondary occupations, so that it spins, weaves for everyone, clothes everyone etc., in short, brings the commodities previously created as direct use values into the form of exchange values, a process which comes about by itself through the separation of the workers from land and soil and from property (even in the form of serf property) in the conditions of production. (1973, 512)[17]

This division of labor involves more than just the commodification of given use values, however; for Marx, it entails a material restructuring and expansion of necessary use values themselves, based on the severing of the producers' prior social ties to natural conditions:

> The crafts themselves do not appear necessary alongside self-sustaining agriculture, where spinning, weaving etc. are done as a secondary domestic occupation. . . . It is therefore chiefly and essentially because agriculture no longer finds the natural conditions of its own production within itself, naturally arisen, spontaneous, ready to hand, but these exist as an independent industry separate from it—and, with this separateness the whole complex set of interconnections in which this industry exists is drawn into the sphere of the conditions of agricultural production—it is because of this, that what previously appeared as a luxury is now a necessity, and that so-called luxury needs appear e.g., as a necessity for this most naturally necessary and down-to-earth industry of all. *This pulling-away of the natural ground from the foundations of every industry,* and this transfer of its conditions of production outside itself, into a general context—hence the transformation of what was previously superfluous into what is necessary, as a historically created necessity—is the tendency of capital. (527–28; emphasis added)

In short, through its broader socialization of needs, the capitalist division of labor makes production less determined by given, particular natural conditions (or by human needs directly bound up with these conditions) and more determined by the complex social connections among producers as mediated by exchange values. At the same time, capitalist production remains a process in which labor and nature both participate. Though less dependent on particular natural conditions than pre-capitalist production, the capitalist division of labor develops in and through the appropriation and technological development of the objects, forces, and life forms present in nature as a whole. It is only "by incorporating both stupendous physical forces, and the natural sciences, with the process of production," that capital "raises the productiveness of labour to an extraordinary degree" (1967a, I, 387). Hence, insofar as it involves increases in relative surplus value (reductions in the work-time necessary to produce the commodities consumed by workers), capital accumulation depends on applications of scientific knowledge that increase the combined productive powers of nature *and* labor.[18] In this way, capital's appropriation of natural conditions helps free up additional social labor time for the development of new branches of production involving new discoveries, appropriations, and applications of useful natural conditions. As Marx indicates:

For the capital and labor which have been set free, a new, qualitatively different branch of production must be created, which satisfies and brings forth a new need. . . . Hence exploration of all of nature in order to discover new, useful qualities in things; universal exchange of the products of all alien climates and lands; new (artificial) preparation of natural objects, by which they are given new use values. The exploration of the earth in all directions, to discover new things of use as well as new useful qualities of the old; such as new qualities of them as raw materials etc.; . . . This creation of new branches of production, i.e., of qualitatively new surplus time, is not merely the division of labour, but is rather the creation, separate from a given production, of labour with a new use value; the development of a constantly expanding and more comprehensive system of different kinds of labour, different kinds of production, to which a constantly expanding and constantly enriched system of needs corresponds. (1973, 408–9)

Capital's profit-driven "development and intensification of productive power" thus takes the form of a striving "for a limitless variety of branches of labour . . . subjecting to itself all aspects of nature" (1994, 19). For Marx, the increasing autonomy of capitalist production from particular natural conditions itself depends on the extensive and intensive development of productive human-nature relations. At the same time, Marx recognizes that this development occurs on the basis of the social separation of the laborers vis-à-vis natural production conditions and the subjugation of *both* to the power of capital in the process of production. The harnessing of workers' living and work conditions to an increasingly social production process evolving according to monetary criteria—a development Marx calls the "real subsumption of labor under capital"—is and must be a process in which nature is likewise treated as a condition of monetary accumulation, both socially and materially. In this sense, *the subsumption of labor under capital implies a parallel subsumption of nature under capital.*[19]

Before investigating the ecological implications of this dual subsumption, I will consider what Marx's analysis has revealed about the natural limits of human production.

Capitalism and Natural Limits

Marx certainly does not downgrade the role of natural conditions in capitalist production. In line with the materialist presupposition that people and society reproduce themselves through a productive metabolism with nature, Marx's analysis shows that capital can only socially reproduce and expand itself as capital by materially exploiting the natural force of human labor power under definite natural conditions. Pursuant to the "decomposition of the original union existing between the labouring man and his means of labour," capital accumulation "reproduces the capital-relation on a progressive scale, more capitalists or larger capitalists at this pole, more wage-workers at that" only through the extensive and intensive appropriation and technological development of natural conditions (Marx, 1976b, 39; 1967a, I, 613). It is the capitalist division of labor and its "cooperation on a large scale, with the employment of machinery, that first subjugates the *forces of nature* on a large scale . . . to the direct production process, converts them into *agents of social labour*" (1994, 31–32).

Marx does suggest that capital's only material requirements are free labor power and conditions under which this labor power can be profitably exploited—conditions that, due to their social separation from the laborers, by no means correspond to those required for a sustainable co-evolution of humanity and nature. At the same time, Marx's analysis helps explain why, compared with previous forms of production, capitalism is much less dependent on *particular* ecosystems and other localized natural conditions (e.g., mineral deposits). Capital accumulation is less constrained by particular terrestrial areas, elements, and extra-human life forms precisely because the social separation of the producers (hence of reproducible means of production) from these natural conditions allows for a broader and deeper scientific development of the combined productive powers of nature and labor. This helps account for the fact that capitalism's historically unprecedented plunder and degradation of natural conditions has not, thus far, seriously threatened the reproduction and expansion of this economic system. Capitalism, more than previous class-exploitative societies, has an ability to destroy or degrade natural phenomena while reproducing and expanding itself both socially and materially (Snyder 1977, 21; Foster, 1994).

In sum, Marx's analysis suggests that capitalism has a twofold effect on the natural limits of human production. On the one hand, through its ruthless discovery and appropriation of use values producible by labor and nature and its expansion of the variety and spatial scope of material production, capitalism relaxes the constraints placed on production by particular natural conditions. On the other hand, with its exploitative scientific development of productive forces, its in-built tendency to "reproduce itself upon a constantly increasing scale," and the attendant extension of production's natural limits to the global, biospheric level, capitalism is the first society capable of a truly planetary environmental catastrophe, one that could ultimately threaten even capital's own material requirements (Marx, 1976b, 39).

CHAPTER 6

Capital's "Free Appropriation" of Natural and Social Conditions

I t is often argued that Marx's value analysis underrates nature's importance as a condition of capitalist production. Even in the "eco-Marxist" literature, one finds assertions that Marx treats natural conditions as valueless, costless, and/or effectively limitless, with no real allowance for natural resource scarcity. Deléage (1994, 48), for example, posits that Marx's labor theory of value "attributes no intrinsic value to natural resources." Similarly, Campbell (1991, 54) refers to "some costs that, according to Marxian lights, are not considered costs at all—namely, the opportunity costs of . . . natural resources." Apparently, Marx, having "formulated his economic theories on the assumption of limitless resources," was unable or unwilling to "factor resource scarcity into his theory" (Carpenter, 1997, 137, 139).

It will be shown that the above assertions are based on a fundamental misunderstanding of Marx's value theory. Specifically, they fail to grasp the distinctions and relations among Marx's conceptions of use value (to which nature always contributes), value (the necessary wage-labor time objectified in *commodity* use values), and exchange value (the monetary price paid for a use value). As an introduction to the basic issues involved, this chapter deals with one aspect of this misunderstanding, involving Marx's treatment of certain natural conditions as "a free gift of Nature to capital" (Marx, 1967a, III, 745). *Capital*'s references to such "free appropriation" of natural conditions are commonly cited as proof that anti-ecological presumptions, or at least a serious disregard of natural resource limits, are built into Marx's value-based analysis of capitalism. Georgescu-Roegen (1971, 2), for example, polemicizes against "Marx's dogma that everything Nature offers is gratis," whereas Carpenter (1997, 147) uses Marx's treatment of certain natural conditions as "available to producers . . . for free" to bolster his own claim that Marx views nature "as an infinitely abundant resource." To see the difficulties with such interpretations, it is necessary to reconstruct capital's free appropriation of natural and social conditions as conceived by Marx.

Definition and Scope of Free Appropriation

According to Marx's definition, capital freely appropriates conditions of production whenever such conditions contribute to the capitalist production of use values without adding to the total value of produced commodities. Given that the substance of value is socially necessary labor time, the conditions being freely appropriated must not be products of commodity-producing labor:

> It is thus strikingly clear, that means of production never transfer more value to the product than they themselves lose during the labour-process by the destruction of their own use-value. If such an instrument has no value to lose, if, in other words, it is not the product of human labour, it transfers no value to the product. *It helps to create use-value without contributing to the formation of exchange-value.* (Marx, 1967a, I, 204; emphasis added)[1]

Note that the use value of which Marx speaks here is not use value in general but rather use value as a condition of value and capital accumulation.[2] The use values to which the freely appropriated conditions of production contribute may be use values in production, in consumption, or both, but they should never be confused with use values other than those serving as vehicles for the production and realization of value and surplus value. Of course, when conditions of production are freely appropriated, their utilization in capitalist production may affect their usefulness for purposes other than monetary accumulation. My point is that when Marx considers *capitalist* free appropriation, he is talking about conditions that help fulfill capital's absolute use-value requirement: the reproduction of exploitable labor power and of conditions under which this labor power may be exploited via the objectification of surplus labor in commodity use values.

"In this class" of freely appropriated conditions of capitalist production, one finds "all means of production supplied by Nature without human assistance, such as land, wind, water, metals in situ, and timber in virgin forests" (1967a, I, 204):

> Natural elements entering as agents into production, and which cost nothing, no matter what role they play in production, do not enter as components of capital, but as a free gift of Nature to capital, that is, as a free gift of Nature's productive power to labour, which, however, appears as the productiveness of capital, as all other productivity under the capitalist mode of production. (1967a, III, 745)

When Marx specifies freely appropriated natural conditions as those "which cost nothing," this is to be taken in terms of value and for capital as a whole, not necessarily in terms of the amount of money paid by individual enterprises or consumers for the use values associated with these conditions. The next section discusses this further.

Since capitalist production is not a purely natural process but instead involves specific social relations, however, Marx emphasizes that capital also freely appropriates important social conditions of production. These include "all those productive forces . . . which derive from the division of labour, cooperation, machinery," and "which cost *nothing*" in terms of additional wage-labor time (Marx, 1991, 146). Capital also freely appropriates scientific knowledge, the productive application of which is, as I have shown, a crucial element in the subsumption of labor and nature under capital.[3] Marx argues that the utilization of freely appropriated natural conditions in production is often informed by scientific knowledge also freely appropriated by capital: "Apart from the natural substances, it is possible to incorporate in the productive process natural forces, which do not cost anything, to act as agents with more or less heightened effect. The degree of their effectiveness depends on methods and scientific developments which cost the capitalist nothing" (1967a, II, 356).

When capital's employment of scientific knowledge about natural forces enhances the productivity of commodity-producing labor, the result is a *reduction* in the values of any given set of produced commodities:

> Natural agents as such cost nothing. They cannot, therefore, add any value to the product; rather they diminish its value in so far as they replace capital or labour, immediate or accumulated labour. In as much as natural philosophy teaches how to replace human labour by natural agents, without the aid of machinery or only with the same machinery as before (perhaps even more cheaply, as with the steam boiler, many chemical processes etc.), it costs

the capitalist, and society as well, nothing and cheapens commodities absolutely. (1968, 553)

In line with his treatment of labor power as a natural and social force, Marx also points out how capital freely appropriates certain natural and social human laboring capacities. Consider, for instance, labor's "preservation of the value of material and instrument," whereby "the *amount* of objectified labour is preserved, because its *quality* as use values for further labour is preserved through contact with living labour." Marx insists that this "preservation of values in the product costs capital nothing" (1987, 523). As a result, this

> vitalising natural power of labour—the fact that by using and expending material and instrument it preserves them in this or that form, hence also preserves the labour objectified in them, their exchange value—becomes a *power,* not of labour, but *of capital,* as does every natural or social power of labour which is not the product of earlier labour or not the product of such earlier labour as must be repeated. (1991, 479)[4]

In general, capital freely appropriates those individual and collective laboring capacities that are the product not simply of the consumption of commodities but also of workers' domestic (family) life *and* of the broader social environment within which workers are brought up and live. It is in this sense that "the worker is not paid for his capacity to think," for example (1991, 479). It is also the sense in which Marx describes "the increase of population" as "a *natural* force of labour, for which nothing is paid" by capital (1973, 400).[5]

Marx analyzes capital's free appropriation of natural and social conditions in the context of capital's overall development of the forces of production, freely appropriated and otherwise. An important motivation for such analysis is that capital only freely utilizes natural and social conditions "to the degree to which their application does not give rise to any costs" (1991, 146):

> We saw that the productive forces resulting from co-operation and division of labour cost capital nothing. They are natural forces of social labour. So also physical forces, like steam, water, &c., when appropriated to productive processes, cost nothing. But just as a man requires lungs to breathe with, so he requires something that is work of man's hand, in order to consume physical forces productively. A water-wheel is necessary to exploit the force of water, and a steam-engine to exploit the elasticity of steam. Once dis-

covered, the law of the deviation of the magnetic needle in the field of an electric current, or the law of the magnetisation of iron, around which an electric current circulates, cost never a penny. But the exploitation of these laws for the purposes of telegraphy, &c., necessitates a costly and extensive apparatus. (1967a, I, 386–87)

In short, although "the forces of nature cost nothing" to capital, "the prime motors on which they act, or through which they are appropriated for the labour process, do cost something" (1991, 477).[6]

Theoretical and Social Significance of Free Appropriation

The preceding exegesis shows that when Marx speaks of capital's "free appropriation" of natural and social conditions, this is not meant to imply that such conditions are costless or infinite from a total, society-wide standpoint. Rather, capitalistic free appropriation only means that no *wage labor* is required to produce certain conditions serving as material or social vehicles of value production and accumulation. This free appropriation certainly does not imply that the conditions being appropriated have no opportunity cost or alternative use from a social point of view. The same could be said about a broader, transhistorical conception of free appropriation covering all those natural and social conditions whose existence, while helping to generate *saleable or unsaleable* use values, does not require the expenditure of any labor time, *commodity-producing or otherwise.*[7] It is obvious that human beings, individually and collectively, appropriate many natural conditions (clean air, for example) that do not require any processing by human labor in order to yield use values. Just as obviously, such conditions are finite and thus have a positive opportunity cost, whether or not they are producible by human labor under the given (current and projected) natural and social conditions. That something can be freely appropriated in the sense that it is "directly" or "spontaneously provided by nature," as Marx (1967a, I, 178, 183) puts it, in no way implies that it is not scarce or valuable from a social (and farsighted) perspective. Stated differently, Marx's description of certain natural conditions as "free gifts" implies no endorsement of *capitalism's* (or any other) tendency toward *prodigality* in their use. Free appropriation need not imply wasteful, destructive, or unsustainable appropriation. The degree to which nature's gifts are cherished and cared for depends on the particular social organization governing their use.

In focusing again on capitalism, one can see that capital freely appropriates use values from the land (its proximity to air, for example); but this does not mean that the quantity of land is infinitely large. Indeed, if land were infinite, it could not be appropriated by capital in such fashion as to exclude labor from this necessary condition of production; hence wage labor and capitalist production would be impossible. As Marx indicates:

> If the land were so easily available, at everyone's free disposal, then a principal element *for the formation of capital* would be missing. A most important condition of production and—apart from man himself and his labour—the only original condition of production could not be disposed of, could not be appropriated. It could not thus confront the worker as someone else's property and make him into a wage-labourer. The productivity of labour . . . in the capitalist sense, the "producing" of someone else's unpaid labour would thus become impossible. And this would put an end to capitalist production altogether. (1968, 43–44)

In short, the social separation of the producers from limited natural conditions, the conversion of these conditions into private capitalist property, and the conversion of natural use values into *freely appropriated* conditions of capitalist production are all aspects of a single process, in Marx's view. That capital's free appropriation of natural conditions does not imply an infinite supply of such conditions is also clear from the previously cited passage in Volume III of *Capital*. Here, Marx discusses situations where a freely appropriated natural condition becomes scarce, leading to a higher price of the commodity produced with its assistance:

> Therefore, if such a natural power, which originally costs nothing, takes part in production, it does not enter into the determination of price, so long as the product which it helped to produce suffices to meet the demand. But if in the course of development, a larger output is demanded than that which can be supplied with the help of this natural power, i.e., if this additional output must be created without the help of this natural power, or by assisting it with human labour-power, then a new additional element enters into capital. A relatively larger investment of capital is thus required in order to secure the same output. All other circumstances remaining the same, a rise in the price of production takes place. (1967a, III, 745)

This analysis of price changes obviously presumes limited availability of the natural force subject to free appropriation. Marx also recognizes, of course, that many natural conditions yield rents (positive exchange values) for individual landowners or enterprises. The collection of such rents itself presumes that the natural conditions in question are scarce relative to the demand for their ownership and/or use by competing firms. Indeed, by their very nature, these rent-yielding "condition[s] for an increase in the productiveness of the invested capital . . . cannot be established by the production process of the capital itself" (1967a, III, 645). The limited quantity of such useful natural conditions is a prerequisite of their monopolization. But these conditions, together with their rents, are freely appropriated insofar as their useful effects can otherwise be produced, if at all, only through an *additional* expenditure of wage-labor time *along with* an expanded utilization of *other* natural conditions.[8]

By now it should be clear that Marx's conception of free appropriation does not downgrade the contribution of natural conditions to the production of use values or wealth. Useful properties are often possessed by natural conditions produced without any assistance by human labor. Indeed, this basis for capital's free appropriation of natural conditions was important enough to be allotted a prominent position in the first section of the very first chapter of *Capital,* Volume I: "A thing can be a use-value, without having value. This is the case whenever its utility to man is not due to labour. Such are air, virgin soil, natural meadows, &c." (1967a, I, 40).

On closer examination, a double error is committed by those who would point to the concept of free appropriation as evidence that *Marx* devalues nature. On the one hand, these critics neglect or downgrade Marx's insistence that value must be embodied in use values, to which nature *and* labor always contribute.[9] Given this requirement, it follows that freely appropriated natural conditions contribute to capital accumulation in the same way as do other, produced means of production: by providing material conditions congenial to capital's extraction of surplus labor and its objectification in vendible use values.[10] Like produced means of production, freely appropriated natural conditions "may serve to absorb additional labour, hence also additional surplus-labour, and therefore create additional capital" (1967a, III, 248). Accordingly, among the "circumstances that . . . determine the amount of accumulation," Marx includes capital's free appropriation not only of "subject[s] of labour . . . furnished by nature gratis, as in the case of metals, minerals, coal, stone, &c.," but also of the soil's "marvellous effect on the amount of [agricultural] product" (1967a, I, 603, 599). Marx emphasizes that only through such free appropriation of useful natural conditions is capital able "to augment the elements of its accumulation beyond the limits apparently fixed by its own magnitude, or by the value and the mass of the means of production, already produced, in which it has its being" (604).

The characterization of natural conditions as "a free gift of Nature to capital" (1967a, III, 745) thus jibes fully with Marx's insistence on the "natural basis of surplus value" (see Chapter 3). For example, the labor-productivity gains pursuant to capital's free appropriation of natural conditions can reduce the value of labor power, *ceteris paribus,* thereby increasing the surplus value appropriated by capital:

> Since these natural agents cost nothing, they enter into the labour process without entering into the valorisation process. They make labour more productive without raising the value of the product, without adding to the value of the commodity. They rather *lessen* the value of the single commodity, since the *quantity* of commodities produced in *the same labour time* is increased, hence the *value* of every aliquot part of this quantity is reduced. Thus, in so far as these commodities enter into the reproduction of labour capacity, the value of labour capacity is thereby reduced, or the labour time necessary for the reproduction of the wage is shortened, and the *surplus* labour is lengthened. To that extent, therefore, the forces of nature themselves are appropriated by capital, not through their raising the value of the commodities, but through their reducing it. (1994, 32)

Little wonder, then, that Marx cites capital's free appropriation of natural conditions as an example of how "*use value,* which originally appears to us only as the material substratum of the economic relations, itself intervenes to determine the economic category" (1991, 146).

On the other hand, precisely insofar as they neglect the crucial role of use value in Marx's analysis of free appropriation, critics bypass the equally crucial distinction between the use value of natural conditions for capital versus the broader conceptions of nature's use value that become possible once use value, and nature's contribution to it, are not reduced to mere conditions of value accumulation. In effect, these critics accuse Marx of "devaluing nature" by reducing it to a condition of capital accumulation, when, in reality, Marx's analysis enables us to more effectively grasp this specifically capitalist devaluation as a basis for envisioning and struggling for a nonexploitative socialization of natural wealth through nonexploitative production relations.[11]

Marx ascribes great social significance to free appropriation, viewing it as an integral element of capital's development of the social character of production via the harnessing of the productive forces latent in labor and nature to the expansionary, transformative impulses of competitive monetary accumulation. At the same time, Marx points out how capital's free appropriation of natural and social conditions reinforces the human alienation built into capital's socialization of production. With capital's increasing dominance over the conditions of production, use value (the social combination of labor and nature to satisfy human needs) becomes less and less the commanding motive behind production and is placed more and more at the service of value accumulation. Once converted into powers of capital, the natural and social conditions of production exert an alienated social power over the producers, who are unable, as long as production remains capitalistic in form, to exert any cooperative control over their material interchange with nature. As Marx indicates, the "conditions of labour" become "an *alien circumstance* to the workers," as "the social character of their labour confronts them to a certain degree as capitalised"; "the same naturally takes place with the forces of nature and science," which "confront the labourers as powers of capital" (1991, 480; 1963, 391):

> The forms of socially developed labour . . . appear as *forms of the development of capital,* and therefore the productive powers of labour built up on these forms of social labour—consequently also science and the forces of nature—appear as *productive powers of capital.* In fact, the unity of labour in co-operation, the combination of labour through the division of labour, the use for productive purposes in machine industry of the forces of nature and science alongside the products of labour—all this confronts the individual labourers themselves as something *extraneous* and *objective,* as a mere form of existence of the means of labour that are independent of them and control them. . . . And in fact all these applications of science, natural forces and products of labour on a large scale . . . appear only as *means for exploitation* of labour, as means of appropriating surplus-labour, and hence confront labour as *powers* belonging to capital. (1963, 390–92)

For Marx, in short, free appropriation is a major factor in the process by which capital develops the natural and social conditions of production, but only by "tearing them away from the individual independent labourer" and "develop[ing] them as powers dominating the individual labourer and extraneous to him" (1963, 392). Through this "alienation of the conditions of social production from the real producers . . . capital comes more and more to the fore as a social power, whose agent is the capitalist" (1967a, III, 264). The "alienated, independent, social power" attained by the conditions of production poses a challenge to society in general and the producers and their communities in particular. This challenge is to replace capital's alienated, class-divided socialization of production with a more democratic socialization via an explicit "transformation of the conditions of production into general, communal, social, conditions" (1967a, III, 264). In this sense, the concept of free appropriation provides a channel for the incorporation of natural conditions into Marx's projections of the transition from capitalism to communism (see Chapters 12 through 14).

CHAPTER 7

Capitalism and Nature: A Value-Form Approach

C apitalism's social separation of workers vis-à-vis necessary conditions of production allows for a competitive, profit-driven development of the combined productive powers of labor and nature.
This separation and combined development, with its increasingly complex
and technologically advanced social division of labor, loosens the constraints placed on production by particular natural conditions. It does so,
however, only by broadening and deepening human appropriation from
and material impacts on nature, in line with the imperatives of competitive profit-making. Capitalism thus overcomes particular natural limits
only by placing increasing pressure on the global biosphere as a whole. The
social roots of capitalism's environmental crisis tendencies are only fully revealed, however, when one considers the tensions with nature built into
the value form of commodities, money, and capital.

The notion that Marx's labor theory of value might provide an important ecological perspective might seem strange, given the popular view that
this theory excludes or downgrades nature's importance as a condition of
and limiting factor in human production. Even among eco-Marxists, the
dominant position seems to be that insofar as Marx achieved any ecological insights, this was despite—not because of—his value theory (Benton,
1989; Deléage, 1994). But the germ of capitalism's tendency to degrade the
natural conditions of human existence is arguably revealed by Marx's basic
analysis of exchange values.

The commodity, like all use values, is a product of both labor and nature. Value, the substance of wealth in its specifically capitalist form, is, however, simply the abstract social labor time objectified in commodities.

Quantitatively, capitalism only ascribes value to nature insofar as its appropriation requires commodity-producing labor, even though nature's contribution to production—and to human life more generally—is not materially reducible to this labor of appropriation. In short, the value form qualitatively and quantitatively abstracts from nature's useful and life-giving characteristics, even though value is a particular social form of wealth—a particular social objectification of both nature and labor.[1] This contradiction helps explain capitalism's tendency to despoil its natural environment, which is the main argument of this chapter. A second, corollary argument is that the common complaint, that Marx's value theory inadequately recognizes the productive role of limited natural conditions, should be redirected toward capitalism itself.

After connecting the value-nature contradiction to the analyses in Chapters 5 and 6, this chapter investigates value's more specific anti-ecological features. Marx's rent theory is then interpreted as a materialist *and* social-relational investigation of the tensions with use value in general and nature in particular that are built into the value form. Finally, the chapter considers the extent to which private and/or state-engineered rents can be expected to resolve the value-nature contradiction on ecologically sustainable terms.

Value and Nature

The wage-labor relation presumes a severing of laborers' social ties to necessary conditions of production and a subordination of the production of necessary use values (workers' consumer goods, plus reproducible means of production) to the economic regulating power of exchange values (see Chapter 5). This subjugation of use value to exchange value may also be viewed as a subordination of both exchange value *and* use value under value as a more general social form;[2] by contrast with the limitation of commodity and money relations by particular use values characteristic of pre-capitalist systems, under capitalism exchange values become particular forms (and use values particular depositories) of value as such—of abstract or homogenous social labor time. With capitalism, "the common substance that manifests itself in the exchange-value of commodities, whenever they are exchanged, is their value," and "exchange-value is the only form in which the value of commodities can manifest itself or be expressed" (Marx, 1967a, I, 38).[3]

The significance of Marx's approach is threefold. First, by positing that exchange value is a form of value and not the reverse, Marx is insisting that value arises only in production, not in the realm of exchange.[4] Indeed, Marx's procedure is the only consistent path to a production-based theory of value that does not *identify* value, exchange value, and use value. This point needs to be emphasized because it seems to have been missed—or at least forgotten—by many of Marx's ecological critics who wish to ascribe value (and not just use value) to nature (see Chapter 8).

Second, the subordination of exchange value and use value as particular forms of value corresponds to the increasing domination of production for profitable sale (M-C-M' in Marx's terms, with M representing money and C commodities) over production for use (in which any monetary exchanges that occur tend to be motivated by the desire for alternative *use values*, as summed up by the circuit C-M-C'). This is how value becomes the underlying "active factor" dominating the movement and development of use value *and* exchange value:

> In the circulation M-C-M, both the money and the commodity represent only different modes of existence of value itself . . . constantly changing from one form to the other without thereby becoming lost, and thus assum[ing] an automatically active character. If now we take in turn each of the two different forms which self-expanding value successively assumes in the course of its life, we then arrive at these two propositions. Capital is money: Capital is commodities. In truth, however, value is here the active factor in a process, in which, while constantly assuming the form in turn of money and commodities, it at the same time changes in magnitude, differentiates itself by throwing off surplus-value from itself. (1967a, I, 153–54)

The increasing domination of value (in the form of money's motive power) in the realm of production and exchange is, in Marx's view, based on the commodification of "free" labor power and means of production, in effect, on the monetary valuation of labor and production itself. I emphasize this domination here in order to anticipate that insofar as value encapsulates capitalism's fundamental antagonism with nature, then any environmental policies under which value remains the "active factor" in human production are unlikely to seriously alleviate ecological crises. This applies especially to private or government-imposed monetary rents on natural resources, which leave the basic class relation between capital and labor intact.

This links up with the third, and for present purposes most important, aspect of Marx's value analysis; that is, since wealth exists only as myriad use values produced by materially variegated forms of labor and nature, the subordination of exchange value and use value under value (*homogenous* social labor time) represents a social abstraction from use value (the material need-satisfying character of production).[5] Value thereby formally abstracts from the natural basis and substance of wealth, in Marx's view. Transhistorically speaking, "material wealth, the world of use values, exclusively consists of natural materials modified by labour"; but under capitalism, "the social form of this wealth, exchange value, is nothing but a . . . social form of the objectified labour contained in the use values" (Marx, 1988, 40).[6]

Stated differently, the contradiction between exchange value and use value intrinsic to the commodity is also a contradiction between wealth's specifically capitalist form and its natural basis and substance.[7] Nature contributes to the production of use values; yet capitalism represents wealth by a purely quantitative, socio-formal abstraction: labor time in general. Capital's "free appropriation" of natural conditions (occurring whenever nature contributes to capitalist use-value production without adding to value production) manifests this contradiction insofar as it is enabled by the system's valuation of nature according to the social labor time necessary for its appropriation in commodity production, not according to the real contribution of nature to wealth or human need satisfaction (see Chapter 6).

All societies must engage in a reproductive allocation of their labor time, and the social relations regulating this allocation always imbue labor with a specific social form (1967a, I, 71). Prior to capitalism, however, productive or need satisfying labor was expended by producers not socially as fully separated from necessary conditions of production. Social labor allocation, including the utilization of any *surplus* labor and products, occurred through relations of direct personal interdependence and/or hierarchical dependence mutually constituted with the laborers' social (including spiritual) ties to the natural conditions of production. As a result, production was mostly for use; and even when some products became commodities, a general regulation of production by socially necessary labor time in the form of exchange values did not take place.[8] In short, although precapitalist people-nature relations were socially mediated, compared to capitalism they were not as socially autonomous from use value's natural basis and substance insofar as the pre-capitalist human producers were not as socially separated from natural conditions.

In Marx's conception, value's formal abstraction from use value and nature is an *antagonistic* contradiction because value is still a form of use-value production—material production being a necessary part of the reproductive people-nature metabolism. Hence, although "use-value . . . is a side issue in capitalist production" (1968, 495), value must be objectified in particular use values; labor interacting with nature is thus a necessary moment of value production and accumulation. Indeed, if capital had no need for nature, it could not have any environmental crisis tendencies, seeing as how such crises must be rooted in historically specific patterns in the use of natural conditions as means of production and disposal—whence the importance of Marx's revelation that value is an alienated form of use value in human, social, and natural terms. With value-formed production, use values are only produced as means of obtaining exchange value, not of satisfying human needs, including the need for a sustainable and fulfilling co-evolution with nature. Capitalism only validates human and extra-human nature as necessary parts of human production insofar as they can be profitably objectified in vendible use values.[9]

Specific Forms of the Value-Nature Contradiction

The substance of value, abstract labor, is a homogenous social entity. Marx says:"As exchange-values in which the qualitative difference between their use-values is eliminated," commodities "represent equal amounts of the same kind of labour . . . uniform, homogenous, simple labour" (1970, 29).[10] It follows that "considered as values, all commodities are qualitatively equal and differ only quantitatively, hence can be measured against each other and substituted for one another . . . in certain quantitative relations" (1973, 141). However, commodity exchange poses the contradiction between the general, homogenous character of value as socially necessary labor time versus the objectification of value as the exchange values of particular use values. In other words, the "natural properties" of commodities "enter into contradiction with their character as exchange values . . . as mere denominated numbers" (1973, 144):

> As a value, the commodity is general; as a real commodity it is particular. As a value it is always exchangeable; in real exchange it is exchangeable only if it fulfills particular conditions. As a value, the measure of its exchangeability is determined by itself; [for] exchange value expresses precisely the relation in which it replaces other commodities; [but] in real exchange it is exchangeable only in quantities which are linked with its natural properties and which correspond to the needs of the participants in exchange. . . . *In its natural existence, with its natural properties . . . the commodity is neither constantly exchangeable nor exchangeable against every other commodity; this it is only as something different from itself, as exchange value.* (141–42; emphasis added).

Marx argues that money, the general equivalent of value, is a necessary form precisely because of this contradiction between the social generality and homogeneity of value versus the material particularity and qualitative variety of commodity use values.[11] The same is true of commodity-producing labor: As Marx emphasizes in his critique of so-called labor money schemes, money is a necessary element of a commodity economy because of the contradiction between the general-quantitative character of abstract labor versus the qualitative variegation of the concrete labors that, socially combined and enmeshed with natural conditions, produce different use values.[12] Money's own use value, that of being the generally accepted representative and carrier of value, both manifests and socially enforces value's formal abstraction from the natural *and* human substance of wealth. For Marx, money is not only "the direct *reification of universal labour-time,* i.e., the product of universal alienation and of the supersession of all individual labour" (1970, 47); it is also "a form of social existence *separated from the natural existence* of the commodity" (1973, 145; emphasis added).[13]

As a measure and objectification of value, money is "wealth . . . in abstraction from its particular modes of existence"; it is a "general form of wealth . . . in contrast to all the natural substances of which wealth consists" (1973, 221). Hence, when a commodity is exchanged for money, "all its natural properties are extinguished; it no longer takes up a special, qualitative relationship towards the other commodities" (141).[14] Money as a representative of value thereby abstracts from the qualitative variegation of nature, from environmental distinctions and relationships—from ecological diversities—insofar as these are not manifested in the *quantity* of social labor time required to appropriate and productively utilize natural conditions. Indeed, money "solves" the contradiction between the generality of value and the particularity of use values by abstracting from the qualitative differentiation of useful labor as conditioned by the material diversity of human and extra-human nature—the true sources of wealth.

It follows that any system of human production regulated by value and money contains a tendency toward what Rachel Carson has termed a "shotgun approach to nature" (1962, 67), that is, toward the appropriation of particular natural conditions as means of production and disposal with little regard for their variety and interconnection. "Our attitude toward plants," for example,

is a singularly narrow one. If we see any immediate utility in a plant we foster it. If for any reason we find its presence undesirable or merely a matter of indifference, we may condemn it to destruction forthwith. . . . Many are marked for destruction merely because, according to our narrow view, they happen to be in the wrong place at the wrong time. (63–64)[15]

Especially when combined with capitalism's division of both labor and nature (see below), money's abstraction from natural diversities and inter-relations helps create a tendency toward simplification and homogeniza-tion of natural conditions. As Foster (1994, 111–12) indicates, when "labor became more homogenous, so did much of nature, which underwent a similar process of degradation.... Natural diversity is destroyed in the same proportion as profits are promoted." Value's abstraction from natural diversity and interconnection is not simply a constant influence in capital-ist development; rather, its social and material power accumulates as the combined productivity of labor and nature is scientifically subsumed under capital (see Chapters 5 and 6).[16]

Since money is a social form of wealth, that is, of people-nature rela-tions, its dequalification of nature also tends to denaturalize human indi-viduality in an alienating fashion. With "money (exchange value) . . . the individual is not objectified in his natural quality, but in a social quality (re-lation) which is, at the same time, external to him" (Marx, 1973, 226). Hence "the individual appears detached from the natural bonds etc. which in earlier historical periods make him the accessory of a definite and lim-ited human conglomerate" (83).[17] Indeed, since value-formed production presupposes the social separation of laborers from natural conditions of production, "exchange value, as the objective basis of the whole system of production, already in itself implies . . . the whole negation of [the worker's] natural existence" (247–48). Based on this separation, "the ob-jectification of land and its products, through commodification" tends to promote "a developing exploitative attitude: that of distancing of—objec-tification of—nature" (Pepper, 1993, 91). From this perspective, capitalism is a system "of self-estranged natural *and* spiritual individuality," because it tends to "turn human beings into abstractions" by "estranging from man (1) nature, *and* (2) himself" (Marx and Engels, 1980, 151, 239; Marx, 1964, 112; emphases added).

One aspect of this estrangement involves the routine destruction of extra-human life associated with capitalism's "shotgun approach to nature" and the effects of this destruction on the human spirit. Hence, after de-scribing the unspeakable suffering imposed on animals as part of the col-lateral damage from pesticide spraying, Rachel Carson asks: "The question is whether any civilization can wage relentless war on life without de-stroying itself, and without losing the right to be called civilized.... By acquiescing in an act that can cause such suffering to a living creature, who among us is not diminished as a human being?" (1962, 99–100).

Alienation from nature is materially quite different for different classes—compare rank-and-file laborers' neighborhoods and workplaces to capitalists' country homes and air conditioned and sunroofed offices, for example—however much such contrasts may "appear as if they [are] *natural conditions*" because they are "not controllable by individuals" (Marx, 1973, 164).[18] To most workers, questions such as Carson's have a distant air about them compared to day-to-day issues of material subsistence, safety, and comfort—which explains why such questions are often posed mostly by members of the upper classes. But this class-differentiated divorce of necessary use values from concerns about human oneness with nature is itself a crucial feature of human estrangement from nature under capitalism (Parsons, 1977, 47).[19] The present, more basic point is that human alienation from nature is intrinsic to value's formal abstraction from use value.

From the qualitative homogeneity of value follows its infinite divisibility. Indeed, "as a value, every commodity is equally divisible; in its natural existence this is not the case" (Marx, 1973, 141).[20] So value and money not only formally abstract from qualitative environmental distinctions and relationships; they also valuate nature so as to enable its artificial division or fragmentation. Marx expresses this fragmentation in terms of the "dissolving effect of money," occurring whenever money serves as "a means of cutting up property" that would otherwise comprise "a mass of inexchangeable, inalienable objects" (871). Such fragmentation need not entail explicit monetary pricing, however; it can also occur via capital's free appropriation of natural conditions. Both forms of nature fragmentation are conditional upon and reinforce value's dequalification of natural diversities and interconnections and of people-nature relations. David Harvey has noted the ecological implications of this aspect of value:

> Money prices attach to particular things and presuppose exchangeable entities with respect to which private property rights can be established or inferred. This means that we conceive of entities as if they can be taken out of any ecosystem of which they are a part. We presume to value the fish, for example, independently of the water in which they swim. The money value of a whole ecosystem can be arrived at, according to this logic, only by adding up the sum of its parts, which are constructed in an atomistic relation to the whole. . . . Indeed, pursuit of monetary valuations commits us to a thoroughly Cartesian-Newtonian-Lockeian and in some respects "anti-ecological" ontology of how the natural world is constituted. (1993, 6)

A brief look at the "unnecessary travel and huge encroachments on green space" as capitalist real estate development intrudes upon wetlands and other eco-systems—or at contemporary agriculture's "complex cycle of pests, pesticides, new pests, soil exhaustion, chemical fertilizers, and water pollution"—establishes the relevance of the value form's dissolving, fragmenting effect for capitalism's environmental degradation tendencies (Wallis, 1993, 151). The simplification of natural conditions associated with capital's development by division and specialization tends to destabilize ecological balances in hazardous ways, as Carson observes: "Nature has introduced great variety into the landscape, but man has displayed a passion for simplifying it. Thus he undoes the built-in checks and balances by which nature holds species within bounds" (1962, 10).

John Bellamy Foster points out that "the disconnection of natural processes from each other and their extreme simplification" is closely bound up with capital's simplification and mechanization of labor; both are integral to the subsumption of labor and nature under capital, which, as discussed in Chapter 5, represents "an inherent tendency of capitalist development" (Foster, 1994, 121; cf. Braverman, 1974). It may be added that value relations, by facilitating the division of nature-provided and other means of production, create a necessary condition for their increased mobility. The money-driven movement of production facilities, commodities, and labor within and between countries reinforces the impermanence of people-nature relations and the accompanying tendency toward short-termist undervaluation of natural conditions—the "slash and burn" mentality characteristic of capitalism.[21]

Finally, there is the quantitatively unlimited character of the goal of monetary capital accumulation (Marx, 1967a, I, 151–52). The limitlessness of capital (money seeking more money) is latent in money's function as a *general* measure and objectification of the values of the limitless variety of *particular* exchangeable use values within its purview (1970, 131–32). In this respect, "use value in itself does not have the boundlessness of value as such" or its universal equivalent, money (1973, 405). Having subordinated production to itself pursuant to the social separation of laborers from necessary conditions of production, money as capital seeks to overcome all particular barriers to its expansion posed by use value and its natural basis and substance:

> However, as representative of the general form of wealth—money—capital is the endless and limitless drive to go beyond its limiting barrier. Every boundary is and has to be a barrier for it. Else it would cease to be capital—

money as self-reproductive. If ever it perceived a certain boundary not as a barrier, but became comfortable within it as a boundary, it would itself have declined from exchange value to use value, from the general form of wealth to a specific, substantial mode of the same. (1973, 334)[22]

The limitless expansionary tendency contained in capital as a social form of wealth contradicts all limiting factors imposed on human production by its natural environment. This is reflected in capitalism's tendency to overcome particular and local natural boundaries by expanding the natural limits of production—the pressure of production on ecosystems and other natural resources—to the global, biospheric level (see Chapter 5). But the goal of value accumulation abstracts even from global limits—a fact that does nothing to negate the material reality of these limits, as Ray Dasmann cogently remarks:

> The concept of limiting factors, combined with a knowledge that the earth is limited in size and in its supplies of energy and materials, leads to the obvious, but sometimes overlooked, conclusion that growth and expansion must have an end. No species, including man, can expand its population indefinitely. Any species, including man, will be better off individually if its growth is limited through its own behavior before the time when environmental limiting factors (shortages in necessities, for example) begin to take effect. (1968, 23)

In sum, while a viable co-evolution of society and nature requires quantitative limits on human production, the value form of wealth by definition imbues production with an expansive character. As a result, capitalist societies are on an unsustainable "treadmill of production" featuring ever-greater quantities of material and energy throughput on the supply (value production) and demand (value realization) sides of capital accumulation (Schnaiberg, 1980; Schnaiberg and Gould, 1994).[23]

When bounded by any given time period, the quantitative limitlessness of the goal of capital accumulation leads to pressures toward short-term calculations and decisions. This helps explain why "the rapidity of change and the speed with which new situations are created" in human production now "follow the impetuous and heedless pace of man rather than the deliberate pace of nature" (Carson, 1962, 7). A prominent example is the failure of capitalist agriculture to heed the limits placed on the sustainable rate of wealth production by the temporal rhythms of organic, ecological processes—the result being widespread erosion and degradation of soil and water resources (Mayumi, 1991; Matson et al., 1997).[24] In *Capital,* Marx posits that the monetization of wealth and the goal of rapid capital accumulation directly contradict environmentally sound and sustainable farming practices. He argues that "in capitalist agriculture . . . all progress in increasing the fertility of the soil for a given time, is a progress towards ruining the lasting sources of that fertility" and that "the vitality of the soil is squandered, and this prodigality is carried by commerce far beyond the borders of a particular state" (1967a, I, 506, and III, 813). In Marx's view,

> the dependence of the cultivation of particular agricultural products upon the fluctuations of market-prices, and the continual changes in this cultivation with these price fluctuations—the whole spirit of capitalist production, which is directed toward the immediate gain of money—are in contradiction to agriculture, which has to minister to the entire range of permanent necessities of life required by the chain of successive generations. (1967a, III, 617)[25]

A similar prognosis applies to forestry. Here, Marx argues that "the long production time . . . and the great length of the periods of turnover make forestry"—as opposed to the simple plunder of forests or anti-ecological tree farming—"an industry of little attraction to capitalist enterprise"; hence capital's activity in this area "has ever evinced itself in such energetic destruction of forests that everything done by it conversely for their preservation and restoration appears infinitesimal" (1967a, II, 244). Marx presciently projected that under capitalism, forests would "only rarely" be "managed in a way more or less corresponding to the interests of society as a whole, i.e., when they are not private property, but subject to the control of the state" (1967a, III, 617).

The artificially fast pace of capital-driven production, when combined with its constant development of new use values extracted and processed largely in abstraction from nature's original life-sustaining qualities and interconnections, has created new uncertainties about the forms and limits of nature's resiliency and the sustainability of human production (Foster, 1994; Briggs, 1997). Rachel Carson's ruminations concerning cancer-causing agents are more relevant today than when they were written, nearly four decades ago:

> Over the eons of unhurried time that is nature's, life reached an adjustment with destructive forces as selection weeded out the less adaptable and only the most resistant survived. These natural cancer-causing agents are still a factor in producing malignancy; however, they are few in number and they belong to that ancient array of forces to which life has been accustomed

from the beginning. . . . With the dawn of the industrial era the world became a place of continuous, ever-accelerating change. Instead of the natural
environment there was rapidly substituted an artificial one composed of new
chemical and physical agents, many of them possessing powerful capacities
for inducing biologic change. Against these carcinogens which his own activities had created man had no protection, for even as his biological her-
itage has evolved slowly, so it adapts slowly to new conditions. As a result
these powerful substances could easily penetrate the inadequate defenses of
the body. (1962, 219–20)

These observations have been corroborated in detail by Steingraber's
(1997) research on environmental sources of cancers. They stand as a warn-
ing that the ecological effects of capital's appropriation, utilization, and disposal of natural conditions are not adequately captured by quantitative
measures of resource depletion, or of the "filling up" of nature's carrying
capacities, or both. They must be conceived in terms of the interactive material effects of capital's in-built drive for unlimited growth and the qualitatively anti-ecological characteristics of value-formed production.
(Chapter 9 sketches such an analysis based on Marx's conception of the
capitalist division between town and country.)

An Introduction to Marx's Analysis of Capitalist Rents

"The last and apparently the decisive objection" to the labor theory of
value, Marx writes in his *Contribution,* "is this: if exchange-value is nothing but the labour-time contained in a commodity, how does it come
about that commodities which contain no labour possess exchange-value,
in other words, how does the exchange-value of natural forces arise? This
problem is solved in the theory of rent" (1970, 63).

Rent is thus posed as the outcome of the contradiction between determination of exchange value by labor time and the fetching of positive market prices by natural conditions not objectifying any human labor. Marx's
solution to this problem, though extremely complex in its details, is
straightforward in terms of its basic principle.[26] He treats "rent of land" as a
redistribution of surplus value, more specifically, as "a surplus profit over and
above the general rate, derived from a monopolised force of nature" (Engels to Schmidt, March 12, 1895, in Marx and Engels [1975, 457]):

Wherever natural forces can be monopolised and guarantee a surplus-profit
to the industrial capitalist using them, be it waterfalls, rich mines, waters
teeming with fish, or a favourably located building site, there the person

who by virtue of title to a portion of the globe has become the proprietor of these natural objects will wrest this surplus-profit from functioning capital in the form of rent. . . . One part of society thus extracts tribute from another for the permission to inhabit the earth, as landed property in general assigns the landlord the privilege of exploiting the terrestrial body, the bowels of the earth, the air, and thereby the maintenance and development of life. (Marx, 1967a, III, 773–74)

The contradiction between "the exchange-value of natural forces" and regulation of exchange value by labor time now appears as the barrier posed by landed property and rents to the competitive formation of an average or general rate of profit:

In a capitalist society, [total] surplus-value . . . is divided among capitalists as dividends proportionate to the share of the social capital each holds. In this form surplus-value appears as average profit which falls to the share of capital, an average profit which in turn divides into profit of enterprise and interest, and which under these two categories may fall into the laps of different kinds of capitalists. This appropriation and distribution of surplus-value, or surplus-product, on the part of capital, however, has its barrier in landed property. Just as the operating capitalist pumps surplus-labour, and thereby surplus-value and surplus-product in the form of profit, out of the labourer, so the landlord in turn pumps a portion of this surplus-value, or surplus-product, out of the capitalist in the form of rent. (1967a, III, 820)

The real underlying tension here, of course, is that between the *use value* of natural conditions and the regulation of production by value. The productive usefulness of scarce and monopolizable natural conditions enables them to command a positive market price—that is, to command a monetary claim on social labor time—despite their production by nature without human assistance. Stated differently, the "barrier" to capitalist competition posed by landed property has a material basis in the variegated and irreplaceable character of natural wealth.[27] This is a further development of the tension between use value and exchange value built into the value form of wealth. That rent, like all exchange values, is still a form of value is clear from the fact that despite the *appropriation* of surplus value by landed property, rents do not affect the total amount of value and surplus value produced:

Profit of capital (profit of enterprise plus interest) and ground-rent are thus no more than particular components of surplus-value, categories by which surplus-value is differentiated depending on whether it falls to the share of capital or landed property, headings which in no whit however alter its nature. Added together, these form the sum of social surplus-value. Capital pumps the surplus-labour, which is represented by surplus-value and surplus-product, directly out of the labourers. Thus, in this sense, it may be regarded as the producer of surplus-value. Landed property has nothing to do with the actual process of production. Its role is confined to transferring a portion of the produced surplus-value from the pockets of capital to its own. (1967a, III, 821)

The redistributive character of rents (the fact that they do not alter the aggregate quantity of value and surplus value) means that the *production* of surplus value is still supported by capital's free appropriation of natural conditions (see Chapter 6). Nonetheless, the rental charges paid by capital on particular natural conditions manifest a tension between this free appropriation and nature's productive use value—a tension deriving from value's abstraction from the natural basis and substance of wealth. The valuation of wealth by abstract labor here meets with a barrier posed by use value and nature in particular, as represented socially by landed property.

Before considering the extent to which rents can resolve the value-nature contradiction, I will emphasize a feature of Marx's rent theory whose relevance extends to his entire investigation of capitalism—its combination of historical specification and materialist analysis. On the historical side, Marx insists on treating rent as a specific social relation peculiar to the capitalist economy. Landed property is, to begin with, a precondition of wage labor insofar as it ensures the social separation of labor power from necessary conditions of production. As Marx indicates,

the landlord plays a role in the capitalist process of production not merely through the pressure he exerts upon capital, nor merely because large landed property is a prerequisite and condition of capitalist production since it is a prerequisite and condition of the expropriation of the labourer from the means of production, but particularly because he appears as the personification of one of the most essential conditions of production. (1967a, III, 821)[28]

Although it is true, moreover, that rents have a "natural basis" in the particular natural conditions that "permit an exceptional increase in the productivity of labour," nonetheless "this increased productivity of labour itself would not be converted into surplus-value were it not for the fact that capital appropriates the natural and social productivity of the labour used by it as its own" (647). Landed property and rents are thus not only preconditions but also *results* of the capital-labor relation and of the entire set of commodity relations enabling natural wealth to be monetized, as the British Marxist Geoffrey Kay observes:

> For the gifts of nature to enter the market alongside commodities requires the existence of the market and the system of property relations associated with it. . . . Consider land and its "price," money-rent, which is the most important economic transaction involving gifts of nature. Historically the emergence of money-rent, the exchange of the use of land for money, followed the development of commodity production; that is to say, it happened only after a decisive proportion of agricultural production had taken the form of commodities. (1979, 49–50)[29]

Marx's treatment of rent as a social relation does not lead him to downgrade the significance of its natural basis, however. In the case of agricultural rent, for example, the issue is "the specific conditions of production and circulation which arise from the investment of capital in agriculture," where "the productivity of labour is dependent on natural conditions, and the same quantity of labour is represented by more or fewer products, use-values, in accordance with such productivity" (1967a, III, 615, 817).[30] A rent represents a "surplus-profit which arises . . . not due to capital, but to the utilisation of a natural force which can be monopolised, and has been monopolised"—a force that is "bound to . . . specific natural conditions prevailing in certain portions of land" and thus "cannot be created by capital out of itself" (645–46). When discussing the rent of land featuring a useful waterfall, Marx emphasizes the point that "it is by no means within the power of capital to call into existence this natural premise for a greater productivity of labour," since "it cannot be established by a definite investment of capital." In short, "those manufacturers who own waterfalls exclude those who do not from using this natural force, *because land, and particularly land endowed with water-power, is scarce*" (645; emphasis added).

Apparently, the critics who condemn Marx for downgrading the productive contribution of limited natural conditions (while ignoring Marx's rent theory) are unaware of these and many similar passages in *Capital* that do precisely the opposite. Far from being isolated fragments, Marx's observations on how natural conditions shape rents and other forms of value and capital are logical, integral elements of his consistently materialist *and* social-relational analysis of capitalism.

Rents and the Value-Nature Contradiction

The foregoing excursus provides essential perspective on the question of whether rents can be expected to alleviate the tensions with nature built into capitalist production. Mainstream economists, in particular, are likely to suggest that the previous value-form analysis overstates the seriousness of the value-nature contradiction by ignoring the role of markets, pricing, and monetary valuation in the signaling of natural resource scarcities and in resource rationing. In this view, limited natural resources are likely to command rents that reduce their appropriation and destruction, and if they do not—that is, if environmental destruction takes the form of privately unpriced "external effects"—the state may assign such rents, using social cost/benefit calculations (Solow, 1976).

Marx's rent theory recognizes that exchange values may be assigned to valueless but scarce and monopolizable natural conditions. In Marx's view, there is no reason why such rents cannot be designed and enforced by the state: In order for a natural condition to yield an exchange value, "nothing more is required than its capacity to be monopolised and alienated," regardless of which of the "many fortuitous combinations" of possible material and juridical forms in which such monopolization and alienation occurs (Marx, 1967a, III, 633). The scope of Marx's analysis is itself notable in this day and age, when corporations are trading rights to pollute (and collecting rents from access to relatively less polluted air), and when oxygen is being sold on the streets of polluted cities.

But even though Marx recognizes "the price of things which have in themselves no value, i.e., are not the product of labour, such as land" (633), he also emphasizes that capitalist rents, like all exchange values, are particular forms of value. Rents represent a redistribution of value (specifically *surplus* value), making them a social derivative of and thus dependent on value production and accumulation.[31] Rents by definition reinforce the monetary valuation of nature, along with all the qualitative and quantitative tensions between value and nature discussed earlier. By contrast, mainstream defenses of the market tend to assert the purported environmental advantages of monetary pricing as if these advantages can be isolated from the entire set of qualitative and quantitative effects of monetary valuation on the people-nature metabolism.

For example, capitalism, with its money economy, has a *tendency* toward the universal commodification and buyability of use values;[32] but this tendency also biases wealth production in favor of those use values capable of being privately produced and/or vended for a profit, as opposed to those serving the requirements of a sustainable or humanly desirable co-evolution of society and nature. The fact that "everything becomes saleable and buyable" (1967a, I, 132) manifests itself not only in environmental impacts stemming from the purchase and sale of natural conditions, and not only in the role of private monetary greed and bribery of government officials in fomenting legal and illegal environmental degradations (e.g., toxic dump sites). The power of money in capitalist society is the primary basis of (1) the "jobs versus environment" tradeoff that capital and its functionaries constantly trumpet in order to profit at the expense of workers' living and work conditions; and (2) the valuation of "environmental assets" by the calculus of (private or "social") monetary profitability. Without recognizing this power of money and the way it biases wealth production in anti-ecological fashion, it is difficult to grasp why any "progress that has been made in the manner in which natural resources within terrestrial areas are protected . . . is blighted by the overuse of technological and scientific discoveries" in the service of "economic necessity" (Osborn, 1968, 12). As Rachel Carson observes, we live in "an era dominated by industry, in which the right to make a dollar at whatever cost is seldom challenged" (1962, 13).

When mainstream economists suggest that natural resource scarcity and the environmental "externalities" of human production can be adequately managed by the price system—including well-defined private property rights and some government tinkering with the market-price vector using taxes and subsidies—they seem to presume that the alternative is no management whatsoever, in effect, completely unconstrained access to natural resources. It is as if one were to support competitive monetary bribes of government officials as an efficient method of political influence, on the grounds that without such "pricing," politics would break down into a physically violent free-for-all, with destructive "external effects." In reality, the alternative to private property and the market may not be a laissez-faire "commons without law, restraint, or responsibility" but rather an institutionalization of the "communal" or "non-moneyed property interest"— one that "provides an essential balance" between individual and collective interests by, in effect, "enabl[ing] so-called externalities to be internalized" into the social decision-making process (Usher, 1993, 100–02). (Chapter 14 explores Marx's projection of such a communal system of explicitly social property.) Although prices can undoubtedly be assigned to many natural phenomena, this does not mean that the alternative is no valuation at all. In this sense, the mainstream argument fails to answer the "fundamental question: why should we give primacy to the market for determining environmental values?" (Phillips, 1993, 111).

Conversely, it is unclear that private and state-engineered resource prices can effectively represent anything other than capitalism's own internal and quite partial criteria of natural-wealth valuation. These prices assume "that the environment is, or can be treated as, a commodity that can be broken into a series of goods and services for sale on a market, real or hypothetical" (Phillips, 1993, 109). By definition, they "ascribe a value to nature only insofar as it has a price" (Altvater, 1990, 15). But natural conditions have an objective communality stemming from their mutual constitution with other natural conditions and from their functioning as conditions of a *social* process of human production. As a result, David Harvey notes: "It is difficult to assign anything but arbitrary money values to assets independently of the market prices actually achieved by the stream of goods and services which they provide" (1993, 6). Elmar Altvater comments on this contradiction that makes "market regulation . . . not adequate to the ecological conditions of economic activity":

> If an attempt is made to base ecological calculation upon monetary values, it will inevitably erect into a principle the characteristics of the commodity form: reification and the screening out of the natural constraints of production and consumption. If, on the other hand, that principle is discarded, the possibility of economic calculation based upon commodification and monetization will be curtailed. (1993, 208)

The difficulties with market-based environmental strategies can be viewed as a necessary outgrowth of the idealist method of neoclassical economics. Specifically, "instead of considering the reproduction conditions of nature" and their co-evolution with society in historically specific fashion, mainstream environmental economics "aims rather at revamping the cost calculations lying at the basis of the concept of economic rationality so that allocation and optimization mechanisms function as the textbooks say they should function" (Altvater, 1990, 11). This approach automatically bypasses or downgrades any natural conditions that, due to their objectively communal or "collective good" character, cannot be priced—*or can only be priced insofar as they are distortedly redefined as private goods.* For example, monetary values may be calculated for privately unpriced natural conditions by asking individuals how much they are willing to pay for their preservation, or how much they would have to be paid to accept their destruction. By such subsumptions of communal interest under individual monetary interest, the neoclassical approach restricts the scope of environmental economics and policy so as to leave out all those unpriceable environmental impacts that do not *directly and immediately* threaten the re-production of the current system of commodity production and exchange conceived in textbook terms.

The bias is exemplified by Robert Solow's argument that "the price system will push our society into faster and more systematic increases in the productivity of natural resources" (1976, 174). According to Solow,

> as the earth's supply of particular natural resources nears exhaustion, and as natural resources become more and more valuable, the motive to economize those natural resources should become as strong as the motive to economize labor. The productivity of natural resources should rise faster than now—it is hard to imagine otherwise. . . . Higher and rising prices of exhaustible resources lead competing producers to substitute other materials that are more plentiful and therefore cheaper. To the extent that it is impossible to design around or find substitutes for expensive natural resources, the price of commodities that contain a lot of them will rise relative to the prices of other goods and services that don't use up a lot of resources. Consumers will be driven to buy fewer resource-intensive goods and more of other things. All these effects work automatically to increase the productivity of natural resources, i.e., to reduce resource requirements per unit of GNP. (175)

For Solow, proper environmental management means adjusting human life to the exhaustion of particular natural resources by increasing their prices, while continuing to strive after the higher purposes of rising productivity and increases in real GNP. This view faithfully reflects capital's ability to continue expanding in both material and value terms by broadening and deepening human appropriation from nature, even as it depletes or destroys particular natural conditions (see Chapter 5). Solow essentially defines the environmental problem as one of keeping the GNP numbers on the rise—much as the goal of monetary capital accumulation recognizes no quantitative limits.

In sweeping the biospheric limits of capitalist production under the rug of rising productivity of *particular* natural resources, Solow's argument ignores two problems. First, it is not obvious that rising natural resource prices even reduce the rate of exhaustion or destruction of the particular resources in question. Rising prices and competition for limited profit-making opportunities may cause firms to step up the exploitation of known resource deposits, especially as firms become aware that these deposits are nearing exhaustion. This problem is best known from the fishing industry. At the same time, upward price pressures are likely to spur on firms' efforts to discover and exploit *new* supply sources, as is clear, for example, from the recent experience of the global forestry sector (Colchester, 1994; Newell and Wilson, 1996; Dauvergne, 1997; Hamilton, 1997). Finally, as Solow himself suggests, higher prices of particular resources tend to increase the exploitation of *substitute* resources. In all these respects, rising resource prices may actually accelerate the overall rate of resource depletion and despoliation. And if it is suggested that rents be applied to the aggregate level of production and/or resource use, then the proper answer is that a zero (or limited) growth solution flatly contradicts the basic inner mechanism of capitalist production. As Altvater observes, although "the 'steady-state principle' is . . . rational within the ecological system," this principle "is irrational in terms of market economics: an economy without profit" (1993, 203).

This brings us to the second difficulty with Solow's argument, namely that private or state-engineered rents apply at most to particular portions of nature, specifically those whose use as means of production or disposal can be quantitatively monitored. Rents are thus a limp instrument for alleviating the environmental impacts of an entire production system driven by the quantitatively boundless goal of capital accumulation—a goal that drives competing enterprises to constantly seek out qualitatively new ways to appropriate and process natural conditions. The competitive search for and extraction of resource rents is, in fact, an important modality of capital's homogenization and fragmentation of nature and people-nature relations, however little this may enter into Solow's GNP calculations (Devine, 1993).

In sum, the value-nature contradiction cannot be resolved by private rents or by grafting "green" tax and subsidy schemes onto an economic system shaped and driven by money and capital. Ecoregulation using monetary and market-based techniques is the pursuit of an "optimum" on capital's terms. Value, with all its anti-ecological features, remains "the active factor" disrupting the co-evolution of society and nature due to its treatment of people and nature as merely "disguised modes" of value itself (Marx, 1967a, I, 153–54). This illustrates a more general phenomenon, namely that whoever "wants to put up barriers to [capitalist] production, from the outside, through custom, law etc." will soon find that such "merely external and artificial barriers would necessarily be demolished by capital" (1973, 411).

CHAPTER 8

Reconsidering Some Ecological Criticisms of Marx's Value Analysis

The preceding chapter showed that Marx's value analysis has much to say about the social roots of capitalism's environmental problems, and that the critics who fault Marx for not ascribing value to nature should redirect their criticisms to capitalism itself. Generally speaking, these critics fail to appreciate the historical and social-relational aspect of Marx's theory—that value as a specifically capitalist form of wealth does not represent Marx's normative valuation of nature's intrinsic worth (e.g., in terms of aesthetic and other use values). In this respect, Marx's critics could have saved much trouble by studying the following passage:

> To what extent some economists are misled by the Fetishism inherent in commodities, or by the objective appearance of the social characteristics of labour, is shown, amongst other ways, by the dull and tedious quarrel over the part played by Nature in the formation of exchange-value. Since exchange-value is a definite social manner of expressing the amount of labour bestowed upon an object, Nature has no more to do with it, than it has in fixing the course of exchange. (Marx, 1967a, I, 82)

Marx's point is clear: since exchange value is a specific social form of wealth, it cannot be treated as being determined by nature. Of course, in order to fetch a positive exchange value (money price) in the market, a commodity must also be a use value. As Marx indicates, although "use-value is in general the bearer of exchange-value, but not its cause," it is still the case that "nothing can have exchange-value unless it has use-value" (1967a, III, 647). Because nature always contributes to use value, it follows that both nature and use value constitute *necessary conditions* of exchange value, even though they do not contribute to its quantity—at least insofar as exchange value is regulated by value.[1] Given that exchange value is a necessary form of value (abstract wage-labor time), it may also be said that nature and use value are necessary conditions of value and of capital accumulation.[2] This approach incidentally explains why Marx is able to describe the natural conditions allowing workers to produce a surplus product as the "natural basis" of surplus value, while simultaneously insisting that because surplus value involves specifically capitalist relations it cannot be treated as naturally determined (see Chapter 3).

Only by clearly demarcating and showing the relations and tensions among value, exchange value, and use value phenomena is Marx able to establish how capitalism's class-exploitative relations shape production together with its human and extra-human natural conditions. At the same time, Marx analyzes how particular sub-forms of value and capital (e.g., money, wages, constant capital, fixed and circulating capital, rent) are themselves shaped by the material conditions of production, that is, by the natural basis and substance of use value. In this way, Marx's value analysis reveals the tensions between wealth in its capitalist form and wealth in the sense of the individual and collective needs of social human beings co-evolving with nature, along with the implications of these tensions for class struggle and the movement toward a new stage of wealth production.

By contrast, many of Marx's ecological critics want to directly attribute value to nature without taking account of the historical specificity of wealth's social forms as determined by particular production relations. As a result, when they try to specify the precise *value-form* taken on by nature (value in terms of what, and for whom?), they are driven to various theoretical contradictions and defaults. The most common contradiction here is the inability to define nature's purported "value" independently of its exchange value and/or its use value, which often leads to (implicit or explicit) *conflations* of the three concepts. These conflations cause the critics in question to ignore or soft-pedal the ecological contradictions of capitalist wealth as revealed by Marx's relational and dialectical approach to value, exchange value, and use value.[3]

Value, Use Value, and the Pricing of Natural Conditions

The contradictions arising from the attribution of value to nature are well illustrated by Gunnar Skirbekk's attempted critique of Marx. Skirbekk argues that labor is the source of value only insofar as production inputs are produced by labor alone, rather than being extracted from nature. In the latter case, Skirbekk suggests, nature adds value to the product:

> The Marxian theory of value founded upon labor is valid for the reproductive forms of production. But in an extractive form of production, value is transferred from resources to profits, which may then be called an extractive surplus profit. This extractive surplus profit can be so large that the entire production process, at all levels, can receive more value from it than the labor itself has created. (1994, 100)

But what *form* does nature's value take? Skirbekk's answer is that nature's value appears in the form of higher *monetary incomes* for the workers and capitalists benefiting from the extraction of natural resources and their use as production inputs (1994, 99–100). These higher monetary incomes correspond to the higher living standards obtained by workers and capitalists at the expense of nature *and* of future generations:

> But who is "exploited" by this extractive surplus profit? Answer: nature, and, indirectly, future generations. Extractive surplus profit represents future pauperization. Oil companies, for example, are not only exempted from accounting for current ecological expenditures, they also omit future expenditures by depriving future generations of vital resources. (101)

In short, nature is "exploited" whenever "a part of the natural resources is used without being restored, without an equal quantity of wealth being returned to nature," and "this destructive extraction of limited natural wealth represents an impoverishment of future generations" (Skirbekk, 1994, 99). The term *exploitation* is thus used to connote both the reduction of natural wealth as such *and* the reduced living standards of future generations resulting from this reduction. Unfortunately, it is not clear how the former can be defined independently of the latter, in which case the attribution of an intrinsic value to nature breaks down. To commensurate exploitation as extraction from nature with exploitation as impoverishment of future generations is to conflate value with use value; because Marx insists on the use value of nature, Skirbekk's critique has already failed. Moreover, whereas Marx's analysis allows one to distinguish natural wealth in general from the more limited role of natural wealth as a condition of value and capital accumulation, Skirbekk's conflation of value and use value allows for no such distinction. Indeed, by limiting the "exploitation" of nature's "value" to "extractive forms of production," Skirbekk seems to naturalize *capitalism's* tendency to treat nature as an inexhaustible reservoir of passively obtainable use values, rather than as a biospheric system co-evolving with human production.

There is another, equally serious contradiction in Skirbekk's argument. It is one thing to recognize that human living conditions depend on the socially organized appropriation of nature-produced use values. Marx's conception of history and his analysis of capitalism in particular certainly do not deny this (see, for example, Chapter 3 of the present work). But it is something else altogether to assert that the utilization of natural conditions involves an extraction of *value* in the form of higher monetary incomes—that is, unless one is willing to conflate value and exchange value. This difficulty becomes clear when Skirbekk considers the question as to how the monetary incomes embodying the extraction of value from nature are actually obtained. On the one hand, he suggests that these incomes depend on the *underpricing* of natural resources in the market, which allows the firms and sectors utilizing the natural resources as inputs to enjoy lower production costs. On the other hand, he argues that in the extractive sectors (the oil industry, for example), nature is exploited insofar as natural resource prices *exceed* the per-unit value added by labor in these sectors, due to the value extracted from nature (1994, 99–101). Apparently, the exploitation of nature involves a simultaneous overpricing and underpricing of natural resources. Which one is it? Stated differently, Skirbekk does not explain why the overpricing of natural resources for extractive sectors does not cancel out the underpricing of natural resources for resource-using sectors, resulting in a zero net monetary gain from resource extraction and thus a zero rate of exploitation of nature.

The problem here is that by defining nature's value and its exploitation in terms of overpricing and underpricing of natural resources, Skirbekk is in effect arguing that value can be increased or decreased in the realm of exchange. In other words, he identifies value with exchange value. Indeed, he even extends this reasoning to the exploitation of *labor power itself,* arguing that workers are exploited insofar as "profit comes from the *underpayment* of the labor included in the product" (1994, 100; emphasis added). More generally, Skirbekk suggests that since "profit equals sales price minus cost price, one can increase profit by raising the sales value, the price, or by lowering the cost price" (100). He does not explain how this reasoning accounts for anything more than the monetary exchange values appropriated by individual firms as opposed to the *value* produced in the economy as a whole. In short, Skirbekk's attempt to attribute value to nature winds up falling prey to the common error of treating unequal exchange as a source of value (see Marx, 1967a, I, Chapter 5). He thus misses Marx's basic point, that whereas a net system-wide appropriation of positive surplus *value* from the purchase and sale of natural conditions is an impossibility (since one agent's gain in exchange is another's loss), the exploitation of *labor power* depends not on unequal exchange but on the ability of workers to expend more labor than required for their own reproduction under the given natural and social conditions. As Elmar Altvater observes:

> In the creation of value, it is in fact only labor that is able to create value and surplus value. From the standpoint of the energy cycle, labor (i.e., the worker) is brought to put more energy (brains, muscle, heart, and hand) in the process than he in the end gets out of it in the form of energy and matter. The surplus goes to the capitalist in the form of surplus value. The worker is brought to this (for him) deficit expenditure of energy by the specific form of the capitalist mode of production. . . . But what about nature? Wherein lies its value-creating power, in what form is value produced by nature, and how does the surplus come about if natural reproduction takes place in accordance with the laws of thermodynamics? (1990, 14)

Skirbekk's attempt to answer Altvater's question founders on the former's conflation of particular exchange values with the more general category of value. It is true that individual exchange values can incorporate surplus profits from the appropriation and productive utilization of scarce natural conditions; Marx deals with such redistributions of value in his analysis of capitalist rents. Skirbekk, however, not only ignores Marx's rent theory but also confuses the redistribution of value in the form of rents with the production of value itself.

Finally, by conceptualizing the "exploitation" of nature in terms of the under- and over-pricing of natural resources, Skirbekk presupposes that the price form can adequately represent nature's use value. This causes him to bypass the contradictions of exchange value as a social form of natural wealth. For example, the notion that natural resources are currently underpriced would seem to suggest that higher prices would resolve the resource-depletion problem. But higher prices would not only worsen the *monetary* exploitation of nature by extractive sectors according to Skirbekk's own logic; they would also spur on capitalist enterprises to seek out and extract new resource deposits and to intensify the extraction of currently known deposits, including deposits of previously unutilized substitute resources—thereby accelerating resource depletion. Whereas Marx's rent analysis can consistently account for this contradiction (see Chapter 7), Skirbekk's framework cannot.

Labor, Value, and Nature's Use Value

Voicing another common variation on the theme that "Marx's labour theory of value" downgrades nature, David Orton complains that for Marx, "nature is valueless, unless worked upon by humans" (1993, 190). It is not clear from the context whether Orton is measuring "valuelessness" in terms of use value or, instead, in terms of value as the social substance of exchange value. In this respect, Orton's criticism at least has the advantage of ambiguity, whereas Geoffrey Carpenter prefers to directly conflate use value and value: "To Marx . . . nature's use-value was realized only at the point of production where nature is transformed by labor into goods or services. 'The purely natural material in which *no* human labour is objectified,' says Marx, 'has no *value,* since only objectified labour is value'" (1997, 146).[4]

Given this confusion of value and use value, neither Orton nor Carpenter provides a viable answer to the basic question raised by any attribution of *value* to nature: namely, what is nature's value-form or, in other words, nature's value in terms of what and for whom?[5] Rather than dismiss their argument, however, I will consider each of the two possibilities in turn. First, did Marx argue that natural wealth is only realized as *use value* in combination with human labor? The answer is certainly yes. This explains why Marx is able to define a use value as "a natural bearer of labour" (1967a, III, 647). Often missed here, however, is Marx's inclusion of primary appropriation (hunting and gathering, fishing, mining—and even more basic actions such as breathing, seeing, hearing, touching, and feeling, especially insofar as one is talking about wealth production in general and not just value-producing labor) in his conception of that labor which is necessary for realizing natural wealth as use values satisfying human needs. That nature-produced use values only satisfy human needs (in production or in consumption) pursuant to their appropriation is as obvious as the fact that these use values must be present in nature in order to be appropriated. Under capitalism, for example, "if the same use-value could be obtained without labour, it would have no exchange-value [apart from rents], *yet it would retain, as before, the same natural usefulness as use-value*" (647; emphasis added).

Second, did Marx ascribe *value* to natural conditions only insofar as they objectify human labor? Once again, the answer is yes. Here, however, it must be kept in mind that Marx's conception of value-creating labor includes only commodity-producing wage-labor. Hence, it includes primary appropriation only insofar as such appropriative labor is *directly* objectified in commodities. Consider, for example, the eating, sleeping, and other restorative activities—not to speak of child-rearing labor and the labor of maintaining residential habitats—undertaken by workers during their "off-hours." These activities certainly involve appropriation of natural wealth including not only extra-human natural conditions (clean air, for example) but also the natural force of household labor power. But the maintenance and development of exploitable labor power associated with such domestic activities is *freely appropriated* by capital. It is a use value, not a value. Capital's free appropriation of the domestic enhancement of labor power increases the *rate* of surplus value insofar as domestic activities *lower* the value of labor power (by raising the productivity of wage-labor or reducing workers' commodified consumption requirements). Hence, if they want to be consistent, the critics of Marx's value analysis should blame him for not attributing value to domestic labor *and* to the natural wealth freely appropriated by capital. Unfortunately, such an argument broadens the confusion of value with use value, thereby worsening the confusion of use value for capital (i.e., as a condition of monetary accumulation) with use value for the working class and society as a whole.

Value as a Social and Material Relation:
A Brief Note

Ted Benton (1989) has enunciated an ecological critique of Marx that, at first sight, appears more sophisticated than the positions considered above. Given the wide influence of Benton's work among eco-Marxists, it is given a detailed treatment elsewhere (Burkett, 1998a and 1998b). Nonetheless, it is useful to establish the close relationship between Benton's interpretation of Marx's value analysis and the criticisms just surveyed. According to Benton, Marx's "labour theory of value" is

> the central conceptual device through which the limits, contradictions, and crises of capital accumulation are rendered thoroughly social-relational. As we saw in the discussion of Ricardo, the labour theory of value either excludes natural scarcity from consideration, or allows it to be recognized only in the form of its displaced manifestation within the internal social-relational structure of the economy. (1989, 76–77).

Consider the basic charge that Marx's value analysis abstracts from all material (as opposed to social) effects of natural scarcity on human production. The presumption here is that insofar as value is a social category, it cannot also be a material one. For Marx, however, value as a specific *social* form of *material* wealth is a contradictory unity of exchange value and use value, and Marx insists that both nature and labor contribute to the production of use values (see Chapter 7). Benton's critique thus artificially dichotomizes value and use value, making his dematerialized interpretation of value equally artificial.

In Marx's analysis, if a useful natural condition of production becomes increasingly scarce (and this includes decreases in its utility due to its degradation), the average productivity of the labor appropriating or utilizing this natural condition is, by definition, reduced in terms of material use values producible per hour of work, *ceteris paribus*. The *values* of the commodities produced with the increasingly scarce natural condition will, accordingly, be increased due to the greater amount of social labor time now required to produce the same use values. (This includes any additional necessary labor expended in the appropriation and utilization of *substitute* natural conditions.) These effects are clearly set out not only in Marx's discussions of the natural basis of surplus value but also in Marx's analyses of crises of capitalist reproduction due to crop failures (see Chapters 3 and 9, respectively).

In short, even abstracting from the effects of rents on the level and pattern of resource appropriation (see Chapter 7), natural scarcity most certainly can have material impacts within the purview of Marx's value analysis. More interesting for present purposes, however, is how Benton's artificial dichotomization of value and use value really represents the flip side, or mirror image, of the conflations of value and use value considered above. The difference is that whereas Benton's "value" is supposed to be Marx's conception of abstract labor, the "value" referred to by the other critics is purportedly the intrinsic value of extra-human nature somehow defined apart from its appropriation by social labor. I have shown that the other critics are unable to establish any value-form for nature without identifying value, use value, and exchange value. Similarly, having dematerialized value by dichotomizing it vis-à-vis use value, Benton is left without a consistent social *and* materialist conception of use value itself, one that does not reduce wealth in general to capitalist wealth in particular (see Burkett, 1998b, for details).

CHAPTER 9

Capitalism and Environmental Crisis

S ocial ecology looks at the mutual constitution, or co-evolution, of society and nature (see Chapter 1). Environmental crises involve discords
in this co-evolution. It is important to recognize that all concepts of
environmental crisis are human-social constructs in the sense that they all
implicitly or explicitly define these discords from the standpoint of the environmental requirements of human and social development. All concepts of
environmental crisis are based on a particular vision of human development
in and through nature and society; a "crisis" occurs when this human development is subjected to "above-normal" restrictions. These restrictions may
be defined in terms of human health, mental and physical capabilities, and
opportunities to appropriate or to co-habitate with natural conditions; or in
terms of breakdowns in the reproduction of the social relations governing
human production and development. Environmental crisis theory normally
focuses on environmental changes stemming from human interventions into
nature, such changes being the most consistent source of "above-normal"
environmental restrictions on human development.[1]

This chapter shows that Marx's analysis of capitalism contains an environmental crisis theory of the type just defined. Specifically, Marx considers two kinds of environmental crises produced by capitalism: (1) crises
of capital accumulation, based on imbalances between capital's material
requirements and the natural conditions of raw materials production; and
(2) a more general crisis in the *quality* of human-social development,
stemming from the disturbances in the circulation of matter and life
forces that are generated by capitalism's industrial division of town and
country. Whereas disruptions of capital accumulation due to materials

shortages involve natural conditions as conditions of accumulation, Marx's broader conception of environmental crisis focuses on the degradation of natural wealth as a condition of human development.

Nonetheless, the two kinds of crisis overlap considerably insofar as they both involve reductions in the quality *and* quantity of appropriable natural wealth; hence they both implicate capital's free appropriation of natural conditions along with all the qualitative tensions between value and nature (see Chapters 6 and 7). More precisely, capital's tendency to *accelerate material throughput beyond its natural limits* is not just a source of materials shortages and accumulation crises; it is also an integral element in the process of ecological degradation produced by the capitalist division of town and country. Our investigation of Marx's environmental crisis theory accordingly begins with this anti-ecological tendency of capital accumulation.

Capitalism and Material Throughput

Accumulation of capital connotes accumulation of value as represented by money, value's general equivalent. Since value must also be represented in use value, capital also takes the form of "an immense accumulation" of vendible use values or commodities (Marx, 1970, 27). Capital accumulation thus translates into a growing processing of materials serving as bearers of value. This material throughput accelerates with the rising productivity of labor, that is, with the growing amount of use values produced per labor hour, *ceteris paribus*. As Marx indicates: "The growing productivity of labour is expressed precisely in the proportion in which a larger quantity of raw material absorbs a definite quantity of labour, hence in the increasing amount of raw material converted in, say, one hour into products, or processed into commodities" (1967a, III, 108):

> The growth of machinery and of the division of labour has the consequence that in a shorter time far more can be produced. Hence the store of raw materials must grow in the same proportion. In the course of the growth of the productive capital the part of capital transformed into raw materials necessarily increases. . . . [T]he part of productive capital intended for wages becomes smaller and smaller in relation to that which acts as machinery and raw material. (1976a, 431)

Capital's demand for materials is also buoyed by the need for growing materials *stocks* in order to maintain the continuity of production and accumulation. Marx develops this point as part of his analysis of "formation of supply" in Chapter 6 of *Capital,* Volume II:

The material forms of existence of constant capital, the means of production, do not however consist only of instruments of labour but also of materials of labour in various stages of processing, and of auxiliary materials. With the enlargement of the scale of production and the increase in the productive power of labour through cooperation, division of labour, machinery, etc., grows the quantity of raw materials, auxiliary materials, etc., entering into the daily process of reproduction. These elements must be ready at hand in the place of production. The volume of this supply existing in the form of productive capital increases therefore absolutely. In order that the process may keep going . . . there must always be a greater accumulation of ready raw material, etc., at the place of production than is used up, say, daily or weekly. The continuity of the process requires that the presence of its conditions should not be jeopardised by possible interruptions when making purchases daily, nor depend on whether the product is sold daily or weekly, and hence is reconvertible into its elements of production only irregularly. (1967a, II, 141–42)

This inventory demand for materials can be expected to increase considerably during periods of shortage or uncertainty in materials supplies. Another notable aspect of the above passage is Marx's distinction between "materials of labour in various stages of processing, and . . . auxiliary materials." Auxiliary materials are those which, while not forming part of "the principal substance of the product," are nonetheless required "as an accessory" of its production (1967a, I, 181). They help provide necessary conditions of production (heat, light, chemical, and other physical processes) distinct from the direct processing of principal materials by goods-producing labor and its instruments.[2] Here the crucial point is that Marx's analysis formally incorporates capital's growing demand for auxiliary materials used as energy sources, thus capturing the growing energy throughput produced by the accumulation process. As Marx observes: "After the capitalist has put a larger capital into machinery, he is compelled to spend a larger capital on the purchase of raw materials *and the fuels required to drive the machines*" (1976a, 431; emphasis added).

Another source of rising material throughput under capitalism is the moral depreciation of fixed capital—that is, of machinery and buildings—by the development of newer, more productive machinery and structures or by rising labor productivity in the industries producing them (Marx, 1967a, I, 404–05, III, 113–14; cf. Horton, 1997). Through such moral depreciation, "competition compels the replacement of the old instruments of labour by new ones before the expiration of their natural life" (Marx, 1967a, II, 170).[3] The threat of moral depreciation (non-realization of values objectified in machinery and buildings) also drives individual enterprises to accelerate the turnover of their fixed capital stocks by prolonging work-time and intensifying labor, further accelerating material and energy throughput.[4]

In sum, with rising productivity and technological advance there is an increase in the quantity of natural forces and objects that capital must appropriate as materials and instruments of production in order to achieve any given expansion of value and surplus value. Rising productivity means that each hour of abstract labor is now borne in a larger and larger quantity of use values and their material prerequisites. In this sense, capital accumulation involves a growing quantitative imbalance between value accumulation and accumulation as a material process dependent upon natural conditions. With "value . . . represented in a massive quantity of use values," as Marx puts it, "there is an increase in [the] difference between the labour process and the valorisation process" (1988, 325). In relating this imbalance to capitalism's undervaluation of natural conditions, John Bellamy Foster argues that

> capitalism maximizes the throughput of raw materials and energy because the greater this flow—from extraction through the delivery of the final product to the consumer—the greater the chance of generating profits. And by selectively focusing on minimizing labor inputs, the system promotes energy-using and capital-intensive high technologies. All of this translates into faster depletion of nonrenewable resources and more wastes dumped into the environment. (1994, 123)

Foster's analysis is consistent with Marx's insofar as increases in material and energy throughput are required to produce additional commodities containing surplus value. I have shown how the necessity for capital to exploit labor power using natural forces and objects in production is, in Marx's view, the flip side of the conversion of natural conditions into conditions of monetary accumulation (see Chapters 5 and 6).[5] Nonetheless, two amplifications are in order here.

First, from the standpoint of individual competing enterprises, it is obviously not the case that "maximizing the throughput of raw materials and energy" always results in a "greater chance of generating profits." Although opportunities to extract surplus labor from workers, and to objectify it in vendible use values, often entail increases in material and energy throughput, competition penalizes "above-normal" throughputs by not recognizing the labor time objectified in them as socially necessary, value-creating labor. Under capitalism, "all wasteful consumption of raw material or instruments of labour," that is, consumption in excess of the "normal" amount per commodity produced, "is strictly forbidden" in that "what is so wasted, represents labour superfluously expended, labour that does not count in the product or enter into its value" (Marx, 1967a, I, 196). Moreover, the normal waste, the labor objectified in which *does* enter into the value of the product, does *not* include any discarded materials or instruments that *could* have been *profitably* used in the production of other commodities:

> Suppose that in spinning cotton, the waste for every 115 lbs. used amounts to 15 lbs., which is converted, not into yarn, but into "devil's dust." Now, although this 15 lbs. of cotton never becomes a constituent of the yarn, yet assuming this amount of waste to be normal and inevitable under average conditions of spinning, its value is just as surely transferred to the value of the yarn, as is the value of the 100 lbs. that form the substance of the yarn. . . . The same holds good for every kind of refuse resulting from a labour-process, *so far at least as such refuse cannot be further employed as a means in the production of new and independent use-values.* Such an employment of refuse may be seen in the large machine works at Manchester, where mountains of iron turnings are carted away to the foundry in the evening, in order the next morning to reappear in the workshops as solid masses of iron. (1967a, I, 205; emphasis added)

In Marx's analysis, individual enterprises not only have an incentive to avoid any above-normal waste of materials and instruments of production (because such waste represents a waste of capital) but also to reduce waste to sub-normal levels in order to enjoy surplus profits at the expense of their competitors (1967a, III, 194). The latter incentive encompasses the development of new and more efficient methods of profitably recycling and re-employing the material byproducts of production. In these ways, "the capitalist mode of production extends the utilisation of the excretions of production" (101).[6]

Marx's analysis also suggests, however, that such competitive reduction, recycling, and re-employment of waste operates *within* a system of rising labor productivity in the form of mass processing of materials and energy into commodities. Under capitalist competition, "there is a motive for each individual capitalist to cheapen his commodities, by increasing the productiveness of labour" (1967a, I, 317). By lowering an enterprise's private production costs per commodity produced, such productivity gains allow the enterprise to reap surplus profits and/or an increased market share at the expense of competitors. The expanding flow of normal hourly material and energy throughput that accompanies rising labor productivity does not worry the competing enterprise. The enterprise still feels pressure to keep throughput at or below the normal level, but this level is itself a function of the constant competitive pressure and positive profit incentive to boost output per labor hour (hourly commodity throughput).

This analysis leads to the second necessary amplification of Foster's (1994) examination of capitalist throughput—that capital's hunger for materials and energy is not just *quantitatively* anti-ecological. Capitalism's valuation of throughput according to necessary wage-labor time is a *qualitatively* anti-ecological representation of wealth or use value (see Chapter 7). The competitive "efficiency" of rising material and energy throughput stems from the social validation of labor productivity as if the net addition to social wealth from "normal" throughput can be measured simply by the wage-labor time it (directly or indirectly) objectifies. This measurement bypasses all the reductions in the quality of appropriable natural wealth associated with the "normal" appropriation, utilization and disposal of materials and energy. Capitalistically "normal" throughput is determined not by the requirements of a sustainable co-evolution of society and nature of any given quality, but simply and solely by the imperatives of competitive monetary accumulation. As André Gorz observes, the system's "economic imperative of productivity is *totally different* from the ecological imperative of resource conservation" (1994, 32; emphasis added).[7] This basic tension is shown even in the capitalist recycling and "waste management" industries that, rather than contributing to a fundamental restructuring of production in ecologically sustainable directions, have mainly served to create new vehicles of value accumulation "through fresh expenditure of energy and materials," thus becoming "a constitutive part of the problem" (Altvater, 1993, 213; cf. Gellen, 1970; Fairlie, 1992; Karliner, 1994; Horton, 1995).

Capitalism's accelerated throughput involves a conflict between the time nature requires to produce and absorb materials and energy versus the competitively enforced dynamic of maximum monetary accumulation in any given time period by all available material means. This contradiction of nature's time versus capital's not only lessens the quality of the natural conditions of human development but also disrupts the process of capital accumulation itself.

Capital's Material Requirements, Natural Conditions, and Accumulation Crises[8]

Marx insists that the production of surplus value in both industry and agriculture depends on natural conditions enabling workers in agriculture (including livestock raising, forestry and fishing) to produce more than their own means of subsistence.[9] The natural basis of surplus value also includes the natural conditions needed for the production of a supply of principal and auxiliary materials. Natural materials—including animate and inanimate life forms—serve as bearers of value and surplus value when they are processed into vendible use values by wage labor (see Chapters 3, 5, and 6).

Given this background, it should not be surprising to find Marx asserting that the only *truly general* crises of capital accumulation are those that feature short supplies of the major agricultural products serving as workers' means of subsistence or as industrial materials. Such agricultural shortages threaten the material conditions needed for capital to extract surplus labor from workers and objectify it in vendible use values. In Volume III of *Capital,* for example, Marx indicates that "a real lack of productive capital, at least among capitalistically developed nations, can be said to exist only in times of general crop failures, either in the principal foodstuffs or in the principal industrial raw materials" (1967a, III, 484). Similarly, as part of his somewhat premature prediction of the global economic crisis of 1857–58, Marx says: "The state of the winter crops being what it is, I feel convinced that the crisis *will become due.* So long as the *staple article, food,* remains tolerably *abundant* and cheap, and what with Australia, etc., the thing could have been a long time in coming. Now a *stop* will be put to all that" (Marx to Engels, January 29, 1853, in Marx and Engels [1983, 275]).

It is also interesting that when charting the probable course of the crisis he saw looming in late 1853, specifically in "France where, after all, the catastrophe will break out," Marx begins with a "failure of the corn and grape harvests"—and then proceeds to trace in detail the likely effects of this agricultural disruption on capital accumulation, the credit system, class conflict, and the political regime of Louis Bonaparte (Marx to Engels, October 12, 1853, in Marx and Engels [1983, 387–88]).

Marx's formal analyses of materials shortages and accumulation crises are developed on two levels. The first level specifies "the general conditions of crises, in so far as they are independent of price fluctuations (whether these are linked with the credit system or not) as distinct from fluctuations of value" (Marx, 1968, 515). On this level, crisis possibilities are treated in terms of "the general conditions of capitalist production," abstracting from all changes in prices and production that involve competition within and between sectors; hence phenomena such as materials-price speculation and the competitive search for new materials supplies, not to speak of rents, are excluded (515). Price changes are only dealt with on this level insofar as they reflect changes in commodity values. In this context, Marx indicates that "a *crisis* can arise: 1. in the course of the *reconversion* [of money] *into productive capital;* 2. through *changes in the value* of the elements of productive capital, particularly of *raw material,* for example when there is a decrease in the quantity of cotton harvested. Its *value* will thus rise" (515).

Marx's point here is that a crop failure raises materials prices even insofar as these are determined by values, since each hour of agricultural labor time is now objectified in a smaller quantity of use values. Such "a rise in the price of raw material can curtail or arrest the entire process of reproduction if the price realised by the sale of the commodities should not suffice to replace all the elements of these commodities" (1967a, III, 109). These price surges and their disruption of accumulation demonstrate capital's ongoing dependence on natural conditions:

> If the price of raw material rises, it may be impossible to make it good fully out of the price of the commodities after wages are deducted. Violent price fluctuations therefore cause interruptions, great collisions, even catastrophes, in the process of reproduction. It is especially agricultural produce proper, i.e., raw materials taken from organic nature, which . . . is subject to such fluctuations of value in consequence of changing yields, etc. Due to uncontrollable natural conditions, favourable or unfavourable seasons, etc., the same quantity of labour may be represented in very different quantities of use-values, and a definite quantity of these use-values may therefore have very different prices. (117–18)

Materials shortages do not just disrupt accumulation by raising the value of constant capital; they also may *physically disrupt* production by "making it impossible to continue the process on the scale required by its technical basis, so that only a part of the machinery will remain in operation, or all the machinery will work for only a fraction of the usual time" (109). In an interesting passage in *Theories of Surplus Value,* Marx analyzes the combined effects of reductions in the available quantity and increases in the value of materials—once again emphasizing the role of "uncontrollable natural conditions":

> Since the reproduction of raw material is not dependent solely on the labour employed in it, but on the productivity of this labour which is bound up with *natural conditions,* it is possible for the volume, the *amount* of the product of the *same* quantity of labour, to fall (as a result of bad *harvests*). The *value of the raw material therefore rises;* its *volume* decreases, in other words the *proportions* in which the money has to be reconverted into the *various com-*

ponent parts of capital in order to continue production on the former scale, are upset. More must be expended on *raw material,* less remains for *labour,* and it is not possible to absorb the same quantity of labour as before. Firstly, this is *physically impossible,* because of the deficiency in raw material. *Secondly,* it is impossible because a greater *portion of the value of the product* has to be converted into raw material, thus leaving less for conversion into *variable capital.* Reproduction cannot be *repeated* on the same scale. A part of *fixed capital* stands idle and a part of the workers is thrown out on the streets. The *rate of profit* falls because the value of constant capital has risen as against that of variable capital and less variable capital is employed. . . . This is therefore a *disturbance in the reproduction process* due to the increase in the value of that part of constant capital which has to be replaced out of the value of the product. (1968, 515–16)

Although such materials-supply disturbances involve uncontrollable natural conditions, they also implicate uncontrolled capital accumulation. This is partly a matter of anarchic competition precluding the kind of *ex ante* planning required to minimize the disruptive effects of natural events (see below); but there is also a fundamental imbalance between capital's tendency toward limitless expansion and the limits of materials production under the given natural *and* social conditions. Natural conditions thus appear as an ultimate limit, along with the extent of the market, on the feasible growth of industrial production and accumulation:

So soon, however, as the factory system has gained a certain breadth of footing and a definite degree of maturity, and, especially, so soon as its technical basis, machinery, is itself produced by machinery; so soon as coal mining and iron mining, the metal industries, and the means of transport have been revolutionized; so soon, in short, as the general conditions requisite for production by the modern industrial system have been established, this mode of production acquires an elasticity, a capacity for sudden extension by leaps and bounds that finds *no hindrance except in the supply of raw material* and in the disposal of the produce. (1967a, I, 450–51; emphasis added)

Marx emphasizes that the barrier to accumulation posed by limited materials supplies manifests a contradiction between capital's acceleration of production and investment on the one hand, and the natural laws and temporal rhythms governing materials production on the other:

It is in the nature of things that vegetable and animal substances whose growth and production are subject to certain organic laws and bound up with definite natural time periods, cannot be suddenly augmented in the same degree as, for instance, machines and other fixed capital, or coal, ore, etc., whose reproduction can, provided the natural conditions do not change, be rapidly accomplished in an industrially developed country. It is therefore quite possible, and under a developed capitalist system even inevitable, that the production and increase of the portion of constant capital consisting of fixed capital, machinery, etc., should considerably outstrip the portion consisting of organic raw materials, so that demand for the latter grows more rapidly than their supply, causing their price to rise. (1967a, III, 118)

A "full development" of this tension between nature's time and capital's must incorporate "the credit system and competition on the world market"; Marx left the bulk of this second level of analysis for the "eventual continuation" of *Capital,* which he was never able to embark upon (110). Nonetheless, "for the sake of completeness," the modification of capitalism's general tendency toward materials-supply disturbances by competition is "discussed in a general way" in Volume III of *Capital* (110, 118). Here, Marx points out that increases in materials prices are likely to elicit three competitive responses seemingly mitigating the disruptive effects of materials shortages. First, the "raw materials" in question can now "be shipped from greater distances, since the mounting prices suffice to cover greater freight rates"; hence there may be increased "importation from remote and previously less resorted to, or entirely ignored, production areas" (118–19). Second, higher prices may eventually elicit a positive supply response even from traditional suppliers, although this "increase in their production . . . will probably not, *for natural reasons,* multiply the quantity of products until the following year" (118; emphasis added). Finally, "rising prices of raw materials naturally stimulate the utilisation of waste products" as well as "the use of various previously unused substitutes" (101, 118).

Marx is skeptical about the ability of these responses to ameliorate materials-supply disturbances; indeed, he argues that they are likely to worsen the instability of materials prices. By the time the "rise of prices begins to exert a marked influence on production and supply it indicates in most cases that the turning-point has been reached at which demand drops on account of the protracted rise in the price of the raw material and of all commodities of which it is an element, causing a reaction in the price of raw material" (118). With the "supply of raw materials" now "exceeding the demand . . . a collapse of these high prices occurs"; and this "sudden collapse of the price of raw materials checks their reproduction" (119). All of this leads to "convulsions . . . in various forms through depreciation of capital," as "the sphere of production of raw materials is, by fits, first suddenly enlarged, and then again violently curtailed" (118, 120). Even with the fall of materials prices, however, the investments in new and old materials production areas during the preceding boom—including investments in the production of substitute materials—create a permanent broadening and deepening of the capital invested in materials production. As Marx puts it: "Due to the impetus it has had, reproduction of raw material proceeds on an extended scale" (119). This results in intensified competition among materials producers, a competition that, in reinforcing the temporary depression of materials prices, naturally favors those "producing countries, which enjoy the most favourable conditions of production" (119).[10]

Competition thus tends to accentuate "the ever-recurring alternation between relative appreciation and the subsequent resulting depreciation of raw materials obtained from organic nature" (121). This provides an incentive for capitalists to form cartels to stabilize materials prices, either at high levels (cartels of materials *producers*) or low levels (cartels of materials *purchasers*). Marx argues that such cartels are unlikely to achieve any long-term stabilization of materials prices:

> During the period in which raw materials become dear, industrial capitalists join hands and form associations to regulate production. . . . But as soon as the immediate impulse is over and the general principle of competition to "buy in the cheapest market" (instead of stimulating production in the countries of origin, as the associations attempt to do, without regard to the immediate price at which these may happen at that time to be able to supply their product)—as soon as the principle of competition again reigns supreme, the regulation of the supply is left once again to "prices." All thought of a common, all-embracing and far-sighted control of the production of raw materials gives way once more to the faith that demand and supply will mutually regulate one another. And it must be admitted that such control is on the whole irreconcilable with the laws of capitalist production, and remains for ever a pious wish, or is limited to exceptional co-operation in times of great stress and confusion. (119–20)

The ephemerality of materials agreements owes much to the opportunities for individual capitalists to profit from the stockpiling of materials and from speculation on materials prices. Such practices are most common during periods of shortage, when material "elements of productive capital are . . . withdrawn from the market and only an equivalent in money is thrown on the market in their place," the result being a further "rise in the prices of productive materials as well as means of subsistence" (1967a, II, 315). Indeed, "speculation in these commodities counts on further rise in prices and the easiest way to make them rise is to temporarily withdraw a portion of the supply from the market" (1967a, III, 514). These operations are fueled by an increasingly well-developed credit system, which services the growing "demand for loan capital . . . in order to pay for the purchased commodities without selling them" (514).[11] Nonetheless, the demand for credit for speculative purposes may place upward pressure on the rate of interest:

> Speculative stock-piling could also occur, either for the purpose of taking advantage of the most favourable moment for production purposes, or in expectation of a future rise in prices. In this case, the demand for loan capital could grow, and the rise in the rate of interest would then be a reflection of capital investment in surplus stock-piling of elements of productive capital. . . . The higher rate of interest then reflects an artificial reduction in the supply of commodity capital. (514–15)

The ability of materials speculators to pay these higher interest rates without incurring large financial losses often depends on a continuation of the materials price run-up. When the downturn of prices occurs, therefore, it generates a large upward pressure on speculators' demand for money as a means of payment—a demand that the speculators, whose creditworthiness is now in question, may only be able to satisfy by distress sales of materials inventories and paper claims thereon, thereby hastening the price deflation (1967a, III, 516). In sum, the use of credit accentuates the instability of materials prices on both the upside and the downside, making it even more difficult to maintain materials cartels among competing capitalists.

Still, the more fundamental basis of materials supply disturbances and price fluctuations is the imbalance between industrial capital's accelerating material demands and the natural conditions of materials production. This imbalance tends to worsen as capitalism matures to the point of developing its own machine-building industries:

> The greater the development of capitalist production, and, consequently, the greater the means of suddenly and permanently increasing that portion of constant capital consisting of machinery, etc., and the more rapid the accumulation (particularly in times of prosperity), so much greater the relative over-production of machinery and other fixed capital, so much more frequent the relative under-production of vegetable and animal raw materials,

and so much more pronounced the previously described rise of their prices and the attendant reaction. And so much more frequent are the convulsions caused as they are by the violent price fluctuations of one of the main elements in the process of reproduction. (118–19)[12]

In Marx's view, one "moral of history" regarding capitalism's materials-supply problems "is that the capitalist system works against a rational agriculture, or that a rational agriculture is incompatible with the capitalist system" (121). The same moral applies to the mining industry; in both cases, a "common, all-embracing and far-sighted control of the production of raw materials" requires "the control of associated producers" (120–21). It is important to establish another motivation for the revolutionary transformation of production and material throughput in Marx's view—one more primary than capitalist materials-supply disturbances and accumulation crises. I refer to capitalism's tendency toward environmental crisis understood as a crisis of human development. This tendency implicates the spatial organization of capitalist production.

Town and Country under Capitalism

Marx and Engels often analyze the environmental impacts of capitalist development in terms of the division and interaction between agricultural and non-agricultural industry and the attendant "antithesis between town and country" (Engels, 1939, 323). Of course, "the separation between town and country" predates capitalism; indeed, Marx goes so far as to assert not only that it is "the foundation of every division of labour that is well developed," but also that "the whole economic history of society is summed up in the movement of this antithesis" (1967a, I, 352). In *The German Ideology*, Marx and Engels assert that the "contradiction between town and country begins with the transition from barbarism to civilisation, from tribe to state, from locality to nation, and runs through the whole history of civilisation to the present day" (1976, 72).[13] At the same time, they argue that "the contrast between town and country . . . has been brought to its extreme point by present-day capitalist society," and that "far from being able to abolish this antithesis, capitalist society on the contrary is compelled to intensify it day by day" (Engels, 1979, 51). It is necessary to understand the forces underpinning this compulsion in order to grasp the environmental implications of the town/country division.

To begin with, the genesis of capitalist production and the creation of its home market involve a separation of agriculture and industry via the expropriation of mainly rural producers from necessary conditions of production, especially the land (see Chapter 5). In this process, activities such as "spinning and weaving become divorced from 'domestic' industry and agriculture," whereupon "all those [still] engaged in agriculture become a market for spinners and weavers" (Marx, 1971, 269):

> Thus, hand in hand with the expropriation of the self-supporting peasants, with their separation from their means of production, goes the destruction of rural domestic industry, the process of separation between manufacture and agriculture. And only the destruction of rural domestic industry can give the internal market of a country that extension and consistence which the capital mode of production requires. . . . Formerly, the peasant family produced the means of subsistence and the raw materials, which they themselves, for the most part, consumed. These raw materials and means of subsistence have now become commodities; the large farmer sells them, he finds his market in manufactures. Yarn, linen, coarse woollen stuffs—things whose raw materials had been within the reach of every peasant family, had been spun and woven by it for its own use—were now transformed into articles of manufacture, to which the country districts at once served for markets. (1967a, I, 747–48)

The process by which "capital destroys craft and artisan labour [and] working small-landownership" culminates with the development of "Modern Industry," which "alone, and finally, supplies, in machinery, the lasting basis of capitalistic agriculture, expropriates radically the enormous majority of the agricultural population, and completes the separation between agriculture and rural domestic industry" (1973, 512; 1967a, I, 748–49). It remains to be explained, however, how this "setting free of a part of the agricultural population" leads to an increased *urban concentration* of industry and population (1967a, I, 745). A crucial point here is that with the "thinning-out of the independent, self-supporting peasants," the means of manufacturing production such as "spindles, looms, [and] raw material" are "now transformed from means of independent existence for the spinners and weavers, into means of commanding them and sucking out of them unpaid labour" (746). Insofar as supervision of free labor power requires the gathering together of large numbers of laborers under one roof, this capitalist control over means of production translates into a greater spatial concentration of workers and means of production. As Marx indicates, "spindles and looms, formerly scattered over the face of the country, [were] now crowded together in a few great labour-barracks, together with the labourers and the raw material," and this "brought about the crowding together of the industrial proletariat" (1967a, I, 745–46).

There were other powerful forces compelling capital to concentrate industrial activity in increasingly large individual workplaces and urban agglomerations. For one thing, the laborers being set free from rural conditions of production were attracted by the potential job openings and other subsistence opportunities offered by pre-existing towns. In this way, Marx notes, the "expropriation and expulsion of the agricultural population, intermittent but renewed again and again, supplied the town industries with a mass of proletarians entirely unconnected with the corporate guilds and unfettered by them" (745). Apart from this growing supply of exploitable labor power and other advantages of pre-existing towns (e.g., superior access to extant financial, communications, and transport facilities), large concentrations of population created more opportunities for division of labor within and among enterprises. As indicated in *Capital*: "Just as a certain number of simultaneously employed labourers are the material pre-requisites for division of labour in manufacture, so are the number and density of the population, which here correspond to the agglomeration in one workshop, necessary conditions for the division of labour in society" (352). Marx develops this point in somewhat more detail in *Theories of Surplus Value:*

> The proper development of the division of labour presupposes a certain density of population. The development of the division of labour in the workshop depends even more on this density of population. This latter division is, to a certain extent, a pre-condition for the former and in turn intensifies it still further. It does this by splitting formerly correlated occupations into separate and independent ones, also by differentiating and increasing the indirect preliminary work they require; and as a result of the increase in both production and the population and the freeing of capital and labour it creates new wants and new modes of satisfying them. (1971, 269)

Marx also argues that physically larger production units tend to outcompete smaller production units, *ceteris paribus,* due to scale economies in the processing of materials and productive instruments into commodities bearing surplus value.[14] For example, capital's "employment of forces of nature on a large scale is only possible where machinery is employed on a large scale, hence also where there is a corresponding *conglomeration* and cooperation of workers subsumed under capital" (1994, 32). Similarly, in *The Condition of the Working-Class in England,* Engels argues that "manufacture centralises property in the hands of the few" insofar as it "requires large capital . . . to erect the colossal establishments that ruin the petty trading bourgeoisie and with which to press into its service the forces of Nature, so driving the hand-labour of the independent workman out of the market" (1973, 60). Another method by which "means of production [are] economised by concentration on a vast scale" involves "instruments of labor which, from their very nature, are only fit for use in common, such as a system of machinery" (Marx, 1967a, I, 623). These "conditions of social, or socially combined, labour," including buildings, "are commonly consumed in the process of production by the aggregate labourer, instead of being consumed in small fractions by a mass of labourers operating disconnectedly" (1967a, III, 79).[15]

The competitive impetuses toward centralization of means of production and labor power are reinforced by and in turn reinforce the agglomerating effects of the division of labor among firms. Closer proximity of enterprises producing related use values may increase their ability to reap "external economies" from one another and from the grouping of production units as a social whole. In addition to potential economies from common utilization of large-scale communication and transport facilities, "the productivity of labour in one branch of industry" may serve "as a lever for cheapening and improving the means of production in another, and thereby raising the rate of profit" (1967a, III, 85). Here, "the development of the productive power of labour in any *one* line of production, e.g., the production of iron, coal, machinery, in architecture," results in "a reduction of the value, and consequently the cost, of means of production in *other* lines of industry, e.g., the textile industry, or agriculture" (81). Given transport costs, the spatial grouping of enterprises may enable them to more easily profit from such effects.

Once production is agglomerated at a given location to a certain degree, it naturally attracts an additional migration of exploitable labor power that, from the standpoint of individual enterprises, appears as virtually a public good—one imparting its own momentum to the agglomeration process. There is an interesting discussion of this point in *The Condition of the Working-Class in England,* in which Engels describes the development of an industrial urban area from a small village:

> Population becomes centralised just as capital does; and, very naturally, since the human being, the worker, is regarded in manufacture simply as a piece of capital for the use of which the manufacturer pays interest under the name of wages. A manufacturing establishment requires many workers em-

ployed together in a single building, living near each other and forming a village of themselves in the case of a good-sized factory. They have needs for satisfying which other people are necessary; handicraftsmen, shoemakers, tailors, bakers, carpenters, stonemasons, settle at hand. The inhabitants of the village, especially the younger generation, accustom themselves to factory work, grow skillful in it, and when the first mill can no longer employ them all, wages fall, and the immigration of fresh manufacturers is the consequence. So the village grows into a small town, and the small town into a larger one. The greater the town, the greater its advantages. It offers roads, railroads, canals; the choice of skilled labour increases constantly, new establishments can be built more cheaply because of the competition among builders and machinists who are at hand, than in remote country districts, whither timber, machinery, builders, and operatives must be brought; it offers a market to which buyers crowd, and direct communication with the markets supplying raw material or demanding finished goods. Hence the marvellously rapid growth of the great manufacturing towns. (1973, 60–61)

Marx and Engels point to certain factors qualifying capitalism's urban agglomeration of industry and population. There are, for example, physical limits to the packing of industrial activity in a given space, and these limits produce a contrary tendency toward spatial widening of facilities: "It is true that, compared with handicrafts, large-scale industry may concentrate much production in a small area. Nevertheless, a definite amount of space is always required at any given level of productivity, and the construction of tall buildings also has its practical limitations" (Marx, 1967a, III, 781).

Urban industrial concentrations may also erode the local natural conditions of production to the point of spurring a migration of capital to less industrialized and less urbanized zones. Engels makes this point using the example of industrial water supplies:

Though water-power was necessarily confined to the countryside, steam-power is by no means necessarily confined to the towns. It is the capitalist mode of its utilisation which concentrates it mainly in the towns and changes factory villages into factory towns. But in so doing, it at the same time undermines the conditions of its own exploitation. The first necessity for the steam engine, and a main requirement of almost all branches of production, is relatively pure water. The factory town, however, transforms all water into stinking ditch water. However much therefore concentration in the towns is a basic condition of capitalist production, each individual capitalist is constantly striving to get away from the large towns necessarily created by it, and to move towards exploitation in the countryside. (1939, 322)

Such industrial decentralization may be further spurred on by the search for lower wage costs, especially if large latent reserves of exploitable labor power remain in rural areas and smaller villages. This motivation is strengthened insofar as urban workers are more effectively organized in trade unions.[16] As Engels indicates: "The country . . . has the advantage that wages are usually lower than in town, and so town and country are in constant competition; and, if the advantage is on the side of the town to-day, wages sink so low in the country to-morrow, that new investments are most profitably made there" (1973, 61).

Apart from these positive centrifugal forces, there are certain general conditions *enabling* capital to decentralize. Economically speaking, "density is more or less relative," in that a "thinly populated country, with well-developed means of communication, has a denser population than a more numerously populated country, with badly-developed means of communication" (Marx, 1967a, I, 352–53). The same goes for the means of transport (384). The development of transport and communications may support more decentralized patterns of production, both across an entire country and *within* particular urban areas. On the institutional level, a prime factor enabling decentralization is the contrast between the division of labor *within* enterprises, as determined by capitalists and their managerial functionaries, and the division of labor *among* enterprises, as determined by anarchic market competition:

> The division of labour in the workshop implies concentration of the means of production in the hands of one capitalist; the division of labour in society implies their dispersion among many independent producers of commodities. While within the workshop, the iron law of proportionality subjects definite numbers of workmen to definite functions, in the society outside the workshop, chance and caprice have full play in distributing the producers and their means of production among the various branches of industry. (355)

The above observations suggest another potential vehicle of industrial decentralization, namely, the tendency for new enterprises or "additional capitals" to be "formed in the normal course of accumulation," as "portions of the original capitals disengage themselves and function as new independent capitals" (625, 628).[17] This tendency partly offsets "the transformation of many small into few large capitals," as "the increase of each functioning capital is thwarted by the formation of new and the sub-division of old capitals," thereby qualifying the tendency toward centralization of larger quantities of labor power and means of production in individual enterprises and workplaces, *ceteris paribus*. Capital accumulation now "presents itself on the one hand as increasing concentration of the means of production, and of the command over labour; on the other, as repulsion of many individual capitals one from another" (625).

Marx and Engels suggest that these decentralizing tendencies are insufficient to offset the centripetal forces compelling industrial capital toward urban agglomeration. Insofar as decentralization is potentially led by newly formed enterprises, it is blocked by the growing tendency for such capitals to be "already massed together by the centralisation movement," both institutionally and spatially (Marx, 1967a, I, 628).[18] Improved means of communication and transport may make decentralization more feasible, but their production requires large-scale industrial facilities, thereby reinforcing the spatial concentration of labor power and means of production (384–85).

Most importantly, the decentralization of industrial facilities itself serves to promote new growth centers of capital accumulation, hence new urban agglomerations. As Engels puts it: "Every new factory built in the country bears in it the germ of a manufacturing town," and "modern capitalist industry is constantly bringing new large towns into being by constantly fleeing from the towns into the country" (1973, 61; 1939, 322). As a result, "the centralising tendency of manufacture continues in full force," but on an extended basis (1973, 61). Stated differently, the agglomeration of industry is not impeded but rather is broadened by capitalist decentralization. Improvements in communications and transport thus translate into increased economic density, not only in the monetary sense but also in the sense of increasingly dense social interchanges (and environmental throughputs) of matter and energy over *extended* industrial zones.[19]

The profitability of capitalism's industrial agglomerations reveals the anti-ecological characteristics of value and capital. In these areas, competing enterprises freely appropriate the productive potentials of their natural and social environment as means of exploiting labor power. In doing so, they ignore the combined impacts of growing industrial throughput and materially dense industry and population on the distinct ecological networks and biospheric connections constituting the ultimate natural basis of human development. Marx and Engels' analysis of the town/country antithesis addresses these impacts through its treatment of the interchanges between agriculture and manufacturing industry under capitalism.

Capitalism and the Natural
Conditions of Human Development

Capitalism's spatial and technological transformation of production vitiates the quality of natural wealth as a condition of human development. The agglomeration of industry and population in urban areas, and the industrialization of agriculture based on the reduced self-sufficiency and depopulation of rural economy, produce a social circulation of matter that is environmentally unsustainable and directly hazardous to human health. This environmental critique of capitalist production is a recurring theme in the writings of Marx and Engels.

Industrial–capitalist cities generate two types of rising material and energy throughput. As noted earlier, the growing productivity of industrial labor translates into rising "normal" levels of material and energy throughput required for the profitable production and sale of commodities. This throughput is accelerated insofar as industrial labor productivity is itself boosted by agglomeration. The adverse effects of industrial waste on the health of the urban population are chronicled in detail by Engels in *The Condition of the Working-Class in England* (1973). In addition, however, a good share of urban throughput takes the form of "excretions of consumption . . . produced by the natural exchange of matter in the human body and partly [as] objects that remain after their consumption" (Marx, 1967a, III, 101). The urban health impacts of these excretions, especially in working-class districts lacking adequate housing and sanitation facilities, are described not only in Engels' classic early work but also in Volume I of *Capital,* especially in Marx's case studies of "The Badly Paid Strata of the British Industrial Class" and "The Nomad Population," illustrating the "accumulation of misery, corresponding with accumulation of capital" (1967a, I, 645, 654–67).[20]

Quite often, Marx and Engels analyze the urban health effects of consumption excretions as part of their broader critique of the circulation of matter produced by capitalism's division of agriculture and urban industry. They argue that the problem of urban waste grows in step with the declining fertility of the soil, as urban industrial agglomerations disrupt the previous recycling of materials through the land itself:

> Capitalist production, by collecting the population in great centres, and causing an ever-increasing preponderance of town population, . . . disturbs the circulation of matter between man and the soil, i.e., prevents the return to the soil of its elements consumed by man in the form of food and clothing; it therefore violates the conditions necessary to lasting fertility of the

soil. By this action it destroys the health of the town labourer and the intellectual life of the rural labourer. (Marx, 1967a, I, 505)

Clearly, Marx's analysis of how capitalism "upset[s] the naturally grown conditions for the maintenance of [the] circulation of matter" encompasses both agricultural and urban-industrial areas (505–6). It is important to establish this point, seeing as how many have argued that Marx's recognition of capitalism's environmental malfunctions is basically limited to agriculture.[21] The connection between urban-industrial concentration and declining soil fertility is reiterated, for example, in Volume III of *Capital,* where Marx suggests that

> large landed property reduces the agricultural population to a constantly falling minimum, and confronts it with a constantly growing industrial population crowded together in large cities. It thereby creates conditions which cause an irreparable break in the coherence of social interchange prescribed by the natural laws of life. As a result, the vitality of the soil is squandered. (1967a, III, 813)

In the same volume, Marx laments over the large-scale waste of potential agricultural raw materials associated with this "break" with "the natural laws of life"—specifically the failure to recycle "excrements of consumption":

> Excrements of consumption are the natural waste matter discharged by the human body, remains of clothing in the form of rags, etc. Excretions of consumption are of the greatest importance for agriculture. So far as their utilisation is concerned, there is an enormous waste of them in the capitalist economy. In London, for instance, they find no better use for the excretion of four and a half million human beings than to contaminate the Thames with it at heavy expense. (101)[22]

Capitalism's contrast of industrial town and agricultural country creates a circulation of matter that corrodes the quality of natural conditions not only for agricultural production but for human development more generally. It does so by violating the "demand," as formulated by the great agricultural chemist, Justus Liebig, "that man shall give back to the land what he receives from it" (Engels, 1979, 92).[23] And it is not just the "existence of the towns, and in particular the big towns," which precludes capitalism from fulfilling Liebig's demand (92). The industrialization of agriculture further despoils the natural wealth of the land, over and above the effects of urban-industrial waste and the failure to recycle excretions of urban consumption (see Chapter 7). Under the competitive pursuit of profit, agricultural technology is transformed using machines and other inputs provided by urban industry. The depletion of the soil is thereby accelerated side by side with intensified exploitation of agricultural labor power that, given the ruining of non-agricultural rural industries, is itself employed largely on a seasonal basis. As Marx indicates: "All progress in capitalistic agriculture is a progress in the art, not only of robbing the labourer, but of robbing the soil" (1967a, I, 506).[24] The joint impacts of capitalist agriculture and urban industry on labor power and its natural conditions are summarized in Volume III of *Capital:*

> Large-scale industry and large-scale mechanised agriculture work together. If originally distinguished by the fact that the former lays waste and destroys principally labour-power, hence the natural force of human beings, whereas the latter more directly exhausts the natural vitality of the soil, they join hands in the further course of development in that the industrial system in the country-side also enervates the labourers, and industry and commerce on their part supply agriculture with the means for exhausting the soil. (Marx, 1967a, III, 813)

In sum, Marx's analysis of capitalist environmental crisis encompasses more than the environmental effects of agriculture and urban industry considered separately. It covers the entire process by which capitalism "develops technology, and the combining together of various processes *into a social whole*" (1967a, I, 506–07; emphasis added). Capitalism "concentrates the historical motive power of society" in urban areas, thereby creating wasteful and ecologically disruptive concentrations of material throughput; but in doing so, it also "completely tears asunder the old bond of union which held together agriculture and manufacture in their infancy" while harnessing agriculture to the quantitatively unlimited goal of monetary accumulation—a goal pursued using the class-exploitative and anti-ecological factory-farm technologies provided by urban industry (505). By this total process, capital winds up "sapping the original sources of all wealth, the soil and the labourer" (507).

Some Interpolations of Marx's Analysis

Marx's conception of capitalist environmental crisis implicates the total spatial and technological organization of capitalist production. As such, it not only relies on but also is the culmination of Marx's entire analysis of capital accumulation in agriculture and urban industry. (Certain additional aspects of Marx's analysis, involving capital's overstretching of the limited resiliency of labor power and its natural conditions, are discussed in Chapter 10.) This section shows that Marx's analysis is open to an incorporation of three additional issues that must be confronted by any realistic perspective on environmental crisis: the use of non-biodegradable synthetics in production and consumption; the global scope of environmental crisis; and the effects of rising energy throughput from human production, given the second law of thermodynamics.

Marx could not have been aware of capitalism's increasingly large-scale development and disposal into the environment of synthetic materials not easily absorbed by pre-existing ecological processes. For one thing, such synthetics are by and large a post–World War II development, whereas Marx optimistically projected that the transition to an environmentally sustainable communist system of production would occur well before capitalism reached its full potential for wreaking ecological havoc (Foster, 1997, 287). But synthetic commodities and throughput do fit into Marx's analysis of capital's powerful tendency to divide and simplify labor and nature in general disregard of the ecological interconnections required for the reproduction of natural wealth of any given quality (see Chapter 7). At the same time, synthetics are a symptom of value's fundamental indifference to the kinds of use values in which it is objectified as long as they are vendible (see Chapter 11). Overall, then, capitalism's wasteful and unhealthy circulation of synthetic *and* organic matter within and between town and country clearly manifests the anti-ecological characteristics of value and capital as revealed by Marx's analysis. Together, capitalism's urban-industrial concentrations and industrialized agriculture have generated artificial material throughputs and land-use patterns inconsistent with natural species diversities (both animate and inanimate), thereby "sapping" the rich variegation and resiliency of natural wealth.[25]

To what extent does Marx's perspective encompass the biospheric sweep of these ecological disruptions? Although Marx and Engels are often somewhat ambiguous about the exact spatial scope of their analyses of town and country, including the interactions of agriculture and urban industry, it seems clear that the basic dynamics are meant to apply not only within individual regions and countries but also on a global scale. As evidence, one can point, first, to Marx's analysis of the expanding sphere of capitalist raw materials production. I have shown how cyclical materials shortages and price rises stimulate the development of new agricultural (and mining) regions.[26] The spatial extension of materials production and exchange is also a natural outgrowth of the world market, the international division of labor, and the overall expansion of industrial production under the spur of competitive monetary accumulation. This general process is outlined in the *Manifesto:*

> All old-established national industries have been destroyed or are daily being destroyed. They are dislodged by new industries, whose introduction becomes a life and death question for all civilised nations, by industries that no longer work up indigenous raw material, but raw material drawn from the remotest zones. (Marx and Engels, 1968, 39)

Rosa Luxemburg provides an even more colorful description of materials globalization in her classic work, *The Accumulation of Capital:*

> In general, capitalist production has hitherto been confined mainly to the countries in the temperate zone, whilst it made comparatively little progress in the East, for instance, and the South. Thus, if it were dependent exclusively on elements of production obtainable within such narrow limits, its present level and indeed its development in general would have been impossible. From the very beginning, the forms and laws of capitalist production aim to comprise the entire globe as a store of productive forces. Capital, impelled to appropriate productive forces for purposes of exploitation, ransacks the whole world, it procures its means of production from all corners of the earth, seizing them, if necessary by force, from all levels of civilisation and from all forms of society. The problem of the material elements of capitalist accumulation, far from being solved by the material form of the surplus value that has been produced, takes on quite a different aspect. It becomes necessary for capital progressively to dispose ever more fully of the whole globe, to acquire an unlimited choice of means of production, with regard to both quality and quantity, so as to find productive employment for the surplus value it has realised. (1964, 358)

This passage reveals the systemic roots of the dark "ecological shadows" cast over primary-materials producing nations and regions by industrialized nations and regions (Dauvergne, 1997). In emphasizing the temperate zone's extraction of materials from a less industrialized East and South, Luxemburg comes close to recognizing the town/country antithesis on a world scale. This is not surprising, seeing as how Marx had previously sketched a global town/country analysis in Volume I of *Capital:*

> On the one hand, the immediate effect of machinery is to increase the supply of raw material in the same way, for example, as the cotton gin aug-

mented the production of cotton. On the other hand, the cheapness of the articles produced by machinery, and the improved means of transport and communication furnish the weapons for conquering foreign markets. By ruining handicraft production in other countries, machinery forcibly converts them into fields for the supply of its raw material. . . . By constantly making a part of the hands "supernumerary," modern industry, in all countries where it has taken root, gives a spur to emigration and to the colonisation of foreign lands, which are thereby converted into settlements for growing the raw material of the mother country. . . . A new and international division of labour, a division suited to the requirements of the chief centres of modern industry springs up, and converts one part of the globe into a chiefly agricultural field of production, for supplying the other part which remains a chiefly industrial field. This revolution hangs together with radical changes in agriculture. (1967a, I, 451)

The basic elements of the town/country antithesis are all present in this passage, but now on a world scale. This provides a framework within which one can treat the ecological and even biospheric disruptions produced by capitalism's global circulation of matter—including disturbances from the importation of non-indigenous species into distinct ecological zones (Vitousek et al., 1997, 498).

The global scope of capitalism's town/country antithesis seems a proper note on which to turn to the final issue to be considered, namely, whether Marx's framework is capable of incorporating the biospheric effects of rising energy throughput. Here, Marx's analysis of capital's growing material throughput explicitly incorporates the processing of fuels and other accessory materials. When combined with Marx's recognition of the limitlessness of monetary accumulation as the goal of production, this analysis helps us understand capitalism's tendency to convert increasing amounts of energy into less organized, more entropic forms in disregard of the earth's limited supply of non-renewable energy resources and limited capacity to absorb entropy without serious climactic and biospheric dislocations.

The often-incisive ecological economist Juan Martínez-Alier has recently questioned whether Marx's critique of political economy provides any meaningful insight into capitalism's unsustainable processing of energy resources—his main evidence being what he terms "Engels's own negative reaction to Sergei Podolinsky's attempt in 1880 to introduce human ecological energetics into Marxist economics" (Martínez-Alier, 1995a, 71). But, when one looks into the relevant Engels-Marx correspondence, a more nuanced picture emerges. Engels observes, for example, that "the working individual is not only a stabiliser of *present* but also, and to a far greater extent, a squanderer of *past,* solar heat" in the form of non-renewable energy sources as well as forests. He goes on to lament "what we have done in the way of squandering our reserves of energy, our coal, ore, forests, etc. . . . accumulated from the past" (Engels to Marx, December 19, 1882, in Marx and Engels [1992, 411]). Is this simply a "negative reaction"?

Engels' recognition of the second law of thermodynamics is less important than the *methodological content* of his comments on Podolinsky. What bothers Engels is not the introduction of ecological energetics into Marx's critique of political economy but rather Podolinsky's attempt to "express economic conditions in terms of physical measures" pure and simple—an effort that, given the social-relational character of all economic phenomena, is "a sheer impossibility." Engels' complaint is that "Podolinski went astray . . . because he sought to find in the field of natural science fresh evidence of the rightness of socialism" without applying "his very valuable discovery" in the context of an analysis of capitalism's specific social forms of material production. This is the sense in which Podolinsky "has confused the physical with the economic" (Engels to Marx, December 19, 1882, in Marx and Engels [1992, 411–12]). Viewed in this light, Martínez-Alier's characterization of Engels' comments as a "negative reaction" is terse to the point of distortion.

The really crucial question here is whether Marx's critique of political economy denies all natural limits to capitalist production, even historically specific ones.[27] Marx's analyses of capitalism's materials-supply disturbances, and of the town/country antithesis with its despoliation of the natural conditions of human development, clearly recognize the limited character of the natural wealth appropriated by capital. Further evidence of this recognition is presented in the next chapter.

CHAPTER 10

Marx's Working-Day Analysis and Environmental Crisis

T he brilliant Russian Marxist political economist I. I. Rubin once observed that "in capitalist society, . . . permanent, direct relations between determined persons who are owners of different factors of production, do not exist" (1972, 18). This impermanence applies not only to relations between workers and capitalists but also to people-nature relations. Under capitalism, the reproduction of both relations is normally dependent on their monetary profitability. Both relations tend to be utilized, reshaped, extended, and abandoned in line with the imperatives of private profitability and competitiveness, not according to any social and ecological criteria of permanence or sustainability.

This parallel between labor and nature as vehicles of monetary accumulation helps explain why Marx treats capitalism's alienation of labor jointly with capitalism's alienation of nature vis-à-vis the producers. In terms of capitalism's environmental crisis tendencies, an important aspect of the parallel is this: the limits to capital's exploitation of human labor power, like the limits to capital's exploitation of natural conditions, are not fully determined by capital itself. In both cases, the limits involve certain material characteristics not subject to alteration by the specific social form of production. The limits to capital's exploitation of labor and nature are, however, elastic limits, this elasticity being partly due to the natural characteristics of labor power and extra-human nature, and partly to the socially defined character of the limits themselves.[1] Capital's damaging effects on labor power and nature result from its tendency to take advantage of this elasticity as the pressures of competitive monetary accumulation stretch human and extra-human natural forces to the breaking point—necessitating social restraints on capital's exploitation of the two basic sources of wealth. From this perspective, Marx's analyses of work-time, child labor, and the struggle over the working day contain important insights for ecological socialists.

Capital and the Natural and Social Limits to Work-Time

The above-mentioned parallel can be discerned from Marx's analyses of the "ultimate, although very elastic boundaries" to the length of the work-day and capital's tendency to extend work-time "beyond its natural limits—until legislation is obliged to take a hand" (1976b, 57; 1988, 319). Marx suggests that because "the variation of the working-day" is subject to "physical and social bounds," capital's "tendency . . . to obtain the greatest possible quantity of living labour time" is itself "held in check in part by physical conditions, and in part by social obstacles" (1967a, I, 232; 1988, 180).

In Marx's view, capital has an in-built tendency to dissolve all social obstacles to the extension of work-time. Here capital takes advantage of the downward flexibility of the laborer's needs—a flexibility basic to labor power's character as a socially and naturally reproduced force.[2] In order to absorb "the active existence of the human being" as surplus labor, capital exploits the elasticity of the worker's need for "time for satisfying his intellectual and social wants, which are conditioned by the general state of social advancement" (1991, 493; 1967a, I, 232). This contraction of the worker's "space for development" represents an "appropriation of the *life*, the mental and physical life, of the worker" (1991, 493). Capital exploits not only the social but also the natural elasticity of labor power's requirements, for the forces of monetary accumulation and competition impel it "to go beyond the natural limits of labour time" and to "produce thus . . . not only the deterioration of human labour-power by robbing it of its normal, moral and physical, conditions of development and function," but also "the premature exhaustion and death of this labour-power itself" (1991, 386; 1967a, I, 265).[3]

Capital's infringement of the "natural barriers to the duration of the daily labour time," its "constant tendency . . . to stretch it to the utmost possible length, because in the same degree surplus labour, and consequently the profit therefrom, will be increased," is shown by its alteration of the social definitions of day and night so that work-time can be extended (1988, 181; 1976b, 52). For Marx, nightwork itself, regardless of the total length of daily work-time, entails an unnatural "signification of 'day' and 'night'" that exploits the flexibility of the worker's need for a healthy metabolism with nature (1988, 223).[4] Under the sway of capital accumulation and competition, "all bounds of . . . day and night were broken down," and "even the ideas of day and night . . . became so confused that an English judge . . . needed a quite Talmudic sagacity to explain 'judicially' what was day and what was night" so far as the extension of work-time was concerned (1967a, I, 278). Such ambiguity "allowed the greatest latitude" for "working-days of 8, 10, 12, 14, 16, 18 hours, i.e., of the most different lengths," to the point where even "Malthus, by no means a man whom you would suspect of a maudlin sentimentalism, declared . . . that if this sort of thing was to go on the life of the nation would be attacked at its very source" (232; 1976b, 53).[5]

Capital thus abuses the elastic limits of the laborer's recuperative powers as much as it abuses the absorptive capacity and resilience of particular ecosystems, in both cases leading to the vitiation of natural forces. And just as capital threatens biospheric havoc with its ability to destroy particular local and regional ecosystems while continuing to function by utilizing others, it also, within certain ultimate limits, applies the same slash-and-burn treatment to the laboring class on an inter- and intragenerational basis. From capital's point of view, "a succession of unhealthy and short-lived generations will keep the labour market as well supplied as a series of vigorous and long-lived generations" (1976b, 57).[6] The availability of labor power despite the unnatural extension of work-time is supported by capital's "constant absorption of . . . physically uncorrupted elements from the country," that is, by the "surplus-population" set free by the capitalization of agriculture and the competitive ruin of handicraft industry domestically and globally (1967a, I, 269, 642). Capitalistic employment of children (see below) should also be located in this context of capital's efforts to "leap over the *natural* limit formed by one individual's living, working day . . . by positing *another* working day alongside the *first* at the same time—by the spatial addition *of more simultaneous working days*" (1973, 400).[7] The supply of exploitable labor power is also replenished by capital's tendency, through mechanization and intensification of labor, to "set free, render disposable a definite number of labour capacities," that is, to "eject them from . . . different spheres of production as superfluous labor power" (1994, 186).[8]

By increasing the capitalistically employed portion of the global population and by producing redundant laborers through mechanization and rising productivity, capital temporarily evades labor power's natural limits by, in effect, "increasing the mass of living labour capacities which forms the basis for exploitation by capital; the animate material from which surplus value is extracted" (1994, 10–11). However, just as in the case of extra-human nature, capital's apparent freedom from these natural limits is only obtained at the cost of a broader and deeper exploitation and despoliation of natural forces (here, the natural forces of labor power).

Natural and Social Aspects of Child Labor

The abuse of labor power's natural and social elasticity is an integral aspect of capital's employment of children. Child labor sheds important light on the exploitative nature of capitalism, not least because "the true character of each epoch come[s] alive in the nature of its children" (Marx, 1973, 111). To Marx, the degradation of human beings to a sub-natural state was evident not only from "the physical deterioration . . . of the children and young persons" employed by capital, but also from the "moral degradation caused by [this] capitalistic exploitation" (1967a, I, 397, 399). Marx describes "the intellectual desolation artificially produced by converting immature human beings into mere machines for the fabrication of surplus-value" as "a state of mind clearly distinguishable from that natural ignorance which keeps the mind fallow without destroying its capacity for development, its natural fertility" (399).[9]

Natural and social degradation are thus inseparable aspects of capitalist child labor, in Marx's view. The employment of children involves capital taking advantage of labor power's "natural diversity" ("the difference between the labour-power . . . of children and adults") in order to lower its wage bill and obtain more pliant labor forces (519). But capital's exploitation of children also means that the dominant social conceptions of what constitutes an able-bodied worker, and even of childhood and adulthood as such, have to be modified. Hence, "according to capitalistic anthropology, the age of childhood ended at 10, or at the outside, at 11" (280). At the same time, child labor implicates particular material and social processes *within* the capitalist economic framework.

For example, the employment of child labor was encouraged by capital's mechanization of production, since "in so far as machinery dispenses with muscular power, it becomes a means of employing labourers of slight muscular strength, and those whose bodily development is incomplete, but whose limbs are all the more supple" (394). Such "mechanical workshops" further promoted child labor via a relative reduction in the demand for "skilled labour, the learning of which can only be begun at a more mature age, and then can only be brought to the required level of virtuosity through long years of apprenticeship" (1991, 493). In Marx's view, the child's physical and mental development is lowered to a sub-natural path when capital "takes control of [the] mind and body when it is still in an *immature* state," the problem being that such "machine labour does away with the all-round exertion of the muscles," and "offers no opportunity for physical activity; nor does it allow any mental activity" (494).

Moreover, once child labor was generalized to a certain extent, it became a normal, involuntary means of supporting the family. When children "emerged as competitors of the other workers," parents were, in effect, forced into "conducting a slave trade," as they "endeavor[ed] to recover by the *sale of children* what the adult worker loses through the competition of child labour" (1991, 492). Here, capital takes advantage of the lower physical subsistence requirements of individual children (and of discrimination against women and children) to gain "economies of scope" from employment of multiple family members when the value of labor power is determined on a family rather than an individual basis. As Marx phrases it (using the example of a traditional family with two children), the employment of children (and of women) "spreads the value of the man's labour-power over his whole family" in such a way that capital "raises the degree of exploitation," because "in order that the family may live, four people must now, not only labour, but expend surplus-labour for the capitalist" (1967a, I, 395). This extension of the family's wage-labor time also involves a replacement of domestic activities with purchases of commodities, so that "the diminished expenditure of labour in the house is accompanied by an increased expenditure of money." In this way, the extent and quality of home life are reduced while "the cost of keeping the family increases, and balances the greater income" (395).[10]

Overall, Marx's analysis of child labor illustrates a real parallel between capital's treatments of human and extra-human nature. Just as capitalism tends to reshape the social standards of what are acceptable natural conditions in line with the conversion of these conditions into conditions of monetary accumulation (unless forcibly constrained from doing so), this system also has a powerful in-built tendency to reduce the standards of social and material existence of the laboring class within and across generations, at home and at work, by extending the wage-labor time of "every member of the workman's family, without distinction of age or sex" (394). It should come as no great surprise that this parallel was explicitly drawn by Marx himself, and repeatedly so.

Capitalism and the Overstretching
of Natural and Human Limits

Marx often notes the parallel between capital's depletion of the natural force of labor power by extension of work-time beyond the limits of human recuperative abilities, and capital's overstretching of the regenerative powers of the land by its plunder of extra-human natural forces. In considering the origins of legal restraints on work-time in England, for example, Marx suggests that "the limiting of factory labour was dictated by the same necessity which spread guano over the English fields. The same blind eagerness for plunder that in the one case exhausted the soil, had, in the other, torn up by the roots the living force of the nation" (1967a, I, 239).

Capital's plunderings of labor power and extra-human nature both involve the extraction of short-run gains at the expense of long-run sustainability:

> Anticipation of the future—real anticipation—occurs in the production of wealth in relation to the worker and to the land. The future can indeed be anticipated and ruined in both cases by premature overexertion and exhaustion, and by the disturbance of the balance between expenditure and income. In capitalist production this happens to both the worker and the land. . . . What is shortened here exists as power and the life span of this power is shortened as a result of accelerated expenditure. (1971, 309–10)

To Marx, capital's dual exploitation of the natural limits of labor power and extra-human nature entails a twofold theft of natural forces. Just "as a greedy farmer snatches increased produce from the soil by robbing it of its fertility," so capital "usurps the time for growth, development and healthy maintenance of the body" and "steals the time required for the consumption of fresh air and sunlight" (1967a, I, 265). Marx's treatment of the overextension of work-time as a robbery of natural forces is reflected in his description of capital as a social-material parasite that, "vampire-like, only lives by sucking labour, and lives the more, the more labour it sucks" (233).[11] What is being robbed here is more than the labor power of private individuals: it is "the prime energy" or "the vital power of the people," nothing less than the "reserve fund for the regeneration of the vital force of nations" (269; 1967a, III, 813). This robbery has a broader social significance stemming from the role of human labor power as a social life-force. From the standpoint of the reproduction and development of society, labor power is a common pool resource—one with definite (albeit elastic) natural limits. Capital vitiates this life-force both materially and socially when it plunders it as a condition of private monetary accumulation.

The notion that Marx treated the overextension of work-time as a theft of a common pool resource may seem farfetched; but Marx does analyze this capitalist threat to the reproduction of human beings in just such terms. From the perspective of individual competing capitalists, the supply of exploitable labor power appears to be unlimited and in any case exogenous with respect to their individual efforts to plunder it. Nonetheless, the exploitation of the laboring class by capital as a whole vitiates and threatens the reproduction of this basic human-social life-force. Marx treats this dynamic in terms of a "tragedy of the commons" model developed by analogy with speculative bubbles in the stock exchange:

> What experience shows to the capitalist generally is a constant excess of population, i.e., an excess in relation to the momentary requirements of surplus-labour-absorbing capital, although this excess is made up of generations of human beings stunted, short-lived, swiftly replacing each other, plucked, so to say, before maturity. . . . Capital that has such good reasons for denying the sufferings of the legions of workers that surround it, is in practice moved as much and as little by the sight of the coming degradation and final depopulation of the human race, as by the probable fall of the earth into the sun. In every stock-jobbing swindle every one knows that some time or other the crash must come, but every one hopes that it may fall on the head of his neighbor, after he himself has caught the shower of gold and placed it in safety. *Après moi le déluge!* is the watchword of every capitalist and of every capitalist nation. Hence Capital is reckless of the health or length of life of the labourer, unless under compulsion from society. (1967a, I, 269–70)

In sum, Marx emphasizes that the same in-built tendency to endanger its own material bases is exhibited in capital's exploitation of labor power and its despoliation of natural conditions. In both cases, the overstretching of natural limits and the movement toward an eventual day of reckoning for society results from capital's ability to gain access to its immediate material requirements (exploitable labor power and conditions allowing for its exploitation), despite the ongoing vitiation of these natural conditions by capitalist exploitation itself. Capital's ability to accumulate in the meantime, despite its corrosive effects on its own human and extra-human conditions, starkly manifests how its use value requirements are alienated from the necessary basis of use value in a sustainable co-evolution of people and nature.

The Significance of Social Restraints
on Capitalist Exploitation

One additional dimension of Marx's work-time analysis has great significance for ecological politics. It involves Marx's suggestion that the social protection of human laboring capacity from capital's "unnatural extension of the working-day" must "take on the form of a class struggle, and thereby call forth the intervention of the state power" (1967a, I, 266; 1988, 184). Marx's reasoning is as follows:

> As to the *limitation of the working day,* in England, as in all other countries, it has never been settled except by *legislative interference.* Without the working men's continuous pressure from without that interference would never have taken place. But at all events, the result was not to be attained by private settlement between the working men and the capitalists. This very necessity of *general political action* affords the proof that in its merely economic action capital is the stronger side. (1976b, 59).

There are several interrelated arguments in this well-packed statement. To begin with, Marx asserts that effective regulation of work-time cannot be achieved privately. Here and elsewhere, Marx treats a sustainable working-day (one consistent with a day-to-day rejuvenation of the natural force of labor power) as a kind of public good. This jibes with Marx's recognition of labor power as a limited common pool resource from the standpoint of society's reproduction and development. Even neoclassical economics recognizes that public goods may be undervalued by unregulated markets, due to the forces of competition and the "free rider" problem. However, Marx's analysis of this public good problem is informed by the class relations of capitalism.[12] As such, it recognizes that the degree of undervaluation of labor power's daily reinvigoration (i.e., of the worker's free time) depends on the relative bargaining power of capital and labor as a whole. Here, Marx suggests that without "legislative interference" in response to "general political action" and "continuous pressure" by workers, the overall balance of class forces—as conditioned by capital's control over the means of employment and the reproduction of a reserve army of unemployed ("its merely economic action")—will tend to favor capital over labor, the result being "an unlimited and reckless extension of the working-day" (1967a, I, 298).

Marx's case for the necessity of *general* working-class pressure and state action to impose safeguards against excessive work-time is thus based on the combined importance of the class-biased economic dynamics of capitalism *and* the social character of labor power as natural wealth. This is the holistic reasoning behind Marx's otherwise inexplicable suggestion that "the measureless demands of capital could never be held in check by the isolated efforts of the worker," so that "the determination of what is a working-day, presents itself as the result of a struggle, a struggle between collective capital, i.e., the class of capitalists, and collective labour, i.e., the working class" (1988, 184; 1967a, I, 235).[13] Once one recognizes that extra-human natural conditions *and* workers' free time *both* have important public good and common pool resource characteristics linked to their special roles in the daily rejuvenation and long-run reproduction of labor power, the relevance of Marx's reasoning for environmental regulation clearly emerges.

Up until this point, it has been presumed that capital's interests lie in the prolongation of work-time to the greatest possible extent. But Marx also recognizes that from a long-term perspective, there are certain ways in which limitations on work-time appear to be rational even for capital. Aside from the long-run threat it poses to capital's absolute use-value requirement (exploitable labor power), unlimited work-time may place upward pressure on wage costs by augmenting workers' subsistence consumption requirements. Beyond a certain boundary, the extension of work-time

> shortens the length of life of the individual labourer, and therefore the duration of his labour-power, [so that] the forces used up have to be replaced at a more rapid rate and the sum of the expenses for the reproduction of labour-power will be greater; just as in a machine the part of its value to be reproduced every day is greater the more rapidly the machine is worn out. *It would seem therefore that the interest of capital points in the direction of a normal working-day.* (1967a, I, 266; emphasis added)

Moreover, the negative "external costs" of unregulated work-time may afflict capitalists and workers alike. Marx mentions how, "as a result of . . . excesses" in work-time, "there broke out epidemics whose devastating effects were equally threatening to capitalists and workers," so that "the state . . . was compelled to introduce normal days in the factories" (1988, 216). Legal caps on work-time may also "free the capitalist from some of the brutality natural to a man who is a mere embodiment of capital, and . . . give him time for a little 'culture'" (1967a, I, 302).[14] The question thus arises as to why Marx places so much stress on *working-class* pressure as a condition for effective regulation of work-time. After all, one could agree, based on "public good" and "externality" arguments, that "it is only government compulsion that can limit labour time," while disagreeing with Marx's view that "the rebellion of the working class itself" is "the main driving force" in the imposition of such compulsion (1988, 226; 1991, 386). Indeed, Marx himself notes that British work-time legislation was "made by a state . . . ruled by capitalist and landlord" (1967a, I, 239). Whence the need for and the significance of explicit *working-class* pressure?

Marx's answer to this apparent puzzle seems to be twofold. First, this is one case where the individual and collective interests of workers correspond more effectively to the interests of the whole present and future society than do the long-term or the short-term interests of capital. The underlying basis of workers' general political action to limit work-time is the close affinity between, on the one hand, workers' interest in their own sustainable and healthy reproduction and, on the other hand, the historical progress of society in terms of the development and fulfillment of human needs and capabilities. By contrast, even from the long-run perspective, capital as such (money seeking more money) requires restraints on work-time solely to ensure a supply of exploitable labor power, with no necessary concern for the present and future wealth of society holistically considered. Clearly, the working-class standpoint is better situated to take the leading ideological position in any "reaction on the part of society, the very sources of whose life are menaced" by competing capitalists' "immoderate lengthening of the working-day" (1967a, I, 409).[15]

The second key aspect here is that explicit social regulation of work-time contradicts the basic principles of capitalist competition. Such regulation represents an encroachment of collective social planning into territory previously ruled by capital and its market forces. Although work-time legislation may be supported by individual socially enlightened capitalists, capital as a whole organized politically at the level of the state will generally not restrict the sphere of capitalist and market-oriented decision-making in favor of explicit social decision-making on behalf of labor unless pressured to do so by the working-class. In this sense, work-time legislation is a great victory not only for workers under capitalism but also for socialism. As Marx indicates, with reference to the English Ten Hours Bill,

> besides its practical import, there was something else to exalt the marvelous success of this working men's measure. . . . This struggle about the legal restriction of the hours of labour raged the more fiercely since, apart from frightened avarice, it told indeed upon the great contest between the blind

rule of the supply and demand laws which form the political economy of the middle class, and social production controlled by social foresight, which forms the political economy of the working class. Hence the Ten Hours Bill was not only a great practical success; it was the victory of a principle; it was the first time that in broad daylight the political economy of the middle class succumbed to the political economy of the working class. (1974a, 79)

So concludes Marx's analysis of how capital's tendency "to go beyond the natural limits of labour time . . . forcibly compels even the society which rests on capitalist production . . . to restrict the normal working-day" (1991, 386). The significance of this analysis for ecological politics should be clear. Just as a rational regulation of work-time contradicts the principles of free capitalist competition and requires "social production controlled by social foresight," so people can only "rationally regulate their interchange with nature" insofar as their actions are not determined by the imperatives of competitive capital accumulation (1967a, III, 820). At the same time, Marx's analysis suggests that one need not wait until "after the revolution" for working-class struggle to achieve important historical progress in terms of the sustainability of production.

For Marx, work-time legislation (and, by extension, meaningful environmental legislation) does not manifest the "modernization" or "humanization" of capitalism as such. Rather, it represents an anti-capitalist development within capitalism—one prefiguring a new system of socially planned production in which the needs of the producers and their communities within and across generations take precedence over the needs of capital, with its profit-driven supply and demand forces. Marx does insist, however, that significant progress toward a sustainable utilization of society's life-forces and the use of such progress as a launching pad for further struggles depend on the incursion of explicit social decision-making into areas previously reserved for capital and the market. This imperative for "general political action" stems from the fact that capital requires the forces of human and extra-human nature only as conditions of monetary accumulation, whereas workers, like society as a whole, obviously have a more holistic interest in natural conditions as conditions of present and future human development (see Chapter 13).

PART III

Nature and Communism

CHAPTER 11

Nature and the Historical Progressivity of Capitalism

Perhaps the most common ecological criticism of Marx is that in applauding capitalism's development of the productive forces as a precondition of communism, he succumbs to a "Promethean" or "productivist" conception of history. Prometheanism, firmly rooted in the Enlightenment tradition, says that human progress hinges on the subjugation of nature to human purposes. Human development thus involves a struggle between people and nature in which people come out on top. The critics labeling Marx a Promethean typically suggest that he foresees a continuation and even an intensification of human domination over nature under communism, conceived as a society of ever-expanding per capita levels of material production and consumption with reduced worktime as enabled by the further development of the mechanized technologies bequeathed by capitalism. In arguing that "the continued 'development' of industrial production coheres with socialist ideology," for example, Andrew McLaughlin suggests:

> Marx praises capitalism for the development of the means of production which, under socialism, will make possible the reduction of the amount of labor required of all humans, and he envisions a general material abundance as the substratum of communism. . . . Labor falls within the realm of necessity. Marxism promises the maximum possible emancipation from this realm, a freedom which is based on the development of the means of production and a rationally administered social organization. For Marxism, there is simply no basis for recognizing any interest in the liberation of nature from human domination. (1990, 95)

Enzo Mingione also detects a Prometheanism in Marx that explains "how difficult it is to reconcile [the] development of Marxism with an approach that seriously considers the question of 'nature'":

Marx believed capitalism to be a necessary step—however painful, unjust and disruptive—in the historical development of human society. He did not see much room for argument on this point, and regarded the organization of human relations and the relations between humans and nature as quite rigid in the capitalist mode of production. From this sprang a social critique which formed the basis for political movements and trade unions and focused on the producers' overturning the exploitive relationships between capital and labor. This whole process was associated with the necessity of developing the forces of production along industrial lines, both quantitatively and qualitatively. (1993, 86)

Similarly, Ted Benton asserts that Marx's vision of capitalism as "preparing the conditions for future human emancipation" shares "the blindness to natural limits already present in . . . the spontaneous ideology of 19th-century industrialism":

Modern industrial production, fostered by capitalist economic relations, is a precondition for the future communist society. The "historical task" of capitalism is precisely to transcend the conditional and limited character of earlier forms of interaction with nature. . . . Elsewhere there is a recognition that *some* element of "struggle" with nature for the necessaries of life is inevitable, the content of emancipation being given in the reduction to a minimum of the time taken up in this struggle. Either way, the possibility of human emancipation is premissed upon the potential for the transformative, productive powers of associated human beings to transcend apparent natural limits, and to widen the field of play for human intentionality. (1989, 74–77)

The notion that Marx believed in the historical progress of humanity *over* nature—and that this belief blinded him to all natural limits of human production under capitalism and communism—is quite common not just in the socio-ecological literature but among Marxologists of all political persuasions. Lewis Feuer, for example, claims that "Marx and Engels . . . placed so much faith in the creative dialectic" of economic history "that they could not seriously entertain the hypothesis that modern technology interacting with the earth's physical environment might imbalance the whole basis of advanced industrial civilization" (1989, xii).[1]

Now, a priori, the Promethean interpretation appears to be consistent with many statements by Marx concerning the historical necessity of capitalism. In *Capital,* for example, he says that the "development of the productive forces of social labour is the historical task and justification of capital. This is just the way in which it unconsciously creates the material requirements of a higher mode of production" (1967a, III, 259).

So the Promethean interpretation is right about capitalism creating prior conditions for communism, in Marx's view. Nonetheless, I shall argue that Marx's belief in the historical progressivity of capitalism is not based on an anthropocentric preference for material wealth over nature. Given Marx's insistence on natural conditions as a necessary part of wealth and on the natural *and* social character of the human producers, such a preference would be self-contradictory, to say the least. For Marx, capitalism's progressivity does not entail an overcoming of all natural limits to human production, if for no other reason than that this would require an infinite supply of exploitable labor power and of material conditions requisite to its exploitation. Rather, capitalism is progressive insofar as through its development and socialization of the human and extra-human conditions of production, it negates the historical necessity (absolute material-scarcity rationale) of exploitative class relations while removing other pre-capitalist *restrictions* on the natural and social development of human beings. Marx's vision of the *less restricted* human development potentiated by capitalism is qualitatively richer and more conducive to ecological values than the image of mass production and consumption presented by the Promethean interpretation.

The Promethean interpretation also discounts Marx's argument that whereas capitalism develops and socializes production, thereby creating the basis for a transcendence of earlier, more restricted forms of human development, "it does so only in *antithetical form*" due to its own class-exploitative and alienating relations of production (1973, 528). For Marx, "the conditional, limited character of earlier forms of interaction with nature" (Benton, 1989, 75) does not refer to ahistorical natural limits; nor does it just refer to the restricted character of pre-capitalist people-nature relations (though it partly involves this). It refers above all to the exploitative, anarchic, and insecure character of human production and people-nature relations endemic to all class societies. *This* conditional and limited character, and the limits it places on the development of people as natural and social beings, is reproduced and in some ways even worsened by capitalism, with its extreme social separation of the producers from necessary conditions of production, including natural conditions. Hence, the real transcendence of humanity's heretofore conditional and limited development only occurs with communism; it is not simply bequeathed by capitalism but requires a long struggle by the producers and their communities for a social union with the conditions of production and the transformation of these conditions into "conditions of free and associated labour" (Marx, 1985, 157). In sum, the Promethean interpretation seriously misinterprets the historical progressivity of capitalism and the tasks of communism, in Marx's view.

In reassessing the ecological connotations of Marx's perspective on capitalism and historical progress, I first detail the importance Marx ascribes to the social separation of the producers vis-à-vis necessary conditions of production and to the corresponding tendency toward universalization of the social and material network of human development. Next, I consider capitalism's effects on the development and application of natural science and on ecological consciousness. Finally, I reinvestigate Marx's position on capitalism's historical necessity and limits from the standpoint of human needs and consumption. Once the antithetical character of capitalist development is taken into account, Marx's perspective appears much less Promethean. (The purported Prometheanism of Marx's projection of communism, with its vision of increased free time, is taken up in Chapter 14.)

Fundamental Basis and Limits of Capitalism's Historical Progressivity

Even in his early *Economic and Philosophical Manuscripts,* Marx asserts the historical necessity and limits of capitalism as a form of human progress: "Precisely in the fact that division of labour and exchange are embodiments of private property [in the means of production] lies the two-fold proof, on the one hand that human life required private property for its realization, and on the other hand that it now requires the supercession of private property" (1964, 163).

Marx's later statements of capitalism's historical progressivity tend to be couched more in terms of the interplay between the capital-labor relation and the development of the combined productive powers of nature and social labor. In this context, Marx places great stress on capitalism's social separation of the producers from necessary conditions of social production as a prerequisite for the development of productive forces. Such development is hindered by the direct *and restricted* social ties between laborers and production conditions characteristic of pre-capitalist forms, including peasant and petty-bourgeois forms based on "private property of the labourer in his means of production" (1967a, I, 761). Although "petty industry, whether agricultural, manufacturing, or both" may be "an essential condition for the development of social production and of the free individuality of the labourer himself," it nonetheless

> pre-supposes parcelling of the soil, and scattering of the other means of production. As it excludes the concentration of these means of production, so also it excludes co-operation, division of labour within each separate process of production, the control over, and the productive application of the forces of nature by society, and the free development of the social productive powers. It is compatible only with a system of production, and a society, moving within narrow and more or less primitive bounds. (761–62)

Development of the wealth-creating powers of labor and nature required an extensive and complex social division of labor that was incompatible with localized and socially restricted ties of laborers to production conditions:

> The original unity between the worker and the conditions of production (abstracting from slavery, where the labourer himself belongs to the objective conditions of production) has two main forms: the Asiatic communal system (primitive communism) and small-scale agriculture based on the family (and linked with domestic industry) in one form or another. Both are embryonic forms and both are equally unfitted to develop labour as *social* labour and the productive power of social labour. Hence the necessity for the separation, for the rupture, for the antithesis of labour and property (by which property in the conditions of production is to be understood). The most extreme form of this rupture, and the one in which the productive forces of social labour are also most powerfully developed, is capital. (1971, 422–23)

Advances in production meant that the wealth-creating powers of labor and nature had to become collective-social powers, and this was inconsistent with individual (personal, family, or local community) ties of labor to the conditions of production. As Marx indicates: "The individual worker could only be restored as *an individual* to property in the conditions of production by divorcing productive power from the development of labour on a large scale" (1994, 109). Capitalist property in the conditions of production is, however, an antagonistic form of property precisely because it separates property from labor, thereby causing the combined productive powers of labor and nature to take the form of a growing power of *private* capital over *social* production and human need satisfaction.[2] Nonetheless, "this separation of property from labour . . . is a necessary transition to the conversion of property in the conditions of production into *social* property" insofar as "the individual's ownership of the conditions of production [is] not only unnecessary but incompatible with . . . production on a large scale" (109).

In short, capitalism's separation of property from labor is progressive insofar as it "revolutionizes, through the organization of the labour-process and the enormous improvement of technique, the entire economic structure of society in a manner eclipsing all former epochs" (1967a, II, 35). It must be kept in mind, however, that Marx does not reduce this progressivity to rising levels of production and consumption per capita. That would be confusing ends and means. For Marx, the content of historical progress resides in the development of people as a social and natural species, and this is not reducible to rising material consumption. Capitalism is progressive not just because it develops productive forces, but because (1) by doing so, it negates any material-scarcity rationale for class monopolies over the disposition of society's surplus labor time and products, hence over opportunities for human development insofar as such opportunities are a function of the distribution of free time *and* the level and security of material living standards; (2) it does so by developing the cooperative and social form of labor and production, thereby enabling humanity to overcome the socially and naturally restricted forms of development characterizing pre-capitalist societies. The first aspect is set out by Marx in *Capital:*

> It is one of the civilising aspects of capital that it enforces surplus-labour in a manner and under conditions which are more advantageous to the development of the productive forces, social relations, and the creation of the elements for a new and higher form than under the preceding forms of slavery, serfdom, etc. Thus it gives rise to a stage, on the one hand, in which *coercion and monopolisation of social development (including its material and intellectual advantages) by one portion of society at the expense of the other are eliminated;* on the other hand, it creates the material means and embryonic conditions, making it possible in a higher form of society to combine this surplus-labour with a greater reduction of time devoted to material labour in general. (1967a, III, 819; emphasis added)

Engels makes the same point even more forcefully in *The Housing Question,* arguing that the "industrial revolution has raised the productive power of human labour to such a high level that—for the first time in the history of mankind—the possibility exists, given a rational division of labour among all, of producing not only enough for the plentiful consumption of all members of society and for an abundant reserve fund, but also of leaving each individual sufficient leisure so that what is really worth preserving in historically inherited culture—science, art, forms of intercourse—may not only be preserved but converted from a monopoly of the ruling class into the common property of the whole of society, and may be further developed. And here is the decisive point: as soon as the productive power of labour has risen to this height, every excuse disappears for the existence of a ruling class. After all, the ultimate basis on which class differences were defended was always: there must be a class which need not plague itself with the production of its daily subsistence, in order that it may have time to look after the intellectual work of society. This talk, which up to now had its great historical justification, has been cut off at the root once and for all by the industrial revolution of the last hundred years. (1979, 26–27)

The second element of capitalism's historical progressivity, mentioned above, involves the socialization of production that enables humanity to overcome the restricted forms of human development typical of pre-capitalist societies. The *Grundrisse* presents a three-stage outline of this perspective:

Relations of personal dependence . . . are the first social forms, in which human productive capacity develops only to a slight extent and at isolated points. Personal independence founded on *objective* dependence is the second great form, in which a system of general social metabolism, of universal relations, of all-round needs and universal capacities is formed for the first time. Free individuality, based on the universal development of individuals and on their subordination of their communal, social productivity as their social wealth, is the third stage. The second stage creates the conditions for the third. (Marx, 1973, 158)

Clearly, the factors distinguishing the three stages are the social separation of the producers from necessary conditions of production in the second (capitalist) stage (hence the "objective dependence" of labor on capital), and the "personally dependent" or restricted form of non-separation from production conditions in the first (pre-capitalist) stage. The third (communist) stage thus represents a return to the unity of laborers and production conditions characteristic of the first stage but in the less restricted form of the associated producers' conscious management of the socialized wealth-creating powers of labor and nature. The third stage's more "universal development of individuals" itself hinges upon an explicit communalization of the "universal relations, all-round needs, and universal capacities" developed under capitalism. This accords with the first aspect of capitalism's historical progressivity, namely, the negation of scarcity rationales for class monopolization of human-developmental opportunities.

Marx is generally laudatory toward capitalism's creation of an increasingly broad and complex social network of human production.[3] For Marx, capitalism's development of "the universality of intercourse, hence the world market" connotes "the possibility of the universal development of the individual . . . not an *ideal or imagined* universality of the individual, but the universality of his *real and ideal relations*" (1973, 542; emphases added). It is with this human-social development in mind, and not the development of production and consumption for their own sake, that Marx praises "the universality of individual needs, capacities, pleasures, productive forces etc., created through universal exchange" under capitalism (488).

If I have spent what may seem to be an inordinate amount of space distinguishing the human-developmental content from the productive form of capitalist progress, it is mainly because this distinction reveals the error of viewing Marx's historical vision through the productivist blinkers of the Promethean interpretation. Marx does not see capitalism's necessity in terms of a simple floating of humanity on a rising tide of material goods and free time created at nature's expense. The key potential Marx sees prefigured by capitalism is for a *less restricted* form of human development, both socially and vis-à-vis nature. Capital's development of productive forces (hence the negation of scarcity rationales for class limits on human development), along with its extensive and intensive development of the social division of labor and exchange (hence the potential universalization of free human individuality), are the vehicles here, not the human-evolutionary content.

That the Promethean interpretation represents a one-sidedly productivist distortion becomes clearer when Marx's historical vision is considered more closely from the standpoint of people-nature relations. Marx does not ascribe a progressivity to capitalism based on a human conquering of nature or an uncoupling of production from natural conditions and limits. Rather, capitalism is progressive insofar as it creates a basis for *less restricted* relations between people and nature. "Less restricted" need not connote "anti-ecological" in this context; rather, it could signify *richer, more universal* people-nature relations—relations not unconducive to ecological and biospheric consciousness. For Marx, this universalization of people-nature relations is just as progressive as the universalization of socio-economic relations that it is a function of; both are integral to capitalism's creation of the potential for free human development unencumbered by class limits and other material and social restrictions.

Stated conversely, Marx does not view capitalism as more advanced than pre-capitalist societies based on a failure of the latter to subdue nature. The relative historical backwardness of pre-capitalist societies resides in their *more restricted* relations with nature, and this corresponds to their more restrictive social relations from the standpoint of free individual development. In *The German Ideology,* for example, Marx argues that in pre-capitalist societies, "the restricted attitude of men to nature determines their restricted relation to one another, and their restricted attitude to one another determines men's restricted relation to nature" (Marx and Engels, 1976, 50). Elsewhere, in a digression on "ancient social organisms of production," Marx suggests that they

> are, as compared with bourgeois society, extremely simple and transparent. But they are founded either on the immature development of man individually, who has not yet severed the umbilical cord that unites him with his fellowmen in a primitive tribal community, or upon direct relations of subjection. They can arise and exist only when the development of the productive power of labour has not risen beyond a low stage, and when, therefore, the social relations within the sphere of material life, between man and man, and between man and Nature, are correspondingly narrow. This narrowness is reflected in the ancient worship of Nature, and in the other elements of the popular religions. (1967a, I, 79)

It is testimony to the power of productivist ideology that Marx's comments on the relatively *restricted* character of pre-capitalist relations with nature are often taken as evidence of an *anti-natural* bias, rather than as validations of the freer, more universal relations with nature potentiated by capitalism. When Marx praises "the great civilizing influence of capital," with its "universal appropriation of nature as well as of the social bond itself by the members of society," he is not downgrading nature or the natural character of human beings; rather, he is recognizing the possibility of a less restricted, more conscious form of human co-evolution with nature "in comparison to which all earlier ones appear as mere *local developments* of humanity and as *nature-idolatry*" (1973, 409–10). Insofar as the freely developing individuals prefigured by capitalism's universalizing tendencies will be capable of "grasping [their] own history as a *process,*" they will also be capable of a freer "recognition of nature . . . as [their] real body" (1973,

542). They will, as Engels puts it, "not only feel but also know their oneness with nature" (1964a, 183).

Promethean interpretations also tend to downplay the contradictory character of capitalist progress in Marx's view—thus falsely ascribing to Marx an overly positive verdict on capitalism's appropriation of natural conditions. While recognizing that capital's "infinite drive for enrichment" translates into a "striv[ing] for the infinite increase of the productive forces" that potentiates less restricted forms of human development, Marx hardly endorses "the alienated form which the objective conditions of labour . . . assume against living labour" in capitalist society (1994, 11, 29). Under capitalism, "every increase in the productive powers of labour . . . appears as a productive power of capital, independent of labour and confronting it" (11, 227). This alienation of "the general social powers of labour" encompasses "natural forces and scientific knowledge," which also "appear most emphatically as forces not only alien to the worker, belonging to *capital,* but also directed in the interests of the capitalists in a hostile and overwhelming fashion against the individual worker . . . as the *quintessence* of the social forces and forms of the individual worker's common labour confronting him" (29–30).

Although capitalism's development and socialization of production expands the historical possibilities for free human development involving less restricted forms of human interaction with society and nature, this is not the primary orientation of capital. For capital, the goal is simply and solely the expansion of value, of monetary accumulation; hence "forces of production and social relations—two different sides of the development of the social individual—appear to capital as mere means, and are merely means for it to produce on its own limited foundation" (Marx, 1973, 706). This, combined with the social separation of the producers vis-à-vis necessary conditions of production, creates a situation in which "the social characteristics of their labour come to confront the workers so to speak in a capitalized form" (1977, 1055). This is how "the forces of nature and science," now also subjected to capital's exploitative form of socialization, "confront the workers as powers of capital" (1055). Alienation of workers from natural conditions is thus a central aspect of capitalism's "reduction of individual labour to the level of helplessness in face of the communality represented by and concentrated in capital" (1973, 700).

Under capitalism, natural conditions, rather than serving as material and aesthetic vehicles for the development of more universal, variegated forms of human individuality, instead "appear directly as weapons" which, with the help of capital's appropriation of science (see the next section), "are used partly to throw the worker onto the streets, to posit him as a *surplus object,* partly to break down his special skill and the claims based on the latter, partly to subject him to the thoroughly organised despotism of the factory system and the military discipline of capital" (1994, 29). Capitalism thus converts the development of the "conditions of labour" into "an *alien circumstance to the workers,*" one "which the individual worker endures passively, and which progresses at his expense" (1991, 480; 1977, 1055). This alienation is not just manifested in the fact that the "application of social labour to science, the forces of nature and the products of labour . . . appears as no more than the means for the exploitation of labour" (1977, 1055); it is also shown by the narrow viewpoint on nature's utility necessarily adopted by "the individual capitalists, who dominate production and exchange" (Engels, 1964a, 185). As Engels observes, competing capitalists

> are able to concern themselves only with the most immediate useful effect of their actions. Indeed, even this useful effect—inasmuch as it is a question of the usefulness of the article that is produced or exchanged—retreats far into the background, and the sole incentive becomes the profit to be made on selling. . . . In relation to nature, as to society, the present mode of production is predominantly concerned only about the immediate, the most tangible result; and then surprise is expressed that the more remote effects of actions directed to this end turn out to be quite different. (1964a, 185–86)

The anti-ecological effects of the conversion of (human and extra-human) nature into a condition of monetary accumulation were discussed in Part II. The point to be emphasized here is that these environmental tensions are logically encompassed by Marx's broader historical conception of capitalist "progress." This casts further doubt on Promethean interpretations according to which Marx saw in capitalism's "domination" of nature the qualitative basis for a high production and high consumption road leading directly to communism. Given capitalism's development and so-cialization of material productive forces, a non-exploitative and sustainable co-evolution of society and nature requires explicit social control over these productive forces by the producers and their communities. But communist production, with its freer development of human individuality, is not simply inherited from capitalism, needing only to be signed into law by a newly elected socialist government. It requires "long struggles, through a series of historic processes, transforming circumstances and men" (Marx, 1985, 76). In a draft of *The Civil War in France,* Marx makes it clear that among these long struggles will be a struggle for new material forms of production:

> The working classes know that they have to pass through different phases of class struggle. They know that the superseding of the economical conditions of the slavery of labour by the conditions of free and associated labour can only be the progressive work of time (that economical transformation), that they require not only a change of distribution, but a new organization of production, or rather the delivery (setting free) of the social forms of production in present organised labour (engendered by present industry) of the trammels of slavery, of their present class character, and their harmonious national and international co-ordination. They know that this kind of regeneration will be again and again relented and impeded by the resistance of vested interests and class egotisms. (1985, 156–57)

This call for a new, disalienated organization of production contradicts Promethean interpretations, which have Marx endorsing capitalism's mechanized mass processing of human and extra-human nature into material goods as a qualitatively appropriate basis for communist development (Mingione, 1993, 86).[4] That Marx and Engels do not see capitalism as directly providing the technical foundations of communist people-nature relations becomes clearer upon closer consideration of their stance on capitalism and science.

Capitalism, Science, and Nature

Historically, "capital does not create science"; nonetheless, "it exploits it, appropriates it to the production process" (Marx, 1994, 33).[5] Indeed, "it is the capitalist mode of production which first puts the natural sciences to the service of the direct production process" on a systematic and routine basis (32). Chapters 5 and 6 touched upon the role of capital's appropriation of science in its exploitative development and socialization of production. It is only by "utilising science itself just as much as all the physical and mental qualities" that "production founded on capital creates universal industriousness . . . a system of general exploitation of the natural and human qualities" (1973, 409). Whether freely appropriated or not, capital's productive *application* of science helps explain how it "tear[s] down all the barriers which hem in the development of the forces of production, the expansion of needs, the all-sided development of production, and the exploitation and exchange of natural and mental forces" (410). It thus also helps explain how capital opens up possibilities for less restricted forms of human development, as it constantly "drives beyond national barriers and prejudices as much as beyond nature worship, as well as all traditional, confined, complacent, encrusted satisfactions of present needs, and reproductions of old ways of life" (410).

The fact that science is systematically "enlisted by capital" does not exhaust capitalism's progressivity in this area (1994, 38). Marx also argues that capitalism positively encourages "the development . . . of the natural sciences to their highest point" (1973, 409). The fundamental basis of this positive evaluation is that "knowledge . . . becomes independent of labour" precisely insofar as it "enters the service of capital"; in other words, "this process belongs in general to the category of the attainment of an independent position by the conditions of production vis-à-vis labour. This separation and autonomisation, which is at first of advantage to capital alone, is at the same time a condition for the development of the powers of science and knowledge" (1994, 57).

Capitalism thus encourages the development and application of scientific knowledge in the same way it accelerates the development of all productive forces: by socially separating this condition of production from the control of the direct producers and converting it into a vehicle of competitive monetary accumulation. With capitalism, there is

> a *separation of science,* as *science applied* to production, from *direct labour,* whereas at earlier stages of production the restricted measure of knowledge and experience is directly linked with labour itself, does not develop as an autonomous power separated from labour, and therefore in general never gets beyond a collection of procedures carried on traditionally and only expanding very slowly and little by little. (1994, 33)

Capitalism's separation of science from direct labor thus involves a "concentration" and "development into a science of the knowledge, observations and craft secrets obtained by experience and handed down traditionally, for the purpose of analysing the production process to allow the application of the natural sciences to the material production process" (34). This reformation and "application of science" by capital "rests entirely on the separation of the intellectual potentialities of the process from the knowledge, understanding and skill of the individual worker, just as the concentration and development of the [other] conditions of production . . . rests on the divestiture—the separation—of the worker from those conditions" (34; cf. Braverman, 1974).

Once the capitalistic appropriation of science is recognized as part of the process by which labor and its necessary conditions are socially separated and recombined in pursuit of private profit, it becomes clear how scientific developments are encouraged by capital's appropriation and application of natural conditions in production. The use of "implements of labour, in the form of machinery" as means of exploitation not only requires a prior deskilling of labor, but also "necessitate[s] the substitution of natural forces for human force, and the conscious application of science, instead of rule of thumb" (Marx, 1967a, I, 386). In this sense, capitalism "is the first mode of production where practical problems are [routinely] posed which can only be solved scientifically" (1994, 32). Moreover, capital's "employment of . . . forces of nature *on a large scale* is only possible where machinery is employed on a large scale, hence also where there is a corresponding conglomeration of workers and cooperation of workers subsumed under capital" (32; emphasis added). Such *concentrated* "employment of the natural agents" itself encourages "the development of scientific knowledge as an independent factor in the production process" (32).[6] In this way, too, capitalist production naturally elicits scientific developments by making it "the task of science to be a means for the production of wealth [as] a means of enrichment" (32). At the same time, capitalist development "provides the means for the theoretical subjugation of nature" in the very practical sense that it "generally first produces the sciences' material means of research, observation and experiment" while enhancing the monetary incentives for scientific work, especially of the more "practical" type:

> In so far as the sciences are used as a means of enrichment by capital, and thereby become themselves a means of enrichment for those who develop them, the men of science compete with each other to discover practical applications for their science. Moreover, invention becomes a *métier* by itself. With capitalist production, therefore, the *scientific factor* is for the first time consciously developed, applied, and called into existence on a scale which earlier epochs could not have imagined. (32, 34)

While noting capitalism's encouragement of scientific activity, Marx recognizes the less progressive features of capital's "exploitation of science, of the theoretical progress of humanity" (1994, 33). With the social separation of the producers vis-à-vis necessary conditions of production, and the scientific development of these conditions as powers of capital, "science appears as a potentiality alien to labour, hostile to it and dominant over it" (34). For example,

> in so far as machinery develops with the accumulation of society's science, of productive force generally, general social labour presents itself not in

labour but in capital . . . and confronts the worker physically as *capital*. In machinery, knowledge appears as alien, external to him; and living labour [as] subsumed under self-activating objectified labour. (1973, 694–95)

Capital's "application of science upon the process of production," and the resulting deskilling and mechanization of labor, thus

coincides with the suppression of all intellectual development in the course of this process. Admittedly, a small class of higher workers does take shape, but this does not stand in any proportion to the masses of "deskilled" workers. . . . It is capitalist production which first transforms the material production process into the application of science to production—science put into practice—but it does so only by subjecting labour to capital and suppressing the worker's own intellectual and professional development. (1994, 34, 38)

The fact that the productive utilization of science and nature occurs only under conditions of labor's subjection to capital obviously hampers the social diffusion of scientific knowledge about the natural conditions of human production and reproduction, *ceteris paribus*.

The subjection of science to capital has an anti-ecological character rooted in capital's treatment of nature as a vehicle for the production of vendible use values. With capitalist production, "nature becomes purely an object for humankind, purely a matter of utility; ceases to be recognized as a power for itself; and the theoretical discovery of its autonomous laws appears merely as a ruse so as to subjugate it under human needs, whether as an object of consumption or as a means of production" (1973, 410). This instrumental processing of nature, driven by the quantitatively unlimited and qualitatively homogenous goal of monetary accumulation, proceeds without any fundamental concern for the diversities, interconnections, and limited adjustment capacities governing the reproduction of human and extra-human nature (see Chapter 7). As a result, the so-called "human victories over nature" achieved by capitalism often turn out to be illusory, as Marx's life-long comrade points out: "For each such victory nature takes its revenge on us. Each victory, it is true, in the first place brings about the results we expected, but in the second and third places it has quite different, unforeseen effects which only too often cancel the first" (Engels, 1964a, 182).

Engels also observes how the subsumption of labor and nature under capital places an anti-ecological stamp on the development of science. For example, the concern of competing capitalists "only with the most immediate useful effect of their actions" appears, in a refracted form, in the failure of scientific practice to take adequate account of ecological interconnections: "In nature nothing takes place in isolation. Everything affects and is affected by every other thing, and it is mostly because this manifold motion and interaction is forgotten that our natural scientists are prevented from gaining a clear insight into the simplest things" (1964a, 185, 180).[7]

Another factor inhibiting the development and application of ecological knowledge is capitalism's tendency to undervalue scientific knowledge in general. As Marx indicates: "All scientific labour, all discovery and all invention . . . depends partly on the utilisation of the co-operation of the living, and partly on the utilisation of the labours of those who have gone before" (1967a, III, 104). As a result, the value of "the product of mental labour—science—always stands far below its [real] value, because the labour-time needed to reproduce it has no relation at all to the labour-time required for its original production" (1963, 353). This undervaluation not only inhibits the general development of science but also biases scientific work toward the production of *monopolizable* forms of knowledge capable of yielding rents. The development and operationalization of the kinds of ecological insights needed for society to sustainably co-evolve with nature thus tends to be socially underprioritized.

Capitalism, with its increasingly globalized and intensive appropriation of nature, its new environmental dysfunctions, and its development of the natural sciences (however biased), cannot help but generate new, more universal forms of ecological consciousness. "Present-day ecology" is undoubtedly "a reflection of the socializing and naturalizing processes already at work in human society—the processes that bind man to man and man to nature"; it cannot help but "reflect man's mode of production, his socialized life and work in relation to nature" (Parsons, 1977, 88–89). In this sense, capitalism does create the potential for a less antagonistic *and* less restricted human co-evolution with nature:

> Thus at every step we are reminded that we by no means rule over nature like a conqueror over a foreign people, like someone standing outside nature—but that we, with flesh, blood and brain, belong to nature, and exist in its midst, and that all our mastery of it consists in the fact that we have the advantage over all other creatures of being able to learn its laws and apply them correctly. . . . And, in fact, with every day that passes we are acquiring a better understanding of these laws and getting to perceive both the more immediate and the more remote consequences of our interference with the traditional course of nature. (Engels, 1964a, 183)

Nonetheless, as long as human production is shaped by value and capital, by the market and private profit-making, this ecological potential will remain a relatively underdeveloped and underutilized "positive externality" languishing on the margins of a predominantly anti-ecological capitalist development. Useful, environmentally sound pre-capitalist *and* contemporary technologies will continue to be displaced in favor of commercially "viable" processes and products.[8] Ecology itself will remain, for the most part, one scientific specialty among many (albeit an interdisciplinary one)—often co-opted for commercial or official "development" purposes but not effectively operating as an overarching framework ensuring that scientific practice as a whole works toward a sustainable and humanly progressive co-evolution of society and nature.

That capitalism puts humanity "in a position to realise, and hence to control, even the more remote natural consequences of [its] production activities" does not mean that this potential can be realized under capitalism; such "regulation . . . requires something more than mere knowledge. It requires a complete revolution in our hitherto existing mode of production, and simultaneously a revolution in our whole contemporary social order" (Engels, 1964a, 183–84). An important task of this revolution will be to "convert science from an instrument of class rule into a popular force," and thereby "convert the men of science themselves from panderers to class prejudice, place-hunting state parasites, and allies of capital into free agents of thought." For "science can only play its genuine part" when the producers are no longer socially alienated vis-à-vis material conditions of their production and reproduction, which is to say, "in the Republic of Labour" (Marx, 1985, 162).

Capitalism and Consumption: An Anti-Ecological Vision?

I have shown that the Promethean interpretation, in which Marx applauds capitalism for building a high-production road to communism at nature's expense, fails to account for Marx's qualitative critique of capitalist production. While arguing that capitalism creates the potential for *less restricted* forms of human development, Marx insists that this system's class-exploitative relations and its narrowly profit-driven appropriation of nature prevent it from realizing this potential. This realization requires a qualitative restructuring of the productive forces and relations developed under capitalism, pursuant to the collective appropriation of these conditions by the producers and their communities. Here I assess the notion, also basic to the Promethean interpretation, that Marx's vision of historical progress hinges on a social broadening and deepening of the same basic kind of anti-ecological mass consumption produced by capitalism. Once again, I will show that the Promethean interpretation bypasses the real human developmental potential created, in Marx's view, by capitalism—a potential not reducible to increases in mass consumption—as well as Marx's qualitative critique of capitalist consumption relations.

Because the Promethean interpretation bypasses Marx's qualitative analysis of capitalism as a specific class form of production, it also ignores Marx's analysis of the "particular mode of consumption" associated with this "specific mode of production . . . as one of its forms" (Marx, 1988, 69).[9] The historical progressivity of this mode of consumption stems first and foremost from the fact that capitalism "is a form of production not bound to a level of needs laid down in advance" (1977, 1037).[10] Competitive monetary accumulation "impels the development of human productive capacity and thereby the activation of human dispositions in fresh directions," producing "an extension of the sphere of social needs and the means for their satisfaction" (1988, 199). As was discussed in Chapter 5, "it is precisely the productivity of labour, the mass of production, of population and of surplus population created by this mode of production that constantly calls new branches of industry into being" (1977, 1035). Individual firms producing use values with their profitable vendibility in mind do not limit themselves to use values satisfying previously expressed needs. They not only compete for the customers previously served by *other* firms but also try to create new market sales, through cost- and price-cutting strategies as well as by differentiating their products and developing new ones satisfying new needs. With the deskilling and mechanization of production and, hence, the employment of large agglomerations of fixed capital, "continuity of production becomes absolutely necessary" for competing enterprises, providing further impetus to sales efforts and the creation of new needs in production and consumption (1987, 530). In this way, "instead of the scale of production being controlled by existing needs, the quantity of products made is determined by the constantly increasing scale of production dictated by the mode of production itself" (1977, 1037–38). Even though each capitalist's "aim is that the individual product should contain as much unpaid labour as possible, . . . this is achieved only by producing for the sake of production" (1038). This, along with the "creation of new branches of production" mentioned above, means that capitalism cannot help but create "a constantly expanding and constantly enriched system of needs" (Marx, 1973, 409).

The human potentialities Marx sees in this process of need creation cannot be reduced to an anti-ecological mass consumerism. To begin seeing this, consider a passage in the *Grundrisse* where Marx lists three ways in which capital's "production of surplus value, based on the increase and development of the productive forces, requires the production of new consumption; requires that the consuming circle within circulation expands as did the productive circle previously." Marx states: "Firstly quantitative expansion of existing consumption; secondly: creation of new needs by propagating existing ones in a wide circle; *thirdly:* production of *new* needs and discovery and creation of new use values" (1973, 408).

Notice that of these three requirements, only the first is purely quantitative. The second is qualitative insofar as it involves a broader access to use values (more below on this point). Meanwhile, the third requirement (the one Marx emphasizes) is purely qualitative, referring as it does to enrichment of the *composition* of use values rather than increases in the general level of consumption. Taken together, the three requirements are consistent with a vision of qualitatively *less restricted* human consumption, not only in the sense that consumption opportunities are broadened to those previously excluded from them but also in the sense of a richer, more variegated natural and social *content* of these opportunities and the needs they satisfy. Indeed, shortly after the above listing, Marx specifies the human potential prefigured by capitalism's "discovery, creation and satisfaction of new needs" in just such qualitative terms, as

> the cultivation of all the qualities of the social human being, production of the same in a form as rich as possible in needs, because rich in qualities and relations—production of this being as the most total and universal possible social product, for, in order to take gratification in a many-sided way, he must be capable of many pleasures, hence cultured to a high degree. (1973, 409)

This qualitative interpretation is also consistent with Marx's assertion that "the greater the extent to which historic needs—needs created by production itself, social needs—needs which are themselves the offspring of social production and intercourse, are posited as *necessary,* the higher the level to which real wealth has been developed" (1973, 527). The qualitative enrichment Marx is referring to here is actually twofold, since it involves the socialization not only of needs in general but of "necessary" needs in particular, that is, the needs of the direct producers. Implicit in capitalism's socialization of the producers' needs is the potential for a less socially and naturally restricted development of these producers as human beings. Marx develops this point in terms of the supersession of prior antitheses between luxury and necessity: "*Luxury* is the opposite of the *naturally necessary.* Necessary needs are those of the individual himself reduced to a natural subject. The development of industry suspends this natural necessity as well as this former luxury" (1973, 528).

Through its development of an extensive and complex network of labor more and more universally and intensively enmeshed with natural conditions, and the attendant increases in the combined wealth-creating powers of labor and nature, capitalism loosens prior social and material restrictions on the universality of needs in general. But it does more than that: it also negates the historical rationale for the monopolization of relatively less socially and naturally restricted needs by a minority, surplus-appropriating class. In both ways, capitalism creates a basis for a "suspension" of the luxury/necessity dichotomy.

This line of argument leads to another historically progressive aspect of capitalism's mode of consumption, one that further highlights the class-relational basis of Marx's argument. According to Marx, capitalism's social separation of the producers from necessary conditions of production paradoxically entails an advance in the social status of the laboring class as regards the sphere of consumption—compared, that is, to systems in which workers and their consumption are socially tied to particular material conditions (cf. Fine and Leopold, 1993; Fine, 1994). Unlike feudalism, for example, where the worker's "way of life [is] prescribed purely by the (feudal) estate," under capitalism "the worker can do what he likes with his money"—so in this sense, at least, capitalism is the first system in which "everything patriarchal falls away" and the laborers first become "free of their subjection to a given relationship" (Marx, 1976a, 436–37). Indeed, once the worker obtains a money-wage in exchange for her/his labor power, she/he "as its possessor maintains . . . the same relationship in the general circulation as any other" possessor of money (1987, 507). Just as it does for all other market agents, this money (at least "within the scope of its value magnitude") represents "universal wealth, wealth in its universal social form . . . a possibility of all gratification" (507):

> Since he exchanges his [labor power] for the general form of wealth, he becomes co-participant in general wealth up to the limit of his equivalent. . . . [H]e is neither bound to particular objects, nor to a particular manner of satisfaction. The sphere of his consumption is not qualitatively restricted, only quantitatively. This distinguishes him from the slave, serf etc. (1973, 283)

In short, the wage-laborer's "consumption . . . falls outside the economic relation" between capital and labor, and this "essentially modifies his relation by comparison to that of workers in other social modes of production" (283–84). Some implications of this modification for ecological struggles are taken up in Chapter 13; what is relevant here is Marx's qualitative, relational approach to the consumption opportunities opened up to the laboring class by the capital-labor relation. His main emphasis is on the less restricted, richer character of workers' consumption opportunities, not on the mere quantity of material goods available to and consumed by workers. When discussing how the worker can "widen the sphere of his pleasures at the times when business is good," for example, Marx does not refer to binges of hedonistic material consumption but to "the worker's participation in the higher, even cultural satisfactions, the agitation for his own interests, newspaper subscriptions, attending lectures, educating his children, developing his taste etc., his only share of civilization which distinguishes him from the slave" (287). There is, in short, nothing inherently anti-ecological about this aspect of capitalism's historical progressivity in the realm of consumption.

In sum, it is true that Marx ranked capitalism's development of a social and material basis for a higher level and improved quality of working-class consumption as one of the more important aspects of this system's historical progressivity. Who can fault Marx for insisting on this point, given the abysmally low level and quality of consumption among workers in his time or even among the majority of the earth's workers today? Nonetheless, it is only by ignoring the qualitative and relational character of Marx's argument that he can be pictured as supporting capitalism's anti-ecological forms of mass material consumption as an historically progressive basis of human development. This becomes clearer when one considers Marx's critical analysis of the quality of working-class consumption opportunities under capitalism. The basic starting point of this analysis is that whereas "in exchange," the worker appears as "an equal vis-à-vis the capitalist, like every other party in exchange," in fact "this equality is already disturbed" by "the worker's relation to the capitalist . . . outside that of exchange," in production (1973, 284).[11]

How is working-class consumption "disturbed" by the capital-labor relation? For starters, in order for the worker to acquire a money wage at all, the exploitation of the worker's labor power in production must be a profitable proposition for the capitalist. This restricts the money wage the capitalist can pay, thereby restricting workers' consumption insofar as it requires purchases of commodities. It is not only the quantity of consumption that is constrained here but also the quality, seeing as how the restricted level of wages forces workers to consume inferior goods:

> Why are cotton, potatoes and spirits the pivots of bourgeois society? Because the least amount of labour is needed to produce them, and, consequently, they have the lowest price. Why does the minimum price determine the maximum consumption? . . . [I]t is because in a society founded on *poverty* the *poorest* products have the fatal prerogative of being used by the greatest number. (1978a, 57)

Although capitalism tends to dissolve prior material and social restrictions underpinning the luxury/necessity dichotomy, "it does so only in *antithetical form,* in that it itself only posits another specific social standard as necessary, opposite luxury" (1973, 528). This "specific social standard" of "necessity" is restricted by capital's absolute material requirement: the reproduction of an exploitable labor force and conditions for its profitable exploitation (see Chapter 5). As a result, the antithesis between luxury and necessity is reproduced in a new form, as the luxury consumption of capitalists and other surplus-appropriating classes becomes necessary for capital to realize the surplus value extracted from workers in production. "In so far as machine labour . . . increases the quantity of commodities which are produced in the same labour time," for example, this rising productivity is often utilized as "an increase in the amount of labour . . . applied to produce commodities that do *not* enter into the consumption of the workers," thus "extend[ing] the basis, upon which can be reared a large upper class" rather than loosening restrictions on the quality and quantity of working-class consumption. As Marx says, "luxury goods are absolutely necessary for a mode of production which creates wealth for the non-producer and which therefore must provide that wealth in forms which permit its acquisition only by those who enjoy" (1977, 1046).[12] Capital's tendency to produce a wider, less restricted circle of consumption thus runs into a barrier posed by its own class-exploitative nature, namely that the "extension of the sphere of needs and the means for their satisfaction is conditioned by the worker's being chained to the necessary requirements of life" (1988, 199). In this sense, capitalism's "multiplication of needs and of the means of their satisfaction breeds the absence of needs and of means" among the producers themselves (1964, 149).

Capitalism's restriction of working-class life encompasses a dequalification of workers' *natural needs* in both production and consumption. As for consumption, Marx notes that, especially among the lowest-paid workers:

Even the need for fresh air ceases for the worker. Man returns to a cave dwelling, which is now, however, contaminated with the pestilential breath of civilization, and which he continues to occupy only precariously, it being for him an alien habitation which can be withdrawn from him any day—a place from which, if he does not pay, he can be thrown out of any day. For this mortuary he has to *pay*. . . . Light, air, etc.—the simplest *animal* cleanliness—ceases to be a need for man. *Filth,* this stagnation and putrefaction of man—the *sewage* of civilization (speaking quite literally)—comes to be the *element of life* for him. Utter, *unnatural* neglect, putrefied nature, comes to be his *life-element*. None of his senses exist any longer, and not only in his human fashion, but in an *inhuman* fashion, and therefore not even in an animal fashion . . . even his *animal* needs cease to exist. (1964, 148–49)

This reduction of workers to a sub-natural state by the capitalistic de-qualification of their natural consumption needs is an important, even central, theme throughout the writings of Marx and Engels (see, for example, Marx, 1967a, I, 654–67; Engels, 1973, *passim;* 1979, 40–46). As for the de-qualification of workers' natural needs in the realm of production, Chapter 10 discussed Marx's analysis of capital's in-built tendency toward an unnatural extension of work-time. The reduction of the worker to a sub-human "beast of burden" is also shown by capital's economization on fixed capital and other outlays at the expense of workplace safety—subjecting workers to avoidable industrial "accidents," "lack of ventilation," and "poisoned air, etc." (Marx, 1971, 257; 1967a, III, 94).[13] Such "dissipation of the labourer's life and health" in production itself reduces the quality of workers' free time and consumption to sub-natural levels (1967a, III, 86). Indeed, insofar as work-time involves a "robbing" of the worker's "normal, moral and physical, conditions of development and function" (1967a, I, 265), how can it *not* vitiate the quality of consumption, free time, and home life?[14] The alienation experienced in production, where "the worker's activity is not his spontaneous activity [but] is the loss of his self," tends to create a situation in which

the worker only feels himself freely active in his animal functions—eating, drinking, procreating, or at most in his dwelling and in dressing-up, etc.; and in his human functions he no longer feels himself to be anything but an animal. What is animal becomes human and what is human becomes animal. Certainly eating, drinking, procreating, etc., are also genuinely human functions. But abstractly taken, separated from the sphere of all other human activity and turned into sole and ultimate ends, they are animal functions. (Marx, 1964, 111; cf. Engels, 1973, 141–42)

The resonation of alienated labor in free time and consumption thus further alienates workers from their own natural being and from nature, as Engels points out using the example of mechanized factory labor:

> The worker's activity is made easy, muscular effort is saved, but the work itself becomes unmeaning and monotonous to the last degree. It offers no field for mental activity, and claims just enough of his attention to keep him from thinking of anything else. And a sentence to such work, to work which takes his whole time for itself, leaving him scarcely time to eat and sleep, none for physical exercises in the open air, or the enjoyment of Nature, . . . how can such a sentence help degrading a human being to the level of a brute? (1973, 158)

For Engels, one of the tragedies of industrial working-class life is that the worker "never gets the slightest glimpse of Nature in his large town with his long working-hours" (1973, 275). This perspective is certainly difficult to square with anti-ecological interpretations of Marx and Engels. Here again, however, the overarching point is that Marx and Engels treat the capitalist development of needs and consumption in dialectical, qualitative and relational terms. While recognizing the *less restricted* forms of human development potentiated by capitalism, they point out how this system's class-based limits on need satisfaction prevent it from realizing this potential qualitatively *or* quantitatively. The stark difference between this approach and Promethean, mass-consumerist interpretations is further illustrated by Marx's critical comments on the kinds of use values capable of embodying value and surplus value.

First of all, "with the development of capitalist production" and increases in labor productivity, "there [is] an increase in the *quantity of goods,* in the *number* of articles that must be sold"; hence "a constant *expansion of the market* becomes a necessity for capitalist production" (1977, 967). Capital's efforts to fulfill this necessity are assisted by value's formal abstraction from the particularity of use value (see Chapter 7), which means that "the nature of the use value, the particular use value of the commodity is, as such, irrelevant" to capital (1973, 284). Since all that matters is the commodity's ability to be profitably vended—to serve as a vehicle for the monetary realization of surplus value—its "use value for society, i.e., the buyers," may be "real or imagined" (1988, 315). Accordingly, capital constantly tries to overcome the limitations its own class relations place on effective demand and "searches for means to spur [workers] on to consumption, to give his wares new charms, to inspire them with new needs by constant chatter etc." (1973, 287). In this way, capitalism's "extension of products and needs falls into *contriving* and ever-*calculating* subservience to inhuman, unnatural and *imaginary* appetites" (1964, 147). The capitalist

> puts himself at the service of the other's most depraved fancies, plays the pimp between him and his need, excites in him morbid appetites, lies in wait for each of his weaknesses—all so that he can demand the cash. . . . Industry speculates on the refinement of needs, but it speculates just as much on their *crudeness,* but on their artificially produced crudeness, whose true enjoyment, therefore, is *self-stupefaction.* (148, 153)

With capitalism's crassly commercialized consumption relations, "victories of art" are increasingly "bought by the loss of character," and "production for production's sake appears as its precise opposite . . . not as the development of human productivity; but as the display of material wealth in antithesis to the productive development of the human individual" (1969, 500; 1994, 109). This alienation of use value represents a further development of the social power of money "as purely abstract wealth, in which every specific use value is extinguished"; in "every individual relation between possessor and commodity," this power tends to convert the individual into "an abstract person, relating to his individuality as totally alien and extraneous" (1987, 451). Given that the social power of money is rooted in capital's power over labor and nature in production (see Chapters 5 and 7), it should not be surprising to find Marx relating this alienation of use value to "the absorption of the labour process *in its material character* as a mere moment of the realization process of capital" (1973, 693; emphasis added). Indeed, capital's mechanized "production in enormous mass quantities . . . destroys every connection of the product with the direct need of the producer, and hence with direct use value." Marx insists that this outcome "is already posited in the form of the product's production and in the relations in which it is produced, i.e., that it is produced only as a conveyor of value, and its use value only as condition to that end" (694):

> As the universally necessary form of the product . . . the commodity palpably comes into its own in the large-scale production that emerges in the course of capitalist production. The product becomes increasingly one-sided and *massive in nature.* This imposes upon it a social character, one which is closely bound up with existing social relations, while its immediate use-value for the gratification of the needs of its producer appears wholly adventitious, immaterial and inessential. (1977, 953)

Marx could not have foreseen the precise anti-ecological forms that capitalism's "increasingly one-sided and massive" production and consumption would eventually take on during the twentieth century. But Marx and Engels did point out the unhealthy disturbances to the natural circulation of matter and the tendency to overstretch (human and extra-human) natural limits, which inevitably result from the conversion of labor and nature into conditions of competitive monetary accumulation (see Chapters 7, 9, and 10). Marx's critical comments on capital's mode of consumption—especially on its artificial creation of needs so that its "mass product" can be "absorbed into commerce" (1977, 953)—certainly bear additional insights into capitalism's fundamentally anti-ecological character. All of this demonstrates the distorted onesidedness of the Promethean interpretation, according to which Marx uncritically envisions life under communism as basically a quantitative enhancement of capitalistic mass production and consumption.

Concluding Comment

Marx argues that even though capitalism creates the potential for a less restricted form of human development, this potential can only be realized with communism's qualitative transformation of the forces and relations of production developed under capitalism. The Promethean interpretation arbitrarily converts Marx's qualitative vision of less restricted human development into a de-socialized, mainly quantitative conception of human progress as mass production and consumption at nature's expense. This false identification ignores Marx's qualitative and class-relational critique of capitalist production and consumption. Perhaps what throws Marx's critics onto the wrong track here is their failure to recognize that the socially antagonistic and restricted character of human development, up to the present, stems from its class-exploitative character. By negating the material-scarcity rationale for class exploitation, capitalism negates the historical necessity of such social antagonisms and restrictions:

> The bourgeois mode of production is the last antagonistic form of the social process of production—antagonistic not in the sense of individual antagonism but of an antagonism that emanates from the individuals' social conditions of existence—but the productive forces developing within bourgeois society create also the material conditions for a solution of this antagonism. The prehistory of human society accordingly closes with this social formation. (Marx, 1970, 21–22)

Although Marx does not make the point explicitly in his 1859 Preface, his analysis of capitalism suggests a correspondence between class antagonisms and antagonistic people-nature relations. It would then follow that capitalism closes the prehistory of human society in the additional sense that it is the last form of human production based on antagonistic people-nature relations. From this perspective, the Promethean interpretation conflates the antagonistic, restricted forms of human development characterizing the class-divided prehistory of humanity with the less restricted, socially non-antagonistic forms of development promised by communism in Marx's view. Just as human development under communism will no longer occur at the expense of the majority of individual human beings, so it will no longer occur at the cost of a vitiation of the natural conditions of human existence.[15] Indeed, given the natural and social character of human beings in Marx's view, these two features of the movement out of human prehistory necessarily coincide (see Chapters 4 and 14).

CHAPTER 12

Nature and Capitalism's Historical Limits

This chapter locates nature and environmental crises in the context of Marx's analysis of capitalism's historical limits. These historical limits involve more than the tendencies toward overaccumulation and falling profitability of capital that were pointed out by Marx. They also encompass an overall crisis of capitalist relations as the historical culmination of the fundamental contradiction between production for profit and production for human needs—a contradiction that takes on many forms, including (but not solely) accumulation crises.[1] By analyzing environmental crises as part of this historical crisis of capitalist relations, one can see the potential role of ecological conflicts in the transition from capitalism to communism.

Marx himself did not make the connection between ecological crises and capitalism's historical crisis, even though he did analyze capitalism's antagonism toward nature as well as the environmental sustainability that would have to be built into any communism worthy of the name (see Chapter 14). The reason for this gap in his analysis is straightforward: "Marx, who tended toward revolutionary optimism, believed that capitalism would be replaced by a society of freely associated producers . . . long before the kinds of ecological problems that he observed could become truly critical" (Foster, 1997, 287). Nonetheless, this chapter shows that capitalism's ecological crisis tendencies are not only consistent with but considerably enrich Marx's projection of capitalism's historical crisis. This provides a basis not only for incorporating ecological concerns into Marx's projection of the transition to communism but also for countering the fashionable view that Marx's analysis of capitalist crisis is irrelevant to environmental problems, including the prospect of biospheric crisis.

The latter view is exemplified by Thomas Weisskopf (1991), who suggests that for Marx, "the mechanism generating crises . . . was the internally contradictory nature of the accumulation process under the capitalist mode of production; as he expressed it in *Capital,* volume 3: 'the *real barrier* of capitalist production is *capital itself*'" (71). This interpretation relegates the natural and social conditions of production to the exterior of Marx's analysis of "capital itself" as the "real barrier" of capitalist production, thus reducing Marx's analysis of capitalist crisis to the modeling of denaturalized and desocialized profitability problems that "disrupt the process of accumulation" (71). Hence, Weisskopf describes any "concern about the limits on economic activity imposed by an ultimately finite environment" as "more Ricardian than Marxian," while any "concern about the destructive social consequences of an unfettered market system" is deemed "fundamentally Polanyian" (86, 89).[2] Bypassing Marx's analysis of how capitalism's fundamental contradiction, and not just cyclical or secular profitability crises, would "ultimately threaten the viability of the mode of production itself," Weisskopf deems "Marxian crisis theory—*in any form*" to be "increasingly irrelevant . . . for analyzing the evolution and potential contradictions of contemporary capitalism" (70, 71, 74; emphasis added). In short, one is counseled to abandon Marxism without any serious investigation of the merits of Marx's historical vision as a window on capitalism's tendency toward "generalized crisis" (70).

In sounding a cautionary note against such a simple and hasty scrapping of Marx's approach to capitalism's historical limits, I first specify Marx's conception of capitalism's fundamental contradiction and the role of natural conditions therein. This conception appears repeatedly in Marx's writings from 1844 onward. I then document Marx's treatment of accumulation crises as one of many *manifestations* of capitalism's fundamental contradiction. Marx's projection of the historical crisis of capitalist relations can be interpreted as the intensification of this fundamental contradiction by capitalist development, as "private property" in the means of production "contradicts itself and abolishes itself in all points" (Marx and Engels, 1980, 52). Finally, I incorporate environmental crises into Marx's vision of capitalism's historical crisis and contrast this vision with an alternative conception of capitalism's contradictions recently proposed by James O'Connor (1988, 1991a, 1998).

Capitalism's Fundamental Contradiction

According to Marx, capitalism's fundamental contradiction lies in the "antithetical character" of the "mass of forms of social unity" through which it develops "the material conditions of production and the corresponding relations of exchange" (1973, 159). The antithesis Marx is talking about here is the contradiction between production for private profit and production for human needs, as is clear from the passage quoted in part by Weisskopf (1991, 71):

> The *real barrier* of capitalist production is *capital itself.* It is that capital and its self-expansion appear as the starting and the closing point, the motive and purpose of production; that production is only for *capital* and not vice-versa, the means of production are not mere means for a constant expansion of the living process of the *society* of producers. (Marx, 1967a, III, 250)

Clearly, Marx does not *identify* capitalism's "real barrier" with profitability crises. Instead, this barrier is located at the more basic level of production's "motive and purpose" being private profit ("capital and its self-expansion") rather than human needs and, in particular, the socially developed needs or "living process" of the producers. Indeed, several pages later, Marx specifies this same barrier or limit to capitalist production as the determination of production "by a definite rate of profit, rather than the relation of production to social requirements, i.e., to the requirements of socially developed human beings" (1967a, III, 258). This alienation of production's motivation and purpose from human-social needs involves a profit-driven appropriation and development of necessary conditions of production, pursuant to the social separation of the producers vis-à-vis these conditions (see Chapter 5). The historical "genesis of capital" is thus "a process of divestiture of labour, of alienation, whereby its own social forms are presented as alien powers" (1988, 311). It follows that capitalism's fundamental contradiction or "real barrier" can be expressed as "the alienation of the conditions of social production personified in the capitalist from the real producers" (1967a, III, 264).

In Marx's view, the "independent position achieved by the social conditions of production vis-à-vis the real creators of those conditions" represents a "barrier to *capital*" precisely because its "entire development . . . the working-out of the productive forces, of general wealth etc., knowledge etc., appears in such a way that the working individual *alienates* himself; relates to the conditions brought out of him by his labour as those not of his *own* but of an *alien wealth* and of his own poverty" (1991, 144; 1973, 541). The "social character" of workers' "own labour," and "the social character with which the conditions of production are endowed, as the conditions of production of the combined labour of the *community,*" are both alienated insofar as they "appear as *capitalistic,* as something independent of the workers and intrinsic to the conditions of production themselves," operating as a "force existing outside them . . . as no more than the means for the exploitation of labour" (1977, 1052–53, 1055).

With this alienation of labor and conditions of production, "the development of the *social* productive powers of labour and the conditions for this development appear as *acts of capital*" rather than of collective labor enmeshed with nature (Marx, 1963, 392). Capital's private control over production "comes more and more to the fore as a social power, whose agent is the capitalist . . . an alienated, independent, social power, which stands opposed to society as an object" (1967a, III, 264).[3] "In fact the rule of the capitalist over the worker is nothing but the rule of the independent *conditions of labour* over the worker, conditions that have made themselves independent of him" (1977, 989). Hence, capitalism's "real barrier" or fundamental contradiction can also be expressed as "the contradiction between the general social power into which capital develops . . . and the private power of the individual capitalists over these social conditions of production" (1967a, III, 264). This "incompatibility of social production with capitalist appropriation" (Engels, 1939, 296) accordingly plays a key role in Marx and Engels' projections of capitalism's historical crisis (see below).[4]

In sum, the conflict between production for profit and production for human needs, the alienation of the conditions of production vis-à-vis the producers and their communities, and the tension between social production and private appropriation, are all equivalent expressions of capitalism's fundamental contradiction in Marx's view. Whichever expression is used, this "real barrier of capitalist production" clearly encompasses capital's profit-driven appropriation of natural conditions and the attendant alienation of these conditions from the needs of the producers and the "living process" of society as a whole. Chapters 6 and 11 documented how Marx's analysis of the "alienation of the conditions of production" explicitly incorporates "the natural elements themselves" (Marx, 1963, 345). Marx includes "natural forces" among the conditions of production, which, under capitalism, "appear only . . . as means of appropriating surplus-labour and hence confront labour as powers belonging to capital" (391–92). For Marx, the natural environment—like all necessary conditions of production—is endowed with a social character to the extent that it serves as a condition of the combined labor of the community. This social character is capitalistic insofar as nature is appropriated, reshaped, and despoiled by capital in line with the imperatives of competitive monetary accumulation (see Chapters 7 through 10). Alienation of the natural conditions of production, which causes the producers to become "nature's bondsmen," to experience "the sensuous external world, . . . nature, as an alien world inimically opposed to them," is thus central to the fundamental contradiction of capitalism posited by Marx: "production set by the profit of the capitalist and in no way by the needs of the producers" (1964, 109, 111; 1968, 527).

Here, it should be noted that the characterization of capitalist production as "production in contradiction, and indifference, to the producer" appears throughout Marx's writings (1977, 1037). In his Paris Manuscripts of 1844, Marx asserts that under capitalism, "the increasing value of the world of things proceeds in direct proportion [to] the devaluation of the world of men," since "the more powerful labour becomes, the more powerless becomes the worker; the more ingenious labour becomes, the less ingenious becomes the worker" (1964, 107, 109). As a result, the worker's "human qualities" as a social and natural being "only exist in so far as they exist for capital *alien* to him" (120). The young Marx often expresses capitalist alienation in terms of the estrangement of a spirit common to all people as social beings:

> Men through the activation of their nature create and produce a human common life, a social essence which is no abstractly universal power opposed to the single individual, but is the essence or nature of every single individual, his own activity, his own life, his own spirit, his own wealth. . . . However, so long as man does not recognize himself as man and does not organize the world humanly, this common life appears in the form of alienation, because its subject, man, is a being alienated from himself. (1967b, 271–72)

Although some might argue that such expressions betray the presence of idealistic residues in the young Marx, even the *Grundrisse* (surely a "mature" work) suggests that under capitalism, "the *social spirit of labour* obtains an objective existence separate from the individual workers" insofar as "living labour appears as a mere means to realize objectified, dead labour, *to penetrate it with an animating soul while losing its own soul to it*" (1973, 529, 461; emphases added). In any case, the important thing is not the spiritual mode of expression but the continuity of the basic theme regarding the fundamentally contradictory, alienating nature of capitalist production. This theme also appears in the first work bearing the full stamp of Marx and Engels' materialist conception of history, namely *The German Ideology*. In it, the authors state that the alienated "fixation of social activity" in capitalism and other class societies,

> this consolidation of what we ourselves produce into a material power above us, growing out of our control, thwarting our expectations, bringing to naught our calculations, is one of the chief factors in historical development up till now. The social power, i.e., the multiplied productive force, which arises through the co-operation of different individuals as it is caused by the division of labour, appears to these individuals . . . not as their own united power, but as an alien force existing outside them, of the origin and goal of which they are ignorant, which they thus are no longer able to control. (1976, 53–54)

Moreover, "the abolition of [this] alien attitude of men to their own product" requires a "communistic regulation of production" whereby "men once more gain control of exchange, production, and the way they behave to one another" (54). The negation of capitalism's fundamental contradiction is thus a core principle in Marx's projection of communism (see Chapter 14).

Capitalism's Fundamental Contradiction and Accumulation Crises

For Marx, capitalism's fundamental contradiction is not reducible to accumulation crises; rather, such crises "reveal" this fundamental contradiction, thereby showing that capitalism is "only a transitional, historical form" of production (1971, 84). As Marx puts it in the *Grundrisse*, the "incompatibility between the productive development of society and its hitherto existing relations of production *expresses itself* in bitter contradictions, crises, spasms" (1973, 749; emphasis added).[5] In *Capital*, one is told that the "specific barrier of capitalist production," namely, the "collision" between production for profit on the one hand and "the creation of wealth" for the producers and their communities on the other, "*appears partly* in periodical crises" (1967a, III, 263–64; emphasis added). Marx expands on this relationship in the context of a discussion of the tendency of the rate of profit to fall:

> The limitations of the capitalist mode of production come to the surface: (1) In that the development of the productivity of labour creates out of the falling rate of profit a law which at a certain point comes into antagonistic conflict with this development and must be constantly overcome through

crises. (2) In that the expansion or contraction of production are determined by . . . a definite rate of profit, rather than the relation of production to social requirements, i.e., to the requirements of socially developed human beings. (258)

Clearly, Marx does not reduce capitalism's fundamental contradiction to "the mechanism generating crises" along the lines suggested by Weisskopf (1991, 71). Rather, the historical "limitations" of capitalism, as a system based on production for profit rather than for human-social requirements, "come to the surface" in the form of falling profitability—a tendency that "must be constantly overcome through crises." For example, insofar as capital overcomes crises by imposing lower wages, intensified labor, regressive state budgetary policies, or "by enforced destruction of a mass of productive forces" as conditions for a recovery of the rate of profit, this hardly signals an overcoming of capitalism's fundamental contradiction (Marx and Engels, 1968, 41). Rather, such attacks on "the living process of the society of producers" alongside "violent destruction of capital . . . as a condition of its self-preservation" graphically demonstrate the extent to which the conditions of social production have become alien wealth driven by the requirements of competitive monetary accumulation rather than those of socially developed human beings. In short, crises *and recoveries* of capital accumulation are "the most striking form in which advice is given [capitalism] to be gone and to give room to a higher state of social production" (Marx, 1973, 749–50).[6]

An important implication of this perspective is that working-class struggles for improved living and work conditions take on added significance during periods of crisis and capital restructuring, when the contradiction between private profitability and human-social needs is most intense. In Marx's view, the overall success of these struggles depends on the extent to which their protagonists first recognize "crises [as] the general intimation which points beyond" capitalism, and then creatively act upon this "urge which drives towards the adoption of a new historical form" (1973, 228). It can be anticipated that capital's attempts to enhance private profitability by further capitalization of nature (through emasculation or evasion of environmental regulations and privatization of natural resources), and popular struggles against such capitalization and for new, more sustainable and human-need driven forms of interaction with nature, enter quite naturally into Marx's strategic approach to crises.

The basic point here is that accumulation crises are a *manifestation* of capitalism's fundamental contradiction and should never be *identified* with it; for such an identification presumes that what is good *for capital* is inherently good *for society*. The present interpretation is indirectly supported by the numerous other manifestations of capitalism's fundamental contradiction discussed by Marx. For example, with capital's "alienated social power" over production, "constantly increasing masses of people are thereby deprived of the conditions of production" (1991, 144). In *Capital*, Marx refers to this growing unemployment—which is by no means limited to crisis periods—as "the absolute general law of capitalist accumulation" (1967a, I, 644). Moreover, as I have shown, the alienation of production vis-à-vis the direct producers takes the form of a deskilling of labor, as capital "combines mass labour with skill, but in such a way that the former loses its physical power, and the skill resides not in the worker but in the machine and in the specific combination of both as a whole in the factory" (1973, 529). As a result, capitalism's fundamental contradiction is manifested in a tendency for "the conditions of labour to dominate labour even technologically and, at the same time, [to] replace it, suppress it and render it superfluous in its independent forms" (1977, 1055). The conflict between production for profit and human-social needs is further manifested in capitalism's "anarchical system of competition," with its "outrageous squandering of labour-power and of the social means of production, not to mention the creation of a vast number of employments, at present indispensable, but in themselves superfluous" (1967a, I, 530). Finally, capital's tendency to develop the forces of production "only by sapping the original sources of all wealth—the soil and the labourer" (507) is also an important *manifestation* of capitalism's "real barrier" or fundamental contradiction (see Chapters 9 and 10).[7]

The Historical Crisis of Capitalist Relations[8]

The preceding section showed that Marx treats accumulation crises as one of many *symptoms* of capitalism's fundamental contradiction. This sheds serious doubt on the notion that Marx reduces the "structural crises" that "ultimately threaten the viability of the mode of production itself" to crises of falling profitability (Weisskopf, 1991, 71). The historical crisis of capitalist relations envisioned by Marx is best interpreted as a culmination of capitalism's fundamental contradiction—alienation of production from the needs of the producers—rather than as a simple function of worsening accumulation crises. Stated differently, even in the absence of profitability problems it is in principle quite possible for capitalism to experience an historical crisis in terms of its ability to satisfy human needs. This could occur, for example, if the measures capital requires to restore private profitability in the wake of accumulation crises *increasingly* conflict with the needs of the producers and their communities.[9]

As noted previously, capitalism's social separation of the producers from necessary conditions of production has an historically progressive side insofar as it enables the productive powers of labor and nature to be more universally developed as *social* productive forces, thereby creating the potential for a less restricted development and satisfaction of human needs. The downside, of course, is that this development occurs only as a means of competitive monetary accumulation. The forms in which capital develops and exploits labor and nature are not directly determined by the requirements of a less restricted human development enmeshed with nature but by the imperative to produce and realize surplus value through the extraction of surplus labor from workers and its objectification in profitably vendible use values. Capital's socialization of production is an exploitative, alienated socialization, as represented by the private power of capitalists over the conditions of social production.

The fact that capitalism is both historically progressive and alienating vis-à-vis human needs suggests that its historical limits involve an in-built tendency for the alienation to become greater and greater relative to the historical progressivity. This would occur, for example, when capital's development of production *itself* makes capitalist relations increasingly inadequate to the further development of the productive forces, where these forces are defined in terms of the ability to satisfy the needs developed by capitalism. The alienation of the producers from the conditions of production, and the exploitation of their labor and these conditions as vehicles of competitive monetary accumulation, always create tensions in capitalist society. The question is when these tensions will reach the point at which their manageability contradicts the reproduction of the class relation between capital and labor. In Marx's view, this occurs when the productive development generated in and through this class relation becomes incompatible with or creates needs that are inconsistent with the reproduction of the class relation. At that point, "capital itself"—understood as the class relation between capital and labor—shows itself to be the "real barrier of capitalist production" (1967a, III, 250).

If the problem is posed in this way, then the basic source of capitalism's historical crisis is not hard to find. It reduces to the fact that even though capitalism develops the wealth-creating powers of labor and nature through the socialization of production, this socialization *itself* makes private, competitive monetary accumulation less and less adequate to the further development of production in terms of effective human need satisfaction. As Marx puts it: "The *inner* progress of capitalist production consists in an ever increasing supersession of *private production,*" so that "the worker's relation to the *conditions of production* develops into a relation to *common, social magnitudes*" (1994, 230–31). Eventually, capital's "centralisation of the means of production and socialisation of labour . . . reach a point where they become incompatible with their capitalist integument," that is, "the monopoly of capital becomes a fetter on the mode of production, which has sprung up and flourished along with, and under it" (1967a, I, 763).[10]

Marx and Engels consider this historical crisis of capitalist relations from three inter-connected angles: the intensifying contradiction between social production and private appropriation; the increasing inadequacy of value as a measure of wealth; and the growing inappropriateness of class exploitation as a social form for the development of production.

The growing tension between social production and private appropriation stems partly from the fact that capital's socialization of production "destroys the basis of commodity production in so far as the latter involves independent individual production and the exchange of commodities between owners [as] the exchange of equivalents" (Marx, 1977, 951). This is eloquently summed up in *Anti-Dühring,* where Engels first describes a hypothetical pre-capitalist system of commodity production by private individual laborers owning their own means of production—a system in which appropriation is "based upon . . . own labour" (1939, 295). With capitalism and its social separation of laborers from means of production now controlled by the capitalist, however,

> came the concentration of the means of production in large workshops and manufactories, their transformation into means of production that were in fact social. But the social means of production and the social products were treated as if they were still, as they had been before, the means of production and the products of individuals. . . . Now, the owner of the instruments of labour continued to appropriate the product, although it was no longer *his* product, but exclusively the product of *other's labour.* Thus, therefore, the products, now socially produced, were not appropriated by those who had really set the means of production in motion and really produced the products, but by the *capitalists.* Means of production and production itself had in essence become social. But they were subjected to a form of appropriation which has as its presupposition private production by individuals, with each individual owning his own product and bringing it on the market. The mode of production is subjected to this form of appropriation, although it

removes the presuppositions on which the latter was based. In this contradiction, which gives the new mode of production its capitalist character, *the whole conflict of today is already present in germ.* The more the new mode of production gained the ascendancy on all decisive fields of production and in all countries of decisive economic importance, supplanting individual production except for insignificant relics, the *more glaring necessarily became the incompatibility of social production with capitalist appropriation.* (295–96)

In this way, the tension between private appropriation and social production manifests itself in an increasingly arbitrary, discordant nexus of the private rewards from and contributions to social production. This arbitrariness involves more than the *unequal* rewards accruing to capital and labor, and more than the fact that workers' wages are themselves paid mostly out of accumulated surplus value previously extracted from workers by capital.[11] More fundamentally, it tells us that capital is the private appropriation of wealth produced by society's collective labor with nature's assistance. Viewed in this way, the tension between social production and private appropriation represents a further development of the contradiction between use value and exchange value built into the commodity itself. By transforming production into an objectively collective operation in which "externalities" are the norm rather than the exception, capital itself negates the social rationality of private monetary calculation, competition, and profit-making.[12]

Marx has a proposal for gauging the extent to which capitalistic appropriation is contradicted by the "organization of labour itself into social labour": he suggests looking at the extent to which "contradictory forms" have arisen whereby capitalism "abolishes [individual] private property *and* private labour" without abolishing capitalist appropriation *in toto* (1967a, III, 266; emphasis added). Among such contradictory forms Marx places great emphasis on financial capital, especially stock companies, as signifying "the abolition of capital as private property within the framework of capitalist production itself." As Marx indicates,

> this expropriation appears within the capitalist system in a contradictory form, as appropriation of social property by a few . . . the conversion in the form of stock still remains ensnared in the trammels of capitalism; hence, instead of overcoming the antithesis between the character of wealth as social and as private wealth, the stock companies merely develop it in a new form. (436, 440)

However, this category of class-exploitative yet quasi-social property rights also encompasses "forms which, by restricting free competition, seem to make the rule of capital more perfect, but are at the same time the heralds of its dissolution and of the dissolution of the mode of production resting on it" (Marx, 1973, 651). One has only to turn to recent NAFTA and GATT "free trade" agreements, with their plethora of stipulations for private monopolization of socially produced knowledge, and for the capitalization of nature, to find examples of such forms in which capital "seeks refuge . . . as soon as it begins to sense itself and become conscious of itself as a barrier to development" (1973, 651). The mushrooming of these contradictory forms of social property shows the extent to which capitalist production has become a parasitical rent-seeking process feeding off of socially generated productive capabilities, in the process restricting their utilization and development in line with the imperatives of competitive monetary accumulation.[13] This degeneration of capitalism's historical progressivity cannot be reduced to distortions of relative rates of return at the level of individual enterprises and sectors; rather, it involves an increasing weight of capital's *free appropriation* of social and natural conditions in the returns accruing to *capital as a whole*.

The increasing tension between social production and private appropriation is also shown by the system's constant creation of new social maladies and malfunctions (and its constant recreation of old ones) that can only be resolved collectively. This tendency is further heightened by misguided attempts to resolve such collective problems using the nexus of market, wage-labor, and private property in its individual or quasi-social forms. Examples include the efforts to "eliminate" unemployment and welfare dependency by forcing people into labor markets completely on capital's terms, to "solve" the problem of supporting an aging population by privatizing social security, to "balance" state budgets by privatizing public services, and to improve "quality" in education by corporatizing schools or reducing the job security of teachers. Basically, in all such cases, the problem being addressed is redefined as one of monetary profitability and competitiveness—with any real costs of the "solution" in terms of human need satisfaction borne by the working class and its communities. The challenge posed to society by the contradiction between social production and private appropriation, namely, to find new collective-democratic mechanisms appropriate to a system of objectively socialized production, is evaded in favor of a reproduction and reinforcement of class rule. The "accumulated disjunction between our technological inventiveness and our imbecility in social organization" thus remains in place (Singer, 1993, 210). As a result, the system's monetary indicators of prosperity (GDP, profits, stock-market values) become more and more disconnected from human well-being. The problem is that in a world of increasingly social-ized production, the further loosening of restrictions on human capabili-ties and needs is less and less achievable by a system of competitive monetary accumulation that not only generates more losers than winners but also biases the process of wealth production in line with the *private-profit interests* of the winners. This contradiction was colorfully described in an 1856 speech by Marx:

> On the one hand, there have started into life industrial and scientific forces, which no epoch of the former human history had ever suspected. On the other hand, there exist symptoms of decay, far surpassing the hor-rors recorded of the latter times of the Roman empire. In our days every-thing seems pregnant with its contrary. Machinery, gifted with the wonderful power of shortening and fructifying human labour, we behold starving and overworking it. The new-fangled sources of wealth, by some strange weird spell, are turned into sources of want. The victories of art seem bought by the loss of character. At the same pace that mankind mas-ters nature, man seems to become enslaved to other men or to his own in-famy. Even the pure light of science seems unable to shine but on the dark background of ignorance. All our invention and progress seem to result in endowing material forces with intellectual life, and in stultifying human life into a material force. This antagonism between modern industry and science on the one hand, modern misery and dissolution on the other hand; this antagonism between the productive powers, and the social rela-tions of our epoch is a fact, palpable, overwhelming, and not to be con-troverted. (1969, 500–1)

The historical crisis Marx saw as imminent is arguably now in full swing: "On the present false base, every fresh development of the produc-tive powers of labour must tend to deepen social contrasts and point social antagonisms" (Marx, 1974a, 77–78).

A related factor making capitalist relations an increasingly "false base" for human development is the growing inadequacy of value as a measure of wealth. The problem is that the socialization of production reduces the relative importance of the labor time directly objictified in commodities (including the labor directly objictified in machinery and other elements of constant capital) as a source of use values. Goods and services more and more become communal products of the social division of labor and its appropriation of natural conditions using socially developed scientific knowledge, rather than private products of the labor expended in indi-vidual enterprises. Hence, over and above value's basic abstraction from nature's contribution to wealth (see Chapter 7), direct labor time becomes less and less appropriate as a social measure of use value, as Marx indicates:

> To the degree that . . . direct labour and its quantity disappear as the determinant principle of production—of the creation of use values—and is reduced both quantitatively, to a smaller proportion, and qualitatively, as an, of course, indispensable but subordinate moment, compared to general scientific labour, technological application of natural sciences on one side, and to the general productive force arising from social combination in total production on the other side . . . capital thus works towards its own dissolution as the form dominating production. (1973, 700)

With the decreasing correspondence between use value and direct labor, capital's utilization of natural and social conditions as bearers of value and surplus value increasingly takes the form of its *free appropriation* of these conditions.[14] The growing inadequacy of value as a measure of wealth and the heightening tension between private appropriation and social production are thus tightly connected. As Marx indicates, insofar as the commodity is "the product of isolated direct labour," then "in direct exchange, individual direct labour appears as realized in a particular product or part of the product, and its communal, social character—its character as objectification of general labour and satisfaction of the general need" is more or less adequately "posited through exchange alone" (1973, 709). With capital's development "of large-scale industry," however, "direct labour as such ceases to be the basis of production, since . . . the combination of social activity appears, rather, as the producer" (709). The values realized in private commodity sales thus become less and less appropriate as a measure of individual enterprises' contributions to society's wealth; "hence exchange value must cease to be the measure of use value" (705).[15]

The declining adequacy of value as a measure of wealth signals the historical limits of capitalistic exploitation as a social form of production. With the socialization of production, wealth becomes more and more a function of the social division of labor and general scientific knowledge combined with natural conditions, and less and less dependent upon individual direct labor and its particular material instruments. As a result, *advances* in wealth production become less dependent on capital's extraction of direct *surplus* labor and its reinvestment (as surplus *value*) in larger and larger agglomerations of material means of production. In other words, "the appropriation of alien labour time ceases, with its development, to make up or to create wealth" (Marx, 1973, 709):

But to the degree that large industry develops, the creation of real wealth comes to depend less on labour time and on the amount of labour employed than on the power of the agencies set in motion during labour time, whose "powerful effectiveness" is itself in turn out of all proportion to the direct labour time spent on their production, but depends rather on the general state of science and on the progress of technology, or the application of this science to production. . . . The *theft of alien labour time, on which the present wealth is based,* appears a miserable foundation in face of this new one, created by large-scale industry itself. (704–5)

From this perspective, capital's growing reliance on free appropriation of objectively communal conditions (especially the division of labor, science, and natural conditions) itself signals the fact that the "*surplus labour of the mass* has ceased to be the condition for the development of general wealth" (Marx, 1973, 705). This is doubly true insofar as the utilization and redevelopment of these communal conditions as forms of a less restricted human development require that the producers and their communities grasp their production as an increasingly universal natural and social process. As Marx indicates, with socialized production: "It is neither the direct human labour [the worker] performs, nor the time during which he works, but rather the appropriation of his own general productive power, his understanding of nature and his mastery over it by virtue of his presence as a social body—it is, in a word, the development of the social individual which appears as the great foundation-stone of production and of wealth" (705). Capital itself creates the potential for the development of the producers into such social individuals insofar as it negates the correspondence between social wealth and direct labor—thereby negating the historical necessity of "the non-labour of the few, for the development of the general powers of the human head" (705). But by doing so it negates the historical rationale for the wage-labor relation.

Capitalism is historically progressive insofar as it develops and socializes production to the point at which further advances in production as a system of human-need satisfaction depend primarily on the universal development of people as natural and social beings. But it is precisely the latter task for which capitalist relations are singularly ill-fitted. Instead of promoting the universal development of the producers and their communities, capital freely appropriates natural and social conditions and converts them into means of exploiting the producers, thereby restricting the development of workers and communities in line with competitive monetary accumulation. "Forces of production and social relations—two different sides of the development of the social individual—appear to capital as mere means, and are merely means for it to produce on its own limited foundation" rather than to serve universal human development itself (1973, 706).[16] Capital socializes human production and development; but capital "makes one-sided, limits, etc. the main force of production, the human being himself" (422). That is how capital creates its own historical limits as a form of human production.[17]

Capitalism's Historical Limits and Environmental Crises

The foregoing exegesis shows that Marx does not reduce capitalism's historical limits to capital's self-generation of worsening accumulation crises. For Marx, capitalism's historical crisis is the intensification of the contradiction between production for profit and production for human needs by capital's socialization of production. It thus represents a generalized crisis of capitalist relations *as a form of human-need satisfaction and human development,* and this cannot be reduced to long-run profitability problems. Marx did not explicitly incorporate environmental crises into this projection; his framework lends itself to such an incorporation, however, because of the way it treats capitalism's historical crisis as a crisis of a particular class-exploitative form of socialization of the conditions of production.

Marx's analysis of the growing tension between social production and private appropriation tells us that given capitalism's development of production as a socialized, universal process of appropriation of nature by labor, the question is no longer whether society *should* appropriate nature for human purposes but rather *what* these purposes should be. Given the social structuring of human purposes, this question reduces to the *kinds* of social relations that, in and through their metabolic enmeshment with natural conditions, will lend themselves to less restricted and more sustainable forms of human development. In a word, whether nature is to be socialized is a moot point; the real question is what kind of socialization will take place (cf. Harrington, 1989, 8–9, 17, 196). Will it be socialization within the confines of competitive monetary accumulation or, instead, socialization regulated by the requirements of a sustainable human development that recognizes nature's eternal contribution to human wealth, including its contribution to aesthetic and spiritual use values—to the human spirit in its infinite variety?

Capital's alienated socialization generates collective problems that it cannot solve in connection with natural conditions as much as it does vis-à-vis all conditions of social production (Harrington, 1989, 184–85). The competitive, profit-driven development of production creates an increasingly intensive, large-scale, and biospheric system of appropriation from nature that calls out for a collective-democratic form of social regulation, not only to protect the natural wealth that remains but also to restructure socialized labor and production into forms more appropriate to natural and social human beings. The socialization of labor, by socializing the people-nature metabolism, creates a valid stake for *all society,* the producers and communities on a global scale, in the transformation of this metabolism into one that supports a less restricted but sustainable development for themselves and their children.

Even though capital transforms the appropriation of nature into a universal-communal endeavor, this wealth-creation process continues to be a process of competitive monetary accumulation. With the socialization of production, the private accumulation process becomes increasingly reliant on free appropriation of natural conditions, both directly and via free appropriation of the socially produced scientific knowledge and forms of cooperation by which nature is appropriated into production. Far from recognizing the communal stake of current and future generations in nature and society as conditions of human development, capital converts natural and social conditions into mere means of exploitation and monetary accumulation. The resulting tendencies toward ecological crisis illustrate how any socio-economic system whose primary forms of regulation (in this case, value, capital, and competition) systematically alienate the system's necessary conditions from human needs will tend to create imbalances in these conditions, where "imbalance" is defined in terms of the sustainability of the quality and quantity of wealth production. Capital's alienated socialization increasingly disrupts the necessary unity of human production with its natural and social conditions (see Rader, 1979, 86, 119–20). This is how capitalism winds up restricting human development despite its own loosening of prior restrictions on the same.

Similar implications emerge from Marx's analysis of value's historical limits as a form of wealth. For Marx, capital's development of socialized productive forces reduces the importance of direct labor time as a source of wealth, with use values more and more becoming the product of the whole system of labor and universal appropriation from nature as informed by socially produced scientific knowledge. Socialization of labor and socialization of nature proceed in tandem, based on the social separation of labor from natural conditions and their exploitative recombination by capital as material vehicles of competitive monetary accumulation (see Chapter 5). Viewed in this way, the historical limits of value as a form of wealth represent a further development, on a more universal level, of the basic value-nature contradiction discussed in Chapter 7. Value always formally abstracts from nature's contribution to wealth, but capital's socialization of production accentuates this distortion in wealth's social representation. Whereas production is an increasingly universal-social metabolism with nature, value continues to represent wealth by privately organized abstract direct labor time in monetary form.

Value always abstracts from all ecological use values not privately registered as monetary exchange values—however much their disruption affects prospects for a continuation of any given quality and quantity of capitalistic wealth production, let alone the broader prospects for a richer, less restricted human co-evolution with nature. The socialization of production accentuates this problem, however, insofar as it makes environmental use values and ecological disruptions more and more unregisterable as market prices, precisely due to their increasingly universal-communal character. The choice increasingly becomes free appropriation and distorted valuation *by capital* on the one hand, versus explicit social valuation and regulation on the other—thereby challenging (global) society to construct collective-democratic forms of the latter (see Chapter 14). Once again, Marx's approach reveals the environmental problem as one that involves conflicting forms of socialization of nature, not the abstract question as to whether nature should be socialized.

Just as *total* value corresponds less and less effectively to *total* wealth and human needs in a system of increasingly socialized production, so does *surplus* value become less and less appropriate as a measure and form of the *growth* in the combined need-satisfying powers of socialized labor and nature. There are two basic ways in which surplus value inadequately represents the human requirements associated with appropriation of nature—over and above value's qualitative anti-ecological characteristics (see Chapter 7). First, the human appropriation of any given set of use values from nature is subject to quantitative ecological and biospheric limits—limits that, if exceeded, impose a qualitative deterioration in appropriable natural wealth. The goal of monetary surplus value accumulation, however, is quantitatively unlimited: regardless of its environmental impacts, capital can and will continue to accumulate both materially and socially so long as it can access a supply of living, exploitable labor power and material conditions amenable to the production of vendible use values. We may not like it, but the fact is that capitalism can survive any ecological catastrophe short of the extinction of human life. This, combined with its tendency to intensify and universalize the processing of natural wealth, is precisely why capitalism's potential for generating environmental crises surpasses that of all previous socio-economic systems—at least from the standpoint of natural human needs, as opposed to the insanely minimal natural requirements of value accumulation (see Chapter 5).

Second, as discussed in the previous section, the socialization of production increasingly means that the growth of wealth no longer hinges on the extraction of surplus value from workers and its reinvestment in material means of production but rather on the universal development of communal productive forces—especially of science and its application in and through the collective division of labor and its natural conditions. The further loosening of restrictions on human development no longer depends on the many performing surplus labor for the few but on the ability of the producers and their communities to take command of and redevelop their universal-social system of labor and appropriation from nature. In short, the universalization of opportunities for individual human development has become the main "productive force" needed for a further development of the need-satisfying capacities of human production. With that, class exploitation in general, and capitalist exploitation in particular, have exhausted their historical necessity. Note that because this historical exhaustion is defined in terms of ineffective satisfaction of human needs, including the need for a healthy, sustainable interchange with nature, it is quite consistent with continued growth of commodity production and capital accumulation as measured, for example, by real per capita GDP. Unlike Weisskopf's (1991) interpretation, in which capitalism only reaches its historical limits when accumulation is blocked by profitability crises, Marx's conception of historical crisis encompasses social and environmental crises in human terms not effectively registered by the monetary forms of value and capital.

Capitalism's Historical Limits and O'Connor's "Two Contradictions"

Capital's appropriation of natural and social conditions plays a key role in Marx's analysis of capitalism's fundamental contradiction and historical limits. O'Connor (1988, 1991a, 1998) has formulated an alternative analysis of the contradictions generated by the use of people and their natural and social conditions as means of capital accumulation. According to O'Connor, capitalism suffers from two basic contradictions that together explain why "capital and the state today" are "totally confused as to the new form of regulation which might provide a coherent framework for capital accumulation" (1991a, 108).

O'Connor's first contradiction involves the danger of accumulation crises due to a failure to realize the surplus value objectified in commodities through commodity sales. Such crises are rooted in the limitation of working-class consumption relative to value produced, a limitation owing to the rising rate of exploitation (surplus value divided by the value of wages paid). The basic problem here is that "capital exercises [too] much power over labor," and the resulting tendency toward underconsumption is manifested in the "vast credit structure, aggressive marketing, constant product innovation, and intensified competition" undertaken by capital to cope with the heightened "risk of a realization crisis" (107).

O'Connor then argues that capital accumulation suffers from a *second* contradiction that is manifested in profitability problems due to *rising costs*. In O'Connor's view, this second contradiction more directly involves the natural and social conditions of production. Specifically, capital has a tendency to erode its own conditions of production, especially "when individual capitals . . . externalize costs on to conditions of production (nature, laborpower, or the urban) with the aim of defending or restoring profits." The "unintended effect" of this degradation of the conditions of production "is to raise costs on other capitals (and, at the limit, capital as a whole), lowering produced profits" (1991a, 108). Profits are further reduced when "social movements demand that capital better provide for the maintenance and restoration" of natural conditions, for example, "when they demand better health care, protest the ruination of soils, and defend urban neighborhoods in ways that increase capital costs or reduce capital flexibility" (1998, 242).

O'Connor's "two contradictions" framework is pleasing insofar as it implies that neither Keynesian demand-side policies nor neoclassical supply- or cost-side policies can overcome the contradictions of capital accumulation. Moreover, O'Connor's second contradiction, like Marx's conception of capitalism's fundamental contradiction and historical limits, recognizes that capital's development of production is based on the conversion of natural and social conditions into vehicles of competitive value accumulation, and that this conversion has irrational results from the standpoint of capitalism's growth and development as a system of wealth production. Nonetheless, there are some serious problems with O'Connor's conception.

The basic difficulty is that O'Connor artificially separates his first contradiction from the conditions of production—even asserting that the "first contradiction of capitalism . . . has nothing to do with the conditions of production, whether these are interpreted economically or in sociopolitical terms" (1991a, 107). Yet if the first contradiction is generated by a rising rate of exploitation, one that "expresses capital's social and political power over labor" (107), how can it be separated from the conditions of production? As already discussed, capital's power over labor and increases in the rate of exploitation (especially through increases in labor productivity which reduce the value of labor power) are—at least in Marx's analysis— firmly rooted in capital's appropriation of natural and social conditions and its conversion of these conditions into means of exploiting labor power and objectifying surplus labor in vendible use values. This exploitative appropriation of natural and social conditions occurs not just through their commodification but also through their free appropriation by capital (see Chapters 5 and 6). Hence, from Marx's perspective, O'Connor's attempt to relegate capital's socialization of the conditions of production to a "second," cost-side contradiction is simply implausible.

As per this second contradiction, it is not clear that rising "external costs" from capital's use of natural and social conditions need translate into profitability problems for capital *as a whole*. All capital accumulation requires is exploitable labor power and material conditions conducive to the extraction of surplus labor and its objectification in marketable use values. The qualitative nature of the labor power, production conditions, and produced use values is historically contingent. Pollution control and waste disposal, prisons (with exploitation of imprisoned labor power), and police and security services are all quite profitable sectors, even though they represent private costs and/or tax bills from the standpoint of many individual enterprises. The fact is that the "external costs" of capital accumulation create profitable opportunities for the production and realization of surplus value, not only for individual enterprises but for capital as a whole. On the one hand, capital responds to its overaccumulation problems by developing and marketing new products featuring ecologically and socially destructive use values (e.g., plastic packaging, fast foods, the automobile, pesticides). On the other hand, capital accumulation increasingly takes the form of goods and services whose necessity or usefulness stems from the "external costs" of capitalist production and consumption. The entire automobile/petroleum/real estate complex, for example, feeds off of capitalism's "negative externalities" as much as it helps generate them; the same can be said of the medical and legal industries. The pollution control and waste treatment industry, with annual sales of between $200 and $300 billion in 1990 (more than the entire global aerospace industry) is merely the latest member of this pantheon of externality-based activities (Karliner, 1994).

The profitability of such destructive and/or externality-based activities does not resolve capitalism's "first contradiction." Indeed, insofar as private enterprise naturally gravitates toward the most profitable pollution control and waste management activities, the problem of overaccumulation of potential surplus value may be correspondingly worsened—all the more so insofar as these activities are increasingly monopolized by a small number of larger, relatively profitable corporations. In this respect, the environment industry does not differ from other monopoly capitalist sectors. Still, that the environment industry can contribute to overaccumulation problems shows very clearly that the real fundamental contradiction of capitalism is the alienation of the conditions of production vis-à-vis workers and communities. O'Connor's "two contradictions" are both *symptoms* of this more basic contradiction.

Once the underlying unity of O'Connor's two contradictions is recognized, one can more clearly see the limits of the reformist vision of a green capitalism. The environment industry is not only incapable of solving the problem of overaccumulation; it is also incapable of resolving capitalism's environmental crisis. Pollution control, waste management, and recycling may be profitable activities, but they do not directly address the tension between competitive capitalist growth and the limited character of natural conditions of any given quality. As matters stand, the competitive "success" of the environment industry itself depends on and contributes to the ecologically unsustainable growth of capitalist production. That "environmental maintenance" is itself a "growth industry" reveals the conflict between the conditions required for capital accumulation and the conditions required for a sustainable process of human and social development (Gellen, 1970). To put it bluntly, capital can in principle continue to accumulate under any natural conditions, however degraded, so long as there is not a complete extinction of human life. This makes it essential to distinguish environmental crises of *capital accumulation* from environmental crisis in the sense of *a general deterioration of the conditions for the development of people as a natural and social species.* The latter type of crisis by no means automatically implies the former, even though both are products of capitalism—which is to say that from the standpoint of human development, capitalism is an ecologically and socially irrational system.

O'Connor does note that capital's destructive effects on the conditions of production represent "not only threats to profits and accumulation, but also to the viability of the social and natural environment as means of life and life itself" (1998, 12). He also describes ecological and social movements as struggles "to determine *what kind of use values production conditions will in fact be"* (14). Nonetheless, by treating the conditions of production as "external" to capital's exploitation of labor, O'Connor's "two contradictions" dichotomy tends to soften the distinction between the conditions required by capitalist production and the conditions required for human development. The effect of this softening is to artificially divide labor and ecological struggles—with the latter still basically defined as "non-class" struggles (1998, 14–15).

For Marx, the fundamental contradiction of capitalism is that between wealth *for capital* versus wealth *for the producers and their communities*—where the latter is defined not in terms of the minimalist material and social requirements of capital accumulation but rather in terms of the conditions for a less restricted and more sustainable human development (cf. Lebowitz, 1992b). Marx does not artificially divide capital's power over both labor and its conditions into two separate powers. Rising exploitation, overproduction crises, increasing "external costs" of production, and the degradation of human, natural, and social wealth are all necessary, mutually constituted aspects of capitalism's fundamental contradiction, in Marx's view. As a result, Marx's analysis does not limit labor's interests a priori to an economistic realm of "wages and jobs" and constructs no false divisions between the labor movement and "radical democratic" struggles over ecological concerns (O'Connor, 1998, 14–15). Chapter 13 accordingly considers the pro-ecological potential of Marx's holistic, non-economistic vision of class struggle.

CHAPTER 13

Capital, Nature, and Class Struggle

This chapter considers the role of environmental conflict in the transition from capitalism to communism, conceived as a struggle by the producers and their communities for control over the natural and social conditions of production. Here, just as in Chapter 12, the subject under discussion is not directly addressed by Marx. Although he did incorporate environmental concerns into his projections of communism (see Chapter 14), these concerns are less apparent in his treatments of the *transition* from capitalism to communism. Nonetheless, I will argue that Marx's analytical approach to the transition contains important insights for the unification of environmental and class struggles. In order to appreciate these insights, however, it is necessary to avoid reducing Marx's approach to a one-sidedly industrialist vision. Hence, before addressing the main elements of Marx's general approach and their relevance for environmental struggles, I discuss the limitations of the more standard industrialist interpretation—an interpretation that does seem to have a strong basis in the writings of Marx and Engels.

The Industrialist Vision of Revolution

According to Marx, capitalism's socialization of production negates the necessity of prior class-based restrictions on human development, thereby creating "the historic presuppositions for a new state of society" (1973, 461). This is crucial because "if we did not find concealed in society as it is the material conditions of production and the corresponding relations of exchange prerequisite for a classless society, then all attempts to explode it would be quixotic" (Marx, 1973, 159). At the same time, Marx recognizes capitalism's inability to fulfill the historical potential it creates. More specifically, Marx treats capitalism's historical limits as an outcome of the basic contradiction between production for profit and production for human needs—a contradiction intensified by capital's exploitative socialization of labor and its natural conditions (see Chapter 12). In sum, capital develops production as a "mass of antithetical forms of social unity, whose antithetical character" makes them "so many mines to explode" capitalist society (1973, 159).

Still, someone must detonate these mines and rebuild production and its natural and social conditions on a less class-restricted basis. If this revolutionary agency is to be a plausible one, it must be developed in and through capitalism. Marx and Engels often indicated that this revolutionary force was to be the industrial section of the working class, that is, workers in the goods-producing sectors (industry, mining, agriculture) where the most advanced forces of production were concentrated. The agglomeration and linking together of workers in highly socialized industrial production would bring forth a class-conscious and productively capable industrial proletariat—an appropriate agency for "digging the graves" of capitalism and leading society toward communism. This vision is colorfully phrased in the *Manifesto:*

> But with the development of industry the proletariat not only increases in number; it becomes concentrated in greater masses, its strength grows, and it feels that strength more. . . . The advance of industry, whose involuntary promoter is the bourgeoisie, replaces the isolation of the labourers, due to competition, by their revolutionary combination, due to association. The development of Modern Industry, therefore, cuts from under its feet the very foundation on which the bourgeoisie produces and appropriates products. What the bourgeoisie, therefore, produces, above all, is its own gravediggers. Its fall and the victory of the proletariat are equally inevitable. (Marx and Engels, 1968, 43, 46)

Similarly, in *Capital,* Marx projects that along with the development and socialization of industry, "grows the mass of misery, oppression, slavery, degradation, exploitation; but with this too grows the revolt of the working-class, a class always increasing in numbers, and disciplined, united, organised by the very mechanism of the process of capitalist production itself" (Marx 1967a, I, 763).

This industrialist conception of revolutionary agency has two closely related problems from an ecological perspective. First, it does not seem to adequately safeguard against the possibility that the industrial proletariat, on attaining power over production and its natural conditions, might use and develop them in an instrumentalist fashion not all that qualitatively different from their capitalistic use as mere conditions of competitive monetary accumulation. Stated differently, the industrialist vision of the transition does not adequately register the *communal* interest in natural and social conditions as conditions of the combined labor of the community (not just industrial labor) and as conditions of the entire community's individual and collective development. As a result, the industrialist vision does not seem as open as it should be to the need for a qualitative transformation of production in line with environmental concerns. This contrasts, for example, with Marx's analyses of capitalism's alienation of production and its natural conditions from the entire "living process of the *society* of producers," that is, from "the requirements of socially developed human beings"—analyses that naturally encompass communal environmental issues not limited to the needs of industrial workers as such (1967a, III, 250, 258).

Second, the industrialist vision of revolution is unconvincing insofar as the industrial proletariat that is supposed to take, hold, operate, and transform the conditions of production is the same proletariat which capitalism systematically alienates from these conditions. The picture of a well-disciplined, class-conscious, and economically and politically powerful industrial army painted in the *Manifesto* contrasts sharply with the "virtual paupers" Marx elsewhere shows to be a logical product of capitalistic alienation:

> It is already contained in the concept of the *free labourer*, that he is a *pauper: virtual pauper.* According to his economic conditions he is merely a *living labour capacity.* . . . Necessity on all sides, without the objectivities necessary to realize himself as labour capacity. If the capitalist has no use for his surplus labour, then the worker may not perform his necessary labour; nor produce his necessaries. Then he cannot obtain them through exchange; rather, if he does obtain them, it is only because alms are thrown to him from revenue. He can live as a worker only in so far as he exchanges his labour capacity for that part of capital which forms the labour fund. This exchange is tied to conditions which are accidental *for him,* and indifferent to his *organic* presence. He is thus a virtual pauper. (1973, 604)[1]

Under capitalism, the worker's labor power "is itself merely the possibility of labour, available and confined within the living body of the worker, a possibility which is . . . utterly separated from all the objective conditions of its realisation" (Marx, 1988, 39–40). The latter conditions, indeed "the whole world of material wealth . . . confronts [the workers] as alien commodity and alien money . . . existing independently over against them" (39–40). This powerlessness of labor and massive alienated power of capital seem to provide a very uncongenial setting for the eruption of a revolutionary industrial proletariat. As Marx indicates,

> just as the social productive forces of labour develop in step with the capitalist mode of production, so too the heaped-up wealth confronting the worker grows apace and confronts him as *capital,* as *wealth that controls him.* The world of wealth expands and faces him as an alien world dominating him, and as it does so his subjective poverty, his need and dependence grow larger in proportion. (1977, 1062)

The apparent contradiction between the alienation of industrial labor and its revolutionary mission is nowhere more apparent than in a passage in Volume I of *Capital,* where Marx considers the extent to which the enforcement of the capital-labor relation depends on open coercion:

> It is not enough that the conditions of labour are concentrated in a mass, in the shape of capital, at the one pole of society, while at the other are grouped masses of men, who have nothing to sell but their labour-power. Neither is it enough that they are compelled to sell it voluntarily. The advance of capitalist production develops a working-class, which by education, tradition, habit, looks upon the conditions of that mode of production as self-evident laws of Nature. The organisation of the capitalist process of production, once fully developed, breaks down all resistance. The constant generation of a relative surplus-population keeps the law of supply and demand of labour, and therefore keeps wages, in a rut that corresponds with the wants of capital. The dull compulsion of economic relations completes the subjection of the labourer to the capitalist. Direct force, outside economic conditions, is of course still used, but only exceptionally. In the ordinary run of things, the labourer can be left to the "natural laws of production," i.e., to his dependence on capital, a dependence springing from, and guaranteed in perpetuity by, the conditions of production themselves. (1967a, I, 737)

For my purposes, the important point is not the pessimistic connotations of such statements for proletarian militancy and self-emancipation but the ecological implications of a proletariat that "looks upon" the natural and social conditions produced by capitalism "as self-evident laws of Nature." If the industrial proletariat's extreme subjugation to natural and social conditions *as developed by capital* is really "guaranteed in perpetuity," then it is difficult to see how a revolution led by this same proletariat could be fundamentally pro-ecological. Here again, the problem is how to ensure ecological conditions appropriate to a sustainable yet less restricted human development as a communal process not reducible to industrial production and its direct human agents.

In what follows, I will show that the basic elements of a less one-sidedly industrialist and more pro-ecological approach to revolution are to be found in Marx's analysis of capitalist alienation and working-class organization. This is not to deny the unmistakable basis of the industrialist interpretation in Marx's writings. My intent is to highlight the positive resources that Marx's more general analytical approach can bring to bear on transitional issues involving the ecology. These resources involve three interconnected areas: (1) the tension between use value and exchange value internal to the capital-labor relation; (2) the imperative for the working class to overcome capitalist competition in order to satisfy its needs; and (3) capital's socialization of production and the attendant increase in the strategic importance of the conditions of social production for both capital and labor. After demonstrating the relevance of these three areas for transition issues, I specify their joint connection to environmental struggles.

Capitalism's Fundamental Contradiction Revisited[2]

The previous section highlighted the apparent contradiction between the emancipatory destiny of the working class and the alienation of the same class vis-à-vis the conditions of production. As long as the alienated power of the conditions of production is represented and drawn upon by capital, the corresponding powerlessness of labor would seem to preclude any full-scale working-class revolt against capitalist relations, especially one converting the conditions of production into conditions of a less restricted and more sustainable human development in and through society and nature. Up to this point, however, I have only covered one side of the tensions built into the capital-labor relation. For Marx, the alienation of wealth from labor is only one side of the fundamental contradiction between production for profit and production for human needs. The other side is that capital accumulation requires exploitation of labor power embodied in living, thinking workers for whom exchange value (wages) is a mere means to the end of use value or human development. In this sense, labor represents a structural opposition to capital's treatment of use value as a mere means of value expansion.

Given that labor is "the activity which mediates use values and creates exchange value," capital (money seeking more money) must command "the real use of labour capacity . . . labour itself" (Marx, 1988, 40). Capital is not only based on the alienation of necessary production conditions from the workers: it is also *dependent on the real activity of the workers.* This is not to deny the unequal, exploitative character of the capital-labor relation. The point is that alienated labor and capital's dependence on labor are equally necessary elements of the fundamental tension between production for profit and production for human development. Indeed, that "labour . . . is *the* use value of capital itself . . . the mediating activity through which capital is increased" reveals capitalism's fundamental contradiction as a *living contradiction* between the purely instrumental use value requirements of capital and the *living substance* of these requirements represented by conscious, willful, natural and social human beings (170). Capitalism's fundamental contradiction is thus shown to have both a "negative" and a "positive" side:

As *not-capital, not-objectified labour,* labour capacity appears:

1) *Negatively.* Not-raw material, not-instruments of labour, not-product, not-means of subsistence, not-money: *labour* separated from all the means of labour and life, from the whole of its objectivity, as a mere possibility. This complete denudation, this *possibility of labour* devoid of all objectivity. Labour capacity as *absolute poverty,* i.e., the complete expulsion of objective wealth. The objectivity possessed by labour capacity is only the bodily existence of the worker himself, his own objectivity.

2) *Positively.* Not-objectified labour, the unobjective, subjective existence of labour itself. Labour not as object but as activity, as living source of value. In contrast to capital, which is the reality of general wealth, it is the general possibility of the same, asserting itself in action. (1988, 170–71)

Here Marx expresses capitalism's fundamental contradiction in terms of the tension between human labor as a necessary source of wealth and the alienation of workers vis-à-vis wealth. In Marx's view, this tension grows in step with capital's development of production, because workers' alienation from increasingly socialized conditions of production eventually restricts the production of wealth itself as understood in human developmental terms (see Chapter 12). This tension is built into the capital-labor relation. As Marx indicates: "It is not at all contradictory, or, rather, the in-every-way mutually contradictory statements that labour is *absolute poverty as object,* on one side, and is, on the other side, the *general possibility* of wealth as subject and as activity, are reciprocally determined and follow from the essence of labour, such as it is *presupposed* by capital as its contradiction and as its contradictory being" (1973, 296). Marx often expresses this tension in terms of the "antithesis" between capital as objectified labor and the subjectivity of the labor making up value's living substance:

A further antithesis is this: in contrast to money (or value in general) as *objectified labour,* labour capacity appears as a capacity of the living subject; the former is past labour, labour already performed, the latter is future labour, whose existence can only be the living activity, the currently present activity of the living subject itself. . . . The capitalist, who represents value as such, is confronted by the worker, as labour capacity pure and simple, as worker in general, so that the antithesis between self-valorising value, self-valorising objectified labour, and living value-creating labour forms the point and the actual content of the relation. They confront each other as capital and labour, as capitalist and worker. (1988, 41)

This contrast between objective capital and subjective labor lends itself to a more confrontational and qualitatively more transformational interpretation of capitalism's fundamental contradiction and the transition to communism than does a one-sided focus on the expropriation of industrial capital by previously alienated industrial labor. Labor now appears as a living, active force *structurally opposed* to capital in the sense that labor's opposition to capital is a necessary element of capital itself. Stated differently, capital contains its own negation as a form of wealth. As Marx observes, "the opposite" of capital as "reified" or

past labour, which exists in space, is living labour, which exists in time. As the presently existing unreified (and so also not yet objectified) labour, it can be present only as the *power,* potentiality, ability, as the *labour capacity* of the living subject. The opposite of capital as the independent, firmly self-sufficient objectified labour is living labour capacity itself. . . . *Labour* is the only *use value which can present an opposite and a complement to money as capital,* and it exists in labour capacity, which exists as a subject. Money exists as capital only in connection with non-capital, the negation of capital, in relation to which alone it is capital. *Labour itself is the real non-capital.* (1987, 502–3)

This structural opposition would not be an antagonistic one if capital and labor shared the same goals. But such is not the case, in Marx's view. For capital, the use values of labor power and nature are mere means of value accumulation. For labor, by contrast, value (in the form of wages) is merely a means to obtain necessary use values:

The worker goes through the form of circulation C-M-C. He sells in order to buy. He exchanges his labour capacity for money, in order to swap the money for commodities—to the extent that they are use values, means of subsistence. The purpose is individual consumption. . . . The capitalist, in contrast, goes through M-C-M. He buys in order to sell. The purpose of this movement is exchange value, i.e., enrichment. (Marx, 1988, 135)

Unlike capital, for whom the sole purpose of exchange and production is the competitive accumulation of value, for the worker

> what is essential is that the purpose of the exchange for him is the satisfaction of his need. The object of his exchange is a direct object of need, not exchange value as such. He does obtain money, it is true, but only in its role as coin; i.e., only as a self-suspending and vanishing mediation. What he obtains from the exchange is therefore not exchange value . . . but a means of subsistence, objects for the preservation of his life, the satisfaction of his needs in general, physical, social etc. (1973, 284)

For the worker, exchange value is a necessary means of obtaining use value (not the other way around). This, combined with the alienation of workers' labor in production, means that "for the worker . . . labour only has use value in so far as it *is exchange value,*" that is, insofar as it yields wages (Marx, 1988, 160). The use-value orientation of labor paradoxically manifests itself in the reduction of "labour [to] a *mere exchange value* for the worker" (159):

> But the putting of labour-power into action, i.e., the work, is the active expression of the labourer's own life. And this life activity he sells to another person in order to secure the necessary means of life. His life-activity, therefore, is but a means of securing his own existence. He works that he may keep alive. He does not count the labour itself as a part of his life; it is rather a sacrifice of his life. It is a commodity that he has auctioned off to another. The product of his activity, therefore, is not the aim of his activity. . . . What he produces for himself is *wages.* . . . Life for him begins where this activity ceases, at the table, at the tavern seat, in bed. The twelve hours' work, on the other hand, has no meaning for him as weaving, spinning, boring, and so on, but only as earnings, which enable him to sit down at a table, to take his seat in the tavern, and to lie down in a bed. (Marx, 1933, p.19)

In short, not only do capital and labor occupy structurally opposed positions vis-à-vis wealth, but labor's use-value goals, its *life activities,* are also structurally constrained by capital's conversion of labor into a means of value accumulation. Capital restricts the same subjective human life forces that it must exploit in order to accumulate value. The tension between production for profit and production for "the living process of the *society* of producers" is thus built into "capital itself," understood as the wage-labor relation (1967a, III, 250). A less restricted human development therefore requires an abrogation of this relation.

Competition and Association

The opposed positions of capital and labor vis-à-vis use value and exchange value parallel their equally structural opposition as regards *competition*. Competition is more than a necessary form of social production organized in mutually autonomous enterprises; it is the veritable engine of capital accumulation. It is in market competition that particular private labors are validated (or not validated) as part of society's necessary labor time; the competitive concentration and centralization of capital is as much a prime factor accelerating value accumulation as it is an outcome of the same. In short, capital's "inner nature" or "essential character" as value expansion can only be "realized" in "competition . . . the reciprocal interaction of many capitals with one another, the inner tendency as external necessity" (Marx, 1973, 414). This is not to deny that competition represents a constant threat to *individual capitals;* the point is that "free competition is the adequate form of the productive process of capital" insofar as it compels maximum value accumulation by capital *as a whole.* It is in this sense that "free competition is the real development of capital" (650–51).[3]

For labor, by contrast, competition represents a constant threat not only to individual workers but also to the wages, work conditions, and general living standards of workers as a whole. Competition for the jobs and investments "provided" by capital directly restricts the development of workers and communities. While "for the capitalist," this "competition . . . is a mere question of profit, for the workers it is a question of their existence" (1976a, 423). Workers are also constantly susceptible to various dislocations stemming from the uneven outcomes of competition among capitalist enterprises. For workers and communities, free competition translates into a never-ending stream of actual or threatened business bankruptcies, locational shifts, lay offs, and work speed-ups, with corresponding pressures to keep wage and workplace demands, taxes on capital, as well as health and environmental regulations, within competitive levels lest "business confidence" be eroded. In short, while free competition promotes capital's free development, it systematically restricts the development of the producers and their communities. It follows that to maintain and improve their work and living conditions, workers must "associate among themselves . . . in the form of combinations" (1978a, 168).

This associational imperative is an important feature of Marx's analysis of the transition to communism because unlike the one-sidedly industrialist vision discussed earlier, it does not treat working-class combinations as a simple function of the agglomeration of industrial labor and means of production. The downward pressure of competition on work and living conditions, and the corresponding need to associate in order to defend and improve these conditions, applies not just to industrial workers but to all the producers and their communities. The fact that the associational imperative is not strictly industrialist should at least partly allay concerns about possible anti-ecological bias built into Marx's approach to the transition.

In the writings of Marx and Engels, the role of competitive pressures in instigating working-class combinations tends to be mixed together with the influence of industrial development and agglomeration. This is not surprising, seeing as how industry was the main locus of capitalist development and competition at that time. In *The Poverty of Philosophy*, for example, Marx observes that "the more modern industry and competition develop, the more elements there are which call forth and strengthen combination" (1978a, 166). Similar statements are found in the *Manifesto* (Marx and Engels, 1968, 42–43). At the same time, other passages in these works express the associational impetus generated by competition in terms not limited to the industrial sphere; hence the *Manifesto* states:

> The growing competition among the bourgeois, and the resulting commercial crises, make the wages of the workers ever more fluctuating. The unceasing improvement of machinery, ever more rapidly developing, makes their livelihood more and more precarious; the collisions between individual work-men and individual bourgeois take more and more the character of collisions between two classes. Thereupon the workers begin to form combinations (Trades' Unions) against the bourgeois; they club together in order to keep up the rate of wages; they found permanent associations in order to make provision beforehand for these occasional revolts. (43)

In *The Poverty of Philosophy*, Marx similarly observes that while "competition divides [workers'] interests," it is still the case that "the maintenance of wages, this common interest which they have against their boss, unites them in a common thought of resistance" to this competition, namely "combination" (Marx, 1978a, 168). This associational tendency is not per se industrialist. Rather, the basic point is the irreducible opposition between capitalist competition (required to maximize value accumulation) and working-class association (required to defend and improve workers' human-developmental conditions)—an opposition clearly manifesting the opposed positions of capital and labor vis-à-vis use value and exchange value. This point emerges even more clearly when Marx and Engels consider the prospects for success of workers' wage struggles. Marx and Engels argue that even though "workers are victorious . . . only for a time" in such struggles, the "real fruit of the battles lies, not in the immediate result, but in the ever-expanding union of the workers" (1968, 43). As Marx indicates, although "the first aim of resistance was merely the maintenance of wages, combinations, at first isolated, constitute themselves into groups . . . and in face of always united capital, the maintenance of the association becomes more necessary to them than that of wages" (1978a, 168).

In short, the real victory achieved by working-class combinations is defense of the principle of association over capitalist competition as the determinant of human-developmental conditions (cf. Lebowitz, 1992a, 67). The antagonism between these two principles comes out clearly in *Capital*, when Marx discusses the necessity of association between employed and unemployed workers. Here, Marx points out that "as soon as" the workers

> discover that the degree of intensity of the competition among themselves depends wholly on the pressure of the relative surplus-population; as soon as, by Trades' Unions &c., they try to organise a regular co-operation between employed and unemployed in order to destroy or to weaken the ruinous effects of this natural law of capitalistic competition on their class, so soon capital and its sycophant, Political Economy, cry out at the infringement of the "eternal" and so to say "sacred" law of supply and demand. Every combination of employed and unemployed disturbs the "harmonious" action of this law. (1967a, I, 640)

For Marx and Engels, the maintenance and growth of working-class combinations represents a triumph of association over competition as a mode of organizing human production. As such, it prefigures the transition to communism, in which capital and its competition are replaced by cooperative-democratic control of production.[4] This, and not the exact degree to which they maintain and increase wages, is the standard against which unions and other worker combinations are to be judged:

> If in the associations it really were a matter only of what it appears to be, namely the fixing of wages, if the relationship between labour and capital were eternal, these combinations would be wrecked on the necessity of things. But they are the means of uniting the working class, of preparing for

the overthrow of the entire old society with its class contradictions. And from this standpoint the workers are right to laugh at the clever bourgeois schoolmasters who reckon up to them what this civil war is costing them in fallen, injured, and financial sacrifices. He who wants to beat his adversary will not discuss with him the costs of the war. (Marx, 1976a, 435)

Stated differently, Marx and Engels view working-class combinations as historically significant insofar as they strive for goals that point beyond the wage-labor relation. This means championing not just the wage-interests of particular groups of workers, but rather the broader principle of working-class association against capitalist competition. Of course, day-to-day wage struggles are still significant, for if workers were to abandon such struggles, "they would be degraded to one level mass of broken down wretches past salvation" (Marx, 1976b, 61). Moreover, "by cowardly giving way in their everyday conflict with capital," workers "would certainly disqualify themselves for the initiating of any larger movement" (61). The point is that workers should "not be exclusively absorbed in these unavoidable guerrilla fights incessantly springing up from the never-ceasing encroachments of capital or changes of the market . . . instead of using their organised forces as a lever for the final emancipation of the working class, that is to say, the ultimate abolition of the wages system" (61–62). The latter goal requires that labor's combinations not simply defend the interests of particular worker-groups but also work toward class- and society-wide goals not containable within the competitive wage-labor relation.

Accordingly, in his "Instructions for the Delegates of the Provisional General Council" of the First International, Marx suggests that to maximize "their power of acting against the system of wage slavery itself," workers' combinations should not be "too much aloof from general social and political movements," and indeed "must learn to act deliberately as organising centres of the working class in the broad interest of its *complete emancipation*. They must aid every social and political movement tending in that direction" (quoted in Lapides, 1990, 64–65).

The social breadth of this vision extends far beyond the industrialist conception of the transition elsewhere enunciated by Marx and Engels. Marx reiterates the broader conception in an 1871 interview:

It is necessary that our aims should be thus comprehensive to include every form of working-class activity. To have made them of a special character would have been to adapt them to the needs of one section. . . . The Association does not dictate the form of political movements; it only requires a pledge as to their end. It is a network of affiliated societies spreading all over the world of labor. In each part of the world some special aspect of the problem presents itself, and the workmen there address themselves to its consideration in their own way. (quoted in Lapides, 1990, 81)

Similarly, in an 1881 article Engels looks toward a movement in which "trades unions . . . no longer enjoy the privilege of being the only organisations of the working class" but instead form an integral part of "a general union, a political organisation of the working class as a whole" (quoted in Lapides, 1990, 129). However, the ecological potential of this broadly associational vision can only be fully appreciated in light of capital's socialization of production, which heightens the tension between competition and association as alternative modes of production.

Socialization and the Conditions of Production

Although the socialization of production increasingly creates social needs, capabilities, and problems that call out for collective management, capital's class-exploitative system of private, competitive appropriation stands in the way of cooperative and democratic regulation. As a result, the socialization of production manifests itself in capital's increased reliance on (1) free appropriation of natural and social conditions; (2) undemocratic quasi-social forms of property and market regulation; and (3) outright privatization of state-managed production conditions, as vehicles of value accumulation. These capitalistic forms of social regulation preclude the universalization of human-developmental opportunities (including generalized reductions in wage-labor time) required for the cooperative-democratic management of socialized productive forces as conditions of a less restricted human development. (See Chapter 12's analysis of capitalism's historical limits.)

From labor's standpoint, the growing tension between social production and private appropriation appears as a growth of restrictions on workers' individual and collective self-development—*restrictions increasingly not removable within the confines of the wage-labor relation itself.* Although individual wage and private consumption levels obviously remain important to workers, the problems of working-class life increasingly call out for explicitly social solutions that directly conflict with the principles of privately contracted wage-labor and labor-market competition. Not surprisingly, these problems often involve workers' connections to the conditions of social production that are increasingly being usurped by capital—education, transportation, communications, health care, sanitation, police and security services, and, of course, natural conditions. Capital's alienated socialization of production thus broadens the imperative for workers to combine in order to achieve their use-value goals. This imperative increasingly extends beyond narrowly defined workplace concerns (wages and work conditions) to encompass associational goals only achievable through class-wide organizations of workers and communities.

Hence, the question more and more clearly arises: in whose interests will the social conditions of production be appropriated and developed—those of capital (i.e., ensuring only those use values required for the reproduction of capitalist relations, thus treating people and the conditions of their production as instruments of value expansion) or those of the whole society of producers (placing individual and collective human needs in command of production, thus converting production into a form of free and associated human development)? This is a struggle pitting capital's exploitative, alienated socialization versus a more representative-democratic and self-managed socialization by workers and communities. It is a society-wide class struggle pitting people's needs versus capital's merely instrumental treatment of wealth. Once again, the narrowly industrialist vision of class struggle is superceded. Marx and Engels projected a broadening of class struggle beyond "a purely economic movement" to become "a *political* movement, that is to say, a *class* movement, with the object of enforcing its interests in a general form" (Marx to Bolte, November 23, 1871, in Marx and Engels [1975, 255]).[5] For present purposes, two aspects of this broadening need to be emphasized.

First, given that popular struggles against capital increasingly encompass struggles over non-commodified or partly commodified social conditions of production, any "evaluation of the class struggle from the working-class point of view" must "perceive its point of departure: the self-activity of the class" in all its social sites, not just "workplaces" as defined by capital itself (Cleaver, 1979, 44). Struggles over social conditions apparently "external" to capital are often internal to the real totality of capital as an antagonistic relation between capital and labor and their respective conditions of reproduction and development. That such struggles often take the form of "non-economic" social movements helps explain why the former often develop independently of traditional working-class structures of a more narrowly economic nature, such as official trade unions and affiliated parties. As Harry Cleaver observes, the "reality of autonomy" of these self-activated movements is manifested in their tendency to "repeatedly surge forward . . . autonomously from, and often against, the influence of either trade unions or the Party" (1979, 45, 52).

Once one drops the strictly industrialist conception of production and class struggle, it becomes clear that all self-activated popular struggles over existing social conditions, and for new conditions amenable to a less restricted human development, are integral to the general movement toward an associated form of production conceived as a new union of the producers and the social conditions of their production.[6] This general movement encompasses popular struggles in the realms of culture and individual consumption. Indeed, given the necessity of capital's alienated mode of consumption for its continued capitalization of wealth, and the relative autonomy of working-class consumption and "domestic" life from capitalist commodity production, it would be surprising if the self-activated struggles of producers and communities for less class-restricted conditions of human development did not extend into the spheres of consumption and cultural production and the gender relations comprised therein (see Chapter 11).[7]

Second, despite the evidently "less industrial" character of many contemporary working-class movements, Marx's vision of the transition to communism as a *reappropriation of the social conditions of production* by the producers and their communities retains its importance. Its relevance is not just due to the continued prominence of industrial production and organization as a determinant of human conditions in both the core and the periphery of the global capitalist system. As noted above, the more general socialization of production has increased the importance of *non-industrial conditions of production* for both capital and labor. Capital accumulation increasingly depends on these conditions not only as necessary "background" conditions for production and accumulation in traditionally private industry and services (consider, for example, the enhanced role of education and communications in an era of computerized industry and services), but as spheres of profitable accumulation in their own right (via the privatization of previously state-run activities and/or the growth of private service industries, such as "entertainment" and the burgeoning information sector). Meanwhile, workers' human-developmental opportunities (their lifestyles and life chances) are increasingly restricted by their relationship to these same social conditions of production. A young person's developmental opportunities can be largely shaped by whether her or his parent(s) have jobs featuring health insurance coverage or by the public school and transportation systems in her or his community, for example, not to mention the qualitative effects on one's development stemming from the ever greater commercialization of production, consumption, and culture by corporate capital.

Hence, even allowing for the "less industrial" character of advanced capitalist societies, it is crucial to not throw out the baby of *control over production conditions* with the bathwater of the one-sidedly industrialist vision of revolution. This is especially important insofar as non-industrial conditions of production are or can be co-produced by the employees and consumers in the pertinent sectors.[8] Such co-production applies in particular to the strategically crucial education, communications, transport, and health care sectors. Co-production in these and other areas creates new possibilities for linking traditional workplace concerns with broader social struggles over the conditions of production and consumption. This potential is exhibited not only in defensive battles against privatization of public services but also in struggles for nonhierarchical forms of administration of these services, that is, for *self-administration of the conditions of production by the producers and communities*. Co-production struggles naturally resonate with the traditional struggle to reduce work-time, as workers and consumers in the sectors in question can use increased free time as a resource for self-administration, for enhancing their administrative capabilities, and for planning new forms of co-production—*new forms of wealth*.[9] Self-administered co-production potentially extends, moreover, to the burgeoning private service sector, where it can enable workers and communities to defend and assert their needs and capacities in these heretofore largely nonunionized areas (Negri, 1997). In all these ways, popular struggles against the capitalization of the conditions of production point toward a real conversion of social wealth into communal wealth.[10]

The Struggle for a Real Socialization of Nature

Marx and Engels' approach to class struggle and the transition to communism contains more than the narrowly industrialist dynamics at times highlighted in the *Manifesto* and *Capital*. Marx and Engels envision broader struggles by workers and communities for control over social conditions of production, and for the transformation of production into a condition of free and associated human development. This is not to say that industrial workers and means of production do not play an integral role in the broader conception of transition. Capital's class-exploitative development of industry is still a central source of the deepening tension between private profit and human-social needs, and of the corresponding imperative for workers to associate to achieve their human-developmental goals. I now consider how natural conditions and environmental struggles fit into the broad revolutionary vision outlined in the previous three sections.

Given the natural basis and substance of use value, the opposed positions of capital and labor vis-à-vis use value contain equally opposed positions toward natural conditions.[11] Capital's treatment of use value as a mere means of competitive accumulation carries with it an equally instrumental treatment of natural conditions. For capital, nature is merely an unavoidable prerequisite for the extraction of surplus labor from free labor power and the objectification of this surplus labor in vendible use values. This instrumental treatment of nature is manifested in the value form of labor time, which, as represented in money, makes up the social substance of capital accumulation. The substance of value—abstract labor time—formally abstracts from the natural basis of human labor and wealth—from its qualitative variegation, its interconnection, and its quantitative limits in space and time. Indeed, the homogeneity, divisibility, and limitlessness of value and capital are directly antagonistic to these characteristics of nature as a condition of production (see Chapter 7).

Labor's position as regards use value and nature is quite different. Their social separation from necessary means of production, and their need for use values to survive and develop as human beings, imbues workers' exchange and production activities with a non-instrumental use-value imperative that does not exist in the case of capital. Workers sell their labor power and participate in production not to accumulate value but to obtain use values. For workers, moreover, use values themselves are not means to some other end; they represent human development as both means and end. Workers are both natural *and* social forces; they have a natural substance and they develop as human beings only in and through a constant enmeshment with nature *and* society. It follows that for labor, the wealth of nature is not a mere input into a production function the output of which is human beings but rather the substance of human development itself—the "real body" of labor, as Marx puts it in the *Grundrisse* (1973, 542). It also follows that labor does not share capital's *necessary* antagonism toward nature. Insofar as the free development of human needs and capabilities involves variety, interconnection, and mutual respect and tolerance among human beings, such development lends itself to and indeed requires a caring, nurturing attitude toward the variety, interconnection, and limits of nature—the opposite of capital's tendency toward industrial division, simplification, and overstretching of natural conditions. Then there is the simple fact that a "free" human development based on an unsustainable exploitation of natural wealth is not free at all, insofar as it *unconsciously and anarchically*, and thus *destructively*, generates its own restrictions.[12]

Labor's non-instrumental relationship with nature corresponds, in principle at least, to the kind of valuation of nature as an end in itself that is required for a sustainable and human-developmental appropriation of natural conditions. Whereas from capital's instrumental standpoint, "environmental conditions appear as objectives that limit productive capacity for economic growth," what is needed is a "perspective . . . that integrates ecological productivity with social processes of production" in such fashion that "natural and cultural processes are incorporated in a new dimension of development of the productive forces" (Leff, 1995, 111). Clearly, the latter dimension must be defined in natural *and* social terms not reducible to monetary criteria of profitability, competitiveness, and "cost-effectiveness." The non-instrumental position of labor vis-à-vis natural and social conditions represents an agency, structurally central to capitalist society, that is capable of defining such terms. Indeed, labor's use-value orientation means that its struggles against capital's degradation of nature are just as inevitable as its resistance to capital's exploitation of labor. The two kinds of struggle can be viewed as two aspects of a single resistance to capital's subsumption of human and extra-human nature under value as an alienated end in itself. Both kinds of struggle demonstrate the need for and, under the right circumstances and strategies, help to prefigure and hasten the movement toward the kind of socialization of labor and nature that will enable humanity to produce wealth in a more pro-ecological and human-developmental fashion—a socialization giving both people and nature their due instead of artificially dividing, devaluing, and ruling over them, as the regime of capital does.

Labor's pro-ecological potential only develops historically, in and through popular struggles against the power of capital over production and its natural and social conditions. Its realization depends on the ability of workers and communities to combine and associate around shared ecological interests, and this means overcoming the divisions imposed by the competitive, unevenly developing structure of capital accumulation. Without such association, capital's control over necessary means of production and its threats of mobility and investment strike often force individual workers, worker-groups, and communities to adopt capital's instrumental view of natural conditions—to accept jobs-versus-environment tradeoffs that treat environmental quality as an unaffordable luxury or economic cost rather than as part of the material substance of human development. This leads not only to a competitive "race to the bottom" of environmental quality among workers and communities (Brecher and Costello, 1994) but also to artificial divisions between "labor" and "environmentalists"—as if labor and nature are not equally essential, co-productive sources of wealth; as if labor is not itself a natural force. These factional divisions manifest the artificial splintering of workers' individual and collective development by capital's separation and exploitative recombination of labor and its natural conditions.

The uneven development of capitalist production systematically divides workers into environmental "haves" and "have nots" insofar as the worst human effects of ecological plunder and degradation are often imposed on the poorest, most socially marginalized sections of the working class. Within the developed capitalist countries, the environmental costs of capital accumulation are unequally borne by indigenous and other poor peoples' communities, and this has instigated powerful movements against environmental racism and for environmental justice among these peoples (Churchill, 1993; Taylor, 1996; Chatterjee, 1997; Muwakkil, 1997). In some cases—but not nearly enough—organized labor has taken part in these movements, demonstrating their potential as rallying points in a broader worker and community struggle for less class-restricted natural and social conditions of human development (Foster, 1994, 137–42).

On a global scale, perhaps the most important factor preventing workers from articulating and coalescing around their common ecological interests has been the uneven incidence of ecological plunder and degradation in the developed-core and underdeveloped-periphery countries of the world capitalist system (Crosby et al., 1991). The dominant core-country subsystems of production and consumption have required much more absorption and disposal of natural resources, and much more qualitative degradation of nature, both in total and (especially) on a per capita basis. Yet, although the immediate benefits of this appropriation of nature in terms of consumption, income, and profits have accrued mainly to the core countries (albeit unequally among classes in the core), the costs have been unequally borne by the periphery, whose people and natural resources have been exploited, extracted, and degraded in particularly wanton fashion to serve accumulation models shaped by the profit-seeking activities and use-value requirements of core capital. Foster (1994, Chapter 5) demonstrates the close connections between this "ecological imperialism" and the failure of some peripheral countries to reach the turning point in the so-called demographic transition to lower birth rates and slower population growth.

Rather than being "pure" class discourses (if such be definable), the discourses of popular environmental struggles in the periphery have been rich in indigenous, community, and feminist values developed in and against relations of external domination. These movements have exhibited complex and, at times, tension-filled relations with traditional socialist and other working-class modes of activity and discourse, including trade unionism narrowly defined, especially when the latter have been hierarchically imported through official working-class institutions, be they capitalist or "socialist" (Peet and Watts, 1996). Even though the new "liberation ecologies" may not fit easily into the narrowly industrialist conceptions of class struggle, they are quite consistent with a broader Marxist vision of the communist transition as a worker-community struggle for conditions of free and associated human development.

Marx's revolutionary vision tells us that the ultimate success of the popular resistance to the capitalization of nature depends on its coalescence into a general political movement of the producers and their communities. This movement will have to overcome the false opposition between people and nature by struggling for new social forms of production that validate natural conditions as the very substance of human development, not as mere means to an end. Once again, the question is how to pro-ecologically socialize nature, not whether nature should be socialized. Marx's perspective also tells us that although the movement toward a sustainable and desirable co-evolution of society and nature is not inevitable—since it is an historically contingent outcome of popular struggles in and against capitalist relations—capitalist development does tend to make the *necessity* of a co-operative management of this co-evolution increasingly transparent. In this way, capitalist development itself supports the *historical rationality* of working-class and community struggles against the capitalization of nature and society.[13]

More specifically, ecological problems can be located in the context of capital's alienated socialization of production, which produces problems that can only be solved collectively, as much as capital's relations of private appropriation and competition impede collective solutions. Production driven by competitive capital accumulation creates an increasingly intensive and universal appropriation of nature by social labor; but this appropriation is still anarchically regulated by private competition among class-divided capitals. The goal of this competition is simply and solely monetary accumulation, with people and their natural and social conditions treated as a means to this qualitatively abstract and quantitatively limitless end (see Chapter 7). The need for a communal and pro-ecological regulation of society's increasingly large-scale and qualitatively diverse interchange with nature, both in production and in consumption, clearly falls under the category of collective problems created by the tension between private appropriation and social production. As the problem of ecological regulation becomes increasingly variegated and biospheric in scope, labor's use-value orientation, and the imperative for workers and communities to combine and associate to fulfill their human-developmental needs, become correspondingly complex and universal, both materially and socially. This, in turn, heightens the imperative for workers and communities to convert scientific knowledge from an instrument of capital accumulation into a more universally appropriated condition of free human development.

Especially since the Second World War, the scientific development and utilization of productive forces in the service of private profit has created a radical quantitative and qualitative disjuncture between human production and the laws governing the reproduction of natural wealth. The combination of absolute growth of production and material throughput on the one hand, and the development of non-biodegradable and downright poisonous forms of production, consumption, and disposal on the other, has caused global capitalism to enter "a new stage of planetary crisis in which human economic activities begin to affect in entirely new ways the basic conditions of life on earth" (Foster, 1994, 108). The insufficiency of the competitive price system to deal with capitalism's biospheric malfunctions is shown by the threat of global warming. Here, even the proponents of market-based "solutions" must admit that tax/subsidy systems and artificial markets for greenhouse gas emissions are at best imperfect *instruments* for achieving pre-determined emissions levels (Passell, 1997). Hence, private and state-regulated environmental rents only validate and rationalize capital's appropriation of nature at the microeconomic level, in line with capital's power over production and worker-community resistance to this power (Nelson, 1993). For greenhouse gases, this is an exceptionally big problem, since emissions targets must be negotiated internationally. The uneven development of global capitalism, when combined with capital's prioritization of competitiveness and maximum value accumulation over long-run sustainability, makes it impossible to adequately regulate greenhouse gas emissions through market channels and their political superstructures. At best, elite-level negotiations promise a slowing of the rate of increase in greenhouse gas concentrations grossly inadequate to meet the challenge posed (*Economist,* 1997a and 1997b; Stevens, 1997). It would be foolish to expect otherwise, given the clear tendency of recent international trade and investment agreements to codify and enforce the competitive race to the bottom in environmental and social standards (Brecher and Costello, 1994; Bleifuss, 1997).

One must also question the sufficiency of market-based policy instruments to achieve even predetermined emissions and environmental quality goals. Not only do state-engineered rents validate all the anti-ecological characteristics of value and capital (see Chapter 7), but their enforcement may also be contradicted by the power and influence of competing capitalists. In the United States, for example, the recent movement toward market-based instruments has been paralleled by an increased laxity in the enforcement of existing environmental regulations and by state assent to a growing secrecy of corporate environmental violations (Tokar, 1996; Montague, 1997). Even with "green" tax/subsidy systems and markets for pollution rights in place, individual enterprises have an incentive to create and utilize any and all opportunities to externalize environmental costs onto the rest of society, so that competition tends to limit information flows concerning environmentally disruptive activities (Pepper, 1993, 83).[14] Often, this information blockage is combined with the dissemination of outright disinformation by large corporations, business associations, and their various think tanks and journalistic mouthpieces as regards the environmental effects of production and the likely disruptions from environmental regulation. In the case of greenhouse gases, for example, powerful capitalist interests have been busily filling the popular media with propaganda minimizing the significance of the global warming problem relative to prospective regulatory disruptions of production and consumption (Breslow, 1997; Levy, 1997).

Market-based environmental policies codify and rationalize capital's restricted identification of natural wealth as a condition of monetary accumulation. This is clear from the key role of such policies in the more general market-based policy reform packages used to enhance private profitability at the expense of labor and communities in both core and periphery (Kolko, 1988). As capital and its state functionaries respond to the problem of overaccumulation by attacking workers' private and social wages simultaneous with efforts to marketize natural and social conditions, the true scope of capital's human-developmental irrationality becomes apparent. This awareness has been heightened by the confluence of renewed globalization of capital (with intensified competitiveness pressures on workers and communities) and the globalization of ecological crisis (Burkett, 1995). The twin globalizations, combined with the failures of market environmentalism, have incubated new forms of environmental struggle that are working-class, internationalist, and anti-capitalist insofar as they recognize "that in order to halt, or even significantly slow down, the rate of environmental deterioration, capitalist commodity society will have to give way to environmental necessity" (Foster, 1994, 130; cf. Brecher et al., 1993; Danaher, 1994; Peet and Watts, 1996).

Insofar as capitalism's ecological and biospheric conflicts boil down to the antagonism between capital's monetary valuation of nature versus nature's use value for workers and communities, Marx's conception of the transition to communism as a conversion of the conditions of production into forms of free and associated human development retains its strategic relevance for popular struggles. The same goes for the projection that this conversion will involve self-administered co-production of the conditions of production by workers and communities (Negri, 1997). Whereas the free and associated co-evolution of human beings hinges on a sustainable co-evolution of society and nature, the reverse is also true (Schnaiberg and Gould, 1994; Gowdy, 1994a, 1994b). Self-administered co-production of natural and social wealth can play a central role in this total system of co-evolution.

For instance, free and associated human development is, by definition, a richly variegated development of human needs and capabilities unrestricted by exploitative class relations; such development has a two-way complementarity with the evolving variegation of nature. By protecting and nurturing nature's variety and interconnection, society not only reproduces the richness and resiliency of natural ecosystems but also diversifies the opportunities for human development. Insofar as human-developmental opportunities do involve a variety of conscious engagements with ecological and biospheric systems, there is an improvement in society's *capability* to protect and nurture natural wealth. The result here is a sustainable, co-evolutionary, and resilient enmeshment of human and natural variety. As Enrique Leff observes, this path involves the social adoption of a "new productive paradigm

> . . . one that articulates the laws of thermodynamics, of ecology, and of social production. This emergent productive rationality will integrate the conditions for the primary productivity of natural ecosystems, the technological productivity of productive processes, and the social productivity of the labor process, supported by socially controlled, scientific-technological progress. (1995, 67)

Self-administered co-production is a natural vehicle for this path insofar as it integrates all workers and community members (really two sides of the same individuals) in the communal appropriation and management of natural wealth. This co-production will only be truly self-administered if it brings technological development under the cooperative control of workers and communities, and this is a function of their command of relevant scientific, including ecological, knowledge. The de-alienation of scientific expertise vis-à-vis workers and communities is required, not just for the development of a social system of material and energy throughput healthily enmeshed with the broader circulation of matter and life-forces but also for a real democratization of the social valuation of natural wealth. The latter process will inevitably require conflict resolution even after class-based restrictions on ecological values are removed.[15] Democratic co-management of natural wealth thus presumes increased free time for workers to develop their technological and administrative capabilities and to engage in cooperative administration. Clearly, these are activities that, as André Gorz suggests, qualify as deserving "to be done on their own account" under any "social project of the Left"; that is, "activities on which the meaning and quality of life, and individual development and sovereignty, depend, but to which, as a result of the dominance of economic rationality, time and social recognition have never been granted. The point, then, is to act so that social time becomes available for these activities" (Gorz, 1994, 35).

Such are the basic principles of natural wealth management based on a "privileging of use values above the production of exchange values . . . an ecodevelopment strategy oriented toward a decentralized, democratic, and participatory development" (Leff, 1995, 112–13). The self-administered co-production of natural wealth is the only worker-community response adequate to the human-developmental potential and the ecological and biospheric threats posed by capital's exploitative appropriation of nature. But does Marx's projection of communism adequately encompass such concerns?

CHAPTER 14

Nature and Associated Production

It is often suggested that Marx's vision of communism not only treats natural conditions as effectively limitless but also embraces an anti-ecological ethic of human domination over nature. In Alec Nove's interpretation, for example, Marx thought that "the problem of production had been 'solved'" by capitalism, so that the future system of associated production would "not require to take seriously the problem of the allocation of scarce resources." Marx's communism thus presumes that "natural resources [are] inexhaustible," and that there is no need for "an environment-preserving, ecologically conscious, employment-sharing socialism" (Nove, 1990, 230, 237). Evidently, Marx projected post-capitalist society as one of "abundance"—defined as "a sufficiency to meet requirements at zero price" (or what amounts to the same thing in Nove's view, production of goods and services at close to zero resource cost). This projection forced Marx into the absurd presumption that "scarce resources (oil, fish, iron ore, stockings, or whatever) . . . would not be scarce" under communism (Nove, 1983, 15–16). Similarly, Andrew McLaughlin asserts that Marx "envisions a general material abundance" and provides "no basis for recognizing any interest in the liberation of nature from human domination" (1990, 95).[1]

Chapters 11 and 12 responded to such "Promethean" interpretations by focusing on the role of natural conditions in Marx's analysis of capitalism's historical progressivity and historical limits. It was shown that Marx's vision of the less restricted, more universal human development potentiated by capitalism is not anti-ecological, and that Marx recognizes the barriers capitalism poses to the use of socially developed productive forces for a sustainable, healthy co-evolution of human and extra-human nature. Marx's projection of future human development cannot be reduced to a growth of free time and mass consumption based on the further expansion and technical perfection of capitalism's anti-ecologically developed productive forces. Rather, Marx foresees a qualitative *enrichment* of people-nature relations *and* of relations among human beings, based on a pro-ecological *and* pro-human transformation of the system of socialized labor and nature (including the scientific knowledge) bequeathed by capitalism. Chapter 13 showed that struggles for democratic worker-community control over the development and utilization of natural and social conditions fit comfortably into Marx and Engels' less industrialist and more broadly social projections of communist revolution.

Nonetheless, a complete response to the Promethean charge must demonstrate that Marx's projection of associated production adheres to specific pro-ecological principles of economic organization. This task is rendered all the more necessary by the sweeping, slashing character of most ecological critiques of Marx's communism. Generally speaking, these critiques do not address the ecological implications of some of the most fundamental characteristics of post-capitalist society as projected by Marx and Engels. Apparently, the critics have mostly labored under the common misperception that Marx and Engels, eschewing all "speculation about imaginary socialist utopias," thought very little about the system to follow capitalism, and that their entire body of writing on this subject is represented by "the *Critique of the Gotha Program,* a few pages long, and not much else" (Auerbach and Skott, 1993, 195).[2]

Leaving such assertions aside, this chapter evaluates the basic organizing principles of Marx's communism from an ecological point of view. The next section provides a benchmark for this evaluation by setting out some general criteria for the ecological soundness of economic systems. These criteria recognize the natural limits of human production as well as the special responsibility of human society to manage natural conditions. The basic features of associated production in Marx's projection are then outlined, followed by a consideration of their ecological significance in terms of the previously proposed criteria.

To avoid unnecessary misunderstanding, three things should be noted about this ecological evaluation of Marx's communism. First, my purpose is not to prove the technical and/or social feasibility of associated production as projected by Marx but to determine whether there is anything fundamentally anti-ecological about its basic principles. Second, my central (not sole) concern is whether Marx's projection of communism's less restricted, more universal human development can be reconciled with an adequate recognition of natural conditions and limits, including an ethic that does not reduce nature to a passive raw material for mass industrialized production and consumption. Third, even though my main concern is with ecological correctness rather than overall feasibility, establishing the inner consistency of Marx's communism is still important for my argument. The organizing principles of associated production must together constitute a coherent vision—one meshing in a reasonable way with the free human development projected by Marx. Otherwise, Marx's communism would be a bootless vision, both ecologically and politically.

Some Requirements of an Ecologically Sound System

Most basically, a healthy and sustainable co-evolution of humanity and nature requires a socio-economic system with a built-in recognition of humanity's responsibility to manage its appropriation of nature, both qualitatively and quantitatively. For this purpose, the quality of natural conditions must be seen as encompassing aesthetic use values, not just nature's usefulness as a condition of industrial labor.

As four eminent ecologists recently pointed out, "humanity's dominance of earth means that we cannot escape responsibility for managing the planet"; even "maintaining the diversity of 'wild' species and the functioning of 'wild' ecosystems will require increasing human involvement" (Vitousek et al., 1997, 499). Given the biospheric impacts of human production, the question is no longer whether nature will be largely humanized but whether this humanization will be pro- or anti-ecological. Although a pro-ecological human production will not try to brutally force nature into desired shapes and forms, it will still need to gently and cautiously guide natural conditions in carefully chosen directions (Carson, 1962, 275, 296). Socially developed human production cannot be purely natural in the same sense as the reproduction of other species *sans* human intervention. It follows that "the integration between humanity and nature" must be "consciously considered" in terms of "the mutual well-being of both" (Morrison, 1995, 182). And as is noted by the social ecologist Ray Dasmann, the management of natural conditions in line with any given quality of human and natural life requires the explicit formulation and pursuit of social *and* ecological goals on local, national, and global levels—otherwise, "by default the options will close" (Dasmann, 1972, 221).

Society's responsibility to manage natural conditions leads to a second ecological criterion: the encouragement of "efforts to understand Earth's ecosystems and how they interact with the numerous components of human-caused global change" (Vitousek et al., 1997, 499). For this ecological knowledge to be applied throughout society's system of production and consumption, it will have to be thoroughly diffused among and grasped by producers and communities. This requires, for example, "a system of alternatives assessment in which facilities regularly evaluate the availability of alternatives" to toxic forms of production and consumption, "coordinated with active attempts to develop and make available nontoxic alternatives for currently toxic processes and with systems of support for those making the transition" (Steingraber, 1997, 271). Of course, the kind of practical knowledge a pro-ecological system needs will often be of a different type than that developed under capitalism—even when the two types have a common scientific basis. Ecological knowledge will often involve ways and means of *limiting* and *channeling* society's productive capabilities so as to maintain and improve the quality of natural conditions. It will, as Lewis Mumford suggests, assist the task of "inventing a social discipline for handling" the "burdensome technique of overproduction" bequeathed by capitalism; as such, it will have to combine social and natural scientific insights (1954, 52).[3] It is in this connection that one must recognize the possibility of an ecologically sound system making use of technologies developed prior to capitalism, even though it will not be possible to avoid making "selective use, involving both assimilation and rejection, of capitalist legacies" (Wallis, 1993, 155). Based on their survey of the soil damage associated with contemporary agriculture, for example, Matson et al. argue for "the development of more ecologically designed agricultural systems that reintegrate features of traditional agricultural knowledge and add new ecological knowledge" (1997, 508).[4]

Nonetheless, even with all efforts to increase, disseminate, and apply knowledge about the environmental impacts of human production, a pro-ecological society will recognize that human knowledge regarding nature and the effects of human interventions therein can never be complete. Society must have an acute awareness of the limits to effective *and safe* human control over natural processes. This awareness must be codified in regulatory measures that restrict any uses of natural conditions having uncertain ecological impacts. Various forms of this environmental risk aversion criterion have been proposed. "Many indigenous peoples," for example, "take the position that all social policies should be entered into only after consideration of their likely implications, both environmentally and culturally, for descendants seven generations in the future. Consequently a number of seemingly good ideas for solving short run problems are never entered into because no one can reasonably predict their longer term effects" (Churchill, 1993, 451). In a similar vein, ecologist Sandra Steingraber suggests three basic principles for dealing with uncertain toxic effects of human production: the *precautionary principle,* which "dictates that indication of harm, rather than proof of harm, should be the trigger for action" limiting the source of toxic effects; the *principle of reverse onus,* under which "it is safety, rather than harm, that should necessitate demonstration," thus effectively "shifting the burden of proof off the shoulders of the public and onto those who produce, import, or use the [potentially toxic] substance in question"; the *principle of the least toxic alternative,* which "presumes that [potentially] toxic substances will not be used as long as there is another way of accomplishing the task" (Steingraber, 1997, 270–71).

Environmental risk aversion also motivates Vitousek et al.'s suggestion that society should "work to reduce the rate at which we alter the Earth system," because "ecosystems and the species they support may cope more effectively with the changes we impose, if these changes are slow" (1997, 499). The risk aversion criterion draws further support from "the need to keep a range of resource use options available to future generations" when, for example, "making a decision to develop hitherto untouched land" (Dasmann et al., 1973, 24). In the same spirit, Dasmann (1975) suggests that "preindustrial land-use systems . . . with a long history of successful adaptation to their environments and continuing productivity . . . should, if possible, be left alone," and that "all proposed changes in existing forms of land use, where the existing forms are successful, or show evidence of continuing success, must be subjected to careful ecological and sociological evaluation" (124–25). Here, the risk aversion criterion is quite consistent with and is even complemented by the ecological knowledge criterion.

Many ecological thinkers would add *cooperation* to the list of core prerequisites for effective social management of natural conditions. Referring to the ecological threat posed by nuclear technology and inadequately regulated "technics" in general, Lewis Mumford goes so far as to assert: "If man fails to take the path toward world co-operation, on every level from government upward, there is no alternative that will not prove monstrous. . . . Unconditional co-operation on a world scale is, therefore, the only alternative" (1954, 32–33). Building an ecologically sound system of production is by nature a cooperative endeavor, because it involves not just resource management but also a reconstruction of the social institutions regulating the use of natural conditions. In such a process, both nature and society "evolve as part of the living world: their relationship and network are dynamic, not hierarchical" (Morrison, 1995, 181). Although many

economists support the market as an efficient substitute for explicit cooperation, even they must admit that the pricing of natural conditions is—
apart from other shortcomings—only an instrument for achieving
predetermined goals. Insofar as these goals are not determined in cooperative-democratic fashion, the true use value of nature in all its ecological
and social variety is unlikely to be represented (see Chapters 7 and 13).

The cooperative character of all socio-ecological endeavors becomes
even clearer once the criterion of *variety and diversity* is taken into account.
To begin with, the diversity of natural conditions means that any systemic
eco-rationality must encourage the maintenance and development of diverse ways of life. An ecologically sound system will thus "reserve certain
areas of our planet, land and water" for "the preservation of older and simpler ways of living," while supporting efforts by modern-day "communi-
tarians" to "develop viable communities that [are] increasingly independent
of inputs from technological society" (Dasmann, 1972, 212; 1975, 136–37).
The preservation of such alternative paths of living will require cooperation
at all levels, based on a widely diffused knowledge of the ecological practices involved and the potential losses to society should they be "swamped
out" by the dominant, more industrial forms of production.

The variety and diversity criterion is not based simply on the need for
humanity to adapt its development to a variegated environment. It is a positive social value insofar as it signifies a rich plurality of paths for human
fulfillment and for developing peoples' natural and social capabilities. An
ecologically sound system must be cooperatively managed by producers
and communities willing and able to make prudent, ecologically informed
decisions on a day-to-day basis. Such a society will have to provide a variety of channels for individual fulfillment, based on "an extraordinary diversity of community lifeways" (Morrison, 1995, 181). Many have
recognized this connection between ecological soundness and human-
social diversity. David Harvey, for example, observes:

> Socialism is not necessarily about the construction of homogeneity. The ex-
> ploration of our species potential can presumably also be about the creative
> search for and exploration of diversity and heterogeneity. Socio-ecological
> projects, much more in tune with resolving questions of alienation and
> opening up diverse possibilities for self-realisation, can be regarded as fun-
> damentally part of some socialist future. (1993, 44–45)[5]

Respect for variety and diversity can also help society avoid the misuse
of ecological thinking as a rationale for a new tyranny of the collective

over the individual (Pepper, 1993, 125). An ecologically sound system "must take into account varying needs and desires based on age, background, and personal preference"; otherwise, "there will be very little support" for such a system (Wright, 1983, 84). Without individual freedom and choice, the system cannot be an effective "vehicle for debate and experimentation that helps test what works best for different circumstances and objectives" (Brecher and Costello, 1994, 172).

An ecologically sound management of human production presumes, however, that people share a fundamental ecological ethic, however diverse its forms. Ray Dasmann provides a wide-ranging consideration of this ethical criterion. He points out that because "environmental conservation represents a goal toward which we must work [together]," it is "not something that can be achieved tomorrow by appeal to [individual] self-interest"; it will thus "require a basic change of attitude on the part of many people" (Dasmann, 1968, 95). There must be "an *extension of ethics* from people to the land, and with this the development of an *ecological conscience*" in which people "feel a deep sense of personal responsibility toward the land" (95). Given the cooperative requirements of ecological management, people will need to "regain a sense of community," and this "recovery of self-identity and awareness" as a social and natural species "can come only through education":

> Not conservation education in the old sense, which too often has emphasized only the economically profitable aspects of resource management, but a new type of education based firmly upon a knowledge of human needs and land ecology. A knowledge of psychology and the social sciences, physical science and engineering, and biology are all an integral part of the requisite educational pattern. The education must reach not just the experts and specialists in conservation but must filter through to everyone who is responsible for the land. (Dasmann, 1975, 158–59; 1968, 96)

Ethical considerations clearly reinforce the important role of widely diffused combinations of natural and social scientific knowledge in an ecologically sound system.

Ecologically informed ethics cannot thrive unless they are routinely validated, both materially and socially, by the system of production, distribution, and consumption. The system must define "wealth" in human and ecological terms, thereby promoting "a consistent change in the habits of production" (Bahro, 1978, 428). As Mumford puts it: "We need more wealth, but a wealth measured in terms of life rather than profit and prestige" (1954, 113).[6] According to the brilliant Green-Red theorist Rudolf Bahro, this *ecological wealth criterion* means giving "primacy" to "simple reproduction with the employment of existing energies and resources," while generally promoting "improvement in quality as against the mere number of finished products" (Bahro, 1978, 429–30). Ecological soundness requires that we no longer "gratuitously assume, as we constantly do, that the mere existence of a mechanism for manifolding or mass production carries with it an obligation to use it to the fullest capacity" (Mumford, 1954, 51). The system must have a built-in recognition that due to the "dangers to the earth's non-renewable resources, and to the natural environment of human civilization and human life . . . consumption of material goods and services cannot grow in an unlimited way" (Mandel, 1992, 207). In short, wealth must be defined not in terms of growth of production and consumption for their own sake but in terms of a healthy, humanly fulfilling, and sustainable co-evolution of human and extra-human nature.

Basic Principles of Associated Production

The most basic feature of communism in Marx's projection is its overcoming of capitalism's social separation of the producers from necessary conditions of production. The new union between the producers and production conditions involves a complete decommodification of labor power plus a new set of communal property rights. On this basis, social production is collectively administered in line with specific use-value goals arrived at in cooperative-democratic fashion. Associated production is production planned and carried out by the producers and communities themselves, without the class-based intermediaries of wage-labor, market, and state. Marx often illustrates these basic features with reference to the primary means and end of associated production— that of free human development.[7]

As I have shown, Marx specifies capitalism as the "decomposition of the original union existing between the labouring man and his means of labour" (Marx, 1976b, 39). In *Value, Price and Profit* (1865), Marx describes communism as the outcome of "a new and fundamental revolution in the mode of production" that "restore[s] the original union in a new historical form" (1976b, 39). Several years earlier, in drafting *Theories of Surplus Value,* Marx had referred to communism as "the historical reversal" of "the separation of labour and the worker from the conditions of labour"—adding that "the original unity can be re-established only on the material foundation which capital creates and by means of the revolutions which, in the process of this creation, the working class and the whole society undergo" (1971, 271–72, 423). Communism "will," as Engels phrases it, "emancipate human labour power from its position as a *commodity*" (1939, 221).[8] Under capitalism's wage system, "the means of production employ *the workers*"; under communism, "the workers, as subjects, employ the means of production . . . in order to produce wealth for themselves" (Marx, 1968, 580).

Production jointly controlled by the associated workers "is only possible where the workers are the owners of their means of production" (1971, 525).[9] This communist property codifies and enforces the new form of the original union of the producers with production conditions. Accordingly, in notes for his famous 1881 letter to Vera Zasulich, Marx describes communism as "replacing capitalist production with cooperative production, and capitalist property with a *higher form* of the archaic type of property, i.e., communist property" (1989d, 362).

Communist property cannot, of course, be individual private property in the conditions of production. The latter form "excludes co-operation, division of labour within each separate process of production, the control over, and the productive application of the forces of Nature by society, and the free development of the social productive powers" (Marx, 1967a, I, 762). In other words, "the individual worker could only be restored as *an individual* to property in the conditions of production by divorcing productive power from the development of labour on a large scale" (1994, 109). As stated in *The German Ideology*, "the appropriation by the proletarians" is such that "a mass of instruments of production must be made subject to each individual, and property to all. Modern universal intercourse cannot be controlled by individuals, unless it is controlled by all. . . . With the appropriation of the total productive forces by the united individuals, private property comes to an end" (Marx and Engels, 1976, 97).

Besides, given capitalism's prior socialization of production, "private" property in the means of production is already a kind of social property, even though its social character is class-exploitative.[10] From capital's character as "not a personal, [but] a social power" it follows that when "capital is converted into common property, into the property of all members of society, personal property is not thereby transformed into social property. It is only the social character of the property that is changed. It loses its class-character" (1968, 47).[11]

Communism thus involves a "reconversion of capital into the property of producers, although no longer as the private property of the individual producers, but rather as the property of associated producers, as outright social property" (Marx, 1967a, III, 437). This explicit socialization of the conditions of production should not be mistaken for a complete absence of individual property rights, however. Although communism "does not re-establish private property for the producer," it nonetheless "gives him individual property based on the acquisitions of the capitalist era: i.e., on co-operation and the possession in common of the land and of the means of production" (1967a, I, 763). Marx posits that "the *alien property* of the capitalist . . . can only be abolished by converting his property into the property . . . of the *associated, social individual*" (1994, 109). In *The Civil War in France*, Marx even asserts that communism will "make individual property a truth by transforming the means of production, land and capital, now chiefly the means of enslaving and exploiting labour, into mere instruments of free and associated labour" (1985, 75). Stated differently, for communism to overcome the class-based separation between individuals and their conditions of existence, communist property must represent a new combination of individual *and* collective property rights.[12]

Communist property is collective precisely insofar as "the material conditions of production are the co-operative property of the workers" *as a whole,* not of particular individuals or sub-groups of individuals (1966, 11). As Engels puts it: "The 'working people' remain the collective owners of the houses, factories and instruments of labour, and will hardly permit their use . . . by individuals or associations without compensation for the cost" (1979, 94). The collective planning and administration of social production requires that not only the means of production but also the distribution of the total product be subject to explicit social control. With associated production, "it is possible to assure each person 'the full proceeds of his labour' . . . only if [this phrase] is extended to purport not that each individual worker becomes the possessor of 'the full proceeds of his labour,' but that the whole of society, consisting entirely of workers, becomes the possessor of the total product of their labour, which product it partly distributes among its members for consumption, partly uses for replacing and increasing its means of production, and partly stores up as a reserve fund for production and consumption" (Engels, 1979, 28). The latter two "deductions from the . . . proceeds of labour are an economic necessity"; they represent "forms of surplus-labour and surplus-product . . . which are common to all social modes of production" (Marx, 1966, 7; 1967a, III, 876).[13] Further deductions are required for "general costs of administration," for "the communal satisfaction of needs, such as schools, health services, etc.," and for "funds for those unable to work." Only then "do we come to . . . that part of the means of consumption which is divided among the individual producers of the co-operative society" (1966, 7–8). The use-value goals that Marx envisions as guiding these allocation decisions are further discussed below. At this point it should just be noted that "what the producer is deprived of in his capacity as a private individual benefits him directly or indirectly in his capacity as a member of society" (8).

Communist property relations also protect the individual's right to a share in the total product (net of the above-mentioned deductions) for her or his private consumption. The *Manifesto* is unambiguous on this point: "Communism deprives no man of the power to appropriate the products of society; all that it does is to deprive him of the power to subjugate the labour of others by means of such appropriation" (Marx and Engels, 1968, 49). In this sense, "social ownership extends to the land and the other means of production, and private ownership to the products, that is, the articles of consumption" (Engels, 1939, 144). An equivalent description of the "community of free individuals" is given in Volume I of *Capital:* "The total product of our community is a social product. One portion serves as fresh means of production and remains social. But another portion is consumed by the members of society as means of subsistence" (Marx, 1967a, I, 78).

This, of course, raises the question as to how the distribution of individual workers' consumption claims will be determined. In *Capital,* Marx envisions that "the mode of this distribution will vary with the productive organisation of the community, and the degree of historical development attained by the producers." He then suggests ("merely for the sake of a parallel with the production of commodities") that one possibility would be for "the share of each individual producer in the means of subsistence" to be "determined by his labour-time" (1967a, I, 78). In the *Critique of the Gotha Programme,* the conception of labor time as the measure of individual consumption rights is less ambiguous, at least for "the first phase of communist society as it is when it has just emerged after prolonged birth pangs from capitalist society" (1966, 10). Here, Marx forthrightly projects that

the individual producer receives back from society—after the deductions have been made—exactly what he gives to it. What he has given to it is his individual amount of labour. . . . The individual labour time of the individual producer is the part of the social labour day contributed by him, his share in it. He receives a certificate from society that he has furnished such and such an amount of labour (after deducting his labour for the common fund), and with this certificate he draws from the social stock of means of consumption as much as the same amount of labour costs. The same amount of labour which he has given to society in one form, he receives back in another. (8)[14]

The basic logic behind labor-based consumption claims is that "the distribution of the means of consumption at any time is only a consequence of the distribution of the conditions of production themselves"; given that the conditions of production are the property of the producers, it stands to reason that the distribution of consumption claims will be more closely tied to labor time than under capitalism, where it is *money* that rules. However, insofar as the individual labor-time standard merely codifies the ethic of equal exchange regardless of the connotations for individual need satisfaction and individual development, it is still infected by "the narrow horizon of bourgeois right." Marx therefore goes on to suggest that "in a higher phase of communist society," labor-based individual consumption claims can and should "be fully left behind and society inscribe on its banners: from each according to his ability, to each according to his needs!" (1966, 10).[15]

Overall, communist property is individual insofar as it affirms each person's claim, as a member of society, for equal access to the conditions and results of production as a conduit to her or his development as an individual "to whom the different social functions he performs are but so many modes of giving free scope to his own natural and acquired powers" (Marx, 1967a, I, 488). Marx and Engels envision communism as "a society organised for co-operative working on a planned basis to ensure all members of society the means of existence and the full development of their capacities" (Engels, 1939, 167). Especially in its higher phase, communism's "mode of distribution . . . allows *all* members of society to develop, maintain and exert their capacities in all possible directions" (221). Accordingly, "the individual consumption of the labourer" becomes that which "the full development of the individuality requires" (Marx, 1967a, III, 876). "In place of the old bourgeois society, with its classes and class antagonisms," communist property relations will codify "an association, in which the free development of each is a condition for the free development of all" (Marx and Engels, 1968, 53).

Naturally, communist society will place certain responsibilities on individuals. Even though free time will expand, individuals will still have a responsibility to engage in productive labor insofar as they are physically and mentally able to do so. Under capitalism and other class societies, "a particular class" has "the power to shift the natural burden of labour from its own shoulders to those of another layer of society" (Marx, 1967a, I, 530); under communism, "with labour emancipated, everyman becomes a working man, and productive labour ceases to be a class attribute" (1985, 75). More generally, individual self-development is not only a right but a responsibility under communism. Hence, "the workers assert in their communist propaganda that the vocation, designation, task of every person is to achieve all-round development of all his abilities, including, for example, the ability to think" (Marx and Engels, 1976, 309).

Marx's vision of human development under communism is further explored below; but first it is important to note the absence of market relations from Marx's projection. This is not an oversight on Marx's part, for there are many places where Marx contrasts communism's *directly* social labor with capitalism's *ex post* establishment of commodity-producing labor as social labor. In Marx's view, a system of freely associated producers, socially unified with necessary conditions of production, by definition excludes commodity exchange and money as forms of social production.

Marx argues that the domination of social production by the value form of wealth, including its component forms of money and price, is specific to a situation in which social production is carried out in independently organized production units on the basis of the producers' social separation from necessary conditions of production. Although the latter separation enables social (abstract) labor time to become the substance of wealth in its specifically capitalist form, it remains the case that the labors expended in the mutually autonomous production units can only be validated as part of society's reproductive division of labor *ex post,* according to the prices their products fetch in the market. In short, "commodities are the direct products of isolated independent individual kinds of labour" that cannot be directly "compared with one another as products of social labour"; hence "through their alienation in the course of individual exchange they must prove that they are general social labour, in other words, on the basis of commodity production, labour becomes social labour only as a result of the universal alienation of individual kinds of labour" (Marx, 1970, 84–85).

By contrast, "communal labour-time or labour-time of directly associated individuals . . . is *immediately social* labour-time" (85). As a result, "where labour is communal, the relations of men in their social production do not manifest themselves as 'values' of 'things'" (1971, 129):

> Within the co-operative society based on common ownership of the means of production, the producers do not exchange their products; just as little

does the labour employed on the products appear here *as the value* of these products, as a material quality possessed by them, since now, in contrast to capitalist society, individual labour no longer exists in an indirect fashion but directly as a component part of the total labour. (1966, 8)

The *Grundrisse* contains an important passage describing the difference between the indirect, *ex post* establishment of labor as social labor under capitalism and the direct, *ex ante* establishment of labor as social labor "on the basis of common appropriation and control of the means of production" (1973, 159):

> The communal character of production would make the product into a communal, general product from the outset. The exchange which originally takes place in production—which would not be an exchange of exchange values but of activities, determined by the communal needs and communal purposes—would from the outset include the participation of the individual in the communal world of products. On the basis of exchange values, labour is *posited* as general only through *exchange*. But on this foundation it would be *posited* as such before exchange; i.e., the exchange of products would in no way be the *medium* by which the participation of the individual in general production is mediated. Mediation must, of course, take place. In the first case, which proceeds from the independent production of individuals . . . mediations take place through the exchange of commodities, through exchange values and through money. . . . In the second case, the *presupposition is itself mediated;* i.e., a communal production, communality, is presupposed as the basis of production. The labour of the individual is posited from the outset as social labour. . . . The product does not first have to be transposed into a particular form in order to attain a general character for the individual. Instead of a division of labour, such as is necessarily created with the exchange of exchange values, there would take place an organization of labour whose consequence would be the participation of the individual in communal consumption. (171–72)

The immediately social character of labor and products is thus a logical outcome of the new communal union between the producers and the conditions of production. This union negates the necessity for the producers to engage in monetary exchanges as a means of establishing a reproductive allocation of their labor enmeshed with natural and social conditions. The fact that the elimination of the commodity/money form and the overcoming of workers' social separation from the conditions of production are two aspects of the same phenomenon explains why, in at least one instance, Marx defines communism simply as "dissolution of the mode of production and form of society based on exchange value. Real positing of individual labour as social and vice versa" (1973, 264).[16] The close connection between the de-alienation of production conditions and communal, non-market control over production is reiterated in another passage in the *Grundrisse*:

> The very necessity of first transforming individual products or activities into *exchange value*, into *money*, so that they obtain and demonstrate their social *power* in this *objective* form, proves two things: (1) That individuals now produce only for society and in society; (2) that production is not *directly* social, is not "the offspring of association," which distributes labour internally. Individuals are subsumed under social production; social production exists outside them as their fate; but social production is not subsumed under individuals, manageable by them as their common wealth. (158)

In sum, commodity exchange is only "the bond natural to individuals within specific and limited relations of production"; the "alien and independent character" in which this bond "exists *vis-à-vis* individuals proves only that the latter are still engaged in the creation of the conditions of their social life, and that they have not yet begun, on the basis of these conditions, to live it" (Marx, 1973, 162).[17] Communist social life is, by contrast, disalienated insofar as it is based on "freely associated" production "consciously regulated . . . in accordance with a settled plan" (1967a, I, 80). With "the means of production in common, . . . the labour-power of all the different individuals is consciously applied as the combined labour-power of the community . . . in accordance with a definite social plan [which] maintains the proper proportion between the different kinds of work to be done and the various wants of the community" (78–79). Under communism, in short, "united co-operative societies are to regulate national production upon a common plan, thus taking it under their own control, and putting an end to the constant anarchy and periodical convulsions which are the fatality of capitalist production" (1985, 76). This "cooperative labor . . . developed to national dimensions" is not to be governed by any centralized state power; rather, "the system starts with the self-government of the communities" (1974a, 80; 1989b, 519). In this sense, communism can be defined as "the people acting for itself by itself," or "the reabsorption of the state power by society as its own living forces instead of as forces controlling and subduing it" (1985, 130, 153).

As noted earlier, Marx envisions associated production not just as a co-operative planning project but, more important, as a condition and result of free human development—a development already advanced by the revolutionary process leading to the establishment of the worker-community association.[18] This projection is most prominent in *The German Ideology,* where Marx and Engels observe that "the all-round realisation of the individual will only cease to be conceived as an ideal . . . when the impact of the world which stimulates the real development of the abilities of the individual is under the control of the individuals themselves, as the communists desire" (1976, 309). In class-exploitative societies, "personal freedom has existed only for the individuals who developed under the conditions of the ruling class"; under the "real community" of communism, "individuals obtain their freedom in and through their association" (87). Instead of opportunities for individual development being obtained mainly at the expense of others, as in class societies, the future "community" will provide "each individual [with] the means of cultivating his gifts in all directions; hence personal freedom becomes possible only within the community" (86). Among the means of individual self-development under communism are the consumption claims discussed earlier, which include not only private consumption claims (labor- or need-based, depending on whether the association is in its lower or higher phase), but also individual benefits from the "public goods" (e.g., education, health services, utilities, and old-age pensions) that are financed by deductions from the total product prior to its distribution among individual workers. Such public-good consumption is, according to Marx, "considerably increased in comparison with present-day society and it increases in proportion as the new society develops" (1966, 7).

Communism can represent a real union of *all* the producers with the conditions of production only if it ensures each individual's right to participate to the fullest of her or his ability in the cooperative utilization and development of these conditions. The highly socialized character of production means that "individuals must appropriate the existing totality of productive forces, not only to achieve self-activity, but, also, merely to safeguard their very existence" (Marx and Engels, 1976, 96). In order to be an effective vehicle of human development, this appropriation must not reduce individuals to minuscule, interchangeable cogs in a giant collective production machine operating outside their control in an alienated pursuit of "production for the sake of production." Instead, it must enhance "the development of *human* productive forces" capable of grasping and controlling social production at the human level in line with "the development of the richness of human nature as an end in itself" (Marx, 1968, 117–18; emphasis added). Although communist "appropriation [has] a universal character corresponding to . . . the productive forces," it also promotes "the development of the individual capacities corresponding to the material instruments of production." Because these instruments "have been developed to a totality and . . . only exist within a universal intercourse," their effective appropriation requires "the development of a totality of capacities in the individuals themselves" (Marx and Engels, 1976, 96). In short, "the genuine and free development of individuals" under communism is enabled by "the universal character of the activity of individuals on the basis of the existing productive forces" (465).

At the same time, Marx suggests that "the true realm of freedom," in the sense of "that development of human energy which is an end in itself . . . lies beyond the actual sphere of material production," that is, beyond that "labour which is determined by necessity and mundane considerations." Communism's "shortening of the working-day" enables this true realm of freedom to "blossom forth" by giving individuals more free time in which to enjoy the "material and intellectual advantages . . . of social development" (Marx, 1967a, I, 819–20). Free time is "time . . . for the free development, intellectual and social, of the individual" (530).[19] As such, "free time, *disposable time,* is wealth itself, partly for the enjoyment of the product, partly for free activity which—unlike labour—is not dominated by the pressure of an extraneous purpose which must be fulfilled, and the fulfillment of which is regarded as a natural necessity or a social duty" (1971, 257). Accordingly, with communism "the measure of wealth is . . . not any longer, in any way, labour time, but rather disposable time" (1973, 708). This is true even though labor is still a fundamental "substance of wealth," and labor time is still an important "measure of the *cost* of [wealth's] production . . . even if exchange-value is eliminated" (1971, 257).

In Marx's projection, the enhancement of free human development via reductions in work-time resonates positively with the development of human capabilities in the realm of production. The "quite different . . . free character" of directly associated labor, where "labour-time is reduced to a normal length and, furthermore, labour is no longer performed for someone else," means that "direct labour time itself cannot remain in the abstract antithesis to free time in which it appears from the perspective of bourgeois economy" (257; 1973, 712). The next section considers the ecological significance of free time as a measure of wealth together with the communist articulation of free time and work-time.

Associated Production Ecologically Considered

Many have questioned the economic practicality of associated production as envisioned by Marx—most prominently Nove (1983), who argues that a "feasible socialism" must use both central planning and commodity exchange to allocate resources.[20] However, even Marx's critics must admit that his vision of free human development based on cooperatively planned and administered production differs greatly from the regimented, statist 'socialisms' of the ex-U.S.S.R. and its satellites. But does Marx's projection offer a *pro-ecological* alternative to Soviet communism?[21] Here I consider whether Marx's communism represents a desirable form of society as measured by the seven ecological criteria proposed earlier: (1) the explicit recognition of society's *managerial responsibility* toward nature and its human appropriation; (2) systemic increases in *ecological knowledge and its social diffusion* among producers and communities; (3) *ecological risk aversion* based on a recognition of the limits to human knowledge of and control over natural processes; (4) social *cooperation* to effectively regulate human ecological impacts from the global level on down; (5) respect for and encouragement of *variety and diversity* in human ways of life; (6) an *ecological ethics* involving a shared sense of membership in a human community enmeshed with natural conditions; and (7) new, *pro-ecological definitions of wealth* explicitly recognizing the contribution of extra-human nature to human production and the limited character of natural conditions of any given quality.

Marx clearly envisions post-capitalist society as recognizing its responsibility to manage its use of natural conditions. This responsibility manifests itself in the eclipse of capitalist notions of land *ownership* by communal *user rights:*

> From the standpoint of a higher economic form of society, private ownership of the globe by single individuals will appear quite as absurd as private ownership of one man by another. Even a whole society, a nation, or even all simultaneously existing societies taken together, are not the owners of the globe. They are only its possessors, its usufructuaries, and, like *boni patres familias,* they must hand it down to succeeding generations in an improved condition. (1967a, III, 776)

The ecological significance of Marx's conception of communal property is further discussed below; the point worth emphasizing here is that Marx does not see this property as conferring a right to overexploit land and other natural conditions in order to serve the production and consumption needs of the associated producers. Instead, the association treats "the soil" and other natural conditions "as *eternal* communal property, an *inalienable* condition for the existence and reproduction of a chain of successive generations of the human race" (1967a, III, 812; emphases added). This built-in limitation of communal property rights to ensure long-run sustainability is strikingly similar to the position held by many indigenous American peoples, who believe that "the notion that any human, or group thereof, has sovereignty over any part of Mother Earth is a myth based upon the white man's Origin Story" (Hillerman, 1997, A23).[22]

Marx's insistence on the future society's responsibility toward the land follows from his projection of the unity of human and extra-human nature being realized in a higher form under communism. For Marx and Engels, people and nature are not "two separate 'things'"; hence they speak of people having "an historical nature *and* a natural history" (1976, 45; emphasis added). They observe how extra-human nature has been greatly altered by human production and development, so that "the nature that preceded human history . . . today no longer exists"; but they also recognize the ongoing importance of "natural instruments of production" in the use of which "individuals are subservient to nature" (46, 71). Communism, far from rupturing or trying to overcome the necessary unity of people and nature, makes this unity more transparent and places it at the service of a sustainable development of people as natural *and* social beings. Engels thus envisions the future society as one in which people will "not only feel but also know their oneness with nature" (1964a, 183). The young Marx goes so far as to define communism as "the unity of being of man with nature" (1964, 137). In a more practical vein, Marx refers to the ongoing necessity for communist society to "wrestle with Nature to satisfy [its] wants, to maintain and reproduce life." This involves "the associated producers rationally regulating their interchange with nature, bringing it under their common control" (1967a, III, 820). Such a rational regulation or "real conscious mastery of Nature" presumes, of course, that the producers have "become masters of their own social organisation" (Engels, 1939, 309).

Communism's acceptance of humanity's managerial responsibility toward nature is reflected in its "abolition of the contradiction between town and country," with its disruptive circulation of matter, as "one of the first conditions of communal life" (Marx and Engels, 1976, 72). As Engels puts it, the

> abolition of the antithesis between town and country is not merely possible. It has become a direct necessity of industrial production itself, just as it has become a necessity of agricultural production and, moreover, of public health. The present poisoning of the air, water and land can only be put an end to by the fusion of town and country. . . . Only a society which makes

possible the harmonious co-operation of its productive forces on the basis of one single vast plan can allow industry to settle in whatever form of distribution over the whole country is best adapted to its own development and the maintenance of development of the other elements of production. (1939, 323)[23]

In *Capital*, Marx foresees communism being built on a "higher synthesis" of "the old bond of union which held together agriculture and manufacture in their infancy." This new union is to work toward a "restoration" of "the naturally grown conditions for the maintenance of that circulation of matter" but "as a system, as a regulating law of social production, and under a form appropriate to the full development of the human race" (1967a, I, 505–6).[24]

The future communist society contains several features that could greatly enhance the level and diffusion of the knowledge needed for sound ecological management of production. Marx envisions an expansion of "technical schools (theoretical and practical) in combination with the elementary school" (1966, 20).[25] The "theoretical and practical" learning taking place in these schools will evidently represent new combinations of natural and social science. In the Paris Manuscripts, Marx projects that

natural science . . . will become the basis of *human* science, as it has already become the basis of actual human life, albeit in an estranged form. One basis for life and another basis for science is *a priori* a lie. . . . Natural science will in time incorporate into itself the science of man, just as the science of man will incorporate into itself natural science: there will be *one* science. (1964, 143)

The unification of natural and social science follows from communism's social re-unification of the producers with the conditions of production. Capitalism alienates science (and other production conditions) vis-à-vis the producers (see Chapter 11). By placing all kinds of scientific knowledge at the service of an exploitative division of labor, capital pushes the artificial division of natural and social science to an historical extreme. Communism's de-alienation of the conditions of production converts these conditions into means of the natural *and* social development of human beings, thereby negating the basis for false divisions between natural and social science.[26]

Marx also suggests that the younger members of communist society will experience "an early combination of productive labour with education"—presuming, of course, "a strict regulation of the working time according to the different age groups and other safety measures for the protection of children" (1966, 22).[27] Indeed, as noted at the end of the previous section, Marx foresees a positive interchange between the intellectual development of *all* the producers during work-time and (expanded) free time, respectively. The point is developed in the *Grundrisse:*

> Free time—which is both idle time and time for higher activity—has naturally transformed its possessor into a different subject, and he then enters into the direct production process as this different subject. This process is then both discipline, as regards the human being in the process of becoming; and, at the same time, practice, experimental science, materially creative and objectifying science, as regards the human being who has become, in whose head exists the accumulated knowledge of society. (Marx, 1973, 712)

Thus, for Marx, communism's expanded free time is not filled by orgies of consumption for consumption's sake but is rather a necessary condition for the free intellectual development of social individuals capable of mastering the scientifically developed forces of nature and social labor in environmentally *and* humanly rational fashion. The "increase of free time" appears here as "time for the full development of the individual" capable of "the grasping of his own history as a *process,* and the recognition of nature (equally present as practical power over nature) as his real body" (542). The intellectual development of workers during free time *and* work-time is clearly central to the process by which communist labor's "social character is posited . . . in the production process not in a merely natural, spontaneous form, but as an activity regulating all the forces of nature" (612).

As to the possible utilization of pre-capitalist ecological practices in post-capitalist society, I have already noted the similarity between Marx's conception of communist user rights and certain pre-capitalist traditions rejecting social *or* private sovereignty over the land. This similarity helps explain Marx's otherwise startling projection, near the end of his life, that the Russian commune could "become the *direct starting point* for the economic system towards which modern society tends" (1989d, 368). In Marx's view, this "still archaic" village-level system of "communal ownership of the land" could "form the natural basis of collective production and appropriation," provided the villages could be organized into a planned system of "cooperative labour . . . on a vast, nationwide scale" (356, 368). True, Russia could only convert its communes into a "fulcrum of social regeneration" by adapting the "positive results" of capitalism to her specific natural and social conditions; it would especially have to apply "the tools, the manure, the agronomic methods, etc.," that is, "all the means that are indispensable to collective labour" in agriculture (356, 362, 371). But there is no evidence of any innate aversion on Marx's part to the potential use of more traditional commune productive practices as appropriate. Indeed, Marx argues that the extant commune organization could "ease the transition from parcel labour to collective labour, which [the Russian peasant] already practises to a certain extent in the undivided grasslands, in land drainage and other undertakings of general interest" (356; cf. Foster, 1997, 288).

Marx and Engels do not refer directly to the shaping of communist production decisions by environmental risk aversion. But in pointing out the need to use a portion of the surplus product as a "reserve or insurance fund to provide against mis-adventures, disturbances through natural events, etc.," Marx does indicate that uncertain natural conditions and incomplete human control over natural processes continue to play a role even with communally planned production, especially in agriculture (1966, 7). These uncertainties are to be dealt with through "a continuous relative overproduction" based partly on a "calculation of probabilities" (1967a, II, 469; 1966, 7). "There must be on the one hand a certain quantity of fixed capital produced in excess of that which is directly required; on the other hand, and particularly, there must be a supply of raw materials, etc., in excess of the direct annual requirements (this applies especially to means of subsistence)" (1967a, II, 469).[28] Marx repeatedly emphasizes the need for such an insurance fund due to unpredictable and uncontrollable natural conditions:

> Entirely different from the replacement of wear and tear and from the work of maintenance and repair is *insurance,* which relates to destruction caused by extraordinary phenomena of nature, fire, flood, etc. . . . Considered from the point of view of society as a whole, there must be continuous overproduction, that is, production on a larger scale than is necessary for the simple replacement and reproduction of the existing wealth . . . so as to be in possession of the means of production required to compensate for the extraordinary destruction caused by accidents and natural forces. (177)

Far from connoting any complete human control or overcoming of natural limits, "this sort of over-production is tantamount to control by society over the material means of its own reproduction" in the limited sense of a more rational social regulation of the productive interchange between the producers and uncontrollable natural conditions (469). Hence, in his marginal notes on Adolph Wagner's *Lehrbuch der Politischen Oekonomie,* Marx projects that the associated producers "will direct production from the outset so that the yearly grain supply depends only to the very minimum on the variations in the weather; *the sphere of production—the supply-and the use-aspects thereof—is rationally regulated*" (1975, 188; emphasis added). It makes perfectly good sense for "the producers themselves . . . to spend a part of their labour, or of the products of their labour to insure their products, their wealth, or the elements of their wealth, against accidents, etc." (Marx, 1971, 357–58). "Within capitalist society," by contrast, uncontrollable natural conditions impart a needless "element of anarchy" to social production (1967a, II, 469).[29]

As noted above, Marx and Engels do envision a great expansion and broader social application of natural scientific knowledge under communism. But they see this knowledge as enhancing "real human freedom," not through a one-sided human domination of nature but rather through "an existence in harmony with the established laws of nature"—in line with the heightened social consciousness of the unity of humanity and nature referred to earlier (Engels, 1939, 126):

> Freedom does not consist in the dream of independence of natural laws, but in the knowledge of these laws, and in the possibility this gives of systematically making them work towards definite ends. This holds good in relation both to the laws of external nature and to those which govern the bodily and mental existence of men themselves—two classes of laws which we can separate from each other at most only in thought but not in reality. . . . Freedom therefore consists in the control over ourselves and over external nature which is founded on natural necessity. (125)

This conception of freedom does not deny the existence of definite limits to human knowledge and control over nature. The "established laws of nature" may, for example, encapsulate randomness and chaotic behavior in natural processes, thereby demarcating limits to the purposeful human manipulation of natural conditions. Presumably, in order to effectively "control" production "in harmony with" nature's laws, the associated producers must take such limits into account.[30] In this sense, at least, the Marx/Engels vision of communal production control is quite consistent with the principle of ecological risk aversion.

Marx's projection of communal property in the conditions of production arguably represents the kind of cooperative framework needed for an ecologically sound management of production. Here, it should first be noted that Marx and Engels insist on the extension of communal oversight to land and other natural "sources of life" (Marx, 1966, 5).[31] The "Association, applied to land" not only "brings to realization the original tendency inherent in land division, namely, equality" but "also reestablishes, now on a rational basis, no longer mediated by serfdom, overlordship and the silly mysticism of property, the intimate ties of man with the earth, since the earth ceases to be an object of huckstering" (1964, 103). As with other conditions of production, this "common property" in land "does not mean the restoration of the old original common ownership, but the institution of a far higher and more developed form of possession in common" (Engels, 1939, 151).

The potential for ecological management through a communalization of natural conditions is clear from Elinor Ostrom's survey of communal property systems in common pool resources (CPRs) (Ostrom, 1990), and from Peter Usher's analysis of "aboriginal property systems in land and resources" in Canada (Usher, 1993). Both authors argue that communal management is a credible alternative to either private property with markets or centralized government control. Experience shows, however, that communal systems are most effective when they are run through associations set up and governed by resource users themselves, where "user" is defined in the broad sense of anyone whose well-being is significantly dependent on the CPRs in question. These associations ensure "the formal recognition of a non-moneyed property interest . . . a property right that arises from use" (Usher, 1993, 102). This basically corresponds to Marx's conception of "self-government of the producers" based on communal appropriation of the conditions of production (Marx, 1985, 72).

In aboriginal-Canadian systems, for example, there was "universal involvement and consensus in management," so that "management and production were not separate functions." As a result, "management 'data' included accumulated historical experience" directly grasped by resource users themselves (Usher, 1993, 96). Similarly, Ostrom's broader survey of communal systems suggests that in the most successful ones, all (or at least most) of the "individuals affected by the operational rules" for appropriating CPRs "can participate in modifying" these rules (1990, 93). Normally, "the rights of appropriators to devise their own institutions are not challenged by external government authorities" (101). At the same time, the monitoring of compliance with appropriation rules (including audits of CPR conditions), and the imposition of sanctions against rules violators, are under the control of the appropriators themselves, either directly or via directly accountable agents (94). Successful systems also often feature "rapid access to low-cost local arenas to resolve conflicts among appropriators" (100).

In short, the successful communal CPR system is typically, just as in Marx's projection, "a working, not a parliamentary, body, executive and legislative at the same time"—with producers and communities wielding the knowledge needed to self-manage their system of appropriation from nature (Marx, 1985, 71). In addition, both Marx's projection and extant communal CPR systems contain "rights and obligations that defy a simple 'public or private' categorization." They both feature universal access rights *and* limitations on individual use (communal regulation of appropriation); hence both "resemble neither individualized private property systems nor common property (open access, state management) systems" (Usher, 1993, 93, 95). Both reject the notion that "land or wildlife" should be "considered a commodity that could be alienated to exclusive private possession"; both protect "the right to obtain sustenance" from nature; and they both insist on "obligations that go with the right"—above all the obligation to keep appropriation from nature within sustainable bounds (95–96). For both, in short, communal property is "in effect a right to both individual livelihood and collective identity and existence," one in which "people do not think of themselves as 'owning' land or wildlife in any private sense" (98).

Marxists looking to further extend Marx's vision of communism in ecological directions can learn much from contemporary research on communal CPR management. Ostrom, for example, emphasizes that in the most effective and sustainable systems, user rights are "well-tailored" to the CPRs being appropriated and to the broader system of social production within which such appropriation occurs. Not only do "appropriation rules . . . reflect the specific attributes of the particular resource," but they also "are related to local conditions and to provision rules requiring labor, materials, and/or money" (1990, 92). Penalties for violations of appropriation rules are likewise tailored to the severity of the infractions in both ecological and social terms, that is, in line with the losses of present and future use values (or risks thereof) that they generate (94). In addition, the "individuals or households who have rights to withdraw resource units from the CPR must be clearly defined, as must the boundaries of the CPR itself" (91). Here, Usher notes that aboriginal-Canadian systems often "combined principles of universal access and benefit within the group," with "territorial boundaries that were permeable according to social rules" (1993, 95). This is consistent with Ostrom's observations of communal property in larger-scale CPRs (e.g., regional and national water resources used for irrigation), which indicate the necessity of "multiple layers" of "nested" associations of users to regulate "appropriation, provision, monitoring, enforcement, conflict resolution, and governance activities" (1990, 101). Such research findings can lend some ecological concreteness to Marx's projection of the association as one in which "not only municipal administration, but the whole initiative hitherto exercised by the State [is] laid into the hands of the Commune" (1985, 72).

At the same time, contemporary researchers can learn a thing or two from Marx about the prerequisites of communal CPR management. Along with Marx's acute awareness of the importance of combining natural and social scientific insights, modern researchers could benefit from Marx's analysis of capital's social separation of the producers from necessary conditions of production—a separation that stands directly in the way of an ecologically sound management of these conditions to the benefit of the community as a whole. Any extension of communal CPR management to the entire system of human production—and this is what is required for an ecologically sound system—hinges on a broad diffusion of decision-making powers *and* scientific knowledge among producers and communities. It also hinges, as Marx emphasizes, on large reductions in individual work-times so that the producers will have sufficient free time to engage in communal management and to develop their managerial capabilities.[32] These changes are inconsistent with wage-labor and other key institutions of the capitalist economy (e.g., financial capital and market rents) that separate producers and communities from effective control over the conditions of production. The extension of communal CPR management is thus a direct infringement of the power of capital and its state functionaries. Without a frontal challenge to capitalist relations in favor of communal relations, extant pockets of communal CPR management will be isolated and marginalized by capital's ecologically unsound production on a global scale.

Is Marx's communist vision open to diverse forms of human production and community, as required for society to healthily enmesh itself with the variegated and evolving world of extra-human nature? The answer does not hinge directly on *The German Ideology's* projection of infinitely increased variety in individual human activity once the association dispenses with all specialization of individuals' tasks within its division of labor.[33] Even if this forecast is relevant only for a distant future, Marx's adherence to the variety/diversity criterion is arguably ensured by the potential for free human development that he sees created by capitalism and realized under communism.

Marx argues that capitalism is historically progressive insofar as it broadens and diversifies the natural and social conditions of human production, thereby making possible a richer development of individuals (see Chapter 11). Capitalism's development of *social* production opens up *individual* development to the universal scope and variety of human and extra-human nature. At the same time, however, capitalism restricts and degrades people and nature in line with its requirements of exploitable labor power and conditions amenable to its exploitation. Capital artificially simplifies, divides, and overextends the wealth-creating powers of labor and nature, partly by alienating scientific knowledge from producers and communities (see Chapters 7 and 11). The less restricted, more universal human development potentiated by capitalism can only be realized through an explicit communalization of the conditions of production and their conversion from means of capital accumulation into means of developing human beings. Given capital's socialization of production, free individual development and diversity in human ways of life require a communal regulation of production. Cooperation is thus a necessary means not only of an ecological production but also of individual self-development and human diversity.

Despite his references to the need for a reserve fund to insure against uncontrollable natural events, Marx does not address the diversification of communist production relations under the influence of variegated natural conditions. Nonetheless, Marx's analyses of production in general and capitalist production in particular show an acute awareness of how natural conditions help shape the organization of human production—and this awareness is often expressed in terms suggesting an ongoing mutual constitution of natural conditions and social production relations under communism (see Chapters 2, 3, and 6). In *Theories of Surplus Value,* for example, Marx points to "the fact that, in order to be exploited really in accordance with its nature, land requires different social relations" (1971, 301). In Volumes II and III of *Capital,* Marx analyzes how the circulation of capital and rents are each shaped (albeit anarchically, due to capitalism's exploitative and competitive relations) by the natural conditions specific to different kinds of agricultural and non-agricultural industry (see Burkett, 1998b, for details). These analyses demonstrate the need for an ecologically planned diversification of communism's productive and community organization. Such diversification falls naturally into Marx's vision of the communal regulation of society's material interchange with nature as a condition and result of free human development.

Whatever its exact organizational forms, an ecologically sound system of production can only be sustained socially if it is receptive to and reinforces an ecological ethics. Ecological values are at least as diverse as human ways of life; but to effectively resonate through the system of human appropriation from nature, these values must together constitute a *shared* sense of unity with and responsibility toward the land and other natural conditions as *shared* conditions of human life. In this sense, an ecological ethics is by definition a communal ethics. Marx's projection of the associated producers' shared sense of responsibility toward the land, based on a new system of communal property rights and the planned allocation of social labor enmeshed with natural conditions, has already been noted. Marx sees this communal responsibility as being reinforced by a broad diffusion of scientific knowledge and a correspondingly heightened consciousness of the land as a source of the "permanent necessities of life required by the chain of successive generations" (1967a, III, 617).

As a framework for ecological ethics, the communal setting envisioned by Marx is potentially far superior to capitalist private property and markets. Consider, for example, the market-based approach to greenhouse gas emissions, as championed by the U.S. government and corporate capital. This approach commodifies pollution (or clean air, depending on one's point of view) by "creating an international market in emission credits." As Michael J. Sandel points out, this could "undermine the ethic we should be trying to foster on the environment," because "turning pollution into a commodity to be bought and sold removes the moral stigma that is properly associated with it" (Sandel, 1997, A19). More specifically, "such trading would enable rich countries to buy their way out of commitments to reduce greenhouse gases," thus "mak[ing] pollution just another cost of doing business"—and this "may undermine the sense of shared responsibility that increased global cooperation requires" (A19). By comparison, communal property in the conditions of production and the cooperative utilization of these conditions, as envisioned by Marx, appears much more congenial to the needed sense of shared responsibility. Although there is never anything automatic about the creation of a shared ethics, Marx's communism potentially provides a framework within which alternative ecological values can be articulated, juxtaposed, and reconciled or chosen from—as opposed to their marginalization by or subsumption under monetary exchange values as under capitalism (cf. Stirling, 1993; Booth, 1994; Adams, 1996).

Some would argue that while Marx's communism may foster a shared sense of responsibility toward nature, this responsibility remains wedded to a Promethean conception of nature as primarily an instrument or subject of productive human labor. Alfred Schmidt, for example, suggests that even "when Marx and Engels complain about the unholy plundering of nature, they are not concerned with nature itself but with considerations of economic utility" (1971, 155). However, Marx's conception of use value in general and nature's use value in particular encompasses the full gamut of human needs, including aesthetic use values not reducible to the industrial processing of natural conditions (see Chapter 2). As David Pepper observes: "Marx did see nature's role as 'instrumental' to humans, but to him instrumental value did not mean merely economic or material. It included nature as a source of aesthetic, scientific and moral value" (1993, 64). Insofar as communism places use value in command of production, its wealth-creating priorities and activities will encompass the maintenance and improvement of natural wealth in all its aesthetic and material forms.[34]

Nonetheless, many have suggested that Marx's vision of communist wealth is anti-ecological because it features continued absolute growth of material production. Marx and Engels do, in fact, make many references to ongoing and even accelerated growth in the production of use values in the future association. However, before rushing to the conclusion that Marx's communism violates the ecological wealth criterion, two things should be noted about these growth projections. First, they are always made in close connection with Marx's vision of free and well-rounded human development, not with growth of material production and consumption for their own sake. Second, and of co-equal importance, they always refer to growth of wealth in a general sense not limited to the kinds of wealth involving industrial appropriation and processing of natural conditions.

In discussing the "higher phase of communist society," for example, Marx sets the "to each according to his needs" criterion in a broad human-developmental context, referring to a situation

> after the enslaving sub-ordination of individuals under division of labour, and therewith also the antithesis between mental and physical labour, has vanished; after labour, from a mere means of life, has itself become the prime necessity of life; after the productive forces have also increased *with the all-round development of the individual,* and *all* the springs of co-operative wealth flow more abundantly. (1966, 10; emphases added)

Whether the above projection is anti-ecological depends on the nature of co-operative wealth—especially the amount of material and energy throughput and the disruption of ecological interconnections that it entails. Communism's abundance of wealth and its all-round human development are ecologically sound insofar as they encompass nature's aesthetic and material use values in the context of a shared social responsibility to maintain and improve the quality of land and other natural conditions. The same goes for Engels' projection, in *Anti-Dühring,* of a "more rapidly progressing development of the productive forces, and therewith of a practically limitless growth of production itself" (1939, 308). The ecological connotations of this development and growth clearly hinge on the meaning of "practical" in this context—one closely connected, in Engels' view, with the communist priority "of securing for every member of society, through social production, an existence which is not only fully sufficient from a material standpoint . . . but also guarantees to them the completely unrestricted development and exercise of their physical and mental faculties" (309). Engels' projection is thus "ecologically correct" insofar as his conception of unrestricted individual development encompasses a healthy and sustainable natural *and* social environment.

Similar considerations apply to Marx's projections of growth in communist wealth as formulated in Volume III of *Capital.* Hence, when Marx indicates that the associated producers will "constantly expand reproduction to the extent dictated by social needs," the ecological connotations of such expanded reproduction clearly hinge on the nature of the needs to be satisfied (1967a, III, 876). For Marx, communism's "progressive expansion of the process of reproduction" encompasses the entire "living process of the *society* of producers"—not just material production and consumption (819, 250). And as discussed earlier, Marx specifies the "material and intellectual advantages" of this "social development" in terms of the less restricted development of people as natural *and* social beings, both at work and in free time (819). Hence, when Marx and Engels envision communism as "an organisation of production and intercourse which will make possible the normal satisfaction of needs, i.e., a satisfaction which is limited only by the needs themselves," they do not mean a complete satiation of limitlessly expanding needs of all kinds, including the type of anti-ecological mass consumption characteristic of capitalism (1976, 273). They mean a satisfaction of the needs associated with a less restricted, all-round development of producers and communities. Although communism entails a freer development and satisfaction of some needs, it also involves important changes in the way needs are satisfied and even outright reductions in certain needs generated by capitalism's class-exploitative relations:

> Communist organisation has a twofold effect on the desires produced in the individual by present-day relations; some of these desires—namely desires which exist under all relations, and only change their form and direction

under different social relations—are merely altered by the communist social system, for they are given the opportunity to develop normally; but others—namely those originating solely in a particular society, under particular conditions of production and intercourse—are totally deprived of their conditions of existence. Which will be merely changed and which eliminated in a communist society can only be determined in a practical way. (Marx and Engels, 1976, 273)

As Ernest Mandel points out, this social-relational and human-developmental approach to need satisfaction is quite different from the "absurd notion" of unqualified "abundance" often ascribed to Marx, that is, "a regime of unlimited access to a boundless supply of all goods and services" (Mandel, 1992, 205). In addition to being "a nightmare" both ecologically and socially, the latter notion directly contradicts Marx's historical projection of communist abundance:

A moment of reflection will lead one to realize that to assume the "limitless" expansion of "needs" and individual consumption is actually to deny the feasibility of communism. Material abundance would be impossible, and the mercantile categories, which in fact correspond to a state of semi-scarcity of goods and economic resources, would survive. (1992, 205; 1973, 71)

Although Marx's vision of communist need satisfaction is consistent with a "definition of abundance [as] *saturation of demand,*" this has to be set in the context of a division of needs into a "hierarchy" of "basic needs, secondary needs that become indispensable with the growth of civilization, and luxury, inessential or even harmful needs" (Mandel, 1992, 206–07; see also Mandel, 1986, 14–18).[35] Marx's conception of communist abundance foresees a satiation of basic needs and a gradual extension of this satiation to secondary needs as they develop socially in the context of expanded free time and cooperative worker-community control over social production—*not* a full satiation of all conceivable needs (cf. Sherman, 1970). In Marx's projection, the producers will tend to use their newfound material security and increased free time to engage in a variety of intellectual and aesthetic forms of self-realization and self-development. This development of secondary needs is to be enhanced by the greater opportunities that real worker-community control provides for people to become informed participants in economic, political, and cultural life (as opposed to their current status mainly as hierarchically directed laborers and passive consumers).

It is in this last context that the full ecological significance of free time as a measure of communist wealth becomes clear. For insofar as the secondary needs developed and satisfied during free time are less material and energy intensive, their increasing weight in total needs reduces the pressure of communist reproduction on natural conditions, *ceteris paribus*. Besides, reductions in work-time directly lessen productive material and energy throughput, *ceteris paribus*. In particular, increases in the productivity of social labor do not entail rising material and energy throughput insofar as they are compensated by reductions in work-time (Gorz, 1994). And as noted earlier, Marx envisions the use of free time for developing environmental sensibilities, such that producers and communities become more and more practically aware of the role of natural wealth as an eternal condition of production and of free time itself.

Of course, since labor *and* nature are both still sources of wealth, the amount of social labor time expended in the production of different products is still an important measure of their *cost* under communism. As Marx puts it in *Capital:* "In all states of society, the labour-time that it costs to produce the means of subsistence, must necessarily be an object of interest to mankind" (1967a, I, 71). Social reproduction requires an allocation of labor among need-satisfying activities; hence "*no form* of society can prevent the working time at the disposal of society from regulating production one way or another" (Marx to Engels, January 8, 1868, in Marx and Engels [1975, 187]). As a result:

> On the basis of communal production, the determination of time remains, of course, essential. The less time the society requires to produce wheat, cattle etc., the more time it wins for other production, material or mental. Just as in the case of an individual, the multiplicity of its development, its enjoyment and its activity depends on economization of time. Economy of time, to this all economy ultimately reduces itself. Society likewise has to distribute its time in a purposeful way, in order to achieve a production adequate to its overall needs; just as the individual has to distribute his time correctly in order to achieve knowledge in proper proportions or in order to satisfy the various demands on his activity. Thus, economy of time, along with the planned distribution of labour time among the various branches of production, remains the first economic law on the basis of communal production. It becomes law, there, to an even higher degree. (Marx, 1973, 172–73)

Marx immediately adds, however, that communism's economy of time "is essentially different from a measurement of exchange values (labour or products) by labour time" (1973, 173). His reasoning here is straightforward: communism's economy of time serves use value, whereas capitalism's economy of time reduces use values (including useful labor and natural conditions) to vehicles of value and capital accumulation. For example, the communist economy of labor time supports reductions of work-time (increases in *human* wealth as measured by free time), but capital's economy of time is oriented toward increasing the surplus labor time expended by the producers (increases in *capitalist* wealth as measured by surplus value).[36] This divergence between the two economies of time is ecologically significant, given the positive ecological potential of increased free time and the anti-ecological character of surplus-value accumulation (see Chapter 7).

Marx and Engels never project labor cost as the sole guide for resource-allocation decisions under communism: they only indicate that it is to be *one important* measure of the social cost associated with different use values. Moreover, this use of labor time as a measure of cost "is accomplished . . . by the direct and conscious control of society over its working time— which is possible only with common ownership," unlike the situation under capitalism, where the "regulation" of social labor time is only accomplished indirectly, "by the movement of commodity prices" (Marx to Engels, January 8, 1868, in Marx and Engels [1975, 187]). According to Marx: "It is only where production is under the actual, predetermining control of society that the latter establishes a relation between the volume of social labour-time applied in producing definite articles, and the volume of the social want to be satisfied by these articles" (1967a, III, 187). Obviously, the establishment of *a relation* between labor cost and social want need not imply that labor time is the sole cost taken into account. Alternatively, communist planning could include the maintenance and improvement of natural conditions (along with increases in free time) under the category of "the social wants to be satisfied" by the system of production and consumption.

Whether environmental goals are included under social costs or social benefits is less important than the overriding priority of use value in Marx's projection. Given Marx's insistence on nature's contribution to use value, there is nothing inherently anti-ecological about the continued use of labor time as an important measure of cost in the future association. Marx's communism would, for one thing, dispense with the waste of nature *and* labor associated with capitalism's "anarchical system of competition" and "vast number of employments . . . in themselves superfluous" (1967a, I, 530). Many anti-ecological use values could be eliminated or greatly reduced under a planned system of labor allocation and land-use, among them the excessive processing and packaging of food and other goods, advertising, the automobile/real estate/petroleum complex, and the planned obsolescence of products. All these destructive use values are "indispensable" for capitalism; from the standpoint of an ecologically sound system, however, they represent "the most outrageous squandering of labour-power and of the social means of production" (1967a, I, 530; cf. Bahro, 1978, 428–30; Gorz, 1994, 31–34).

Marx and Engels do not envision communism as prioritizing minimum labor cost over all ecological and other use-value goals. Not only is economy of labor time treated as a means to the higher end of use value, including expanded free time, but there is also strong evidence that the founders of Marxism would gladly accept some increase in necessary labor time in return for a more ecologically sound production. Hence Engels, after describing the "abolition of the antithesis between town and country" as "a direct necessity of . . . production and, moreover, of public health," goes on to ridicule Dühring's projection "that the union between agriculture and industry will nevertheless be carried through even *against* economic considerations, as if this would be some economic sacrifice!" (1939, 323–24). Clearly, what bothers Engels is not just Dühring's inadequate appreciation of nature as a necessary condition of production, but also Dühring's failure to see that if communism is at all distinct from capitalism it is because the former's production is dictated by use value, and that this involves a more human, social, and ecological definition of economic necessity. This is precisely how the ecological wealth criterion is fulfilled by Marx's vision of communism.

Concluding Remark

This chapter has established the consistency of Marx's vision of communism with an ecologically sound human production. Associated production, with increases in free time and material security for the producers, represents a potentially congenial human and social context for healthy and sustainable people-nature relations—relations less pressured by class-exploitative forms of material necessity or "shortage." The realization of this potential hinges on a new social union of producers and communities with the conditions of production, that is, a collective appropriation, utilization, and development of these conditions in line with cooperatively determined use-value goals. Marx envisions this union taking the form of communal property in the conditions of production, where "property" connotes user rights and responsibilities rather than the rights of "owners" (either individuals or society as a whole) to unrestricted use based on "possession." This communal property is designed to promote the free development of human beings (compared to class societies) while protecting the interests of future generations in a sustainable appropriation from nature— one that maintains and even improves the quality of natural wealth. In Marx's vision, the de-alienation of the conditions of production includes a broad diffusion of the scientific knowledge required for effective communal management of natural conditions and their appropriation in the social labor process.

Underlying the ecological potential of Marx's vision is an interesting paradox. Only through "a real social communality," in which "all relations are posited by society, not as determined by nature," does it become possible for society to co-evolve more harmoniously with nature, "the direct wellspring of subsistence" (Marx, 1973, 276). If people want to develop as natural beings, they must develop further as social beings, and achieve an explicit socialization of the natural conditions of production. We cannot overcome natural necessity—we cannot conquer nature; but neither can we ignore the conscious, social, and cumulative character of human production by taking refuge in an idealized, unmediated nature that no longer exists. The development of human production is no longer predetermined by nature as such. So if we want to live with nature, we must master our social organization.

Notes

Foreword

1. John Bellamy Foster, *Marx's Ecology* (New York: Monthly Review Press, 2000), ix. Burkett and I corresponded and inspired each other throughout the 1990s. While he was developing on Marx's ecological-value analysis I was working on the concept of metabolic rift. See John Bellamy Foster, "Marx's Theory of Metabolic Rift," *American Journal of Sociology* 105, no. 2 (September 1999): 366–405. In both areas our work overlapped.

2. It is a testimony to the power of Burkett's analysis that it gave centrality to the concept of value form, a category that has come to be regarded as increasingly central to the interpretation of Marx's value analysis. Part of this was due to the influence of I. I. Rubin's work on Burkett's thinking as well Burkett's own deep appreciation of the logic of Marx's analysis. On this see Burkett, *Marx and Nature*, chapter 3; also I. I. Rubin, *Essays on Marx's Theory of Value* (Detroit: Black and Red, 1972), 107–23; Michael Heinrich, *An Introduction to the Three Volumes of Karl Marx's 'Capital'* (New York: Monthly Review Press, 2012), 52–64.

3. Here it should be mentioned that a brilliant precursor of Burkett's analysis of the ecological implications of Marx's value analysis was Elmar Altvater, *The Future of Money* (London: Verso, 1993). Altvater, however, stopped short of a systematic development of Marx's analysis in this area.

4. The discussion of first-stage and second-stage ecosocialism in this and the following paragraphs draws on John Bellamy Foster, "Environmental Politics: Analyses and Alternatives" (a review), *Historical Materialism* 8 (Summer 2001): 461–77. See also Paul Burkett, " Two Stages of Ecosocialism?: Implications of Some Neglected Analyses of Ecological Conflict and Crisis," *International Journal of Political Economy* 35, no. 3 (Fall 2006): 23–45.

5. See André Gorz, *Capitalism, Socialism, Ecology* (London: Verso, 1994); Ted Benton, "Marxism and Natural Limits," *New Left Review* 178 (November–December 1989): 51–86; James O'Connor, *Natural Relations* (New York: Guilford Press, 1998); Alain Lipietz, " Political Ecology and the Future of

Marxism," *Capitalism, Nature, Socialism* 11 (2000): 69–85; Joel Kovel, *The Enemy of Nature* (London: Zed, 2002).

6. Gorz, *Capitalism, Socialism, and Ecology*, vii, 29; Lipietz, "Political Ecology," 74–75.

7. Raymond Williams, *Problems in Materialism and Culture* (London: Verso, 1980), 185, 106–14.

8. Kovel, *Enemy of Nature*, 210-11.

9. Kovel, *Enemy of Nature*, ix. In a similar way, *An Ecosocialist Manifesto*, authored by Kovel and Michael Löwy in 2001, sees ecosocialism as the heir to what it calls "first-epoch socialism": http://www.iefd.org/manifestos/ecosocialist_manifesto.php.

10. Georg Lukács, *History and Class Consciousness* (London: Merlin Press, 1971), 1.

11. In addition to Burkett's *Marx and Nature*, particularly chapter 9, see Foster, *Marx's Ecology*, 141–77, and John Bellamy Foster, "Capitalism and the Accumulation of Catastrophe," *Monthly Review* 63, no. 7 (December 2011): 1–17.

12. Karl Marx and Frederick Engels, *Collected Works* (New York: International Publishers 1975), vol. 30, 63. Sebastiano Timpanaro's interpretation of Marx's materialism, which suggests that Marx saw nature as "passive" and denies its active principles, is strongly criticized in Foster, *Marx's Ecology*, 258.

13. Karl Marx, *Capital*, vol. 1 (London: Penguin, 1976), 290.

14. Marx, *Capital*, vol. 1, 638.

15. Marx and Engels, *Collected Works*, vol. 30, 63.

16. Karl Marx, *Capital*, vol. 3 (London: Penguin, 1981), 911, 959.

17. See, for example, Hanna Wittman, "Reworking the Metabolic Rift: La Via Campesina, Agrarian Citizenship, and Food Sovereignty," *Journal of Peasant Studies* 36, no. 4 (October 2009): 805–26.

18. Paul Burkett, *Marxism and Ecological Economics: Toward a Red and Green Economy* (Chicago: Haymarket, [2006] 2009), vii.

19. Paul Burkett, "Marx's Vision of Sustainable Human Development," *Monthly Review* 57, no. 5 (October 2005): 34–62.

20. See, for example, Jason W. Moore, "Transcending the Metabolic Rift," *Journal of Peasant Studies* 38, no. 1 (2011): 1–46; John Bellamy Foster, Brett Clark, and Richard York, *The Ecological Rift* (New York: Monthly Review Press, 2010); John Bellamy Foster, "The Ecology of Marxian Political Economy," *Monthly Review* 63, no. 4 (September 2011): 1-16; Ariel Salleh, "From Metabolic Rift to 'Metabolic Value,'" *Organization and Environment* 23, no. 2 (2010): 205–19; and Chris Williams, *Ecology and Socialism* (Chicago: Haymarket, 2010).

21. A high point here was the 2010 Peoples' Agreement in Bolivia, reprinted in Fred Magdoff and John Bellamy Foster, *What Every Environmentalist Needs to Know About Capitalism* (New York: Monthly Review).

Introduction to the Haymarket Edition

1. To avoid misunderstanding, whenever I refer singularly to Marx this is meant to include the work of Engels as well. I do not believe there were any fundamental disagreements between Marx and Engels on the treatment of nature in political economy and history.

2. The main variant of the "Promethean" charge that was *not* addressed in *Marx and Nature* involved Marx's reference to nature as "the inorganic body of man" in his *Economic and Philosophical Manuscripts of 1844* (Karl Marx, *Early Writings* (New York: Vintage, 1974), 328). This statement has often been interpreted as a simple denial of any close ("organic") connection between human beings and nature, and thus as evidence of Marx's anti-ecological leanings, his tendency to treat nature as a purely instrumental value, etc. (The most influential example of this kind of interpretation is John P. Clark, "Marx's Inorganic Body," *Environmental Ethics* 11, no. 3 (Fall 1989), 243–58). In more recent work, John Bellamy Foster and I investigated Marx's use of the term "inorganic" in light of: (1) the prior usage of the organic/inorganic distinction in classical and Hegelian philosophy; (2) Marx's studies of natural science, including Darwin; and (3) Marx's discussions of tools and machines as "organs" of human labor in *Capital* and related writings (John Bellamy Foster and Paul Burkett, "The Dialectic of Organic/Inorganic Relations," *Organization & Environment* 13, no. 4, December 2000, 403–25). We concluded—to quote our reply to two critics of our main article in this area—that "Marx's dialectical reference to nature as the inorganic body of man was meant . . . to convey that human beings and nature were connected together even *bodily* . . . but that human beings related to nature as extensions of their bodies—through tool making—beyond their own bodily organs (i.e., 'inorganically' in this sense). By using the term *inorganic*, Marx was therefore not attempting to divide human beings from nature . . . but merely seeking to define the character and limits of that relationship and the centrality of *tool making* in human evolution as an 'inorganic' extension of mere bodily organs" (John Bellamy Foster and Paul Burkett, "Marx and the Dialectic of Organic/Inorganic Relations," *Organization & Environment* 14, no. 4 (December 2001), 452). Indeed, it turns out that Marx's use of the organic/inorganic concepts finds a close parallel in the modern-day distinction between *endosomatic* and *exosomatic* instruments—as employed by ecological economics "since the days of Alfred Lotka" to help explain ecological crises (ibid). In short, once one unpacks the whole "inorganic" business in a serious way, it ends up testifying not just to Marx's great sensitivity to the role of natural conditions in human production, but to the relevance of his whole approach for the understanding of contemporary ecological problems!

3. Indeed, Marx goes so far as to repeatedly point out the "natural basis of surplus value," specifically the fact that workers in agriculture must be capable

of producing a surplus of foodstuffs in order for any surplus product or surplus value to exist in the economy as a whole—which obviously depends on natural conditions. See chapter 3 below; also Burkett, *Marxism and Ecological Economics*, chapter 1.

4. These processes are the ones Ted Benton labels "eco-regulatory" in his important article "Marxism and Natural Limits," *New Left Review* 178 (November–December 1989), 51–86. For my response to his argument that Marx's analysis leaves such processes out of account, see chapter 3 below and, in somewhat more detail, Paul Burkett, "Labor, Eco-Regulation, and Value," *Historical Materialism* 3 (Winter 1998), 119–44.

5. It is worth noting that Marx develops the basic category of *fixed capital* in similarly dialectical terms, as an outgrowth of tensions between value and the materiality of production.

6. Foster, *Marx's Ecology*.

7. Foster, Brett and York, *Ecological Rift*.

8. John Bellamy Foster and Brett Clark, "Ecological Imperialism," in *Socialist Register 2004: The New Imperial Challenge*, edited by Leo Panitch and Colin Leys (New York: Monthly Review Press, 2004), 230–46; Jason W. Moore, "Environmental Crises and the Metabolic Rift in World-Historical Perspective," *Organization & Environment* 13, no. 2 (June 2000), 123–57.

9. See John Bellamy Foster, *The Ecological Revolution: Making Peace with the Planet* (New York: Monthly Review Press, 2009), chapter 10; Foster, "Environmental Politics: Analyses and Alternatives" Burkett, "Two Stages of Ecosocialism?; Burkett, *Marxism and Ecological Economics*.

10. Marx sees human labor power as a common-pool resource, i.e., as a basic requirement for the sustainable reproduction of society as a whole. As demonstrated in chapter 10 below, Marx's treatment of capital's tendency to overexploit this resource by lengthening and intensifying work time should be seen as a model of environmental crisis—not a crisis in the profitability *of* capital accumulation, but rather one of vitiation of the conditions of human development *by* capital accumulation. For further details on the interesting combination of class and environmental analysis employed by Marx in this context, see Paul Burkett, "Natural, Social, and Political Limits to Work Time: The Contemporary Relevance of Marx's Analysis," in *Working Time: International Trends, Theory and Policy*, edited by Lonnie Golden and Deborah M Figart (London: Routledge, 2000), 143–58.

11. On the importance of recognizing how capital can profit from the damage that it causes to nature, see Paul Burkett, "Fusing Red and Green," *Monthly Review* 50, no. 9 (February 1999), 47–56; also Burkett, "Two Stages of Ecosocialism?," and Burkett, *Marxism and Ecological Economics*, especially chapters 5 and 7–9.

12. The primary sources for these claims are Joan Martinez-Alier, *Ecological Economics* (Oxford: Basil Blackwell, 1987), and Joan Martinez-Alier and

J. M. Naredo, "A Marxist Precursor of Ecological Economics: Podolinsky," *Journal of Peasant Studies* 9, no. 2 (1982), 207–24. For additional writings by Martinez-Alier and others influenced by his arguments, see the citations in the articles referenced in note 13 below.

13. John Bellamy Foster and Paul Burkett, "Ecological Economics and Classical Marxism: The 'Podolinsky Business' Reconsidered," *Organization & Environment* 17, no. 1 (March 2004), 32–60; "Metabolism, Energy, and Entropy in Marx's Critique of Political Economy: Beyond the Podolisky Myth," *Theory and Society* 35, no. 1 (February 2006), 109–56; "The Podolinsky Myth: An Obituary," *Historical Materialism* 16, no. 1 (2008), 115–61; "Classical Marxism and the Second Law of Thermodynamics: Marx/Engels, the Heat Death of the Universe Hypothesis, and the Origins of Ecological Economics," *Organization & Environment* 21, no. 1 (March 2008), 3–37. As part of this effort, Foster and I arranged for the first English-language translations of Podolinsky's work, which had taken the form of four separate but overlapping articles published in French, Italian, German, and Russian. So far we have edited and published translations of the Italian and German versions. For the Italian, see Sergei Podolinsky, "Socialism and the Unity of Physical Forces," translated by Angelo Di Salvo and Mark Hudson, *Organization & Environment* 17, no. 1 (March 2004), 61–75; for the German, see Sergei Podolinsky, "Human Labor and Unity of Force," *Historical Materialism* 16, no. 1 (2008), 163–83.

14. Foster and Burkett, "Classical Marxism and the Second Law."

15. Foster and Burkett, "Ecological Economics and Classical Marxism," 50–54; "The Podolinsky Myth," 133–40.

16. See Foster and Burkett, "The Podolinsky Myth," 145–49; "Metabolism, Energy, and Entropy," 119–29; Burkett, *Marxism and Ecological Economics*, 182–93.

17. Herman E. Daly, *Steady-State Economics*, 2nd ed. (London: Earthscan, 1992), 23. For further discussion of the solar budget constraint, see Burkett, *Marxism and Ecological Economics*, 199–201.

18. Foster and Burkett, "Metabolism, Energy, and Entropy," 130–37; "The Podolinsky Myth," 149–51; Burkett, *Marxism and Ecological Economics*, 193–202.

19. Andreas Malm, "The Origins of Fossil Capital: From Water to Steam in the British Cotton Industry," *Historical Materialism* 21, no. 1 (2013), 15–68.

20. Marx, *Capital*, Volume III (New York: Vintage, 1976), 949–50. As Marx phrases it in one of the preparatory works for *Capital*: "Anticipation of the future—real anticipation—occurs in the production of wealth in relation to the worker and to the land. The future can indeed be anticipated and ruined in both cases by premature overexertion and exhaustion, and by the disturbance of the balance between expenditure and income. In capitalist production this happens to both the worker and the land. . . . What is

expended here exists as power and the life span of this power is shortened
as a result of accelerated expenditure" (*Theories of Surplus Value*, Part III,
Moscow: Progress Publishers, 1971, 309–10). As Foster and I have pointed
out, Marx here and in other passages adapts the energy income and expenditure model of human labor proposed by the German physiologist
Ludimar Hermann, i.e., an explicitly bio-thermodynamic framework, for
analyzing labor power and its exploitation by capital. For this and other
connections between Marx's scientific studies and his political economy,
see Foster and Burkett, "The Podolinsky Myth," 147–48; "Metabolism,
Energy, and Entropy," 120–23.

21. For instance, Martinez-Alier asserts that Marx ignored Podolinsky's work.
But we now know that Marx did no such thing, that he in fact compiled
detailed extract notes and comments on a rough draft of the French ver-
sion of Podolinsky's analysis (the most rudimentary of the four versions
even in its published form). While conferring with Engels on Podolinsky's
work, Marx probably sent comments back to Podolinsky on the copy of
the manuscript he had received. (See Foster and Burkett, "Ecological Economics and Classical Marxism," 49–50.) We hope to publish an English
translation of Marx's notes on Podolinsky in the near future as part of a
book project that synthesizes our research on classical Marxism and thermodynamics.

22. A related, but less influential, critique of Marx argues that the reproduction
schemes in Volume II of *Capital* have the same ecological defects as the "cir-
cular flow" models in mainstream introductory economics textbooks.
Hence Georgescu-Roegen complained that: "In Marx's famous diagram of
reproduction, . . . the economic process is represented as a completely cir-
cular and self-sustaining affair . . . a completely closed system" (Nicholas
Georgescu-Roegen, "The Entropy Law and the Economic Problem," in
Economics, Ideology, Ethics, edited by Herman E. Daly, San Francisco: W. H.
Freeman, 1873, 50). Basically, Georgescu-Roegen argued that Marx's reproduction schemes violated the first and second laws of thermodynamics.
In an article published after *Marx and Nature*, I rebutted this criticism by detailing how: (1) Marx's reproduction schemes encapsulate the dependence
of production on natural conditions as established elsewhere in *Capital*; (2)
these reproduction schemes are not meant to theorize environmental crises,
but merely to set out the basic exchanges necessary for capitalist reproduction as a material and social class process. See Paul Burkett, "Marx's Reproduction Schemes and the Environment," *Ecological Economics* 49, no. 4
(August 2004), 457–67.

23. For more recent work by Michael Lebowitz, see *Beyond Capital: Marx's Political Economy of the Working Class*, 2nd ed. (New York: Palgrave Macmillan, 2003), and *Build It Now: Socialism for the Twenty-First Century* (New
York: Monthly Review Press, 2006).

24. I was not quite as conscious of this shift when I wrote *Marx and Nature* as I became in subsequent years. See, for example, Paul Burkett, "Marx's Vision of Sustainable Human Development," *Monthly Review* 57, no. 5 (October 2005), 34–62. Here again, the work of Michael Lebowitz helped me to more clearly understand the issues at stake. See especially Lebowitz, *Build It Now*.

25. *Capital*, Vol. III (New York: Vintage, 1981), 959.

26. *Marxism and Ecological Economics*, 15. See ibid., Chapter 10.

27. On "accumulation by dispossession," see David Harvey, *The New Imperialism* (Oxford: Oxford University Press, 2003).

28. David Barkin, *Wealth, Poverty and Sustainable Development* (Mexico City: Centro de Ecologia y Desarrollo, 1998).

Introduction

1. See Foster (1997, 279–80) for a useful discussion of the use and abuse of Parsons' (1977) work by Marx's ecological critics.

2. This statement applies to those left-ecological critics who explicitly reject capitalism as a basis for an ecologically sound society. Many of Marx's critics, of course, continue to assert that capitalism is quite capable of providing such a basis. In both cases, however, the real point of contention is the historically specific, class-relational character of value itself and its shaping of people-nature relations. Consider, for example, Löwy's call for a system of "incorporating ecological costs in calculating value" (1997, 34), as if value—the specifically capitalist representation of wealth as abstract labor time—were not, by definition, incapable of such an "incorporation" (see Chapter 7). It is striking to find Löwy apparently endorsing the claims of neoclassical economists that the market system is capable of adequately registering nature's contribution to wealth.

3. This is not to deny that Marx gave considerable thought to the natural sciences. Unfortunately, as pointed out in Pradip Baksi's (1996) very useful account, Marx's evidently voluminous natural science notebooks remain mostly unpublished. Perhaps more important, even Marx's natural scientific investigations were also apparently designed to support his primary goal: "to find out the exact location of the rest of nature in the sociohistorical activities of human beings" (ibid., 268).

4. Some feel that such a "productivist" perspective is inherently anti-ecological, but this involves an overly narrow interpretation of what Marx means by production (see, for starters, Chapter 2).

5. On the importance of the dialectic of social form and material content, especially in Marx's analysis of capitalism, see Rosdolsky (1977), Clarke (1994), and Smith (1990 and 1997).

6. Here as elsewhere, all emphases in quoted passages are as in the original, unless otherwise noted.

7. This auxiliary work, essential as it is to the proper interpretation of Marx, is unfortunately rarely undertaken in any meaningful way by Marx's ecological critics—"eco-Marxists" included.

8. Even in 1844, however, Marx did succeed in specifying the basic problem posed by the value form. For instance, in speaking of exchange as "the social, generic act" under capitalism, he notes that here "private property appears as a representative of private property of a different nature, as the *equivalence* of another natural product. . . . As an *equivalent* its existence is no longer something peculiarly appropriate to it. It has become *value* and immediately *exchange value*. Its existence as *value* is a determination of *itself*, different from its immediate existence, outside of its specific nature, and *externalized*—only a *relative* existence" (Marx, 1967b, 274). This passage has a familiar ring to anyone who has read the value-form analysis in Part I of *Capital*, Volume I, where Marx makes good his earlier promise that "it will be shown elsewhere how this *value* is more precisely determined and how it becomes *price*" (ibid.).

9. This strategy is, of course, diverted insofar as Marx's ecological critics refer to the Paris Manuscripts and other early works in more indiscriminate fashion.

10. Many of the attempts to build methodological walls between Marx and Engels have been designed "to detach Engels' *Anti-Dühring* from Marx's seal of approval" (Draper, 1977–90, I, 24)—despite the fact that Marx not only publicly endorsed the book in 1880, two years after its initial publication (Marx, 1989c), but even contributed a chapter to it, in line with Marx's earlier statement that he and Engels "both work to a common plan and by prior arrangement" (1982, 99). A particularly questionable but influential attempt to discredit *Anti-Dühring* is Terrell Carver's argument that (1) Engels lied about Marx having read and approved the book, and (2) Marx formally endorsed the book (for party publication, no less) because he "felt it easier, in view of their long friendship, their role as leading socialists, and the usefulness of Engels' financial resources, to keep quiet and not to interfere in Engels' work" (Carver, 1980, 360–61)! Carver manufactures these charges on the basis of the relative paucity of surviving correspondence between Marx and Engels concerning the book—ignoring the fact that their correspondence on all issues "naturally fell to an intermittent trickle" when Engels moved to London in 1870, after which "the two talked over issues and affairs virtually every day" (Draper, 1977–90, I, 24). As Draper notes, if *Anti-Dühring* "is basically anti-Marx," it seems strange "that all this anti-Marxism went by Marx's anxious inspection without raising a murmur. Obviously, Marx did not understand Marxism either; only the mythologists do" (25). Paul Sweezy may have pinpointed the real

problem here when he described *Anti-Dühring* as "a masterpiece of exposition and clarification that has too often been neglected or put down precisely because it was addressed to a popular audience rather than to an elite of self-anointed experts" (1981, 17). Paul Kellogg's general critique of the Marx versus Engels myth and its political uses is worthwhile reading in this connection (Kellogg, 1991).

11. It should be noted that the rigorous comparison of Marx's and Engels' respective approaches to natural science has been greatly hampered by the fact that most of Marx's natural scientific writings, and many of Engels', remain unpublished (Baksi, 1996).

12. If this observation is accurate, it makes little sense to reconstruct Marx's conception of nature in abstraction from issues of history, sociology, and political economy. To cite one influential example, it is unsurprising that Reiner Grundmann's *Marxism and Ecology* winds up saddling Marx with a technological-determinist conception of people-nature relations, seeing as how his study "largely excluded questions of epistemology, political economy, and history" (Grundmann, 1991a, 8). When one excludes history and class relations from Marx's approach to nature, the result naturally tends to be one or more forms of crude materialism and/or idealism (see Burkett, 1997 and 1998a, for further discussion).

13. See, for example, Sagoff (1988), Amin (1992), Stirling (1993), Booth (1994), Gowdy and Olsen (1994), Munda, et al. (1995), Adams (1996), Tokar (1996), and Dore (1996).

Chapter 1

1. Although the presentation of the four criteria is motivated by expositional concerns, these criteria are informed by relevant socio-ecological works. See, in particular, Dasmann (1968), Dasmann et al. (1973), Enzensberger (1974), Schnaiberg (1980), Pepper (1993), Gowdy (1994a, 1994b), Leff (1995), and Lewontin and Levins (1997b).

2. "It is impossible, therefore, to exchange social objectivity for any kind of natural objectivity and to ignore the profound distortion undergone, at least by terrestrial nature, with the arrival of man; equally, we cannot exchange biology for sociology. Just as it should also be impossible, on the contrary, to take human practice, let alone *knowledge,* as the *only* objectivity" (Colletti, 1972, 33).

3. From the social *and* material basis of human values, and the role of values in the reproduction of social relations, it follows that "particular attitude[s] to nature" are "determined by the form of society *and vice versa*" (Marx and Engels, 1976, 50 [marginal note by Marx]; emphasis added). But this recognition of the material basis of human values is quite different from the false ascription of human values to nature itself, as with McLaughlin's (1990, 95)

call for a "liberation of nature" and O'Connor's (1991b, 9) reference to "nature's economy."

4. This highlights the affinity between class rule (in which institutional power positions and those holding them operate against societal self-criticism and self-transformation) and ecological problems (involving the alienation of people vis-à-vis their material circumstances). See Junker (1982) for an insightful discussion of this connection.

5. "To regard society as one single subject is . . . to look at it wrongly; speculatively" (Marx, 1973, 94).

6. As I have discussed elsewhere, the fact that many of Marx's ecological critics emphasize the quantitative side of his value theory to the neglect of its qualitative side may help explain their inadequate recognition of its ecological significance (Burkett, 1998b). Sweezy (1970, Chapter 2) also points to the shortcomings of one-sidedly quantitative interpretations of Marx's value analysis.

Chapter 2

1. "Labour is *not the source* of all wealth. *Nature* is just as much the source of use values (and it is surely of such that material wealth consists!) as is labour, which itself is only the manifestation of a natural force, human labour power" (Marx, 1966, 3). "Labour is the source of all wealth, the political economists assert. And it really is the source—next to nature, which supplies it with the material that it converts into wealth" (Engels, 1964a, 172).

2. When positing the "natural productivity of agricultural labour" as the "natural basis of surplus-labour in general," for example, Marx explicitly incorporates "the labour of simple gathering, hunting, fishing and cattle-raising" (1967a, III, 632).

3. In a draft of Volume I of *Capital,* Marx similarly specifies labor as a "universal condition for the metabolic interaction between nature and man . . . a natural condition of human life [that] is independent of, equally common to, all particular social forms of human life" (1988, 63).

4. In *Capital,* Marx likewise insists that "the earth . . . exists independently of man" (1967a, I, 183). Earlier on, Marx and Engels had asserted that under their materialist conception of history, "the priority of external nature remains unassailed," although they immediately noted that "this differentiation has meaning only insofar as man is considered to be distinct from nature" (1976, 46).

5. Marx's treatment of unappropriated but useful natural conditions as wealth is clear from his analyses of the natural basis of labor productivity (see Chapter 3) and capital's "free appropriation" of natural conditions (see Chapter 6).

6. "Individuals producing in society—hence socially determined individual production—is, of course, the point of departure . . . production at a definite stage of social development—production by social individuals" (Marx, 1973, 83, 85).

7. One indication that these characteristics do not fully define human labor is that they exist, albeit in less developed forms, in other terrestrial species. Engels, for example, states that "it would not occur to us to dispute the ability of animals to act in a planned, premeditated fashion," and then gives various examples, including the "acts of cunning on exactly the same level as those of children" that are "constantly" undertaken by "domestic animals" (1964a, 181). Similarly, Marx observes that the production and use of instruments of labor "exist[s] in the germ among certain species of animals" (1967a, I, 179).

8. This conception of production relations as a productive force has important implications for the potential unification of class and ecological struggles (see Chapter 13).

9. "The first premise of all human history is, of course, the existence of living human individuals. Thus the first fact to be established is the physical organisation of these individuals and their consequent relation to the rest of nature. . . . All historical writing must set out from these natural bases and their modification in the course of history through the action of men" (Marx and Engels, 1976, 37). While productive forces are socially constituted, it remains the case that the development of human beings and their social relations largely "coincides with their production, both with what they produce and with how they produce. Hence what individuals are depends on the *material conditions* of their production" (ibid.; emphasis added).

10. I say "now largely counterfactual" because, so far as the earth is concerned, "the nature that preceded human history . . . today no longer exists anywhere"—having long ago been altered by human intervention (Marx and Engels, 1976, 46).

11. As Sweezy (1970, 29) points out: "Nature co-operates both actively and passively in the process of producing use value" in Marx's view. Marx's recognition of the active role of nature in wealth production becomes even clearer in *Capital*'s analyses of agriculture and other forms of production where human labor is necessarily interrupted by natural productive processes (see Chapter 3).

12. Notice that insofar as the use value of nature is defined in and through relations among the human producers, this indicates another sense in which labor is a necessary condition of wealth production, despite the fact that many use values are produced by nature alone.

13. The argument that Marx's labor theory of value itself devalues nature is a specific case of this general tendency to blame Marx for the environmen-

tal contradictions of economic systems—contradictions actually revealed by Marx's analyses (see Chapter 7).

Chapter 3

1. This conception of the natural basis of surplus labor plays an important role in Marx's analysis of capitalist agriculture, landed property, and rents. Marx uses it to help clear up the "confusion between surplus-product and ground-rent" characteristic of prior political economy, enabling him to debunk "the mistaken idea that the rent corresponding to the capitalist mode of production . . . is explained by merely explaining the general conditions for the existence of surplus-value and profit in general" (Marx, 1967a, III, 632, 634).

2. One of Marx's preliminary drafts of *Capital,* Volume I, has a most interesting discussion of the possibility of surplus labor in relation to natural conditions and human needs: "However, the physical possibility of a surplus produce, in which surplus labour is objectified, clearly depends on 2 circumstances: If needs are very limited, then even with a small natural productive power of labour a part of the labour time can suffice to satisfy them, and thus to leave another part over for surplus labour, and therewith for the creation of the surplus produce. On the other hand: If the natural productive power of labour is very high—i.e., if the natural fertility of the soil, the waters, etc., requires only a slight expenditure of labour to be made to gain the means of subsistence necessary to existence, *this natural productive power of labour, or if you please, this productivity of labour of natural and spontaneous origin, naturally functions—if we consider the mere duration of the necessary labour time—in exactly the same way as the development of the social productive power of labour"* (Marx, 1994, 93–94; emphasis added). Such passages make it clear that Marx in no way downgrades the contribution of natural conditions to the production of wealth.

3. "No mystical ideas must in any way be connected, as sometimes happens, with this historically developed productiveness of labour" (Marx, 1967a, I, 512). See Burkett (1998a, 139–40) for a discussion of the political importance of Marx's insistence that both nature and labor contribute to the production of wealth.

4. In a draft of Volume I of *Capital,* Marx observes that "the mere existence of absolute surplus value implies nothing more than such a level of natural fertility, hence a productivity of labour of natural and spontaneous origin, that not all the possible daily labour time of a man is required for the maintenance of his own existence or the reproduction of his own labour capacity. The only further requirement is that he should be compelled . . . to work more than the necessary labour time" (1994, 93). Similarly, in *Theories of Surplus Value,* Marx states: "Both absolute and relative surplus-value

have this in common that they presuppose a certain level of the productive power of labour. If the entire working-day (available labour-time) of a man (any man) were only sufficient to feed himself (and at best his family as well), then there would be no surplus labour, surplus-value and surplus produce. This prerequisite of a certain level of productivity is based on the natural productiveness of land and water, the natural sources of wealth" (1971, 449).

5. "Human labour-power is by nature no more capital than are the means of production. They acquire this specific social character only under definite, historically developed conditions" (Marx, 1967a, II, 35). Clearly, there is nothing natural about workers being "*compelled* to work in excess of the [necessary] time"; rather, "this compulsion is exerted by capital" as a specific social relation (Marx, 1968, 406).

6. Marx normally uses the terms earth and nature interchangeably (see, for example, Marx, 1967a, I, 183, III, 774).

7. "Hence we see that whether a use-value is to be regarded as raw material, as instrument of labour, or as product, this is determined entirely by its function in the labour-process, or by the position it there occupies; as this varies, so does its character" (Marx, 1967a, I, 182).

8. Marx had already developed the distinction between production time and labor time in the *Grundrisse*: "In agriculture (and to a greater or lesser degree in many another branch of production) there are interruptions given by the conditions of the production process itself. . . . The time required here for the product to reach maturity, the interruptions of work, here constitute conditions of production. Not-labour time constitutes a condition for labour time, in order to turn the latter really into production time" (Marx, 1973, 602, 668–69). This "non-identity of production time with labour time can be due generally only to natural conditions, which stand directly in the path of the realization of labour" (669–70).

Chapter 4

1. Marx analyzes the dominant social forms of production under the assumption that the requirements of human-material reproduction are fulfilled *before* he considers the different possibilities for malfunctions in reproduction associated with these forms. Although this procedure may seem strange, it is necessary to specify how a particular form of production occurs at all before one can understand the crisis tendencies of this form.

2. "The different forms of material life are, of course, in every case dependent on the needs which are already developed, and the production, as well as the satisfaction, of these needs is an historical process" (Marx and Engels, 1976, 90).

3. Marx and Engels (1976, 48) go so far as to say that "to begin with" the family "is the only social relation"; this is followed immediately with the qualifying suggestion that "later, when increased needs create new social relations and the increased population new needs," the family relation becomes "a subordinate one." This is related to an important feminist criticism of Marx—namely, that he tends to subordinate family relations, and relations between the sexes more generally, to class relations, especially in his analysis of capitalism. Burkett (1998a, 131–34) considers this question by way of response to Benton's (1989, 72) charge that Marx "assimilate[s] the processes of production and reproduction of the labourer" to the capitalist production of workers' means of consumption.

Chapter 5

1. In this sense, "*no form* of society can prevent the working time at the disposal of society from regulating production one way or another" (Marx to Engels, January 8, 1868, in Marx and Engels [1975, 187]). See also Marx to Kugelmann, July 11, 1868, in Marx and Engels (1975, 196).

2. As Marx indicates in his January 8, 1868 letter to Engels, "in bourgeois society" the "regulation" of production "is accomplished not by the direct and conscious control of society over its working time—which is possible only with common ownership—but by the movement of commodity prices" (Marx and Engels, 1975, 187). Marx specifies the conditions of such indirect regulation in the very first chapter of *Capital* (1967a, I, 72–73): "As a general rule, articles of utility become commodities, only because they are products of the labour of private individuals or groups of individuals who carry on their work independently of each other. The sum total of the labour of all these private individuals forms the aggregate labour of society. Since the producers do not come into social contact with each other until they exchange their products, the specific social character of each producer's labour does not show itself except in the act of exchange. In other words, the labour of the individual asserts itself as a part of the labour of society, only by means of the relations which the act of exchange establishes directly between the products, and indirectly, through them, between the producers."

3. "The labour, however, that forms the substance of value, is homogenous human labour, expenditure of one uniform labour-power. The total labour-power of society, which is embodied in the sum total of the values of all commodities produced by that society, counts here as one homogenous mass of human labour-power" (Marx, 1967a, I, 39). "A commodity has a *value,* because it is a *crystallisation of social labour.* The *greatness* of its value, or its *relative* value, depends upon the greater or less amount of that

social substance contained in it; that is to say on the relative mass of labour necessary for its production" (1976b, 31).

4. Marx thus observes that in a commodity economy, "the labour of the individual producer acquires a two-fold character. On the one hand, it must, as a definite useful kind of labour, satisfy a definite social want, and thus hold its place as part and parcel of the collective labour of all, as a branch of the social division of labour that has sprung up spontaneously. On the other hand, it can satisfy the manifold wants of the producer himself, only in so far as the mutual exchangeability of all kinds of useful private labour is an established social fact, and therefore the private useful labour of each producer ranks on an equality with that of all others. . . . In this way, the character that his own labour possesses of being socially useful takes the form of the condition, that the product must be not only useful, but useful for others" (1967a, I, 73).

5. In this respect, there is a formal similarity between capitalism's undervaluation of natural conditions and its undervaluation of certain human-reproductive activities, including so-called domestic labor. See Burkett (1998a, 134) for a discussion of this connection.

6. See Smith (1990, 100–06) and Chattopadhyay (1995) for detailed elaborations of these points, which also apply, in a modified form, to arguments for "market socialism." As Nell (1988, 73) observes: "The ultimate insight of the labour theory of value in its most general form is that value as a society-wide phenomenon, expressed in universal equivalence with money ('everything has its price'), can arise only in social circumstances of class conflict. No harmony is possible through the market, since class conflict is a precondition for exchange value."

7. Marx repeatedly stresses this connection in Volume I of *Capital*. For example, he describes "the so-called primitive accumulation," that is, "the historical process of divorcing the producer from the means of production," as a "separation of the labourer from *the conditions of labour and their root, the soil*" (1967a, I, 714, 768; emphasis added).

8. In order for capital (money begetting more money) to dominate human production, it must become a "self-positing movement" whose action is not limited to the "merely formal movement of preposited exchange values" in commodity trade or money-lending (Marx, 1987, 492). In other words, the "use value for which money as potential capital . . . exchange[s] itself can only be the use value out of which the exchange value itself arises. And this is labour alone" (504). "The opposite of capital as the independent, firmly self-sufficient objectified labour is living labour capacity itself, and so the only exchange by means of which money can become capital is the exchange between the possessor of capital and the possessor of the living labour capacity, i.e., the worker" (502).

9. True, if money is "to realise itself as capital—i.e., as self-preserving and self-increasing value—it must transform itself into the conditions of labour"; nonetheless, it can "only be transformed into capital through exchange with living labour capacity" (Marx, 1988, 134, 36). "What is essential, therefore, is the component of capital which buys labour capacity. . . . Its transformation into capital requires that it be exchanged, on the one hand, for labour capacity and, on the other, for the material conditions prerequisite to the objectification of labour capacity" (ibid.). "Capital can multiply itself only by exchanging itself for labour-power, by calling wage-labour into life" (1933, 32).

10. This may also be conceptualized as a subordination of exchange value and use value as particular forms of value as such (see Chapter 7).

11. "The production and therefore the circulation of commodities can, however, take place between different communities or between different organs of the same community, even though the major part of what is produced may be produced as use values, for the producers' own direct personal requirements, and therefore may never take on the commodity form. The circulation of money, for its part . . . presupposes nothing more than commodity circulation itself, and crudely developed commodity circulation at that" (Marx, 1988, 39).

12. "Bailey and others remark that 'value', 'valeur' express a property of things. In fact the terms originally express nothing but the use-value of things for people, those qualities which make them useful or agreeable etc. to people. . . . Use-value expresses the natural relationship between things and men, in fact the existence of things for men. *Exchange-value,* as the result of the social development which created it, was later superimposed on the word value, which was synonymous with use-value. It is the *social existence* of things" (Marx, 1971, 296).

13. Hence, with pre-capitalist production, "the minimum produce required for the maintenance of the producers themselves is consequently small, and so is the surplus product. On the other hand, the number of people who live off the surplus product in those circumstances is likewise very small, so that they receive the sum total of the small amounts of surplus product obtained from a relatively large number of producers" (Marx, 1971, 449).

14. "While formerly need determined the extent of production, now production, or rather the *owning of the product,* determines how far needs can be satisfied" (Marx, 1967b, 278).

15. "The capitalist system pre-supposes the complete separation of the labourers from all property in the means by which they can realise their labour. As soon as capitalist production is once on its own legs, it not only maintains this separation, but reproduces it on a continually extending scale" (Marx, 1967a, I, 714). "The loss of the conditions of labour by the work-

ers is expressed in the fact that these conditions become independent as capital or as things at the disposal of the capitalists. Thus primitive accumulation . . . means nothing but the separation of labour and the worker from the conditions of labour, which confront him as independent forces. The course of history shows that this separation is a factor in social development. Once capital exists, the capitalist mode of production itself evolves in such a way that it maintains and reproduces this separation on a constantly increasing scale" (1971, 271–72).

16. This regulating power of exchange values over the division of labor (the "law of value"), depending as it does on the social separation of the laborers from necessary production conditions, is absent even in those pre-capitalist societies engaging in some commodity production. In "classic feudal society," for example, "the law of value actually regulates nothing except commodity exchange. . . . The law of value does not essentially regulate the division of available labor power among the various sectors of the economy. This still depends on the feudal structure, especially the serf's bondage to the soil. In capitalist society, the law of value regulates commodity exchange as well as the division of labor power and economic resources among the various sectors of the economy. But it now regulates indirectly . . . through capital competition and deviations from average profit. Capital flows into sectors where profits are above average and out of sectors where profits are below average" (Mandel, 1973, 81).

17. "In fact, the events that transformed the small peasants into wage-labourers, and their means of subsistence and of labour into material elements of capital, created, at the same time, a home-market for the latter" (Marx, 1967a, I, 747).

18. In Marx's view, capital's "employment of the natural agents—their incorporation so to speak into capital—coincides with the development of scientific knowledge as an independent factor in the production process" (1994, 32). Chapter 11 discusses this further.

19. For the original detailed discussions of the real subsumption of labor under capital, (see Marx 1967a, I, Chapter 15; 1977, 1019–38).

Chapter 6

1. Note that in this passage, "exchange value" is equivalent to "value," the reason being that Volume I of *Capital* does not analyze the deviations of exchange values (money prices) from values (in the sense of socially necessary labor times) that are associated with capitalist competition and rents. Such deviations are only dealt with in Volume III. Interestingly,

Deléage (1994, 48) also quotes from the passage shown in the present text but omits the second and third sentences. This omission has the effect of concealing Marx's insistence on nature's contribution to use value, thus providing an artificial boost to Deléage's claim that Marx devalues nature.

2. "Use-values are only produced by capitalists, because, and in so far as, they are the material substratum, the depositories of exchange-value" (Marx, 1967a, I, 186).

3. "Science, generally speaking, costs the capitalist nothing, a fact that by no means hinders him from exploiting it. The science of others is as much annexed by capital as the labour of others" (Marx, 1967a, I, 386). See Chapter 11 for further discussion of capitalism's positive and negative influences on the development and application of scientific knowledge in connection with the ecology.

4. "The property therefore which labour-power in action, living labour, possesses of preserving value, at the same time that it adds it, is a gift of Nature which costs the labourer nothing, but which is very advantageous to the capitalist inasmuch as it preserves the existing value of his capital" (Marx, 1967a, I, 206). "The maintenance of present capital by the labour which realizes it therefore costs capital nothing and hence does not belong among the production costs" (1973, 366).

5. Marx immediately adds that "all *natural forces of social labour* are themselves historical products" (1973, 400). Insofar as state-sector activities (in education, for example) contribute to the development of individual and collective labouring capacities, the extent to which capital freely appropriates these capacities becomes a matter of struggle over the class distribution of taxes and expenditures (Carchedi, 1991, 129). The same goes for other natural and social conditions of production whose provision involves government activities.

6. "These forces of nature cost nothing as such. They are not the product of human labour. But their appropriation occurs only *by means of* machinery, which does have a cost, is itself the product of past labour. They are therefore only appropriated as agents of the labour process through machinery and by the owners of machinery" (Marx, 1994, 32; emphasis added).

7. This broader definition manifests itself, among other places, in a draft of *The Civil War in France,* where Marx refers to "the means of labour, created by the labourers themselves or forming the gift of nature" under both communism *and* capitalism (1985, 156).

8. The free appropriation of rent-yielding natural conditions clearly manifests the fundamentally *redistributive* character of rents themselves (see Chapter 7). In addition, it clarifies the misconceptions in the following statement by Carpenter (1997, 147): "Marx's evaluation of nature as a priori valueless stems in part from his definition of scarcity. As an infinitely abundant re-

source, Marx assumes nature to be what contemporary economists would call a 'zero-price commodity'. Economists define zero-price commodities as those goods or resources in an economy which are available to producers or consumers for free or that have no unmediated exchange value." Along with his mistaken presumption that only infinitely abundant resources can have zero value, Carpenter ignores the fact that freely appropriated natural conditions can have a price—so that "an object may have a price without having value" (Marx, 1967a, I, 102).

9. "Value is independent of the particular use-value by which it is borne, but it must be embodied in a use-value of some kind" (Marx, 1967a, I, 188). "Lastly nothing can have value, without being an object of utility. If the thing is useless, so is the labour contained in it; the labour does not count as labour, and therefore creates no value" (41).

10. "The amount of labour which a capital can command does not depend on its value, but on the mass of raw and auxiliary materials, machinery and elements of fixed capital and necessities of life, all of which it comprises, whatever their value may be. As the mass of the labour employed, and thus of surplus-labour increases, there is also a growth in the value of the reproduced capital and in the surplus-value newly added to it" (Marx, 1967a, III, 248).

11. Given the tension between nature's use value for capital and less restricted conceptions of nature's use value as revealed by Marx's analysis, one can understand why neoclassical economists—whose basic instinct is to deny capitalist exploitation and the alienation of capitalist production from the producers and nature—are at pains to conflate the concepts of value, use value, and capital while ridiculing Marx's critical demarcation of these categories. Robert W. Campbell provides a clear example of such "common sense" thinking: "Natural resources (such as agricultural land, or deposits of coal underground) are productive, and have value as a consequence of their ability to increase society's output. The income associated with these forms of property is called rent" (Campbell, 1991, 199). "Marxian economics broke off from the mainstream of economic thought at a time in the history of the science before it had been understood [!!!] that the issues of value and allocation are inextricably intertwined" (Campbell, 1974, 175). It is difficult indeed to respond to such an ahistorical "understanding."

Chapter 7

1. As Altvater (1990, 24) puts it: "A natural environment is of no value at all in itself—at least not in the calculus of capitalism—as long as it has not been 'invested with value' by the factors at the disposal of private enterprise. . . . But investing with value in any case means transforming nature

in accordance with principles that investment with value by capital requires, *an abstraction from the concrete circumstances of the environment*" (emphasis added).

2. "Is not *value* to be conceived as the unity of use value and exchange value?
In and for itself, is [not] value as such the general form, in opposition to
use value and exchange value as *particular* forms of it?" (Marx, 1973, 267).

3. As Marx indicates: "The value of a commodity obtains independent and
definite expression, by taking the form of exchange-value. . . . A commodity is a use-value or object of utility, and a value. It manifests itself as
this two-fold thing, that it is, as soon as its value assumes an independent
form—viz., the form of exchange-value" (1967a, I, 60).

4. "Our analysis has shown, that the form or expression of the value of a
commodity originates in the nature of value, and not that value and its
magnitude originate in the mode of their expression as exchange-value"
(Marx, 1967a, I, 60).

5. "As use-values, commodities are, above all, of different qualities, but as exchange-values they are merely different quantities, and consequently do
not contain an atom of use-value"; in this sense, "the exchange of commodities is evidently an act characterised by a total abstraction from use-
value" (Marx, 1967a, I, 37–38). Saad-Filho (1993) provides an insightful
discussion of this aspect of Marx's analysis.

6. "Value as such has no other 'substance' than labour itself" (Marx to Engels,
April 2, 1858, in Marx and Engels [1975, 98]). For Marx, "labour itself" is
"the sole source of wealth in the particular social form wealth has as exchange value" (1988, 40). "Only as a result of production for exchange—
whereby abstraction is made from the fact that materials and energy are
transformed through concrete, quality-changing labour—does the labour
product become a bearer of value and fall under the dynamic of the system of values" (Altvater, 1993, 190).

7. That Marx recognized this connection is clear from the following passage
in the *Grundrisse:* "Because the product becomes a commodity, and the
commodity becomes an exchange value, it obtains, at first only in the head,
a double existence. This doubling . . . proceeds (and must proceed) to the
point where the commodity appears double in real exchange: as a natural
product on one side, as exchange value on the other" (Marx, 1973, 145).

8. "The *private exchange* of all products of labour, all activities and all wealth
stands in antithesis . . . to a distribution based on a natural or political super-
and subordination of individuals to one another . . . regardless of the character of this super- and sub-ordination: patriarchal, ancient or feudal"
(Marx, 1973, 159). In pre-capitalist economy, "exchange proper only runs
parallel" to social production relations, so that "by and large, [it] does not so
much take a grip on the life of entire communities as, rather, insert itself between different communities; it by no means exercises general domination

over all relations of production and distribution" (ibid.). As Marx indicates, the "division of a product into a useful thing and a value becomes practically important, only when exchange has acquired such an extension that useful articles are produced only for the purpose of being exchanged, and their character as values has therefore to be taken into account, beforehand, during production" (1967a, I, 73). This situation where "all, or even the majority of products take the form of commodities . . . can only happen with production of a very specific kind, capitalist production" (169).

9. "Use-values must therefore never be looked upon as the real aim of the capitalist; neither must the profit on any single transaction. The restless never-ending process of profit-making alone is what he aims at" (Marx, 1967a, I, 152–53). "It must never be forgotten, that in capitalist production what matters is not the immediate use-value but the exchange-value and, in particular, the expansion of surplus-value. This is the direct motive of capitalist production" (1968, 495).

10. Similarly, in a preliminary draft of *Capital,* Volume I, Marx refers to abstract labor as "labour of the quality or rather the qualitylessness in which it forms the substance of exchange value" (1988, 81).

11. "From the contradiction between the general character of value and its material existence in a particular commodity . . . arises the category of money" (Marx to Engels, April 2, 1858, in Marx and Engels [1975, 98]; cf. Marx, 1967a, I, Chapter 1, Section 3; 1970, 37–52). See Rosdolsky (1977, 109–18) for a useful exposition of this portion of Marx's value-form analysis.

12. "Labour time cannot directly be money (a demand which is the same, in other words, as demanding that every commodity should simply be its own money), precisely because in fact labour time always exists only in the form of particular commodities (as an object): being a general object, [value] can exist only symbolically, and hence only as a particular commodity which plays the role of money. . . . [Hence] in the form of exchange value, labour time is required to become objectified in a commodity which expresses no more than its quota or quantity, which is indifferent to its own natural properties, and which can therefore be metamorphosed into—i.e., exchanged for—every other commodity which objectifies the same labour time" (Marx, 1973, 168). See Saad-Filho (1993, 72ff) on this point.

13. Money's use value "as materialised universal labour-time" is itself "a formal use-value . . . not related to any real individual need," in the sense that it only "satisfies a universal need arising from the exchange process itself . . . that of being a carrier of exchange-value" (Marx, 1970, 46, 48, 49). Nonetheless, "it is not at all apparent on [money's] face that its character of being money is merely the result of social processes; it *is* money. This is all the more difficult . . . because, in general, the memory of use value, as distinct from exchange value, has become entirely extinguished in this incarnation of pure exchange value. Thus the fundamental contradiction

contained in exchange value, and in the social mode of production corresponding to it, here emerges in all its purity" (1973, 239–40).

14. Any form of measurement connects quality and quantity (Botella, 1993, 408). In the case of money as measure of value, however, the connection is dominated by the quantitative (value) side to the detriment of the qualitative (use value) side, in line with the regulation of production by value in the form of exchange values—whence the abstraction from the natural properties of wealth.

15. Similarly, even though the "soil community . . . consists of a web of interwoven lives, each in some way related to the others," the capitalistic "control of insects seems to have proceeded on the assumption that the soil could and would sustain any amount of insult via the introduction of poisons without striking back. The very nature of the world of the soil has been largely ignored" (Carson, 1962, 56–57).

16. The extent of this power is evident from "the failure of capitalism to produce anything other than the uneven geographical development of bland, commoditized, homogeneity" in the human landscape—especially in the United States, where land use is relatively unregulated compared to other advanced capitalist countries (Harvey, 1993, 45). Dolores Hayden rightly observes that the "space produced by the monopoly-capitalist economy is styled to emphasize superficial differences, and to conceal the uniformity below the facade" (1983, 61). This homogenization of the natural conditions of human life is connected with another of "the consequences of capitalist development," namely, the tendency toward "obliteration of ethnic and regional traditions," which, as Gwendolyn Wright indicates, "a socialist society would try to reverse" (1983, 83).

17. "Before it is replaced by exchange value, every form of natural wealth presupposes an essential relation between the individual and the objects, in which the individual in one of his aspects objectifies himself in the thing, so that his possession of the thing appears at the same time as a certain development of his individuality: wealth in sheep, the development of the individual as shepherd, wealth in grain his development as agriculturalist, etc. *Money, however, as the individual* of general wealth, as something emerging from circulation and representing a general quality, as a *merely social result,* does not at all presuppose an individual relation to its owner; possession of it is not the development of any particular essential aspect of his individuality; but rather possession of what lacks individuality, since this social relation exists at the same time as a sensuous, external object which can be mechanically seized, and lost in the same manner. Its relation to the individual thus appears as a purely accidental one" (Marx, 1973, 221–22).

18. "In fact the 'environmental' threat is *not* equally grave for everyone . . . if they are rich enough, some can still command amenity and a relatively

healthy environment. . . . [E]ven as the earth chokes and suffocates, some can buy their way out of trouble. Class therefore *is* relevant" (Pepper, 1993, 141). Such class-based differentials in environmental conditions are an important concern of Engels in *The Condition of the Working-Class in England*. Engels observes, for example, that the "east and north-east sides of Manchester are the only ones on which the bourgeoisie has not built, because ten or eleven months of the year the west and south-west wind drives the smoke of all the factories hither, and that the working-people alone may breathe" (1973, 99). See also Enzensberger's (1974, 24–28) seminal work on the relations between class inequalities and environmental ideologies.

19. A full treatment of this issue requires prior discussion of capitalism's specific mode of consumption (see Chapters 11 and 13).

20. "For example commodities as use-values are not divisible at will, a property which as exchange-values they should possess" (Marx, 1970, 51).

21. Victor Wallis (1993, 151) emphasizes the ecological and social effects of capitalism's tendency toward "atomization," that is, "the isolation of the individual for purposes of consumption and indoctrination." This tendency is, arguably, grounded largely in the dequalification, fragmentation, and impermanence of people-nature relations under value-formed production.

22. The ecological implications of Marx's analysis are well stated by Habermas (1975, 42–43): "The possible means of averting ecological crises are . . . specific to systems. Capitalist societies cannot follow imperatives of growth limitation without abandoning their principle of organization; a shift from unplanned capitalist growth to qualitative growth would require that production be planned in terms of use values. The development of productive forces cannot, however, be uncoupled from the production of exchange values without violating the logic of the system."

23. See Chapter 9 for a detailed discussion of capitalism's tendency to increase the amount of material throughput in human production, based on Marx's analysis of capital accumulation.

24. "Gradual regenerative processes that allow biotic resources to recuperate and to grow cannot keep pace with accelerated capital reproduction cycles" (Leff, 1995, 24).

25. See Mayumi (1991), Foster (1997), and Foster and Magdoff (1998) for excellent overviews of Marx's analyses of capitalist agriculture as influenced by Justus Liebig's work on soil chemistry.

26. For detailed discussions of Marx's rent theory, see Fine (1979), Harvey (1982, Chapter 11), and Devine (1993).

27. Hence, when speaking of rent-yielding agricultural land in *The Poverty of Philosophy*, Marx states: "If one could always have at one's disposal plots of land of the same degree of fertility; if one could, as in manufacturing in-

dustry, have recourse continually to cheaper and more productive machines, or if the subsequent outlays of capital produced as much as the first, then . . . from this moment rent would have disappeared" (1978a, 152–53). Clearly Marx would have no problem endorsing Enrique Leff's opinion that rents are "conditioned by uneven productivity of natural ecosystems and soil fertility" (1995, 87–88).

28. Capitalism "presupposes, on the one hand, the separation of the direct producers from their position as mere accessories to the land (in the form of vassals, serfs, slaves, etc.), and, on the other hand, the expropriation of the mass of the people from the land. To this extent the monopoly of landed property is a historical premise, and continues to remain the basis, of the capitalist mode of production" (Marx, 1967a, III, 616–17). The mutually supportive relationship of capital and landed property has important practical implications for workers' day-to-day struggles. As Marx observes: "The monstrous power wielded by landed property, when united hand in hand with industrial capital, enables it to be used against labourers engaged in their wage struggle as a means of practically expelling them from the earth as a dwelling-place" (773). Engels and Marx both note the key role played by capital's power of housing eviction in particular strike episodes; see Engels (1973, 221, 293–94; 1979, 53–54), and the excerpts in Lapides (1990, 17–18, 60, 72, 143).

29. "No producer, whether agricultural or industrial, when considered by himself alone, produces value or commodities. His product becomes a value and a commodity only in the context of definite social interrelations. In the first place, in so far as it appears as the expression of social labour, hence in so far as the individual producer's labour-time counts as a part of the social labour-time in general; and, secondly, this social character of his labour appears impressed upon his product through its pecuniary character and through its general exchangeability determined by its price. . . . It is not a singularity of ground-rent, then, that agricultural products develop into, and as, values, i.e., that they confront other commodities as commodities; or that they develop as specific expressions of social labour. The singularity of ground-rent is rather that together with the conditions in which agricultural products develop as values (commodities), and together with the conditions in which their values are realised, there also grows the power of landed property to appropriate an increasing portion of these values, which were created without its assistance; and so an increasing portion of surplus-value is transformed into ground-rent" (Marx, 1967a, III, 638–39).

30. In this connection, it was Marx's great sensitivity to the naturally *and* socially determined variegation of agricultural production conditions that allowed him to "take care of the first false assumption regarding differential rent—still found among West, Malthus, and Ricardo—namely, that it nec-

essarily presupposes a movement toward worse and worse soil" (Marx, 1967a, III, 659).

31. As Geoffrey Kay indicates: "Not only is rent historically subsequent to commodity production, but it is also dependent on it. Ricardo demonstrated this in detail and we have here one of the few parts of classical political economy that was assimilated into neo-classical theory. The magnitude of rent does not determine the prices of commodities; on the contrary, it is determined by these prices" (1979, 50).

32. "Because money is the *general equivalent, the general power of purchasing,* everything can be bought, everything may be transformed into money. . . . There is nothing inalienable, since everything alienable for money. There is no higher or holier, since everything appropriable by money" (Marx, 1973, 838–39). "Since gold does not disclose what has been transformed into it, everything, commodity or not, is convertible into gold" (1967a, I, 132).

Chapter 8

1. The last proviso is necessary because Marx's theory incorporates deviations of *particular* exchange values from underlying values, even though value is by definition equal to exchange value in the aggregate. Among such deviations are the rents collected from ownership of useful and scarce natural conditions (see Chapter 7).

2. The necessity of natural conditions for value and capital accumulation can also be derived from capital's absolute use-value requirement: exploitable labor power and material conditions conducive to its exploitation (see Chapter 5).

3. As Altvater puts it: "The contradiction between economics and ecology . . . is totally ignored when the attempt is made to attribute value to nature, without paying sufficient attention to the particular social form of the 'valuing' of nature" (1994, 87–88).

4. Carpenter uses a secondary translation of the quoted passage from the *Grundrisse,* taken from Schmidt (1971, 30). I have replaced it with the standard English translation by Martin Nicolaus (Marx, 1973, 366).

5. Actually, Orton ignores these questions. Carpenter, however, winds up conflating value, use value, and exchange value with his assertions that (1) only infinitely abundant resources can have zero value; and (2) zero-value resources cannot have a price (see Chapter 6, footnote 8).

Chapter 9

1. The extent of human intervention into nature is now such that even the purely natural character of "natural disasters," such as earthquakes, hurricanes, and precipitation and temperature fluctuations, can no longer be safely presumed. Moreover, even insofar as human development is subjected to "above-normal" restrictions by purely natural events, a social ecology must treat these events in proper historical context. The human impacts of an earthquake, for example, can only be understood in terms of the geographic distribution of production and population, class inequalities in the safety of built environments, and the level and distribution of society's emergency-response capabilities—all of which are a function of historically developed socio-economic relations.

2. Marx's analyses of the growing demand for materials accompanying the growth of labor productivity rarely fail to make this distinction. When treating the rising technical composition of capital in Chapter 25 of *Capital*, Volume I, for example, Marx notes that "with the division of labour in manufacture, and with the use of machinery, more raw material is worked up in the same time, and, therefore, a greater mass of raw material *and auxiliary substances* enter into the labour-process" (1967a, I, 622; emphasis added). Similarly, in Volume III's analysis of materials price fluctuations, Marx states that "raw materials here include auxiliary materials as well, such as indigo, coal, gas, etc.," then adds: "Even in industries which consume no actual raw materials, these enter the picture as auxiliary materials" (1967a, III, 106).

3. Marx's reference to the "natural life" of labor's instruments is not a casual one. The "destructive influence of natural forces" on machines and other means of production is discussed not only in Marx's initial analysis of the labor process in Chapter 7, Volume I, of *Capital* (1967a, I, 183), but also—and in detail—in Chapter 8, Section 2 of Volume II, where Marx carefully distinguishes between "wear and tear [as] a result of use" versus "wear and tear . . . caused by the action of natural forces" (1967a, II, 170). The latter distinction is, in fact, introduced in Volume I: "The material wear and tear of a machine is of two kinds. The one arises from use, as coins wear away by circulating, the other from non-use, as a sword rusts when left in its scabbard. The latter kind is due to the elements. The former is more or less directly proportional, the latter to a certain extent inversely proportional, to the use of the machine" (1967a, I, 404).

4. "The shorter the period taken to reproduce [a machine's] total value, the less is the danger of moral depreciation; and the longer the working-day, the shorter is that period. When machinery is first introduced into an industry, new methods of reproducing it more cheaply follow blow upon blow, and so do improvements, that not only affect individual parts and details of the machine, but its entire build. It is, therefore,

in the early days of the life of machinery that this special incentive to the prolongation of the working-day makes itself felt most acutely" (Marx, 1967a, I, 404–5).Volume III of *Capital* also describes capitalists' resort to "flagrant prolongation of the working-time" and "alternating day and night-shifts, so that the value of the machinery may be reproduced in a shorter time without having to place the figures for wear and tear too high" (1967a, III, 113).

5. Under capitalism, "applications of science, natural forces and products of labour on a large scale . . . appear only as *means for the exploitation* of labour"; although "capital naturally uses all these means only to exploit labour . . . in order to exploit it, it must apply them in production" (Marx, 1963, 391–92).

6. "The general requirements for the re-employment of these excretions are: large quantities of such waste, such as are available only in large-scale production; improved machinery whereby materials, formerly useless in their prevailing form, are put into a state fit for new production; scientific progress, particularly of chemistry, which reveals the useful properties of such waste. . . .The so-called waste plays an important role in almost every industry" (Marx, 1967a, III, 101).

7. "Ecological rationality consists in satisfying material needs in the best way possible with as small a quantity as possible of goods with a high use-value and durability, and thus doing so with a minimum of work, capital and natural resources.The quest for maximum economic productivity, by contrast, consists in selling at as high a profit as possible the greatest possible quantity of goods produced with the maximum of efficiency, all of which demands a maximization of consumption and needs" (Gorz, 1994, 32–33).

8. See Perelman (1987) for further documentation and analysis of the issues treated in this section.

9. This natural basis of industrial surplus value follows from "the time-honoured economic fact that all industrial producers are dependent for their subsistence on the products of agriculture, stock farming, hunting and fishing" (Engels to Marx, December 22, 1882, in Marx and Engels [1992, 413]). For further discussion, see Marx (1988, 192–93).

10. The contemporary relevance of this analysis is clear from Joyce Kolko's brilliant survey of the "intensification of the traditional supply-shortage cycles" in global materials production after the late 1960s (Kolko, 1988, Chapter 9). A full application of Marx's materials-supply analysis to contemporary conditions must, however, incorporate rents and struggles over their distribution; see, for example, Massarrat (1980) and Bina (1989).

11. Financial leveraging of materials stockpiling and speculation is partly a natural outgrowth of the routine use of credit in materials production and trade (Marx, 1967a, III, 481–82).

12. The other factor making materials price fluctuations inevitable is capital's immanent tendency toward overproduction *relative to the market:* "The enormous power, inherent in the factory system, of expanding by jumps, and the dependence of that system on the markets of the world, necessarily beget feverish production, followed by over-filling of markets, whereupon contraction of the markets brings on crippling of production. The life of modern industry becomes a series of periods of moderate activity, prosperity, over-production, crisis and stagnation" (Marx, 1967a, I, 453). See Clarke (1994) for an illuminating overview of this aspect of Marx's analysis.

13. In *Theories of Surplus Value*, Marx suggests that "the accumulation of capital in the towns during the Middle Ages . . . was principally due to the exploitation of the country (by trade as well as by manufacture)" (1968, 232). He goes on to argue that "the urban labour of the Middle Ages already constitutes a great advance and serves as a preparatory school for the capitalist mode of production, as regards the continuity and steadiness of labour" (1971, 434).

14. "The battle of competition is fought by cheapening of commodities. The cheapness of commodities depends, *ceteris paribus,* on the productiveness of labour, and this again on the scale of production. Therefore, the larger capitals beat the smaller" (Marx, 1967a, I, 626).

15. As Marx observes: "The concentration of labourers, and their large-scale co-operation, saves constant capital. The same buildings, and heating and lighting appliances, etc., cost relatively less for the large-scale than for small-scale production. The same is true of power and working machinery. Although their absolute value increases, it falls in comparison to the increasing extension of production and the magnitude of the variable capital, or the quantity of labour-power set in motion" (1967a, III, 82).

16. "But with the development of industry the proletariat not only increases in number; it becomes concentrated in greater masses, its strength grows, and it feels that strength more. . . . Thereupon the workers begin to form combinations (Trades' Unions) against the bourgeois" (Marx and Engels, 1968, 43; cf. Engels, 1973, 161).

17. Such capital spin-offs are often connected with "the division of property within capitalist families" and/or with "the exploitation of new inventions and discoveries, and industrial improvements in general" (Marx, 1967a, I, 625, 628).

18. In this connection, the routinization of inventions and innovations within large-scale firms reduces the relative importance of new, smaller-scale firms in the organization of production, spatial and otherwise (Sweezy, 1943).

19. "If it were possible for this mad rush of manufacture to go on at this rate for another century, every manufacturing district of England would be one great manufacturing town, and Manchester and Liverpool would meet at Warrington or Newton" (Engels, 1973, 61).

20. See Waitzkin (1983) for a survey of subsequent work in this area as well as an updated analysis of the "illness generating social conditions" produced by capitalism in urban areas.

21. Ted Benton, for example, suggests that "it was almost exclusively with respect to agriculture that Marx was able to recognize . . . the tendency of capitalism to destroy its own natural conditions of possibility" (1989, 85).

22. Similarly, in *The Housing Question*, Engels exclaims: "When one observes how here in London alone a greater quantity of manure than is produced by the whole kingdom of Saxony is poured away every day into the sea with an expenditure of enormous sums, and what colossal structures are necessary in order to prevent this manure from poisoning the whole of London, then the utopia of abolishing the distinction between town and country is given a remarkably practical basis. And even comparatively unimportant Berlin has been suffocating in the malodours of its own filth for at least thirty years" (1979, 92).

23. See Mayumi (1991), Foster (1997), and Foster and Magdoff (1998) for the significant influence of Liebig's work on Marx and Engels.

24. "In modern agriculture, as in the urban industries, the increased productiveness and quantity of the labour set in motion are bought at the cost of laying waste and consuming by disease labour-power itself" (Marx, 1967a, I, 506). Indeed, the intensively exploitative and immiserizing character of agricultural wage-labor, along with its seasonality, helps explain agricultural capital's heavy reliance on migrant workers and/or various forms of forced labor (693–96).

25. As observed by Vitousek et al. (1997, 498): "Recent calculations suggest that rates of species extinction are now on the order of 100 to 1000 times those before humanity's dominance of Earth. . . . Land transformation is the single most important cause of extinction, and current rates of land transformation will drive many more species to extinction, although with a time lag that masks the dimensions of the crisis."

26. See the discussion of materials-supply disturbances earlier in this chapter. The following comment by Rosa Luxemburg is also of interest in this connection: "The process of accumulation, elastic and spasmodic as it is, requires inevitably free access to ever new areas of raw materials in case of need, both when imports from old sources fail or when social demand suddenly increases" (Luxemburg, 1964, 358).

27. Martínez-Alier's avoidance of this fundamental question is understandable, given his own tendency toward "confusing the physical with the economic," thereby diluting the specificity of capitalism's environmental problems. He thus misreads David Harvey's (1993) insistence on the historical specificity of natural conditions and limits as a complete denial of their importance (Martínez-Alier, 1995a, 72). Similarly, Hans Enzensberger's (1974) thoughtful materialist *and* class analysis of environmentalism is dismissed as a "reaction . . . of surprise if not repudiation,"

and even of "incomprehension" (Martínez-Alier, 1995a, 71). Meanwhile, Martínez-Alier's recent work on environmental conflicts takes technocratic refuge in Sraffian input/output analysis and zero-sum distributional concerns, bypassing the value form of capitalist production with all its anti-ecological connotations (ibid., 78–81; see also Martínez-Alier, 1995b).

Chapter 10

1. In this connection, it is crucial to remember that capital's only absolute use-value requirement is exploitable labor power, with other material conditions required only insofar as they are absolutely necessary for labor power's reproduction or for the objectification of surplus labor in commodified use values (see Chapter 5).
2. "Man is distinguished from all other animals by the limitless and flexible character of his needs. But it is equally true that no animal is able to restrict his needs to the same unbelievable degree and to reduce the conditions of his life to the absolute minimum" (Marx, 1977, 1068). See Chapter 4 for further discussion.
3. Hence, Marx's emphasis on the elasticity and relative indeterminacy of the natural limits to work-time is not to be confused with a denial that an absolute natural limit exists. For Marx, this "ultimate limit is given by the physical force of the labouring man," so that "if the daily exhaustion of his vital forces exceeds a certain degree, it cannot be exerted anew, day by day" (1976b, 57). "Leaving aside the time required for the intake of food, the individual needs sleep, relaxation, needs a break during which labour capacity and its organ can enjoy the rest without which they are incapable of continuing the work or starting afresh" (Marx, 1988, 181).
4. "The *day* itself can be characterised as the natural measure of labour's duration" (Marx, 1988, 181). Under capitalism, however, "the mere circumstance that fixed capital—factory buildings, machinery, etc.—lies idle during pauses in the labour-process, became one of the motives for an unnatural prolongation of the labour-process and for day-and-night work" (1967a, II, 238).
5. Note, however, that capital's extension of work-time may be constrained by the natural conditions of production. "In agriculture," for example, "the extension of labour-time . . . is only possible to a limited degree. One cannot work by gaslight on the land and so on. True, one can rise early in spring and summer. But this is offset by the shorter winter days when, in any case, only a relatively small amount of work can be accomplished. So in this respect absolute surplus value is greater in industry so long as the normal working-day is not regulated by force of law. A second reason for a smaller amount of surplus-value being created in agriculture is the long period during which the product remains in the

process of production without any labour being expended on it" (Marx, 1968, 20).

6. "If the average age of working-class generations declines, there is always available on the market a superfluous and constantly increasing mass of short-lived generations, and that is all capitalist production needs" (Marx, 1988, 302).

7. Any such expansion of employment is profitable for capital "if the length of the working-day and the necessary labour-time, and therefore the rate of surplus-value are given," in which case "the amount of surplus-value depends on the *number* of workers simultaneously employed by the same capital" (Marx, 1968, 410).

8. Marx also suggests that the low living standards of the reserve army of unemployed will often lead its members to "reproduce more rapidly than the labourer in his natural conditions—because the conditions for his reproduction are of infinitesimal size" (1994, 165). See Burkett (1998a, 129–30) for an elaboration of Marx's anti-Malthusian perspective on this issue.

9. See Parsons (1977, 62) for an excellent discussion of the significance of child labor in Marx's critique of capitalism.

10. "In addition to this, economy and judgement in the consumption and preparation of the means of subsistence becomes impossible" (Marx, 1967a, I, 395). In making these observations, Marx endorses neither the extant distribution of domestic tasks between men, women, and children nor the social undervaluation of the labor and leisure time of women and children relative to male time (cf. Schor, 1992). Indeed, Marx emphasizes that "modern industry, in overturning the economic foundation on which was based the traditional family, and the family labour corresponding to it, had also loosened all traditional family ties. . . . However terrible and disgusting the dissolution, under the capitalist system, of the old family ties may appear, nevertheless, modern industry, by assigning as it does an important part in the process of production, outside the domestic sphere, to women, to young persons, and to children of both sexes, creates a new economic foundation for a higher form of the family and of the relations between the sexes" (Marx, 1967a, I, 489–90). In the *German Ideology,* Marx and Engels castigate the "slavery latent in the family . . . where wife and children are the slaves of the husband," and which features an "unequal distribution, both quantitative and qualitative, of labour and its products" (1976, 38, 52). See also the discussion of familial exploitation in the *Communist Manifesto* (Marx and Engels, 1968, 49–50). Lebowitz (1992a, 112–18) provides an excellent study of the notion of gender-based exploitation in Marx and Engels.

11. In addition to its other appearances in *Capital* (1967a, I, 256, 302), the vampire analogy is used in the Inaugural Address of the International Working Men's Association, where Marx speaks of "British industry, which

vampire-like, could but live by sucking blood, and children's blood too" (1974a, 79). (Marx may have picked up on the analogy from Engels, who had referred to "the vampire property-holding class" in *The Condition of the Working-Class in England* [Engels, 1973, 274].) In *Capital,* Marx similarly cites a "were-wolf hunger for surplus-labour" as driving capital to "over-step not only the moral, but even the merely physical maximum bounds of the working-day" (1967a, I, 265; cf. ibid., 243).

12. Burkett (1986a) criticizes the neoclassical approach to public goods and free riding, based on its lack of a structural analysis of capitalism.

13. "The history of the regulation of the working-day . . . prove[s] conclusively that the isolated labourer, the labourer as 'free' vendor of his labour-power, when capitalist production has once attained a certain stage, succumbs without any power of resistance. The creation of a normal working-day is, therefore, the product of a protracted civil war, more or less dissembled, be-tween the capitalist class and the working-class" (Marx, 1967a, I, 299).

14. This last suggestion obviously holds only for those capitalists who take an active role in management, but it could also be applied to hired managers once the function of supervising labor power is separated from formal cap-ital ownership.

15. This argument is structural in that it presumes that the priorities of indi-viduals are determined, on balance, by their class position in capitalism considered as a specific social form of production.

Chapter 11

1. See Foster (1995, 108–9) for a useful set of additional references to Left-Green charges of Prometheanism against Marx.

2. Hence capitalism's "development of the objective conditions of labour ap-pears as a growing power of these objective conditions over living labour, instead of as a growing power of labour" (Marx, 1994, 196). For Marx, a key "characteristic of the capitalist production process" is that "the objec-tive conditions of labour confront labour in *alienated* and *independent* form, as powers in their own right" socially represented by capital (ibid.). (More below on this point.)

3. "When we consider bourgeois society in the long view and as a whole, then the final result of the process of social production always appears as the society itself, i.e., the human being itself in its social relations. . . . The conditions and objectifications of the process are themselves equally mo-ments of it, and its only subjects are the individuals, but individuals in mu-tual relationships, which they equally reproduce and produce anew. The constant process of their own movement, in which they renew themselves even as they renew the world of wealth they create" (Marx, 1973, 712).

4. The ecological relevance of Marx's vision of "long struggles" for a qualitative transformation of production is indirectly supported by Roy Morrison, who projects that the "struggle for the creation of an ecological commons is the struggle for the building of an ecological democracy—community by community, neighborhood by neighborhood, region by region. It represents the struggle and work of fundamental social transformation from below" (1995, 188).

5. See Noble (1977) and Du Boff (1989) on the history of this process in the United States.

6. As Marx indicates: "With the real subsumption of labour under capital, . . . the development of the productive power of labour takes place, in that the productive forces of social labour are developed, and only at that point does the application of natural forces on a large scale, of science and of machinery, to direct production become possible" (1994, 106).

7. See Levins and Lewontin (1985) for the most detailed Marxist critique of the inadequately dialectical, that is, inadequately relational *and* holistic, character of modern scientific theory and practice. The same authors' recent series of articles in the pages of *Capitalism, Nature, Socialism* is also notable in this regard (Levins and Lewontin, 1994; Lewontin and Levins, 1996a, 1996b, 1997a, 1997b).

8. See Chapter 14 for a discussion of the possible role of pre-capitalist technologies in communism's general disalienation of the producers vis-à-vis the conditions of production.

9. The correspondence between the mode of consumption and the mode of production follows from the determinant role of production posited by Marx (1973, 88–100, especially 92). For an illuminating discussion of this aspect of Marx's thinking, see Fine and Harris (1979, 8–12).

10. Which in turn follows from the fact that capitalism entails "the supercession of the mode of production in which personal consumption is the main purpose of production, and in which only the surplus is sold as a commodity" (Marx, 1988, 69). See Chapters 5 and 7 for further discussion.

11. As Marx puts it in the draft of his *Contribution,* the "buying of the [worker's] labour capacity" by the capitalist "naturally places the buyer and the seller in the act of its use in another relationship to each other than that in the buying of objectified labour existing as an object outside the producer" (1987, 506).

12. There is a discernible continuity on this issue from Marx's earliest writings onward. In his Paris Manuscripts of 1844, for example, Marx notes how capitalism "produces sophistication of needs and of their means on the one hand, and a bestial barbarization, a complete, unrefined abstract simplicity of need, on the other" (1964, 148). Marx's *Capital* similarly refers to "the intimate connexion between the pangs of hunger of the most industrious

layers of the working-class, and the extravagant consumption, coarse or re-
fined, of the rich, for which capitalist accumulation is the basis" (1967a, I,
657). In a draft of the same work, one finds this passage: "The surplus produce increases in quantity and value with the accumulation of capital; it is
therefore possible for an ever greater part to be reproduced in the form of
luxury products . . . means of consumption which do not enter the consumption of the working classes" (1988, 226).

13. The environmental consciousness built into Marx's analysis of capitalist industry is evident from passages like the following: "We shall here merely al-
lude to the material conditions under which factory labour is carried on.
Every organ of sense is injured in an equal degree by artificial elevation of
the temperature, by the dust-laden atmosphere, by the deafening noise, not
to mention danger to life and limb among the thickly crowded machinery. . . . Economy of the social means of production, matured and forced as
in a hothouse by the factory system, is turned, in the hands of capital, into
systematic robbery of what is necessary for the life of the workman while he
is at work, robbery of space, light, air, and of protection to his person against
the dangerous and unwholesome accompaniments of the productive
process, not to mention the robbery of appliances for the comfort of the
workman" (1967a, I, 425–27).

14. This illustrates how "the use of products is determined by the social conditions in which the consumers find themselves placed, and these conditions themselves are based on class antagonism" (Marx, 1978a, 57).

15. As Marx indicates: "Although at first the development of the capacities of
the human species takes place at the cost of the majority of human individuals and even classes, in the end it breaks through this contradiction and
coincides with the development of the individual" (1968, 118).

Chapter 12

1. I agree with Ernest Mandel on this issue: "The crisis of capitalist relations
of production must be seen as an overall social crisis—that is, the historical decline of an entire social system and mode of production, operative
through the whole epoch of late capitalism. This is neither identical with
classical crises of overproduction, nor does it exclude them" (Mandel,
1975, 570). See also Clarke (1994, 279–80).

2. Here Weisskopf ignores, among other things, Marx's analysis of capital's
tendency to extend work-time beyond its natural limits (see Chapter 10).

3. "To be a capitalist, is to have not only a purely personal, but a social *status*
in production. Capital is a collective product, and only by the united action of many members, nay, in the last resort, only by the united action of
all members of society, can it be set in motion. Capital is, therefore, not a
personal, it is a social power" (Marx and Engels, 1968, 47).

4. "All the contradictions of the capitalist mode of production can be summed up in one general and fundamental contradiction, that between *the effective socialisation of production* and the *private, capitalistic form of appropriation*" (Mandel, 1968, 170).

5. Similarly, the *Communist Manifesto* treats "commercial crises," with their "epidemic[s] of over-production," as *symptoms* of "the revolt of modern productive forces against modern conditions of production, against the property relations that are the conditions for the existence of the bourgeoisie and of its rule" (Marx and Engels, 1968, 40).

6. During crises, "there are not too many necessities of life produced, in proportion to the existing population. Quite the reverse. Too little is produced to decently and humanely satisfy the wants of the great mass. . . . Not too much wealth is produced. But at times too much wealth is produced in its capitalistic, self-contradictory forms" (Marx, 1967a, III, 257–58). "In these crises a great part not only of the existing products, but also of the previously created productive forces, are periodically destroyed. In these crises there breaks out an epidemic that, in all earlier epochs, would have seemed an absurdity—the epidemic of over-production. Society suddenly finds itself put back into a state of momentary barbarism; it appears as if a famine, a universal war of devastation has cut off the supply of every means of subsistence; industry and commerce seem to be destroyed; and why? Because there is too much civilisation, too much means of subsistence, too much industry, too much commerce. The productive forces at the disposal of society no longer tend to further the development of the conditions of bourgeois property; on the contrary, they have become too powerful for these conditions" (Marx and Engels, 1968, 40–41).

7. Paul Sweezy has proposed that militarism and war should also be viewed as manifestations of capitalism's fundamental contradiction. His reasoning is worth quoting at length: "Actually the contradiction of capitalism consists in an inability to utilize the means of production 'for an ever expanding system of the life process for the benefit of the society of producers.' Under certain circumstances this manifests itself in stagnation and unemployment, that is to say, in the *non-utilization* of a part of the means of production. Under other circumstances, however, it manifests itself in the utilization of the means of production for the purposes of foreign expansion. Stagnation and unemployment on the one hand and militarism and war on the other are therefore alternative, and to a large extent mutually exclusive, forms of expression of the contradiction of capitalism" (Sweezy, 1970, 343).

8. The conception of historical crisis presented in this section has profited from the prior work of Rader (1979, Chapter 5). See also Michael Harrington's discussion of capitalist socialization in his last work, *Socialism: Past and Future* (Harrington, 1989, 8–9 and *passim*).

9. It may be suggested that this intensifying conflict could itself be due to a worsening of accumulation crises. True enough; but this would not preclude the presence of other factors making it more difficult to restore profitability without marginalizing the producers' needs. Besides, worsening accumulation crises themselves require explanation in terms of the historical contradictions of capitalist relations.

10. This is a direct application of the approach demarcated in Marx's 1859 Preface: "At a certain stage of development, the material productive forces of society come into conflict with the existing relations of production. . . . From forms of development of the productive forces these relations turn into their fetters" (1970, 21).

11. Marx analyzes the latter aspect in Chapter 24, Section 1, of *Capital*, Volume I, under the category of "transition of the laws of property that characterise production of commodities into laws of capitalist appropriation." See also the discussion in the *Grundrisse* (Marx, 1973, 450–58) and the exegesis by Rosdolsky (1977, Chapters 10 and 19).

12. Veblen also sees this growing discord between profits and contributions to social production. He argues that the "returns actually accruing" to the capitalist are "a measure of the differential advantage held by him by virtue of his having become legally seized of the material contrivances by which the technological achievements of the community are put into effect," and that this "capitalisation of technological expedients" grows more regressive as "the capital required to put the commonplace knowledge to effect grows larger" (1961, 186, 200).

13. Combining the insights of Marx and Veblen with a lifelong study of advanced capitalism in the United States and Japan, Shigeto Tsuru suggests that "profits have become an index of the degree of success in *not* making others share the progress in productivity which in the nature of things should redound to all"—so that "net internal surplus under corporate capitalism does not reflect truthfully the socially desired activities" (1993, 222). The problem is that "giant corporations," based on their control over necessary conditions of production, "are capable of perpetuating excess returns to themselves through oligopolistic price maintenance and various other devices such as privatizing particular innovations as well-guarded know-how" (ibid.). See Du Boff (1989) for an historical treatment of this phenomenon.

14. Insofar as these conditions are monopolizable *and* scarce, they may yield rents when they are appropriated; but such rents entail a *redistribution* of surplus value and as such do not negate the fact that the relevant conditions are freely appropriated by capital as a whole (see Chapters 6 and 7).

15. As Mandel observes: "The contradiction between the increasing objective socialisation of labour and the further continuance of private appropriation . . . corresponds to the contradiction between the increasing disap-

pearance of private labour . . . and the survival of the commodity form of exchange value or profit . . . which is based on private labour" (1975, 565).

16. Hence the producers and their communities "find themselves confronted by the *functions* of the capital that lives in the capitalist. The social forms of their own labour—both subjectively and objectively—or, in other words, the forms of *their own* social labour, are utterly independent of the workers. Subsumed under capital the workers become components of these social formations, but these social formations do not belong to them and so rise up against them as the *forms* of capital itself, as if they belonged to capital, as if they arose from it and were integrated within it, in opposition to the isolated labour-power of the workers" (Marx, 1977, 1054–55).

17. This historical barrier shows how capitalism's "historical progress and extension of exchanges develops the contrast, latent in commodities, between use-value and value" (Marx, 1967a, I, 86).

Chapter 13

1. Similarly, in a draft of *Capital,* Volume I, Marx observes that under capitalism, the production of life's necessities "confronts labour as an *alien power,* as an *independent power;* while labour confronts the latter again and again in the same objectlessness, as mere labour capacity" (1988, 113).

2. In reconsidering the capital-labor relation in terms of the opposed positions of capital and labor vis-à-vis use value and exchange value, this section follows a tradition established by Cleaver (1979) and Lebowitz (1992a).

3. Given that "capital exists and can only exist as many capitals," it follows that "its self-determination" necessarily "appears as their reciprocal interaction with one another" (Marx, 1973, 414). "In competition," the "inner tendency of capital" toward self-expansion "appears as a compulsion exercised over it by *alien capital,* which drives it forward . . . with a constant, *march, march!*" (413). For a detailed discussion of Marx's approach to competition, see Burkett (1986b).

4. This is the sense in which Marx describes the struggle over the regulation of work-time as a "great contest between the blind rule of the supply and demand laws which form the political economy of the middle class, and social production controlled by social foresight, which forms the political economy of the working class" (1974a, 79). For Marx, the English Ten Hours Bill "was the victory of a principle," insofar as "the political economy of the middle class succumbed to the political economy of the working class" (ibid.). See Chapter 10 for further discussion.

5. Underlying Engels' call for "a general union, a political organisation of the working class as a whole" was a vision of "the working class . . . awakening to the consciousness that it has for some time been moving in the

wrong groove; that the present movements for higher wages and shorter hours exclusively, keep it in a vicious circle out of which there is no issue; that it is not the lowness of wages which forms the fundamental evil, but the wages system itself" (quoted in Lapides, 1990, 129).

6. It is in this sense that "every movement in which the working class as a *class* confronts the ruling classes and tries to constrain them by pressure from without is a political movement" (Marx to Bolte, November 23, 1871, in Marx and Engels [1975, 254]).

7. Habermas (1975, 71) suggests that capitalism's tendency to commodify and bureaucratize social relations may increase the popularity of autonomous, emancipatory working-class activity in these areas.

8. This paragraph draws from Toni Negri's extremely rich analysis of struggles for reappropriation and co-production of the conditions of production by workers and communities—an analysis informed by the December 1995 explosion in France (Negri, 1997). Ivan Illich's case for co-production—which he calls "convivial" production—is also relevant in this context (Illich, 1973).

9. There is an obvious complementarity between educational struggles and movements centered on other socialized conditions of production whose self-administered co-production could benefit from increased access to educational resources. See Illich (1971) on this point.

10. It is, perhaps, with this conversion in mind that Marx projects: "Society simply does not find its equilibrium until it revolves around the sun of labour" (1989a, 53–54).

11. This paragraph and the next two draw on the analysis in Lebowitz (1992a, 100; 1992b).

12. It may be added that if free human development is inherently anti-natural, there is little hope for a sustainable and desirable co-evolution of society and nature. History and logic both show that human development simply will not and cannot be *universally* restricted. True, the human development of the laboring class has normally been restricted to provide for the less restricted development of the few. This is precisely how human development occurs in class societies (see Chapter 11). In reality, then, those championing the conscious restriction of human development as an "ecological" guide to the problem of co-evolution are effectively calling for a continuation of class rule. For instance, even if one supposes that human development is to be universally restricted in order to "liberate nature," someone must still determine what kinds of restrictions must be imposed, how they will be enforced, and so on. In this way, the premise of universal, equal restriction tends to contradict itself. This difficulty is not shared by Marx and Engels' vision of a universally less restricted human development precisely in and through a universal knowledge of natural and social necessities (see Chapter 14).

13. This statement bucks the currently fashionable denial of all historical logics, especially those based on contradictory evolutionary tendencies built into capitalism. In my opinion, this denial marks the complete break of post modernist ideology from Marx—whatever complex discourses may be concocted to paper over the rupture. For further discussion, see Wood and Foster (1997).

14. Capital's systematic blockage of information makes it doubly difficult to gauge the likely effectiveness of any given regulatory regime insofar as this effectiveness depends on the ability to project the ecological impacts of any inputs and processes substituted for the ones being curbed.

15. Leff observes that the development of ecologically sustainable production "as a material base for the development of new self-managed social forces of production" requires "the creative integration of workers into the innovation of technologies" (1995, 77). "In this way, skill development, an increase in the productivity of labor power, increased efficiency of the productive forces, and the enhancement of ecological potentials would all be embedded in a continuous and integrated process" (70). To be effective, eco-technological integration must encompass not just labor but also communities, insofar as the latter are also users of natural wealth. The democratic valuation of nature as social wealth must also incorporate people as community members, not just as workers (see Chapter 14).

Chapter 14

1. Geoffrey Carpenter also refers to Marx's apparently unqualified "faith in the ability of an improved mode of production to eradicate scarcity indefinitely" (1997, 140). For additional claims along these lines, see the introduction to Chapter 11.

2. By contrast, Paresh Chattopadhyay suggests that Marx's vision of communism "as a free union of producers with the conditions of production excluding private property in the means of production, commodity relations and wage labor along with the state—all symbols of human alienation—appears to be the most thoroughgoing and self-consistent project of social emancipation and hence . . . worth studying as such" (1992, 91). I hope my basic agreement with Chattopadhyay's viewpoint is clear from the present chapter.

3. "We need more knowledge still, but of a different kind from the fragmentary, unco-ordinated triumphs of modern specialists; . . . we need more power, too, the human power to control, to inhibit, to direct, to restrain, to withhold, in direct proportion to our augmented physical power to explode and destroy" (Mumford, 1954, 113).

4. See Wallis (1993, 147–48) for a discussion of the issues involved in such an integrative approach.

5. Similarly, Ray Dasmann projects that "the communities of the future could be places of endless diversity where people could learn once more to enjoy the process of living and the pleasant work that goes with an understanding of the functioning of man and nature" (1975, 159).

6. "Unlimited profit and unlimited power can no longer be the determining elements in technics, if our civilization as a whole is to be saved: social and personal development must take precedence" (Mumford, 1954, 59).

7. My reading of the logic governing Marx's communist vision follows Chattopadhyay (1992, 1994).

8. The decommodification of labor power corresponds to the fact that "society"—not capital and wage-labor responding to market signals—"distributes labour-power and means of production to the different branches of production." Hence, under "socialised production the money-capital" (including the payment of money wages) "is eliminated" (Marx, 1967a, II, 358). "The producers may . . . receive paper vouchers entitling them to withdraw from the social supplies of consumer goods a quantity corresponding to their labour-time"; but such "vouchers are not money" because "they do not circulate" (ibid.). In other words, "the future distribution of the necessaries of life" cannot be treated "as a kind of more exalted wages" (Engels, 1939, 221).

9. Stated conversely, "to say that [the workers] are the owners of the means of production amounts to saying that these belong to the united workers and that they produce as such, and that their own output is controlled jointly by them" (Marx, 1971, 525).

10. Witness Marx's description of joint stock companies as a contradictory form of social ownership, or "the abolition of the capitalist mode of production within the capitalist mode of production itself . . . private production without the control of private property" (1967a, III, 438). Marx treats stock ownership as a form in which "the antagonism" between private appropriation and social production "is resolved negatively," and as a necessary "transition toward the conversion of all functions in the reproduction process which still remain linked with capitalist property, into mere functions of associated producers, into social functions" (ibid., 437, 440).

11. Similarly, in one of the draft manuscripts for *Capital,* Marx suggests that "the individual's ownership of the conditions of production appears as not only unnecessary but incompatible with . . . production on a large scale. This is represented in the capitalist mode of production by the fact that the capitalist—the *non-worker*—is the owner of these social masses of means of production. He never in fact represents towards the workers their unification, their social unity. Therefore, as soon as this contradictory form ceases to exist, it emerges that they own these means of production *socially,* not as *private individuals.* Capitalist property is only a contradictory expression of their social property—i.e., their negated individual property—in the conditions of production" (1994, 108).

12. Marx and Engels insist that in "the community of revolutionary proletarians . . . it is as individuals that the individuals participate," precisely *because* "it is the association of individuals . . . which puts the conditions of the free development and movement of individuals under their control—conditions which were previously left to chance and had acquired an independent existence over against the separate individuals" (1976, 89).

13. "Surplus-labour in general, as labour performed over and above the given requirements, must always remain. . . . A definite quantity of surplus-labour is required as insurance against accidents, and by the necessary and progressive expansion of the process of reproduction in keeping with the development of the needs and the growth of population" (Marx, 1967a, III, 819). For similar formulations, see ibid., III, 847, I, 530; also Marx (1963, 107).

14. The labor-time standard for consumption claims raises important social and technical issues—especially whether and how differentials in labor intensity, work conditions, and skills would be measured and compensated. See Engels (1939, 220–22) and Marx (1966, 9–10).

15. "But one of the most vital principles of communism, a principle which distinguishes it from all reactionary socialism, is its empirical view, based on a knowledge of man's nature, that differences of *brain* and of intellectual ability do not imply any differences whatsoever in the nature of the *stomach* and of physical *needs;* therefore the false tenet, based upon existing circumstances, 'to each according to his abilities', must be changed . . . into the tenet, '*to each according to his need*'" (Marx and Engels, 1976, 566).

16. In Volume I of *Capital,* Marx again describes "directly associated labour" as "a form of production that is entirely inconsistent with the production of commodities" (1967a, I, 94). There is also an extended discussion of this point in *Anti-Dühring* (Engels, 1939, 337–38).

17. Elsewhere, Marx emphasizes capitalism's alienation of "the *social* character of wealth" by pointing out that money and credit "represent independent incarnations" of social life as "a world beyond . . . alongside of and external to the real elements of social wealth" (1967a, III, 573).

18. Marx and Engels argue that the communist "appropriation" of the conditions of production "can only be effected through a union, which by the character of the proletariat itself can again only be a universal one, and through a revolution, in which, on the one hand, the power of the earlier mode of production and intercourse and social organisation is overthrown, and, on the other hand, there develops the universal character and the energy of the proletariat, which are required to accomplish the appropriation, and the proletariat moreover rids itself of everything that still clings to it from its previous position in society" (1976, 97).

19. See Chapter 10 for Marx's view of free time and human development.

20. For Marxist responses to Nove's arguments, see Chattopadhyay (1986), Mandel (1986), and Devine (1988). Both Devine (1988) and Albert and Hahnel (1991) present fully articulated models of cooperative-democratic planning and production without markets.

21. The environmental shortcomings of U.S.S.R.-type "socialism" are well known, and their causes lie outside the bounds of this book. See, however, the useful discussions in Foster (1994, 96–101), Mirovitskaya and Soroos (1995), and O'Connor (1998, 256–65).

22. Consider also the similarity between Marx's projection and Ray Dasmann's call for "a change in attitude toward land. So long as it is regarded as a mere commodity whose value is to be judged only in the market place, we will continue to destroy the earth on which we depend. When land is regarded as the home for people and other living things, as the sole base for humanity's future—then there will be hope" (1975, 126).

23. Similarly, in *The Housing Question,* Engels suggests that "the abolition of the antithesis between town and country is no more and no less utopian than the abolition of the antithesis between capitalists and wage-workers. From day to day it is becoming more and more a practical demand of both industrial and agricultural production" (1979, 92).

24. See Foster (1997) and Foster and Magdoff (1998) for historical analyses demonstrating the contemporary relevance of Marx's vision of a sustainable agricultural-industrial system.

25. In *Capital,* Marx again projects "that when the working-class comes into power, as inevitably it must, technical instruction, both theoretical and practical, will take its proper place in the working-class schools" (1967a, I, 488).

26. The present interpretation follows Bertell Ollman, who speaks of people "becoming conscious of the internal relations between what are today called 'natural' and 'social' worlds, and treating the hitherto separate halves as a single totality. In learning about either society or nature, the individual will recognize that he is learning about both" (1979, 76). This intrinsic unity of social and natural science is a logical corollary of the unity of humanity and nature, in Marx's view. As stated in *The German Ideology:* "We know only a single science, the science of history. One can look at history from two sides and divide it into the history of nature and the history of men. The two sides are, however, inseparable; the history of nature and the history of men are dependent on each other so long as men exist" (Marx and Engels, 1976, 34).

27. Marx argues that "the fact of the collective working group being composed of individuals of both sexes and all ages, must necessarily, under suitable conditions, become a source of humane development" (1967a, I, 490).

28. Marx's projection of planned relative overproduction follows the work of Thomas More, whose Utopians do not consider themselves to have a

"sufficient store of provision . . . until they have provided for the two years following, because of the uncertainty of the next year's crop" (More, 1947, 100).

29. The fact that Marx's conception of a rationally planned agriculture does not involve complete human control over the vagaries of nature is clear from his response to Lewis Henry Morgan's claim, in his book *Ancient Society,* that "mankind are the only beings who may be said to have gained an absolute control over the production of food." Recording this statement in his ethnological notebooks, Marx stressed the words "have gained an absolute control," appending to them only the parenthetical comment: "?!" (Marx, 1974b, 99).

30. A similar interpretation is given by Ollman, who suggests that "when communist people fully comprehend nature they will not desire anything which stands outside their effective reach" (1979, 75).

31. Marx criticizes the Gotha Programme for not making it "sufficiently clear that land is included in the instruments of labour" in this connection (1966, 6).

32. See the discussion earlier in this section. Ernest Mandel suggests that "the half-workday of four hours, or the half workweek of twenty hours, would provide the ideal conditions for self-administration on a mass scale" (1992, 202).

33. Marx and Engels foresee a situation, "in communist society, where nobody has one exclusive sphere of activity but each can become accomplished in any branch he wishes," so that each person can "do one thing today and another tomorrow" (1976, 53).

34. This concern with nature's aesthetic use value extended to Marx and Engels personally. When convalescing in Monte Carlo near the end of his life, Marx penned a letter to Engels, observing: "You will know everything about the charm exerted by the beauties of nature here. . . . Many of its features vividly recall those of Africa" (Marx to Engels, May 8, 1882, in Marx and Engels [1992, 253]). "A really beautiful situation," is how he described it to his daughter in a letter written the same day (Marx to Longuet, May 8, 1882, in Marx and Engels [1992, 255]). Engels' instrumental conception of nature did not prevent his study of "comparative physiology" from instilling in him "a withering contempt for the idealistic exaltation of man over the other animals" (Engels to Marx, July 14, 1858, in Marx and Engels [1975, 102]). For further discussion of Marx and Engels' personal love of nature, see Parsons (1977, 41, 46).

35. Mandel provides a practical definition of demand saturation, according to which a particular product is abundant "when the marginal elasticity of demand for it," that is, the response of monetary demand to a reduction in price, "is around or below zero," at which point "its distribution free of

charge is economically more efficient than further sales at declining 'real' prices, since distribution costs are then sharply reduced" (1992, 206).

36. "The limit of capitalist production is the excess time of the labourers. The absolute spare time gained by society does not concern it. The development of productivity concerns it only in so far as it increases the surplus labour-time of the working-class, not because it decreases the labour-time for material production in general. It moves thus in a contradiction" (Marx, 1967a, III, 264). Elsewhere, Marx relates this angle on capitalism's fundamental contradiction to overproduction crises, observing that capital's "tendency" is "always, on the one side, *to create disposable time, on the other, to convert it into surplus labour.* If it succeeds too well at the first, then it suffers from surplus production. . . . The more this contradiction develops, the more does it become evident that the growth of the forces of production can no longer be bound up with the appropriation of alien labour, but that the mass of workers must themselves appropriate their own surplus labour" (1973, 708).

References

Adams, John. 1996. "Cost-Benefit Analysis: The Problem, Not the Solution." *The Ecologist,* Vol. 26, No. 1, January/February, 2–4.

Albert, Michael, and Robin Hahnel. 1991. *The Political Economy of Participatory Economics.* Princeton: Princeton University Press.

Altvater, Elmar. 1990. "The Foundations of Life (Nature) and the Maintenance of Life (Work)." *International Journal of Political Economy,* Vol. 20, No. 1, Spring, 10–34.

———. 1993. *The Future of the Market: An Essay on the Regulation of Money and Nature after the Collapse of "Actually Existing Socialism."* London: Verso.

———. 1994. "Ecological and Economic Modalities of Time and Space." In *Is Capitalism Sustainable? Political Economy and the Politics of Ecology,* Martin O'Connor, editor, 76–90. New York: Guilford.

Amin, Samir. 1992. "Can Environmental Problems Be Subject to Economic Calculations?" *World Development,* Vol. 20, No. 4, April, 523–30.

Auerbach, Paul, and Peter Skott. 1993. "Capitalist Trends and Socialist Priorities." *Science & Society,* Vol. 57, No. 2, Summer, 194–204.

Bahro, Rudolf. 1978. *The Alternative in Eastern Europe.* London: New Left Books.

Baksi, Pradip. 1996. "Karl Marx's Study of Science and Technology." *Nature, Society, and Thought,* Vol. 9, No. 3, 261–96.

Benton, Ted. 1989. "Marxism and Natural Limits: An Ecological Critique and Reconstruction." *New Left Review,* No. 178, November/December, 51–86.

Bina, Cyrus. 1989. "Some Controversies in the Development of Rent Theory: The Nature of Oil Rent." *Capital & Class,* No. 39, Winter, 82–112.

Bleifuss, Joel. 1997. "Taking Care of Business." *In These Times,* Vol. 21, No. 18, July 28, 12–13.

Booth, Douglas E. 1994. "Ethics and the Limits of Environmental Economics." *Ecological Economics,* Vol. 9, No. 3, April, 241–52.

Botella, Luisa Redondo. 1993. "Engels on the Origins and Development of Mathematics." *Nature, Society, and Thought,* Vol. 6, No. 4, 389–409.

Braverman, Harry. 1974. *Labor and Monopoly Capital: The Degradation of Work in the Twentieth Century.* New York: Monthly Review Press.

Brecher, Jeremy, John Brown Childs, and Jill Cutler. 1993. *Global Visions: Beyond the New World Order.* Boston: South End Press.

Brecher, Jeremy, and Tim Costello. 1994. *Global Village or Global Pillage: Economic Reconstruction from the Bottom Up.* Boston: South End Press.

Breslow, Marc. 1997. "Can We Afford to Stop Global Warming?" *Dollars and Sense,* No. 214, November/December, 21–24.

Briggs, Shirley A. 1997. "Thirty-Five Years with *Silent Spring.*" *Organization & Environment,* Vol. 10, No. 1, March, 73–84.

Burkett, Paul. 1986a. "Critical Notes on the 'Free Rider Problem' in Collective Action." *Forum for Social Economics,* Fall, 29–43.

———. 1986b. "A Note on Competition under Capitalism." *Capital & Class,* No. 30, Winter, 192–208.

———. 1987. "Instrumental Justice and Social Economics: Some Comments from a Marxian Perspective." *Review of Social Economy,* Vol. 45, No. 3, December, 313–24.

———. 1991. "Some Comments on 'Capital in General and the Structure of Marx's *Capital*.'" *Capital & Class,* No. 44, Summer, 49–72.

———. 1995. "Capitalization Versus Socialization of Nature." *Capitalism, Nature, Socialism,* Vol. 6, No. 4, December, 92–100.

———. 1996a. "On Some Common Misconceptions about Nature and Marx's Critique of Political Economy." *Capitalism, Nature, Socialism,* Vol. 7, No. 3, September, 57–80.

———. 1996b. "Value, Capital and Nature: Some Ecological Implications of Marx's Critique of Political Economy." *Science & Society,* Vol. 60, No. 3, Fall, 332–59.

———. 1997. "Nature in Marx Reconsidered: A Silver Anniversary Assessment of Alfred Schmidt's *Concept of Nature in Marx.*" *Organization & Environment,* Vol. 10, No. 2, June, 164–83.

———. 1998a. "A Critique of Neo-Malthusian Marxism: Society, Nature, and Population." *Historical Materialism,* No. 2, Summer 1998, 118–42.

———. 1998b. "A Critique of Neo-Malthusian Marxism: Labor, Nature, and Capital." manuscript under review.

Campbell, Robert W. 1974. *The Soviet-Type Economies: Performance and Evolution,* 3rd ed. Boston: Houghton Mifflin.

———. 1991. *The Socialist Economies in Transition.* Bloomington: Indiana University Press.

Carchedi, Guglielmo. 1991. *Frontiers of Political Economy.* London: Verso.

Carpenter, Geoffrey P. 1997. "Redefining Scarcity: Marxism and Ecology Reconciled." *Democracy & Nature,* Vol. 3, No. 3, 129–53.

Carson, Rachel. 1962. *Silent Spring.* Boston: Houghton Mifflin.

Carver, Terrell. 1980. "Marx, Engels and Dialectics." *Political Studies,* Vol. 28, No. 3, September, 353–63.

Chatterjee, Pratap. 1997. "Toxic Racism: Chippewas Resist Deadly Dumping." *Dollars and Sense,* No. 211, May/June, 13–15.

Chattopadhyay, Paresh. 1986. "Socialism: Utopian and Feasible." *Monthly Review,* Vol. 37, No. 10, March, 40–53.

————. 1992. "The Economic Content of Socialism: Marx vs. Lenin." *Review of Radical Political Economics,* Vol. 24, No. 3–4, Fall/Winter, 90–110.

————. 1994. *The Marxian Concept of Capital and the Soviet Experience: Essay in the Critique of Political Economy.* Westport, CT: Praeger.

————. 1995. "Market and Socialism: A Materialist Point of View." Mimeo. Université du Québec à Montréal.

Churchill, Ward. 1993. *Struggle for the Land: Indigenous Resistance to Genocide, Ecocide and Expropriation in Comtemporary North America.* Monroe, ME: Common Courage Press.

Clark, John P. 1989. "Marx's Inorganic Body." *Environmental Ethics,* Vol. 11, No. 3, Fall, 243–58.

Clarke, Simon. 1994. *Marx's Theory of Crisis.* London: Macmillan.

Cleaver, Harry. 1979. *Reading "Capital" Politically.* Austin: University of Texas Press.

Colchester, Marcus. 1994. "The New Sultans: Asian Loggers Move in on Guyana's Forests." *The Ecologist,* Vol. 24, No. 2, March/April, 45–52.

Colletti, Lucio. 1972. *From Rousseau to Lenin: Studies in Ideology and Society.* London: New Left Books.

Crosby, Alfred W., Elizabeth Dore, John C. Ryan, Sidney W. Mintz, William Roseberry, Daniel Faber, and Warren Dean. 1991. "The Conquest of Nature, 1492–1992." *Report on the Americas,* Vol. 25, No. 2, September, 5–40.

Danaher, Kevin (editor). 1994. *50 years Is Enough: The Case against the World Bank and the International Monetary Fund.* Boston: South End Press in association with Global Exchange.

Dasmann, Raymond F. 1968. *Environmental Conservation,* 2nd ed. New York: John Wiley & Sons.

————. 1972. *Planet in Peril: Man and the Biosphere Today.* New York: New World Publishing.

————. 1975. *The Conservation Alternative.* New York: John Wiley & Sons.

Dasmann, Raymond F., John Milton, and Peter H. Freeman. 1973. *Ecological Principles for Economic Development.* New York: John Wiley & Sons.

Dauvergne, Peter. 1997. *Shadows in the Forest: Japan and the Politics of Timber in East Asia.* Cambridge: MIT Press.

Deléage, Jean-Paul. 1994. "Eco-Marxist Critique of Political Economy." In *Is Capitalism Sustainable? Political Economy and the Politics of Ecology,* Martin O'Connor, editor, 37–52. New York: Guilford.

Devine, James. 1993. "The Law of Value and Marxian Political Ecology." In, *Green On Red: Evolving Ecological Socialism,* Jesse Vorst, Ross Dobson, and Ron Fletcher, editors, 133–54. Winnipeg: Fernwood Publishing in association with the Society for Socialist Studies.

Devine, Pat. 1988. *Democracy and Economic Planning: The Political Economy of a Self-governing Society.* Boulder, CO: Westview Press.

Dore, Mohammed H. I. 1996. "The Problem of Valuation in Neoclassical Environmental Economics." *Environmental Ethics,* Vol. 18, No. 1, Spring, 65–70.

Draper, Hal. 1977–90. *Karl Marx's Theory of Revolution,* 4 vols. New York: Monthly Review Press. (Vol. I: *State and Bureaucracy* [1977]; Vol. II: *The Politics of Social Classes* [1978]; Vol. III: *The "Dictatorship of the Proletariat"* [1986]; Vol. IV: *Critique of Other Socialisms* [1990].)

Du Boff, Richard B. 1989. *Accumulation and Power: An Economic History of the United States.* Armonk, NY: M. E. Sharpe.

Economist. 1997a. "A Warming World: Countries Have Not Lived Up to Their Environmental Promises." June 28, 41–42.

Economist. 1997b. "Global Warming Meets the Prodigal Eagle." October 11, 25–29.

Engels, Frederick. 1939. *Herr Eugen Dühring's Revolution in Science (Anti-Dühring).* New York: International Publishers.

———. 1964a. *Dialectics of Nature.* Moscow: Progress Publishers.

———. 1964b. "Outlines of a Critique of Political Economy." In *Economic and Philosophical Manuscripts of 1844,* by Karl Marx, 197–226. New York: International Publishers.

———. 1973. *The Condition of the Working-Class in England.* Moscow: Progress Publishers.

———. 1979. *The Housing Question.* Moscow: Progress Publishers.

Enzensberger, Hans Magnus. 1974. "A Critique of Political Ecology." *New Left Review,* No.84. Reprinted in *The Greening of Marxism,* Ted Benton, editor, 17–49. New York: Guilford, 1996.

Fairlie, Simon, 1992. "Long Distance, Short Life: Why Big Business Favours Recycling." *The Ecologist,* Vol. 22, No. 6, November/December, 276–83.

Feuer, Lewis S. 1989. "Introduction." In *Karl Marx and Friedrich Engels: Basic Writings on Politics and Philosophy,* Lewis Feuer, editor, vii-xix. Garden City, NY: Anchor Books.

Fine, Ben. 1979. "On Marx's Theory of Agricultural Rent." *Economy and Society,* Vol. 8, No. 3, August, 241–78.

———. 1994. "Consumption in Contemporary Capitalism: Beyond Marx and Veblen—A Comment." *Review of Social Economy,* Vol. 52, No. 3, Fall, 391–96.

Fine, Ben, and Laurence Harris. 1979. *Rereading Capital.* New York: Columbia University Press.

Fine, Ben, and Ellen Leopold. 1993. *The World of Consumption.* London: Routledge.

Foster, John Bellamy. 1994. *The Vulnerable Planet: A Short Economic History of the Environment.* New York: Monthly Review Press.

———. 1995. "Marx and the Environment." *Monthly Review,* Vol. 47, No. 3, July/August, 108–23.

———. 1996. "Sustainable Development of What?" *Capitalism, Nature, Socialism,* Vol. 7, No. 3, September, 129–32.

———. 1997. "The Crisis of the Earth: Marx's Theory of Ecological Sustainability as a Nature-Imposed Necessity for Human Production." *Organization & Environment,* Vol. 10, No. 3, September, 278–95.

Foster, John Bellamy, and Fred Magdoff. 1998. "Liebig, Marx and the Depletion of Soil Fertility: Relevance for Today's Agriculture." *Monthly Review,* Vol. 50, No. 3, July/August, 1–16.

Gellen, Martin. 1970. "The Making of a Pollution-Industrial Complex." In *Eco-Catastrophe,* Editors of *Ramparts,* editors, 73–83. San Francisco: Harper & Row.

Georgescu-Roegen, Nicholas. 1971. *The Entropy Law and the Economic Process.* Cambridge: Harvard University Press.

Gorz, André. 1994. *Capitalism, Socialism, Ecology.* London: Verso.

Gowdy, John M. 1994a. *Coevolutionary Economics: The Economy, Society and the Environment.* Boston: Kluwer Academic Press.

———. 1994b. "The Social Context of Natural Capital: The Social Limits to Sustainable Development." *International Journal of Social Economics,* Vol. 21, No. 8, 43–55.

———. 1995. "Trade and Environmental Sustainability: An Evolutionary Perspective." *Review of Social Economy,* Vol. 53, No. 4, Winter, 493–510.

Gowdy, John M., and Peg R. Olsen. 1994. "Further Problems with Neoclassical Environmental Economics." *Environmental Ethics,* Vol. 16, No. 2, Summer, 161–71.

Grundmann, Reiner. 1991a. *Marxism and Ecology.* Oxford, UK: Clarendon Press.

———. 1991b. "The Ecological Challenge to Marxism." *New Left Review,* No. 187, May/June, 103–20.

Habermas, Jürgen. 1975. *Legitimation Crisis.* Boston: Beacon Press.

Hamilton, Clive. 1997. "The Sustainability of Logging in Indonesia's Tropical Forests: A Dynamic Input-Output Analysis." *Ecological Economics,* Vol. 21, No. 3, June, 183–95.

Harrington, Michael. 1989. *Socialism: Past and Future.* New York: Little, Brown.

Harvey, David. 1982. *The Limits to Capital.* Oxford, UK: Basil Blackwell.

———. 1993. "The Nature of Environment: The Dialectics of Social and Environmental Change." In *Socialist Register 1993: Real Problems, False Solutions,* Ralph Miliband and Leo Panitch, editors, 1–51. London: Merlin.

Hayden, Dolores. 1983. "Capitalism, Socialism, and the Built Environment." In *Socialist Visions,* Steve Rosskamm Shalom, editor, 59–81. Boston: South End Press.

Hillerman, Tony. 1997. "Who Has Sovereignty over Mother Earth?" *New York Times,* September 18, p. A23.

Horton, Stephen. 1995. "Rethinking Recycling: The Politics of the Waste Crisis." *Capitalism, Nature, Socialism,* Vol. 6, No. 1, March, 1–19.

———. 1997. "Value, Waste and the Built Environment: A Marxian Analysis." *Capitalism, Nature, Socialism,* Vol. 8, No. 1, March, 127–39.

Illich, Ivan. 1971. *Deschooling Society.* New York: Harper & Row.

———. 1973. *Tools for Conviviality.* New York: Harper & Row.

Junker, Louis. 1982. "The Ceremonial-Instrumental Dichotomy in Institutional Analysis: The Nature, Scope and Radical Implications of the Conflicting Systems." *American Journal of Economics and Sociology,* Vol. 41, No. 2, April, 141–50.

Karliner, Joshua. 1994. "The Environment Industry: Profiting from Pollution." *The Ecologist*, Vol. 24, No. 2, March/April, 59–63.

Kay, Geoffrey. 1979. "Why Labour Is the Starting Point of *Capital*." In *Value: The Representation of Labour Under Capitalism*, Diane Elson, editor, 46–66. London: CSE Books.

Kellogg, Paul. 1991. "Engels and the Roots of 'Revisionism': A Re-Evaluation." *Science & Society*, Vol. 55, No. 2, Summer, 158–74.

Kolko, Joyce. 1988. *Restructuring the World Economy*. New York: Pantheon Books.

Kovel, Joel. 1997. "The Enemy of Nature." *Monthly Review*, Vol. 49, No. 6, November, 6–14.

Lapides, Kenneth. 1990. *Marx and Engels on the Trade Unions*. New York: International Publishers.

Leacock, Eleanor Burke. 1978. "Introduction." In *The Origin of the Family, Private Property and the State*, by Frederick Engels, 7–67. New York: International Publishers.

Lebowitz, Michael A. 1992a. *Beyond Capital: Marx's Political Economy of the Working Class*. New York: St. Martin's Press.

―――. 1992b. "Capitalism: How Many Contradictions?" *Capitalism, Nature, Socialism*, Vol. 3, No. 3, September, 92–94.

Leff, Enrique. 1992. "A Second Contradiction of Capitalism? Notes for the Environmental Transformation of Historical Materialism." *Capitalism, Nature, Socialism*, Vol. 3, No. 4, December, 109–16.

―――. 1993. "Marxism and the Environmental Question: From the Critical Theory of Production to an Environmental Rationality for Sustainable Development." *Capitalism, Nature, Socialism*, Vol. 4, No. 1, March, 44–66.

―――. 1995. *Green Production: Toward an Environmental Rationality*. New York: Guilford.

Levins, Richard, and Richard C. Lewontin. 1985. *The Dialectical Biologist*. Cambridge: Harvard University Press.

―――. 1994. "Holism and Reductionism in Ecology." *Capitalism, Nature, Socialism*, Vol. 5, No. 4, December, 33–40.

Levy, David. 1997. "Not to Worry, Say Business Lobbyists." *Dollars and Sense*, No. 214, November/December, 20, 24–25.

Lewontin, Richard, and Richard Levins. 1996a. "The Return of Old Diseases and the Appearance of New Ones." *Capitalism, Nature, Socialism*, Vol. 7, No. 2, June, 103–7.

―――. 1996b. "False Dichotomies." *Capitalism, Nature, Socialism*, Vol. 7, No. 3, September, 27–30.

―――. 1997a. "Chance and Necessity." *Capitalism, Nature, Socialism*, Vol. 8, No. 1, March, 65–68.

―――. 1997b. "The Biological and the Social." *Capitalism, Nature, Socialism*, Vol. 8, No. 3, September, 89–92.

Löwy, Michael. 1997. "For a Critical Marxism." *Against the Current*, Vol. 12, No. 5 (n.s.), November-December, 31–35.

Luxemburg, Rosa. 1964. *The Accumulation of Capital.* New York: Monthly Review Press.

Mandel, Ernest. 1968. *Marxist Economic Theory,* Vol. I. New York: Monthly Review Press.

————. 1971. *The Formation of the Economic Thought of Karl Marx.* New York: Monthly Review Press.

————. 1973. "Mercantile Categories in the Period of Transition." In *Man and Socialism in Cuba: The Great Debate,* Bertram Silverman, editor, 60–97. New York: Atheneum.

————. 1975. *Late Capitalism.* London: New Left Books.

————. 1986. "In Defence of Socialist Planning." *New Left Review,* No. 159, September/October, 5–37.

————. 1992. *Power and Money: A Marxist Theory of Bureaucracy.* London: Verso.

Martínez-Alier, Juan. 1995a. "Political Ecology, Distributional Conflicts, and Economic Incommensurability." *New Left Review,* No. 211, May/June, 70–88.

————. 1995b. "Distributional Issues in Ecological Economics." *Review of Social Economy,* Vol. 53, No. 3, Winter, 511–28.

Marx, Karl. 1933. *Wage-Labour and Capital.* New York: International Publishers.

————. 1963. *Theories of Surplus Value,* Pt. 1. Moscow: Progress Publishers.

————. 1964. *Economic and Philosophical Manuscripts of 1844.* New York: International Publishers.

————. 1966. *Critique of the Gotha Programme.* New York: International Publishers.

————. 1967a. *Capital,* Vols. I-III. New York: International Publishers (1977 printing).

————. 1967b. "Excerpt-Notes of 1844." In *Writings of the Young Marx on Philosophy and Society,* Loyd D. Easton and Kurt H. Guddat, editors, 265–82. Garden City, NY: Anchor Books.

————. 1968. *Theories of Surplus Value,* Pt. 2. Moscow: Progress Publishers.

————. 1969. "Speech at the Anniversary of the *People's Paper.*" In *Selected Works* (3 vols.), Karl Marx and Frederick Engels, Vol. 1, 500–01. Moscow: Progress Publishers.

————. 1970. *A Contribution to the Critique of Political Economy.* New York: International Publishers.

————. 1971. *Theories of Surplus Value,* Pt. 3. Moscow: Progress Publishers.

————. 1973. *Grundrisse.* New York: Vintage.

————. 1974a. "Inaugural Address of the International Working Men's Association." In *The First International and After,* David Fernbach, editor, 73–81. New York: Random House.

————. 1974b. *The Ethnological Notebooks of Karl Marx,* Lawrence Krader, editor. Assen, The Netherlands: Van Gorcum.

————. 1975. "Notes on Wagner." In *Texts on Method,* Terrell Carver, editor, 179–219. Oxford, UK: Blackwell.

————. 1976a. "Wages." In *Collected Works,* Karl Marx and Frederick Engels, Vol. 6, 415–37. New York: International Publishers.

———. 1976b. *Value, Price and Profit*. New York: International Publishers.

———. 1976c. "Theses on Feuerbach." In *The German Ideology*, by Karl Marx and Frederick Engels, 615–20. Moscow: Progress Publishers.

———. 1977. "Results of the Immediate Process of Production." In *Capital*, Vol. I, 948–1084. New York: Vintage.

———. 1978a. *The Poverty of Philosophy*. Peking: Foreign Languages Press.

———. 1978b. "Forced Emigration (etc.)." In *Ireland and the Irish Question*, by Karl Marx and Frederick Engels, 64–68. Moscow: Progress Publishers.

———. 1982. *Herr Vogt*. London: New Park.

———. 1985. "The Civil War in France." In *On the Paris Commune*, by Karl Marx and Frederick Engels, 48–181. Moscow: Progress Publishers.

———. 1987. "From the Preparatory Materials." In *Collected Works*, Karl Marx and Frederick Engels, Vol. 29, 430–532. New York: International Publishers.

———. 1988. "Economic Manuscript of 1861–63, Third Chapter." In *Collected Works*, Karl Marx and Frederick Engels, Vol. 30, 9–346. New York: International Publishers.

———. 1989a. "Epilogue to *Revelations Concerning the Communist Trial in Cologne.*" In *Collected Works*, Karl Marx and Frederick Engels, Vol. 24, 51–54. New York: International Publishers.

———. 1989b. "Notes on Bakunin's Book *Statehood and Anarchy.*" In *Collected Works*, Karl Marx and Frederick Engels, Vol. 24, 485–526. New York: International Publishers.

———. 1989c. "Introduction to the French Edition of Engels' *Socialism: Utopian and Scientific.*" In *Collected Works*, Karl Marx and Frederick Engels, Vol. 24, 335–39. New York: International Publishers.

———. 1989d. "Drafts of the Letter to Vera Zasulich," and "Letter to Vera Zasulich (March 8, 1881)." In *Collected Works*, Karl Marx and Frederick Engels, Vol. 24, 346–71. New York: International Publishers.

———. 1991. "Economic Manuscript of 1861–63, Continuation." In *Collected Works*, Karl Marx and Frederick Engels, Vol. 33, 9–352, 372–501. New York: International Publishers.

———. 1994. "Economic Manuscript of 1861–63, Conclusion." In *Collected Works*, Karl Marx and Frederick Engels, Vol. 34, 7–354. New York: International Publishers.

Marx, Karl, and Frederick Engels. 1968. "Manifesto of the Communist Party." In *Selected Works* (1 vol.), Karl Marx and Frederick Engels, 35–63. London: Lawrence and Wishart.

———. 1975. *Selected Correspondence*. Moscow: Progress Publishers.

———. 1976. *The German Ideology*. Moscow: Progress Publishers.

———. 1979. *Marx and Engels on the United States*. Moscow: Progress Publishers.

———. 1980. *The Holy Family, or Critique of Critical Criticism*. Moscow: Progress Publishers.

———. 1982. *Collected Works*, Vol. 38. New York: International Publishers.

————. 1983. *Collected Works,* Vol. 39. New York: International Publishers.

————. 1992. *Collected Works,* Vol. 46. New York: International Publishers.

Massarrat, Mohssen. 1980. "The Energy Crisis: The Struggle for the Redistribution of Surplus Profit from Oil." In *Oil and Class Struggle,* Petter Nore and Terisa Turner, editors, 26–68. London: Zed Press.

Matson, P. A., W. J. Parton, A. G. Power, and M. J. Swift. 1997. "Agricultural Intensification and Ecosystem Properties." *Science,* Vol. 277, No. 5325, July 25, 504–9.

Mayumi, Kozo. 1991. "Temporary Emancipation from Land: From the Industrial Revolution to the Present Time." *Ecological Economics,* Vol. 4, No. 1, October, 35–56.

McLaughlin, Andrew. 1990. "Ecology, Capitalism, and Socialism." *Socialism and Democracy,* No. 10, Spring/Summer, 69–102.

Mingione, Enzo. 1993. "Marxism, Ecology, and Political Movements." *Capitalism, Nature, Socialism,* Vol. 4, No. 2, June, 85–92.

Mirovitskaya, Natalia, and Marvin S. Soroos. 1995. "Socialism and the Tragedy of the Commons: Reflections on Environmental Practice in the Soviet Union and Russia." *Journal of Environment and Development,* Vol. 4, No. 1, Winter, 77–110.

Montague, Peter. 1997. "Right to Know Nothing." *Rachel's Environment and Health Weekly,* No. 552, June 26.

More, Thomas. 1947. *Utopia.* Princeton: D. Van Nostrand.

Morrison, Roy. 1995. *Ecological Democracy.* Boston: South End Press.

Mumford, Lewis. 1954. *In the Name of Sanity.* New York: Harcourt, Brace.

Munda, G., P. Nijkamp, and P. Rietveld. 1995. "Monetary and Non-Monetary Evaluation Methods in Sustainable Development Planning." *Économie Appliquée,* Vol. 48, No. 2, 143–60.

Muwakkil, Salim. 1997. "Greens Get Real: The Environmental Justice Movement." *In These Times,* Vol. 21, No. 18, July 28, 26–28.

Negri, Toni. 1997. "Reappropriations of Public Space." *Common Sense,* No. 21, 31–40.

Nell, Edward. 1988. "On Monetary Circulation and the Rate of Exploitation." In *Post-Keynesian Monetary Economics: New Approaches to Financial Modelling,* Philip Arestis, editor, 72–121. Aldershot, Eng.: Edward Elgar.

Nelson, Eric. 1993. "Pollution Trading: Buying and Selling Pieces of Our Lives." *Z Magazine,* Vol. 6, No. 9, September, 47–51.

Newell, Josh, and Emma Wilson. 1996. "The Russian Far East: Foreign Direct Investment and Environmental Destruction." *The Ecologist,* Vol. 26, No. 2, March/April, 68–72.

Noble, David F. 1977. *America by Design: Science, Technology, and the Rise of Corporate Capitalism.* New York: Knopf.

Nove, Alec. 1983. *The Economics of Feasible Socialism.* London: Allen & Unwin.

————. 1990. "Socialism." In *The New Palgrave: Problems of the Planned Economy,* John Eatwell, Murray Milgate, and Peter Newman, editors, 227–49. New York: Norton.

O'Connor, James. 1988. "Capitalism, Nature, Socialism: A Theoretical Introduction." *Capitalism, Nature, Socialism,* Vol. 1, No. 1, Fall, 11–38.

————. 1991a. "On the Two Contradictions of Capitalism." *Capitalism, Nature, Socialism,* Vol. 2, No. 3, 107–9.

————. 1991b. "Socialism and Ecology." *Capitalism, Nature, Socialism,* Vol. 2, No. 3, 1–12.

————. 1998. *Natural Causes: Essays in Ecological Marxism.* New York: Guilford.

O'Connor, Martin. 1994. "Codependency and Indeterminacy: A Critique of the Theory of Production." In *Is Capitalism Sustainable? Political Economy and the Politics of Ecology,* Martin O'Connor, editor, 53–75. New York: Guilford.

Ollman, Bertell. 1979. "Marx's Vision of Communism." In *Social and Sexual Revolution: Essays on Marx and Reich,* by Bertell Ollman, 48–98. Boston: South End Press.

————. 1993. *Dialectical Investigations.* New York: Routledge.

Orton, David. 1993. "Envirosocialism: Contradiction or Promise?" In *Green On Red: Evolving Ecological Socialism,* Jesse Vorst, Ross Dobson, and Ron Fletcher, editors, 189–203. Winnipeg: Fernwood Publishing in association with the Society for Socialist Studies.

Osborn, Fairfield. 1968. *Our Plundered Planet.* New York: Pyramid Books.

Ostrom, Elinor. 1990. *Governing the Commons: The Evolution of Institutions for Collective Action.* Cambridge, UK: Cambridge University Press.

Parsons, Howard L. 1977. *Marx and Engels on Ecology.* Westport, CT: Greenwood Press.

Passell, Peter. 1997. "Trading on the Pollution Exchange: Global Warming Plan Would Make Emissions a Commodity." *New York Times,* October 24, C1, C4.

Patel, Sujata. 1997. "Ecology and Development." *Economic and Political Weekly,* Vol. 32, No. 38, September 20, 2388–91.

Peet, Richard, and Michael Watts (editors). 1996. *Liberation Ecologies: Environment, Development, Social Movements.* London: Routledge.

Pepper, David. 1993. *Eco-Socialism: From Deep Ecology to Social Justice.* London: Routledge.

Perelman, Michael. 1987. *Marx's Crises Theory: Scarcity, Labor, and Finance.* New York: Praeger.

Phillips, Paul. 1993. "Red and Green: Economics, Property Rights, and the Environment." In *Green On Red: Evolving Ecological Socialism,* Jesse Vorst, Ross Dobson, and Ron Fletcher, editors, 103–17. Winnipeg: Fernwood Publishing in association with the Society for Socialist Studies.

Rader, Melvin. 1979. *Marx's Interpretation of History.* New York: Oxford University Press.

Rosdolsky, Roman. 1977. *The Making of Marx's "Capital."* London: Pluto Press.

Rubin, Isaak Illich. 1972. *Essays on Marx's Theory of Value.* Detroit: Black & Red.

Saad-Filho, Alfredo. 1993. "Labor, Money, and 'Labor-Money': A Review of Marx's Critique of John Gray's Monetary Analysis." *History of Political Economy,* Vol. 25, No. 1, Spring, 65–84.

Sagoff, Mark. 1988. "Some Problems with Environmental Economics." *Environmental Ethics*, Vol. 10, No. 1, Spring, 55–74.

Sandel, Michael J. 1997. "It's Immoral to Buy the Right to Pollute." *New York Times*, December 15, A19.

Schmidt, Alfred. 1971. *The Concept of Nature in Marx*. London: New Left Books.

Schnaiberg, Allan. 1980. *The Environment: From Surplus to Scarcity*. New York: Oxford University Press.

Schnaiberg, Allan, and Kenneth Alan Gould. 1994. *Environment and Society: The Enduring Conflict*. New York: St. Martin's Press.

Schor, Juliet B. 1992. *The Overworked American: The Unexpected Decline of Leisure*. New York: Basic Books.

Sherman, Howard J. 1970. "The Economics of Pure Communism." *Review of Radical Political Economics*, Vol. 2, No. 4, Winter, 39–50.

Singer, Daniel. 1993. "The Emperors Are Naked." *The Nation*, Vol. 257, No. 6, August 23, 208–10.

Skirbekk, Gunnar. 1994. "Marxism and Ecology." *Capitalism, Nature, Socialism*, Vol. 5, No. 4, December, 95–104.

Smith, Tony. 1990. *The Logic of Marx's Capital: Replies to Hegelian Criticisms*. Albany: State University of New York Press.

———. 1997. "Marx's Theory of Social Forms and Lakatos's Methodology of Scientific Research Programs." In *New Investigations of Marx's Method*, Fred Moseley and Martha Campbell, editors, 176–97. Atlantic Highlands, NJ: Humanities Press.

Snyder, Gary. 1977. *The Old Ways*. San Francisco: City Lights Books.

Solow, Robert M. 1976. "Is the End of the World at Hand?" In *Great Debates in Economics*, Vol. 1, Richard T. Gill, editor, 172–80. Pacific Palisades, CA: Goodyear.

Steingraber, Sandra. 1997. *Living Downstream: An Ecologist Looks at Cancer and the Environment*. New York: Addison-Wesley.

Stevens, William K. 1997. "Experts Doubt Greenhouse Gas Can Be Curbed." *New York Times*, November 3, A1, A8.

Stirling, Andrew. 1993. "Environmental Valuation: How Much Is the Emperor Wearing?" *The Ecologist*, Vol. 23, No. 3, May/June, 97–103.

Sweezy, Paul M. 1943. "Professor Schumpeter's Theory of Innovation." *Review of Economic Statistics*, Vol. 25, No. 1, February, 93–96.

———. 1970. *The Theory of Capitalist Development*. New York: Monthly Review Press.

———. 1981. *Four Lectures on Marxism*. New York: Monthly Review Press.

Taylor, Dorceta E. 1996. "Environmental Justice: The Birth of a Movement." *Dollars and Sense*, No. 204, March/April, 22–23, 48–49.

Tokar, Brian. 1996. "Trading Away the Earth: Pollution Credits and the Perils of 'Free Market Environmentalism'." *Dollars and Sense*, No. 204, March/April, 24–29.

Tsuru, Shigeto. 1993. *Japan's Capitalism: Creative Defeat and Beyond.* New York: Cambridge University Press.

Usher, Peter. 1993. "Aboriginal Property Systems in Land and Resources: Lessons for Socialists." In *Green On Red: Evolving Ecological Socialism,* Jesse Vorst, Ross Dobson, and Ron Fletcher, editors, 93–102. Winnipeg: Fernwood Publishing in association with the Society for Socialist Studies.

Veblen, Thorstein. 1961. *The Place of Science in Modern Civilization.* New York: Russell & Russell.

Vitousek, Peter M., Harold A. Mooney, Jane Lubchenco, and Jerry M. Melillo. 1997. "Human Domination of Earth's Ecosystems." *Science,* Vol. 277, No. 5325, July 25, 494–99.

Waitzkin, Howard. 1983. *The Second Sickness: Contradictions of Capitalist Health Care.* New York: Free Press.

Walker, K. J. 1979. "Ecological Limits and Marxian Thought." *Politics,* Vol. 14, No. 1, May, 29–46.

Wallis, Victor. 1993. "Socialism, Ecology, and Democracy." In *Socialism: Crisis and Renewal,* Chronis Polychroniou, editor, 143–69. Westport, CT: Praeger.

Weeks, John. 1981. *Capital and Exploitation.* Princeton: Princeton University Press.

Weisskopf, Thomas E. 1991. "Marxian Crisis Theory and the Contradictions of Late Twentieth-Century Capitalism." *Rethinking Marxism,* Vol. 4, No. 4, Winter, 70–93.

Wood, Ellen Meiksins, and John Bellamy Foster (editors). 1997. *In Defense of History: Marxism and the Postmodern Agenda.* New York: Monthly Review Press.

Wright, Gwendolyn. 1983. "Environmental Pluralism and the Socialist Visions." In *Socialist Visions,* Steve Rosskamm Shalom, editor, 82–86. Boston: South End Press.

Index

Printed in the USA
CPSIA information can be obtained
at www.ICGtesting.com
JSHW022246110324
58926JS00001B/2